CRITICAL APPROACHES TO FOOD IN CHILDREN'S LITERATURE

Children's Literature and Culture
Jack Zipes, *Series Editor*

Pinocchio Goes Postmodern
Perils of a Puppet in the United States
by Richard Wunderlich and
Thomas J. Morrissey

Little Women and the
Feminist Imagination
Criticism, Controversy, Personal Essays
edited by Janice M. Alberghene and
Beverly Lyon Clark

The Presence of the Past
*Memory, Heritage, and Childhood
in Postwar Britain*
by Valerie Krips

The Case of Peter Rabbit
*Changing Conditions of Literature
for Children*
by Margaret Mackey

The Feminine Subject in Children's
Literature
by Christine Wilkie-Stibbs

Ideologies of Identity in
Adolescent Fiction
by Robyn McCallum

Recycling Red Riding Hood
by Sandra Beckett

The Poetics of Childhood
by Roni Natov

Voices of the Other
*Children's Literature and the
Postcolonial Context*
edited by Roderick McGillis

Narrating Africa
George Henty and the Fiction of Empire
by Mawuena Kossi Logan

Reimagining Shakespeare for Children
and Young Adults
edited by Naomi J. Miller

Representing the Holocaust in
Youth Literature
by Lydia Kokkola

Translating for Children
by Riitta Oittinen

Beatrix Potter
Writing in Code
by M. Daphne Kutzer

Children's Films
History, Ideology, Pedagogy, Theory
by Ian Wojcik-Andrews

Utopian and Dystopian Writing for
Children and Young Adults
edited by Carrie Hintz and Elaine Ostry

Transcending Boundaries
*Writing for a Dual Audience of
Children and Adults*
edited by Sandra L. Beckett

The Making of the Modern Child
*Children's Literature and Childhood in the
Late Eighteenth Century*
by Andrew O'Malley

How Picturebooks Work
by Maria Nikolajeva and Carole Scott

Brown Gold
*Milestones of African American Children's
Picture Books, 1845-2002*
by Michelle H. Martin

Russell Hoban/Forty Years
Essays on His Writing for Children
by Alida Allison

Apartheid and Racism in South African
Children's Literature
by Donnarae MacCann and
Amadu Maddy

Empire's Children
*Empire and Imperialism in Classic British
Children's Books*
by M. Daphne Kutzer

Constructing the Canon of
Children's Literature
Beyond Library Walls and Ivory Towers
by Anne Lundin

Youth of Darkest England
*Working Class Children at the Heart of
Victorian Empire*
by Troy Boone

Ursula K. Le Guin Beyond Genre
Fiction for Children and Adults
by Mike Cadden

CRITICAL APPROACHES TO FOOD IN CHILDREN'S LITERATURE

EDITED BY KARA K. KEELING
AND SCOTT T. POLLARD

Routledge
Taylor & Francis Group
NEW YORK AND LONDON

First published 2009
by Routledge
711 Third Avenue, New York, NY 10017

Simultaneously published in the UK
by Routledge
2 Park Square, Milton Park, Abingdon, Oxfordshire OX14 4RN

Routledge is an imprint of the Taylor & Francis Group, an informa business

First published in paperback 2011

Typeset in Minion by IBT Global.

Library of Congress Cataloging in Publication Data

Critical approaches to food in children's literature / edited by Kara K.
Keeling and Scott T. Pollard.
    p. cm.—(Children's literature and culture ; 59)
  Includes bibliographical references and index.
    1. Children's literature—History and criticism.   2. Food in litera-
ture.   I. Keeling, Kara K.   II. Pollard, Scott T.
  PN1009.5.F66C75 2009
  809'.89282—dc22
  2008017665

ISBN13: 978-0-415-96366-4 (hbk)
ISBN13: 978-0-415-80891-0 (pbk)
ISBN13: 978-0-203-88891-9 (ebk)

Contents

Series Editor's Foreword

Dedicated to furthering original research in children's literature and culture, the Children's Literature and Culture series includes monographs on individual authors and illustrators, historical examinations of different periods, literary analyses of genres, and comparative studies on literature and the mass media. The series is international in scope and is intended to encourage innovative research in children's literature with a focus on interdisciplinary methodology.

Children's literature and culture are understood in the broadest sense of the term "children" to encompass the period of childhood up through adolescence. Owing to the fact that the notion of childhood has changed so much since the origination of children's literature, this Routledge series is particularly concerned with transformations in children's culture and how they have affected the representation and socialization of children. While the emphasis of the series is on children's literature, all types of studies that deal with children's radio, film, television, and art are included in an endeavor to grasp the aesthetics and values of children's culture. Not only have there been momentous changes in children's culture in the last fifty years, but there have been radical shifts in the scholarship that deals with these changes. In this regard, the goal of the Children's Literature and Culture series is to enhance research in this field and, at the same time, point to new directions that bring together the best scholarly work throughout the world.

Jack Zipes

Acknowledgments

We owe thanks for this project in many quarters. At Christopher Newport University, we would like to express our appreciation to our successive department chairs, Tracey Schwarze and Jean Filetti, for their support of this project. Thanks are also due to Douglas Gordon as the Dean of the College of Liberal Arts and Sciences, Provost Richard Summerville, and the Christopher Newport University Faculty Senate for their support in the form of faculty development grants and sabbaticals, without which completion of this project would have been impossible.

We would also like to thank our colleagues in the field of children's literature. We owe a particular debt of gratitude to the Children's Literature Association for having chosen our proposal for a special session on Food and Children's Literature for the 2004 Modern Language Association Conference in Philadelphia, and to the many colleagues who attended that session and gave feedback to the scholars who presented papers there. We are particularly grateful to Jan Susina, who generously referred Routledge to us and us to Routledge to carry the project on from that session to book form. Also, we would like to extend a very special thank you to Margaret Mackey, who first suggested to us that a single article on food in Maurice Sendak's work had further possibilities as a topic for longer study.

We are very grateful to our editors at Routledge: Matthew J. Byrnie, who first commissioned the project; Max Novick, who helped us get started; Erica Wetter, who has seen the manuscript through the publication process and patiently answered many questions; and Jack Zipes, the general editor of the series of which this book is a part, who has done so much to extend scholarship in the field of children's literature.

Finally, we would like to thank all our contributors: Genny Ballard, Holly Blackford, Winnie Chan, Lan Dong, James Everett, Leona Fisher, Lisa Rowe Fraustino, Elizabeth Gargano, Robert M. Kachur, Jacqueline M. Labbe, Karen Hill McNamara, Martha Satz, Jodie Slowthower, Jan Susina, Richard Vernon, Annette Wannamaker, and Jean Webb. They have all been enthusiastic with their contributions and patient with the many inquiries required to put this volume together.

Part I
Introduction

.

Chapter One
Introduction:
Food in Children's Literature

Kara K. Keeling and Scott T. Pollard

Food Is Everywhere

> But he struck his chest and curbed his fighting heart:
> "Bear up, old heart! You've borne worse, far worse,
> that day when the Cyclops, man-mountain, bolted
> your hardy comrades down. But you held fast—
> Nobody but your cunning pulled you through
> the monster's cave you thought would be your death."
>
> So he forced his spirit into submission,
> the rage in his breast reined back—unswerving,
> all endurance. But he himself kept tossing, turning,
> intent as a cook before some white-hot blazing fire
> who rolls his sizzling sausage back and forth,
> packed with fat and blood—keen to broil it quickly,
> tossing, turning it, this way, that way.
> (Homer, The Odyssey, Book 20, lines 20–31)

At the beginning of Book 20, Odysseus cannot sleep for the anger that he feels. An insomniac lying in the entranceway of his own house, he is tempted to simply rise up and attack the suitors then and there, disgusted by their abuse of his household (e.g., the butchering of Odysseus's stock of pigs and hogs for their perpetual feasting), but he represses that urge in order to give his cunning the time it needs to devise an attack. He thinks about an analogous moment—Polyphemous eating his crew—when he successfully strategized and executed a plan to save himself and the rest of his men from becoming food. Food leads to food. His anger successfully repressed (food memory as defense mechanism), Odysseus will not let it die out, though, and he keeps himself awake, "tossing, turning." At which point, Homer introduces another food moment, this time as a simile. Odysseus is the cook grilling the sausage, which is also Odysseus, "tossing, turning." He is the cook and the cooked, subject and object, a closed circuit meant to embody Odysseus's management of his anger. As with all cooks, the keys to his success are ingredients, heat, and timing. The cook Odysseus has a hot fire and a well-stuffed sausage, and he has the skill "to broil it quickly" (but not too quickly) in order to serve up his anger to the suitors, with the "fat and blood" at its peak, ready to burst out of the skin. But Odysseus's fire is too hot, and Athena appears to cool his anger and assure him of his revenge:

> Even if fifty bands of mortal fighters
> Closed around us, hot to kill us off in battle,
> Still you could drive away their herds and sleek flocks. (lines 49–51)

Odysseus is promised that he will control the suitors' food stocks. In fifty-one lines, in the lead-up to the climax of *The Odyssey*, the slaying of the suitors, food and food preparation dominate Homer's language as he attempts to capture Odysseus's mindset.

We see here in one of the earliest texts of world literature the integral role of food as cultural signifier, not only the product of a culture but one that gives shape to the *mentalités* that structure thought and expression. The presence of food, food production, and scenes of eating and feasting—all thread through the epic. One can read the epic as an adventure tale, but food is fundamental to the plot and to character interactions, to the very propelling of the adventure forward throughout the story: the ritual barbecues, the feasts, the slaughtering of bulls and pigs and sheep and, occasionally, humans. Polyphemous, whom Odysseus remembers at this crucial moment, kills and eats Odysseus's crew, but until Odysseus's arrival he is primarily a dairy farmer who raises sheep for their milk, out of which he makes cheese. He is a pastoralist who inexplicably turns cannibal.

Readers can take literature from practically any period or cultural tradition and do this kind of analysis about food. In *Gilgamesh*, Enkidu is inducted into civilization through eating cooked food. In *The Iliad*, Priam and Achilles negotiate the release of Hector's body over a meal. In *The Metamorphoses*, Ovid advocates vegetarianism. In the Prologue to *The Canterbury Tales*, Chaucer distinguishes the Prioress from the other pilgrims by her delight in good manners, signified by her dainty eating habits. In *Gargantua and Pantagruel*, Rabelais delights in using food as a positive sign of excess for the vast intellectual and physical capacities of his main characters. Gustave Flaubert spends an entire chapter on the wedding feast in *Madame Bovary*. Marcel

Proust's six-volume *Remembrance of Things Past* is launched by the memory of a cookie.

These are just a few examples; more will occur to any thoughtful reader who reviews his or her repertoire of texts, including those read in childhood. Food is as prevalent and significant in children's literature as it is in literature for any other audience. Taking, for example, Maurice Sendak's *In the Night Kitchen*, Mickey's situation is similar to that of Odysseus: Mickey too is an outsider trying to find his way in. Although he is not angry, as Odysseus is, he is still frustrated at his subordinate, marginalized social position. Whereas Odysseus feels homicidal because his rightful position of power has been usurped, Mickey quests for a new position of power. It is through food—through negotiating his liminal position of cook and almost cooked—that Mickey succeeds. Mickey does not live in a world of threatening suitors; rather, he inhabits a fantastic dreamscape of early twentieth-century commercially prepared staples (bottles of cream of tartar and baking soda, bags of sugar and flour, containers of salt, yeast, and coffee), a dreamscape created from the adult world from which he has so far been excluded. He desires to be coequal with these avatars of the adult world, and it is as both prepared food and as food preparer that Mickey dreams his inclusion. To mix our metaphors, it is in his ability to walk the fine line between those roles that Mickey is able to embrace his rightful position as consumer of a product of whose production he has dreamed himself a part. In the end he has become the knowledgeable consumer who understands from where this food comes and how it is made. As the final illustration of the book suggests, as hero of the tale Mickey becomes the brand, the Mickey-cake, that everyone eats, achieving power not through homicide but through economic ingenuity, through the negotiation and navigation of a food production and distribution system.

Food Is Fundamental to Literature

> Food is important. In fact, nothing is more basic. Food is the first of the essentials of life, our biggest industry, our biggest export, and our most frequently indulged pleasure. Food means creativity and diversity. As a species, humans are omnivores; we have tried to eat virtually everything on the globe, and our ability to turn a remarkable array of raw substances into cooked dishes, meals, and feasts is evidence of astounding versatility, adaptability, and aesthetic ingenuity. (Belasco viii)

If food is fundamental to life and a substance upon which civilizations and cultures have built themselves, then food is also fundamental to the imagination and the imaginary arts. Food is fundamental to the imagination, because food is fundamental to culture, or as Massimo Montanari puts it in the title of his latest book, *Food Is Culture*. If food were plain—if it were nothing more than bland nutrition—perhaps we could leave it to the scientists and technicians to know how nutrition works and to deliver it more efficiently, in pills, for example. But food is seldom plain. Cultures and civilizations will not leave it alone. Cultures elaborate it, not simply as Lévi-Strauss speaks of "elaboration" in "The Culinary Triangle"—the transformation of food from the raw to the cooked—but through its inclusion in cultural rituals, its purpose as cultural signifier, its central position in the creation of culture. Food is also essential to the cultural imagination, or the imagination period. Thus food proliferates as the product of the imagination. As we have already indicated above, food and foodways are a constant thread in literature. Food can be epic in scope, and it can be intimate. It can give bent to joy or anger or mark humankind's mortality.

Food has not always been deemed a subject worthy of literary study, despite its omnipresence in literature. In his autobiography, *The Apprentice*, Jacques Pépin recollects his desire as a graduate student in the 1970s to write his doctoral dissertation on Flaubert's description of the wedding feast in *Madame Bovary*, but his advisor in the French Department at Columbia nixed the idea, telling Pépin "the reason not much has been written on the topic . . . is that cuisine is not a serious art form. It's far too trivial for academic study. Not intellectual enough to form the basis of a Ph.D. thesis." The rejection of his proposal pushed Pépin out of an academic career and back into his first love of food preparation as a chef (Pépin 212). But by 1984 one finds James Brown noting in *Fictional Meals and Their Function in the French Novel: 1789–1848* that "Fictional meals are above all literary signs: consequently they are subject to the same kinds of analysis as any other literary phenomenon" (3).

To better understand the potential for studying food in literature, a brief overview of the development of food studies in the last century is needed. The three fields that have been the primary contributors to food studies have been social sciences (anthropology, sociology, and history), though the field is inherently interdisciplinary and has come to include the arts and humanities as well. But there is little sense of food studies as an interdisciplinary field of its own until long after studies of food had developed in the individual disciplines. Thus in 1999 the field still seems very new, and a certain defensiveness is still noticeable in its early practitioners. In his review of the field that year, "Why Food Matters," Warren Belasco, an influential scholar in the development of food studies, admits his defensiveness about the scholarship he does, noting the "bemused wonder" of other academics in reaction to his work. But Belasco also shows the breadth of the developing field, offering a bibliography of sixty-eight works from the 1920s onwards that covers multiple fields and many varieties of writing, ranging from the impact of food on body image to food history to cookbooks and gastronomic literature. In 2002 an even more comprehensive literature review of food studies, "The Anthropology of Food and Eating," was published. In it Sidney Mintz and Christine Du Bois observe "the staggering increase in the scale of food literature—inside and outside anthropology" (111). They claim that food studies in anthropology began at the end of the nineteenth century but developed most significantly after Claude Lévi-Strauss and Mary Douglas wrote about food and foodways in the mid-1960s. The important turning point came, though, in 1982 with the publication of Jack Goody's *Cooking, Cuisine, and Class: A Study in Comparative Sociology*, after which work in the anthropology of food grew exponentially. Mintz and Du Bois's bibliography cites 233 articles and books on food and foodways; clearly this had already become a productive subfield that has only continued to develop since then. They argue that there are three major trends responsible for the growth of food scholarship: "globalization; the general affluence of Western societies and their growing cosmopolitanism; and the inclusivist tendencies of U.S. society which spurs . . . disciplines . . . and professions, such as journalism and business . . . to consider cross-cultural variations in foodways" (111).

In the field of history, food becomes an important focus with the French historian Fernand Braudel and the French *Annales* school of history. In *The Structures of Everyday Life: The Limits of the Possible*, the first volume of his three-volume history, *Civilization and Capitalism: 15th–18th Century*, Braudel focuses on the material components of the lives of ordinary people (as opposed to the Great Man or political theories of history), in which he has chapters on bread, rice, maize, potatoes, eating habits, etcetera. Stephen Mennell, in the introduction to *All Manners of Food: Eating and Taste in England and France from the Middle Ages to the Present*, notes that Braudel called for a history of food in 1961 (17). Since then, a variety of comprehensive food histories have been written, most notably Reay Tannahill's *Food and History* (1973), Maguelonne Toussaint-Samat's *History of Food* (1987), Jean-Louis Flandrin, et al.'s *Food: A Culinary History* (1996), and Felipe Fernández-Armesto's *Near a Thousand Tables: A Brief History of Food* (2002). A number of histories of specific foods, such as Sidney Mintz's *Sweetness and Power: The Place of Sugar in Modern History* (1986) and Mark Kurlansky's *Salt: A World History* (2002), have received popular acclaim.

A key moment in the development of food studies in the humanities was the founding of *Gastronomica: The Journal of Food and Culture*, which began publishing in 2001. Although other publications devoted to food existed (*Food, Culture & Society* and *Food History News*), they were oriented toward social sciences rather than the arts and humanities. *Gastronomica*'s stated goals include "promoting greater recognition and awareness for the field of food studies"; they explicitly proclaim food studies as an existing field of its own, deserving of its own journal, in which they feature a wide variety of interdisciplinary scholarly and general audience articles. Any issue may include pieces on art, photography, poetry, creative nonfiction, memoir, testimonial, restaurants, table manners, utensils, chef biographies, historical events, and current controversies, all of which explore the pervasiveness of food in cultures around the world and are captured under the umbrella of food studies. In reviewing all the issues of *Gastronomica*, we find literature is the focus of a number of pieces. A scattering of titles includes "Roman Food Poems: A Modern Translation," "The Duchess of Malfi's Apricots, and Other Literary Fruits," and "Scenes of the Apple: Food and the Female Body in Nineteenth- and Twentieth-Century Women's Writing"; these articles suggest food's omnipresence in literature, yet it remains an area ripe for analysis and commentary. *Gastronomica* has also given space to discussions about food in children's lives and children's culture. Among all the disciplines to which it gives voice, *Gastronomica* provides a central outlet for analyses of food in literature; this is much needed, given that although many analyses of food in literature are being produced, there is no strong venue devoted to the topic. The field is now at the point that we need studies exclusively devoted to food and literature.

Some of the most important literary and cultural theorists have addressed food and literature. Perhaps the most outstanding is Mikhail Bakhtin in *Rabelais and His World*, which Carolyn Korsmeyer in *Making Sense of Taste: Food and Philosophy* sees as "Bakhtin's meditations" on food as "a metaphor for power" that focus particularly on Rabelais's "trope of appetite to ferocious excess" (188). In *Mythologies* Roland Barthes pursues semiotic analyses of food in chapters on "Wine and Milk," "Steak and Chips," and "Ornamental Cookery." Barthes uses his article "Toward a Psychosociology of Contemporary Food Consumption" to develop a general semiotic theory of food and culture:

> For what is food? It is not only a collection of products that can be used for statistical or nutritional studies. It is also, and at the same time, a system of communication, a body of images, a protocol of usages, situations, and behavior. (167)

In 1986, Louis Marin wrote *Food for Thought*, in which he develops the idea of the culinary sign through textual analyses of fairy tales, political and religious texts, and Rabelais. For Marin, the culinary sign is multivalent and connects to the methods by which society makes meaning, functioning as what Marin calls a trans-signifier—through metonymy, synecdoche, and metaphor—to facilitate movement among cultural discourses. Conversely, in 1982 Julia Kristeva speaks of food loathing as a means of deconstructing cultural signifying regimes in *Powers of Horror: An Essay on Abjection*. Even in this very quick and selective review, we see how these four major theorists place food at the center of their cultural analyses.

A number of literary critics have also addressed the significance of food in literature; although good work has been done, it has largely been accomplished by writers without a clear sense of participating in a developing subfield. There are a few notable book-length studies of food in literature. James Brown's *Fictional Meals and Their Function in the French Novel: 1789–1848* (mentioned above) discusses the function of meals in the works of Honoré Balzac, George Sand, Victor Hugo, Gustave Flaubert, and Eugene Sue. Gian-Paolo Biasin, in *The Flavors of Modernity: Food and the Novel*, which focuses on food in nineteenth- and twentieth-century Italian novels, questions why the novel superimposes its own signifying system onto the signifying system of cooking and asks, why doesn't the sign system of cooking superimpose itself instead on the novel? He treats food and foodways as something other than a subordinate cultural expression; instead he sees them as powerful creators of cultural meaning, which he explores by treating the novel's and food's signifying powers as equivalent and thus interdependent. Like Biasin, Allen Weiss argues for the equivalency of food and aesthetics as cultural signifiers in his *Feast and Folly: Cuisine, Intoxication and the Poetics of the Sublime*, producing a gastronomic aesthetic theory while focusing primarily on nineteenth- and twentieth-century French texts: "Taste (culinary and otherwise) constitutes a sign of individual style, a mode of constituting the self, a mark of social position, an aesthetic gesture" (85).

Much article-length work on the role of food in literature has been done; articles are, not surprisingly, much more the norm for the young field. The most notable critic for our purposes is Mervyn Nicholson, who has three articles that bridge adult and children's literature: "Food and Power: Homer, Carroll, Atwood and Others," "Magic Food, Compulsive Eating, and Power Poetics," and "The Scene of Eating and the Semiosis of the Invisible." Nicholson analyzes issues of power relations, violence, and transformation through food and eating in works such as Homer's *The Odyssey*, Carroll's *Alice in Wonderland*, Keats's *La Belle Dame sans Merci*, Lewis's *The Lion, the Witch, and the Wardrobe*, and Atwood's *The Handmaid's Tale*. For readers interested in other articles in the field, we recommend the one book-length bibliography of food in literature: Norman Kiell's *Food and Drink in Literature: A Selectively Annotated Bibliography* (published in 1995 and thus now somewhat out of date). Kiell gives a substantial annotated list of both books and articles; much more critical work has been done in the past thirteen years, however.

In our research we have also noted the presence of analyses of food in literature in interdisciplinary texts such as Carolyn Korsmeyer's *Making Sense of Taste: Food and Philosophy* and Michael Symons's *A History of Cooks and Cooking*. Although food in literature is not their primary focus, nor are they conventional literary critics, both Korsmeyer and Symons include discussions of literary texts in their cultural analyses: Korsmeyer on meals in Melville's *Moby Dick*, Woolf's *To the Lighthouse*, and Dinesen's "Babette's Feast," and Symons on women novelists who feature cooks and cooking. We find Symons interesting because he features both historical children's authors (Susan Coolidge, Laura Ingalls Wilder, Louisa May Alcott, L. M. Montgomery) along with contemporary women writers (Laura Esquivel and Nora Ephron).

Food Is Fundamental to Children's Literature

As Nicholson and Symons demonstrate, just as food studies is becoming more important in general literary studies, so too is it becoming important in the field of children's literature. Whether in memoir, fiction, or poetry, writers continually hark back to childhood experiences of food, even when the intended audience is adults rather than children, as with Proust's *Remembrance of Things Past*. Food experiences form part of the daily texture of every child's life from birth onwards, as any adult who cares for children is highly aware; thus it is hardly surprising that food is a constantly recurring motif in literature written for children.

In children's literature scholarship, there have been a few important investigations of food, eating, and manners. Wendy Katz's 1980 article, "Some Uses of Food in Children's Literature," is both one of the first and one of the best general discussions of food in children's literature. Katz's thesis is that to understand the relationship between children and food is to understand the world of the young. Katz illustrates her points with brief analyses of a number of texts: *Alice in Wonderland*; *The Wind in the Willows*; *The Lion, the Witch, and the Wardrobe*; *The Hobbit*; *Anne of Green Gables*; *The Adventures of Huckleberry Finn*; *Nobody's Family Is Going to Change*; and *Higglety Pigglety Pop!* In this short overview of the subject, she identifies a number of themes as they apply to particular texts: civilization, community, identity, emotional stability, meals and food events, empowerment. This early article offers short takes on important thematic ideas that can be further developed within the new context of food studies.

Unlike Katz, J. Ellen Gainor offers a single-work study in her 1992 article "'The Slow-Eater-Tiny-Bite-Taker': An Eating Disorder in Betty McDonald's *Mrs. Piggle-Wiggle*." Gainor's research is primarily focused on male anorexia: the issues of control, identity, and social integration. She focuses on the character of Allen, a boy who alarms his mother by eating less and less, more and more slowly. Gainor looks at table manners as therapy; both society and the child define their relationship to one another through eating and the ways food is consumed. A reading of Gainor's analysis reveals food in this story as a way of understanding character and redefining social relations. The table is a locus of socialization from which Allen isolates himself, and it is Mrs. Piggle-Wiggle who uses that same table, the food served on it, and the table setting to normalize his behavior and reintegrate him into society. Gainor's essay is useful because she widens the scope of literary inquiry beyond food itself to the nexus of manners of consumption.

In the 1990 article, "Maurice Sendak's Ritual Cooking of the Child in Three Tableaux: The Moon, Mother, and Music," Jean Perrot uses Claude Lévi-Strauss and Jacques Lacan against Sendak's own background in psychoanalysis to discuss a variety of Sendak's texts, from *Kenny's Window* to *Outside Over There*. Perrot sees a parallel between Lévi-Strauss's food texts (*The*

Raw and the Cooked and *The Naked Man*) and Sendak's *Where the Wild Things Are* and *In the Night Kitchen*, in that both Lévi-Strauss and Sendak see food as a primary engine in the civilizing process. Perrot consistently frames his analysis of Mickey, the protagonist of *In the Night Kitchen*, with Lévi-Strauss's understanding of cooking as a civilizing trope. For example, Perrot quotes Lévi-Strauss to support his point that "Mickey completes the culinary operations necessary 'as mediatory activities between heaven and earth, life and death, nature and nurture' (Lévi-Strauss, *Raw* 65)" (Perrot 72–73). Perrot represents a significant shift to an approach that utilizes literary theory as a way of discussing the role food plays in children's literature.

Maria Nikolajeva, in *From Mythic to Linear: Time in Children's Literature*, also uses sophisticated theoretical approaches. Although the obvious focus of her 2000 book is the issue of time, she includes an important chapter on food as a means of measuring time: "An Excursus on Significant Meals." Using a variety of theorists from various disciplines (Claude Lévi-Strauss, Carl Jung, Vladimir Propp, and Algirdas Julien Greimas), Nikolajeva reads children's literature as mythic and rejects the notion of realistic fiction. Children's literature functions off the deep structures (mythic, archetypal) embedded in it. She links literary analysis with a mythic hermeneutic, which provides her a closed world of interpretation: known patterns and known symbols. Within that hermeneutic, the consumption of food in human societies functions as significant, ritualized temporal markers that integrate the child into the community (echoing Perrot's Lévi-Straussian analysis of the process by which Mickey becomes civilized). In later chapters, she discusses food in a number of important children's books, including Dahl's *Charlie and the Chocolate Factory*, Linklater's *The Wind of the Moon*, Milne's *Winnie-the-Pooh*, Lewis's Narnia books, and Lindgren's *Pippi Longstocking*, *Mio my Son*, *The Brothers Lionheart*, and *Ronia, the Robber's Daughter*.

Our own first article on food in children's literature, "Power, Food and Eating in Maurice Sendak and Henrik Drescher: *Where the Wild Things Are*, *In the Night Kitchen*, and *The Boy Who Ate Around*" (1999), shows an incipient awareness of the young field of food studies, using the Douglas, Brown, Mennell, and Kristeva texts cited above to discuss the socialization process of table rituals and the means by which Sendak's and Drescher's child protagonists use food consumption as a means of rebellion and self-empowerment. Our 2002 article on Beatrix Potter's *The Tale of Peter Rabbit*, "In Search of His Father's Garden," takes a similar approach but also displays a greater awareness of food studies as a field, citing the above-mentioned Barthes, Fisher, Mennell, and Korsmeyer texts. Additionally, we employed the centerpiece of nineteenth-century British middle-class food life, *Mrs. Beeton's Book of Household Management*, as well as Alan Beardworth and Teresa Keil's *Sociology on the Menu: An Invitation to the Study of Food and Society* and Deane W. Curtin's "Food/Body/Person." Now, in retrospect, our articles seem to be in the mainstream of how children's literature scholars were beginning to integrate critical theory and food studies into analyses of children's literature.

In the literature review that begins her 2002 article, "'What Is the Meaning of All This Gluttony?': Edgeworth, the Victorians, C. S. Lewis and a Taste for Fantasy," Lynne Vallone captures the nascent scholarship of food in children's literature, demonstrating an awareness of not only the work on the topic done in the field of children's literature by Katz and Nikolajeva but also roving more broadly through available scholarship, citing Gian-Paolo Biasin's *The Flavors of Modernity: Food and the Novel,* and even an early example of food studies in the humanities, Margaret Visser's *The Rituals of Dinner: The Origins, Evolution, Eccentricities, and Meaning of Table Manners.* Whereas Katz uses food as a tool for social analysis to define the child's world, Nikolajeva and Perrot speak to how the child is integrated into the larger adult community using myth criticism. Vallone, constructing food as metaphor, demonstrates a shift from didactic Victorian beliefs in self-restraint of good children "in terms of what is eaten, when, how much, and in what manner" as a means of social integration into the adult world to Lewis Carroll's and C. S. Lewis's rejection of "the sterility of the adult community" in favor of a redefined community of wholesome pleasure that leaves children freer to define their relationship to food (53).

Carolyn Daniel has written the longest study of food in children's literature so far. Her 2006 book *Voracious Children: Who Eats Whom in Children's Literature* covers a vast number of children's texts chiefly from the Anglo-Australian tradition. Daniel has done an enormous amount of research and uses most of the children's literature and food scholars mentioned above. Most importantly, she references authors who are important in the field of food studies: Julia Kristeva, Roland Barthes, Mary Douglas, Norbert Elias, Peter Farb, Sidney Mintz, Pierre Bourdieu, and Margaret Visser. Thus she contextualizes her discussion of children's literature within a larger interdisciplinary frame than we have yet seen. The book is trenchantly feminist; Daniel comes to the conclusion that no text can find freedom from or negotiate a space outside the patriarchal monoculture. Basing her work on Lévi-Strauss and Judith Butler, Daniel employs various binaries (adult/child, male/female, boy/girl, good/bad, food/nonfood, human/nonhuman, order/disorder, civilization/barbarity), all of which feed into an overarching binary of patriarchy and its Other. Through these binaries, Daniel portrays power relations in children's texts and how food, eating, and manners act as signifiers that reflect the larger ideological structure of society. The Other (most often female) represents the desire to counter patriarchy and its array of powerful social forces, but inevitably patriarchy (embodied today in the commodity-driven globalized corporate culture) wins. Like Nikolajeva and Perrot, Daniel sees food in children's literature as a means to socialization:

> As far as adult culture is concerned, children must internalize very precise rules about how to maintain a "clean and proper" body, what to relegate to abjection, and how to perform properly in social situations.

Children must also learn all sorts of rules about food and eating. Most important—they must know who eats whom. Food events in children's literature are clearly intended to teach children how to be human. (12)

But whereas Vallone sees the possibility that children's literature can negotiate a space for the child outside the dominant culture, Daniel sees patriarchal domination as nearly all encompassing, an event horizon from which texts, readers, and authors have great difficulty escaping.

Published in a variety of venues over the past twenty-six years, these works of children's literature scholarship demonstrate an uncanny likeness to the interdisciplinary growth of food studies scholarship. All reflect the development of critical theory as analytical tool over the latter half of the twentieth century and into the twenty-first, exploring with increasing sophistication food as a powerful and complex signifying force. All illuminate food as a prime cultural mover. Food makes things happen. It is acted upon (cooked, elaborated), but as a cultural force it also acts. The scholarship reviewed above is the groundwork upon which this volume is built. This book is the first collection of essays on food and children's literature, and we hope that it becomes another important reference point in the development of the subfield. The impetus for this volume came from a 2004 Modern Language Association conference special session on the topic of food and children's literature, sponsored by the Children's Literature Association and chaired by the editors of this volume. The session was quite successful, attracting an amazing number of superb submissions, of which only four could be used for the session. Many of the participants asked if we would consider putting together a scholarly volume on the topic. Looking again at the other submissions, we came to the conclusion that we had the material for a very strong and diverse collection, and we agreed to move forward.

The volume includes seventeen scholars from both inside and outside the field of Anglo-American children's literature. From inside, there are essays from a new scholar (Elizabeth Gargano); people well established in the field (Holly Blackford, Leona Fisher, Lisa Rowe Fraustino, Jan Susina, Annette Wannamaker); and a senior scholar (Jean Webb). From outside, the volume features a variety of scholars with specializations in nineteenth- and twentieth-century British literature (James Everett, Robert Kachur, Jacqueline Labbe, Winnie Chan); another set with global/multicultural foci (Genny Ballard, Lan Dong, Karen McNamara, Richard Vernon); and Jodi Slothower, an independent scholar, cookbook writer, and collector of children's cookbooks. The volume also features an essay by Martha Satz, who contributed an essay, "The Death of the Buddenbrooks: Four Rich Meals a Day," to one of the early, seminal volumes in food studies, *Disorderly Eaters: Texts of Self-Empowerment* (Furst and Graham 1992). For the Anglo-American tradition, we include essays that cover texts from the nineteenth century to the contemporary period. The volume also includes essays on United States multicultural (Asian American) and international children's literature (Brazil, Ireland, Mexico). In terms of genre, the essays discuss picture books, chapter books, popular media and children's cookbooks, and the contributors utilize a variety of approaches: archival research, culture studies, feminism, formalism, gender studies, material culture, metaphysics, popular culture, postcolonialism, post-structuralism, race, structuralism, and theology. As with the prior scholarship touched upon above, the essays in this volume not only look at food as a viable entré to social, cultural, and literary analysis but, full of its own signifying regimes (not an empty vessel), food is a worthy study in and of itself as well as in how it shapes our view of that literature, culture, and society. It is the treatment of food as critical vehicle that distinguishes the scholarship of food, whatever the discipline. Again, food makes things happen.

The volume is organized in five parts to capture some (certainly not all) of the thematic similarities among the chapters, and an intrepid reader will discover other potential groupings. The parts are also meant to reflect issues regularly taken up by food studies (gender, body, globalization, identity). To begin the volume, in a way that emphasizes the inexorable textuality of food (perfect for a book on food and literature), is Part II, Reading as Cooking, which is represented by "Delicious Supplements: Literary Cookbooks as Additives to Children's Texts." Working from Susan J. Leonardi's 1989 *PMLA* essay, "Recipes for Reading," Jodie Slowthower and Jan Susina look at the phenomenon of children's literature cookbooks, exploring the relationship between the original text and the adjunct cookbook as well as the relationship between the books and their dual, adult and child, audiences. In considering the linked cooking and reading texts, and thus the relationship between cooking and reading, the authors also raise interesting issues of power and reception. The cookbooks shift the reading experience from simple passive consumption to empowering the readers to pursue a more interactive and engaged role with the books.

The chapters in Part III—Girls, Mothers, Children—examine gender and generational relations. In "Recipe for Reciprocity and Repression: The Politics of Cooking and Consumption in Girls' Coming-of-Age Literature," Holly Blackford analyzes the mythic and fairy-tale intertextuality of the representation of eating and cooking in girls' literature. Scenes of food production typically sort mother figures into divine sacrificial objects or evil witches, categories to which we can apply a psychoanalytic understanding of child development. Because women and their cooking cross many important boundaries, between raw and cooked, self and other, outside and inside, nature and culture, women's cooking holds both wonder and anxiety in their daughters' imaginations. In "The Apple of her Eye: The Mothering Ideology Fed by Bestselling Trade Picture Books," Lisa Rowe Fraustino reviews all-time best-selling trade picture books depicting mother–child relationships and examines how food is used, both literally and metaphorically, in the reproduction of mothering ideology as defined by feminist theorists, most pertinently Nancy Chodorow in her influential text *The Reproduction of Mothering*.

Part IV—Food and the Body—has two chapters on obesity and one that explores the blurring of the eater/eaten dichotomy vis-à-vis the child. In "Nancy Drew and the 'F' Word," Leona W. Fisher examines food as a central presence in the Nancy Drew novels from the mid-1930s onward. The essay argues that food functions in the series as a marker of class status, a domestic relief from the pressures of dangerous sleuthing, and a signifier of alternative feminine subjectivities (ranging from the "athlete" to the balanced leader to the "boy-crazy romantic"), concluding that the novels' contradictory representations of food illustrate both the series' overt conservatism as well as the implicit acknowledgment that (in Suzie Orbach's famous phrase) "fat is a feminist issue." In "To Eat and Be Eaten in Nineteenth-Century Children's Literature," Jacqueline Labbe discusses instances in Victorian children's literature when food transmutes from nourishment for the child's body to a metonym for the child's body, and when eating is less about satisfying corporeal needs than about symbolizing moral needs. Children's literature then both entertains young readers and implicitly threatens their existence: violence, fear, and the threat of death allow adults to ensure that their children will perform suitably, allowing the playfulness of "I'm going to eat you up" to assume a new and darker meaning. In "Voracious Appetites: The Construction of 'Fatness' in the Boy Hero in English Children's Literature," Jean Webb explores how nineteenth-century Muscular Christianity was a major influence on the construction of the hero in children's literature, establishing the strong athletic heroic image as a desirable role model. In parallel, the image of the sedentary obese child developed as an opposition, being the butt of bullying and a figure of fun.

The five chapters in Part V—Global/Multicultural/Postcolonial Food—have a worldwide reach, extending from Latin America to Europe to Asia. The first two chapters take up the topic of cross-cultural assimilation (or the lack thereof). In "'The Eaters of Everything': Etiquettes of Empire in Kipling's Narratives of Imperial Boys," Winnie Chan examines scenes of eating in Kipling's most influential tales of imperial boys as they developed and acquired an increasingly necessary etiquette of Empire. In "Eating Different, Looking Different: Food in Asian American Childhood," Lan Dong uses Donna Gabaccia's theory from *We Are What We Eat: Ethnic Food and the Making of Americans* (1998) on the intersection between ethnic food and ethnic identity to analyze how food functions as a complex signifier for Asian American children's struggle over identity construction. In "The Potato Eaters: Food Collection in Irish Famine Literature for Children," Karen MacNamara examines the use of food (and its lack) as a complex signifier for socialization and identity construction in Irish Famine texts written for children, arguing that they construct new cultural identities by dispelling feelings of survivor's guilt and shame. The last two essays in this section look at childhood and gender within a Latin context. In "The Keys to the Kitchen: Cooking and Latina Power in Latin(o) American Children's Stories," Genny Ballard explores how food in

Latin American children's literature reflects gender roles and cultural identity and provides linkages for family and community across time (generations) and space (immigration). In "Sugar or Spice? The Flavor of Gender Self-Identity in an Example of Brazilian Children's Literature," Richard Vernon examines how Ana Maria Bohrer's 1992 *A menina açucarada* (The Sugar-coated Girl) uses food as a veiled means to critique dictatorship. Applying the ideas of food theorists Mary Douglas, Pasi Falk, and Paul Rosin concerning taste preferences and the social acceptance and taboo of certain foods, the essay shows how the story's 5-year-old protagonist rejects the sociofamilial role assigned her and accepts one of her own choosing (roles symbolized in the story by sugar and hot sauce respectively).

Part VI—Through Food the/a Self—looks at how food impacts various constructions and deconstructions of childhood identity and agency. In "Oranges of Paradise: The Orange as Symbol of Escape and Loss in Children's Literature," James Everett argues that oranges, both in literature for and about children, hold an odd double value as signifiers that promise one thing and deliver another, complicating a child's identity formation. In "Trials of Taste: Ideological 'Food Fights' in Madeleine L'Engle's *A Wrinkle in* Time," Elizabeth Gargano explores how often-overlooked scenes involving food and eating play a crucial role in L'Engle's valorization of the individual consciousness. In "A Consuming Tradition: Candy and Socio-religious Identity Formation in Roald Dahl's *Charlie and the Chocolate Factory*," Robert Kachur studies how the novel positions food and identity in two ways: first, within the biblical master narrative of creation, paradise, fall, and redemption, thus helping children see themselves and their appetites in relation to the dominant Judeo-Christian tradition; second, how the novel reproduces that master narrative in ways peculiarly resonant for children raised in a postmodern consumer society. In "Prevailing Culinary, Psychological, and Metaphysical Conditions: Meatballs and Reality," Martha Satz looks at how Judi Barnett's picture book *Cloudy with a Chance of Meatballs* constructs a dialectic between the unyielding nature of reality and its tractability in the face of the imagination. Food is associated with plentitude, love, the imagination, and the Real in both its yielding and unyielding aspects, assuring children that they will be able to cope with their existence even when manna ceases to fall from the sky or their parents' refrigerators and that adulthood has its redemptive features. In "'The Attack of the Inedible Hunk!': Food, Language, and Power in the Captain Underpants Series," Annette Wannamaker explores how in Dav Pilkey's novels food, the monstrous, and the grotesque are conflated, sometimes with women and sometimes with children, conflations that represent the power struggle between the adult world and childhood agency.

Lévi-Strauss said that "food is good to think with." Certainly, the scholars in this collection have followed his maxim. There is not only much food but much "with" here as well. We hope that the chapters—whether feast, entrée, appetizer, or snack—have whetted the appetite for more scholarship on food and children's literature. Just as the burgeoning field of food studies has just begun to chart the power of food in culture and history, so too is children's literature scholarship just beginning to grapple with food as an essential interpretive trope for children's literature.

Works Cited

Bakhtin, M. M. *Rabelais and His World.* Bloomington: Indiana UP, 1984.

Barthes, Roland. "Towards a Psychosociology of Contemporary Food Consumption." *Annales E.S.C.* 16 (Sept.-Oct. 1961): 977–986.

———. *Mythologies.* New York: Hill, 1972.

Beardworth, Alan, and Teresa Keil. *Sociology on the Menu: An Invitation to the Study of Food and Society.* London: Routledge, 1997.

Beeton, Isabella. *Mrs. Beeton's Book of Household Management: A First Edition Facsimile.* New York: Farrar, 1969.

Belasco, Warren James. *Meals to Come: A History of the Future of Food.* Berkeley: U of California P, 2006.

———. "Why Food Matters." *Culture and Agriculture* 21.1 (1999): 27–34.

Biasin, Gian-Paolo. *The Flavors of Modernity: Food and the Novel.* Princeton, NJ: Princeton UP, 1993.

Braudel, Fernand. *The Structures of Everyday Life: The Limits of the Possible: Civilization and Capitalism, 15th–18th Century.* New York: Harper, 1981.

Brown, James W. *Fictional Meals and Their Function in the French Novel, 1789–1848.* Toronto: U of Toronto Romance Series, 1984.

Chodorow, Nancy. *The Reproduction of Mothering: Psychoanalysis and the Sociology of Gender.* Berkeley: U of California P, 1978.

Curtin, Deane W. "Food/Body/Person." *Cooking, Eating, Thinking: Transformative Philosophies of Food.* Ed. Deane W. Curtin and Lisa M. Heldke. Bloomington: Indiana UP, 1992.

Daniel, Carolyn. *Voracious Children: Who Eats Whom in Children's Literature.* 2006. New York: Routledge, 2006.

Douglas, Mary. "Deciphering a Meal." *Daedalus* 101.1 (1963): 61–68.

Fernández-Armesto, Felipe. *Near a Thousand Tables: A History of Food.* New York: Free P, 2002.

Flandrin, Jean Louis, Massimo Montanari, and Albert Sonnenfeld. *Food: A Culinary History from Antiquity to the Present.* New York: Columbia UP, 1999.

Food, Culture, & Society. Association for the Study of Food and Society. Biggleswade, UK: Berg, 1996–present.

Food History News. Isleboro, ME: S. L. Oliver, 1989–present.

Furst, Lilian R., and Peter W. Graham. *Disorderly Eaters: Texts in Self-Empowerment.* University Park: Pennsylvania State UP, 1992.

Gabaccia, Donna R. *We Are What We Eat: Ethnic Food and the Making of Americans.* Cambridge: Harvard UP, 1998.

Gainor, J. Ellen. "'The-Slow-Eater-Tiny-Bite-Taker': An Eating Disorder in Betty Macdonald's *Mrs. Piggle Wiggle.*" *Disorderly Eaters: Texts in Self-Empowerment.* Ed. Lilian R. Furst and Peter W. Graham. University Park: Pennsylvania State UP, 1992. 30–41.

Gastronomica: The Journal of Food and Culture. U of California P, 2001–present.

Goody, Jack. *Cooking, Cuisine, and Class: A Study in Comparative Sociology.* Cambridge: Cambridge UP, 1982.

Homer. *The Odyssey.* Trans. Robert Fagles. New York: Penguin, 1997.

Katz, Wendy R. "Some Uses of Food in Children's Literature." *Children's Literature in Education* 11.4 (1980): 192–199.

Keeling, Kara K., and Scott Pollard. "Power, Food, and Eating in Maurice Sendak and Henrik Drescher: *Where the Wild Things Are, In the Night Kitchen,* and *The Boy Who Ate Around.*" *Children's Literature in Education* 30.2 (1999): 127–143.

Kiell, Norman. *Food and Drink in Literature: A Selectively Annotated Bibliography.* Lanham, MD: Scarecrow, 1995.

Korsmeyer, Carolyn. *Making Sense of Taste: Food & Philosophy.* Ithaca, NY: Cornell UP, 1999.

Kristeva, Julia. *Powers of Horror: An Essay on Abjection.* New York: Columbia UP, 1982.

Kurlansky, Mark. *Salt: A World History.* New York: Walker, 2002.

Leonardi, Susan J. "Recipes for Reading: Summer Pasta, Lobster à La Riseholme, and Key Lime Pie." *PMLA* 104.3 (1989): 340–347.

Lévi-Strauss, Claude. "The Culinary Triangle." *Partisan Review* 33 (1966): 586–595.

———. *The Raw and the Cooked.* New York: Harper, 1969.

Marin, Louis. *Food for Thought.* Baltimore: Johns Hopkins UP, 1989.

Mennell, Stephen. *All Manners of Food: Eating and Taste in England and France from the Middle Ages to the Present.* Oxford: Oxford UP, 1985.

Mintz, Sidney W. *Sweetness and Power: The Place of Sugar in Modern History.* New York: Viking, 1985.

Mintz, Sidney W., and Christine M. Du Bois. "The Anthropology of Food and Eating." *Annual Review of Anthropology* 31 (2002): 99–119.

Montanari, Massimo. *Food Is Culture.* New York: Columbia UP, 2006.

Nicholson, Mervyn. "Magic Food, Compulsive Eating, and Power Poetics." *Disorderly Eaters: Texts in Self-Empowerment.* Ed. Lilian R. and Peter W. Graham Furst. University Park: Pennsylvania State UP, 1992. 43–60.

———. "The Scene of Eating and the Semiosis of the Invisible." *Recherches semiotiqie/Semiotic Inquiry* 14.1–2 (1994): 285–302.

———. "Food and Power: Homer, Carroll, Atwood and Others." *Mosaic: A Journal for the Interdisciplinary Study of Literature* 20.3 (Summer 1987): 37–55.

Nikolajeva, Maria. *From Mythic to Linear: Time in Children's Literature.* Lanham, MD: Scarecrow, 2000.

Pépin, Jacques. *The Apprentice: My Life in the Kitchen.* New York: Houghton, 2003.

Perrot, Jean. "Maurice Sendak's Ritual Cooking of the Child in Three Tableaux: The Moon, Mother, and Music." *Children's Literature* 18 (1990): 68–86.

Pollard, Scott, and Kara K. Keeling. "In Search of his Father's Garden." *Beatrix Potter's Peter Rabbit: A Children's Classic at 100.* Ed. Margaret Mackey. Lanham, MD: Scarecrow, 2002. 117–130.

Sendak, Maurice. *In the Night Kitchen.* New York: Harper, 1970.

Symons, Michael. *A History of Cooks and Cooking.* Urbana: U of Illinois P, 2004.

Tannahill, Reay. *Food in History.* New York: Stein, 1973.

Toussaint-Samat, Maguelonne. *A History of Food.* Cambridge: Blackwell, 1993.

Vallone, Lynne. "'What Is the Meaning of All This Gluttony?': Edgeworth, the Victorians, C. S. Lewis and a Taste for Fantasy." *Papers: Explorations into Children's Literature* 12.1 (2002): 47–54.

Visser, Margaret. *The Rituals of Dinner: The Origins, Evolution, Eccenticities, and Meaning of Table Manners.* New York: Grove, 1986.

Weiss, Allen S. *Feast and Folly: Cuisine, Intoxication, and the Poetics of the Sublime.* Albany: State U of New York P, 2002.

Part II

Reading as Cooking

Chapter Two
Delicious Supplements: Literary Cookbooks as Additives to Children's Texts

Jodie Slothower and Jan Susina

Would Jo March in *Little Women* (1868) make cucumber sandwiches? Could Nancy Drew scare up "Ghostly Popcorn," or was she better at investigating "Hidden Staircase Biscuits"? If you could create it, would "Stickjaw for Talkative Parents," from Roald Dahl's *Charlie and the Chocolate Factory* (1964), actually stop parents from talking? Scrambled eggs may always taste the same, as Peter T. Hooper tells his sister in Dr. Seuss's *Scrambled Eggs Super!* (1953), but are the ones they make really so wonderful? How does one make green eggs and ham? Readers of Laura Numeroff's *If You Give a Mouse a Cookie* (1985) know what will happen if you make this offer, but what sort of cookie should they serve? Cookbooks connected to specific children's books answer these questions and provide recipes for these literary foods based on preexisting texts intended for children and adult readers. The best literary cookbooks for children offer a gustatory supplement to the narrative—expanding on readers' interests in and curiosities about characters by creating a community; adding sensory details to the original texts, particularly historical annotations; and hypothesizing what characters might have eaten. The more poorly constructed cookbooks are lightweight confections for the original books' fans that function like a form of literary junk food, somewhat enjoyable and familiar, but hardly nutritious and rarely enlightening.

In this chapter, we limit our examination of the genre of children's cookbooks to those that are specifically connected to children's literature. In her groundbreaking 1989 *PMLA* article "Recipes for Reading," Susan Leonardi has noted that all cookbooks are embedded narratives (340). Cookbooks that are linked to children's texts converse between original text and the cookbook, author and reader, recipe and creator, and various readership communities. To better understand cookbooks that are based on children's books, we will establish several categories within this subgenre along with criteria for what makes the best of these cookbooks successful. The multiple audiences reflect how these children's literature-based cookbooks expand the scope of the narrative, add historical and cultural culinary references, and produce connections to literary and gastronomic communities beyond the original texts. Children's literature-linked cookbooks are elements of the interconnecting parts that Marsha Kinder, in *Playing with Power* (1991), calls children's commercial supersystems. A key assumption underlying our analysis of these cookbooks is the consideration of how they fit into such supersystems. Kinder explains that a children's commercial supersystem is a network of intertextuality constructed around a figure or group of figures from popular culture. Such a system may be a network of products that cut across various forms of production that foster collectability and increase commodification (Kinder 123). Many of these cookbooks serve as narratives to connect readers with historical foodways or the eating habits of literary characters. The overarching consideration in examining these cookbooks is how they transform and enrich the reading of the original text(s) into an interactive experience.

To understand children's literature-linked cookbooks, it is helpful to look briefly at similar cookbooks linked to literature for adults. These adult cookbooks are best exemplified by Linda Wolfe's *The Literary Gourmet: Menus from Masterpieces* (1962). This cookbook features selections from literary texts—such as Marcel Proust's madeleine description in *Swann's Way* (1913) to Mrs. Ramsay's *boeuf en daube* from Virginia Woolf's *To the Lighthouse* (1927)—and then provides recipes to re-create the food described in the text. The publication of Wolfe's cookbook may have inspired a subsequent interest in children's literary cookbooks, as all of the children's cookbooks that we have found were published after 1962. The recipes Wolfe selected are from cookbooks from the period of the original book's publication, thus enabling readers to experience the food as it might have been served during the historical time period of the fictional text. The reproduction of foods that may have inspired the authors is a significant aspect that often reappears in the children's cookbooks.

Recipes in Wolfe's cookbook as well as these children's cookbooks tell stories, which, as Janet Theophano observes in *Eat My Words: Reading Women's Lives Through the Cookbooks They Wrote* (2002), "tell about life and its sustenance in different eras and in different places; they are about enjoyment and desire, family and friendships, stability and change, and the contentment and longings of lives lived in worlds remote from our own" (10). Recipes in children's literature-based texts can provide a significant cultural context to better understand the characters' lives through food. They also have a way of expanding a text, as Sarah Sceats observes: "Written recipes have the peculiar metaliterary status of anticipating the creation of material entities and events beyond the text" (169). Theophano is one of a growing number of culinary experts, food enthusiasts, anthropologists, folklorists, psychologists, sociologists, and literary scholars examining the cultural significance of cookbooks and cooking. Cookbooks, as Barbara Haber observes, are "a vastly underutilized resource" (5). She notes that "in the last several years ... studies in women's history have appeared that demonstrate how customs surrounding food itself reveal important distinctions among women and their connections to the communities in which they live" (4).

Although much has been written about food in children's literature, surprisingly little has been written about children's cookbooks. Sherrie Inness, who edited *Kitchen Culture in America: Popular Representations of Food, Gender, and Race* (2000), focused her chapter on cookbooks and magazine articles about food for children that were published between 1910 and 1960. Inness is one of the few literary scholars to have specifically examined children's cookbooks. She notes the importance of studying this material as "cookbooks do more than teach how to grill a steak or bake a cake; they demonstrate to boys and girls the attitudes that society expects them to adopt towards cooking and cooking-related tasks" (Inness 120). Though her essay focuses primarily on gender roles reflected in children's cookbooks, she acknowledges that "this chapter cannot adequately explore the countless intersections between juvenile cookbooks and girls' (and boys') material culture, which includes dolls, toys, books, and numerous other items" (Inness 120).

Given the abundance of possible texts, we realized the need for a narrower focus within the field of contemporary children's cookbooks. Some stories—such as Alice Waters's *Fanny at Chez Panisse* (1992), Christina Bjork's *Elliot's Extraordinary Cookbook* (1990), and Deborah Hopkinson's *Fannie in the Kitchen* (2001)—intertwine recipes within the narrative and are compelling combinations of fiction and nonfiction texts, but they are beyond the scope of this chapter. Like Nora Ephron's *Heartburn* (1983) and Laura Esquivel's *Like Water for Chocolate* (1993), these children's books interweave recipes and narrative. Esquivel's novel and similar novels with recipes have been analyzed by Sarah Sceats, among others. Our essay is limited to cookbooks that are inspired by children's books, rather than children's books that incorporate recipes into the narrative. However, the cookbooks we examine are intended for both child and adult readers.

Another way to narrow the large number of cookbooks connected to children's literature is through stylistic categories. In one of her many helpful online lists related to children's literature, Kay Vandergrift notes thirty-seven "cookbooks related to children's stories" (Vandergrift Web site). However, she includes some books with recipes woven into the narrative, which we have chosen to exclude. Yet, there are at least thirty-seven, and probably forty to fifty, cookbooks connected to children's books.

Roland Barthes writes in "Toward a Psychosociology of Contemporary Food Consumption," "When he buys an item of food, consumes it, or serves it, modern man does not manipulate a simple object in a purely transitive fashion; this item of food sums up and transmits a situation; it constitutes an information, it signifies" (21). The recipes gathered in these children's literature-based cookbooks not only transform the recipe, they influence the understanding of the original text as well, adding a new flavor to it. Although recipes tell stories on their own, recipes within a cookbook create narratives to bridge to the original text and ask the reader to reflect back, like a mirror. Leonardi observes, "A recipe is, then, an embedded discourse, and like other embedded discourses, it can have a variety of relationships with its frame, or its bed" (340). The interwoven nature of these books becomes increasingly complex. Readers come to these texts prepared to make the connections between the original literary text and the subsequent cookbook. As Leslie Cefali writes, "Children need concrete learning experiences to get involved in the learning process. What better way for them to become a part of a book than to experience cooking and preparing food that is eaten in nursery rhymes and literature?" (v). The complexity of this interactive experience makes cookbooks based on children's literature a literal embodiment of instruction to delight. Just as alphabet books have the overt objective of teaching the shapes and the sequence of letters, most alphabet books have a secondary message that forms their frame, or concept. Similarly, these children's cookbooks are intended to expand the knowledge of the original book and teach children about cooking and sometimes about nutrition.

Categorizing Cookbooks Linked to Children's Books

To help us sift through these cookbooks, we devised five categories that help to analyze the books' success in their strategy of linking to the original texts. The categories range from primarily capitalizing on the original books to those that distinctly enhance and further the primary texts. Although a cookbook that meets the first category requirements is satisfactory, the subsequent categories reflect more positive and intelligent extensions of the original.

1. Awkward Connections. The first category of these cookbooks includes those that merely capitalize on the popularity of an established text, series, or character. Publishers realize that a book or series can be extended through a cookbook. This type of cookbook includes Carolyn Keene's *Nancy Drew Cookbook: Clues to Good Cooking* (1973); through dull design and repetitive writing style, it adds little new insight about cooking or Nancy Drew. The recipes are only faintly linked to the series through titles such as "Hidden Staircase Biscuits" or "Twisted Candles Peach Crisp." Dewey Gram's *Babe's Country Cookbook* (1998) is a similar cookbook; it was intended to capitalize on the popularity of the film version of Dick King-Smith's *Babe the Gallant Pig* (1985). The cookbook cover features a photo from Chris Noonan's 1995 film, rather than a book illustration by Mary Rayner. But it does not take long to ponder the problematic premise of a *Babe* cookbook. The central conflict of the book and film is how Babe manages to avoid becoming Christmas dinner for the Hoggetts. Gram manages to avoid what he calls "a delicate issue" (8) in the cookbook's introduction by explaining that after Babe won the National Grand Challenge Sheep Dog Trials, the Hoggetts decided to go vegetarian, thus saving Babe and his barnyard friends from being featured on a plate. *Babe's Country Cookbook* is a "*meat-free* farm cookbook—perhaps as rare a bird as the Grand National Sheep-Pig himself" (Gram 8). In order to appeal to the child reader, the cookbook has to do some serious revisions to the original text.

2. Text Extenders. These cookbooks use the original text and illustrations of the children's books to extend their scope; these contain recipes that would be appropriate within the cultural context of the original narratives. Fans of Lucy Maud Montgomery's *Anne of Green Gables*, P. L. Travers's *Mary Poppins*, C. S. Lewis's *The Narnia Chronicles*, L. Frank Baum's *Oz* series, and Dr. Seuss's picture books will find that each has an accompanying cookbook. These cookbooks have explicit links to the originals and often expand on the narratives. For instance, an extension of a popular series that makes more sense than the *Babe Country Cookbook* is Laura Numeroff's *Mouse Cookies & More: A Treasury* (2006). Based on *If You Give a Mouse a Cookie* and her subsequent picture books in the series, Numeroff fills this book with stories as well as recipes, songs, crafts and activities appropriate for young children and their parents.

Consider how Baum's *Oz* series has been repositioned into different cookbooks. Monica Bayley's *The Wonderful Wizard of Oz Cook Book* (1981) features illustrations by W. W. Denslow and is organized according to the color scheme of the four sections of Oz, which reflects different parts of the United States. This cookbook is created for the Oz fan and collector. It would be an unusual example of Floyd and Forster's observation that "recipes may be linked with the impulse to rule, hierarchise and differentiate" (5). Sara Key, et al.'s *The Wizard of Oz Cookbook: Breakfast in Kansas, Dessert in Oz* (1993) is published by Turner Entertainment as part of its "Hollywood Hotplate" series. This cookbook includes Denslow's illustrations; it also features stills from Victor Fleming's 1939 movie. This cookbook is organized in a more typical fashion, but the emphasis is on how to hold Oz-related parties, for either adults or children. Like the Emerald City, Key's recipes emphasize appearance over taste. Adam Gopnik astutely observes, "cookbooks are finally more book, than they are cook, and, more and more we know it; for every novel that contains a recipe, there is now a recipe book that is meant to be read as a novel" (85).

Out-of-copyright illustrations are particularly popular for remanipulation in this type of cookbook. Nika Hazelton's *Raggedy Ann and Andy's Cookbook* (1975) clearly is extending the series/brand by reproducing Johnny Gruelle's famous illustrations and occasionally a passage from one of the Raggedy Ann and Andy books. But this cookbook is not just a nostalgic reflection of a once popular children's series. This is a serious, though flawed, cookbook for children by Hazelton, who has written well-received adult cookbooks, particularly on European cuisine. Hazelton's directions on "How to Clean a Small Fish" (54–55) seem inappropriate in a general recipe collection for contemporary children, even if she does suggest having a father, or a mother, present to help. Oddly, it is also accompanied by an illustration of three goldfish jumping out of their bowl and falling on Raggedy Ann. Most of Hazelton's other recipes here reflect more traditional fare.

3. Cookbooks That Combine Multiple Narratives. A third category of children's literature-based cookbooks includes those that link multiple children's texts—such as nursery rhymes, fairy tales, or famous literary characters—into a single collection of recipes. The best of these is Carol MacGregor's *The Storybook Cookbook* (1967), which includes several excerpts from well-known children's books and then offers appropriate recipes. Among the texts featured are Robert Louis Stevenson's *Treasure Island* (1883), Ruth Sawyer's *Roller Skates* (1936), and Lewis Carroll's *Alice in Wonderland* (1865). *The Storybook Cookbook* functions as a children's version of Wolfe's *The Literary Gourmet*. MacGregor features a recipe associated with an excerpt from J. M. Barrie's *Peter and Wendy* (1912) in which Captain Hook leaves a poisonous cake next to the Lost Boys' hideaway. The recipe is for "Captain Hook's Poison Cake" with green frosting (MacGregor 65–67).

Mother Goose has inspired several cookbooks. Lorinda Bryan Cauley's *Pease-Porridge Hot*: *A Mother Goose Cookbook* (1977) features recipes for food described in nursery rhymes and fairy tales. Children may be curious about what "Little Red Riding Hood's Granny's Custards" really taste like (26–27). Lyn Stallworth's *Wond'rous Fare* (1988) features imaginative illustrations and book design, which add to the appeal of recipes such "Toad's Buttered Toast," "Ben Gunn's Toasted Cheese," and "The Mock Turtle's Beautiful Soup." Children may see recipes as a window to a world that is already attractive and appealing. Anne L. Bower notes in *Community Cookbooks: Stories, Histories and Recipes for Reading* (1997):

> Those who do cook also know that a recipe can go beyond formulaic in both content and form . . . And beyond that content level, we also savor the style of a recipe, it can make us laugh, give us a sense of the world from which it originates, incorporates some history, or an inkling of the personality of its writers (7–8).

Two books that use fairy tales as the inspiration for recipes are Jane Yolen and Heidi Stemple's *Fairy Tale Feasts: A Literary Cookbook for Young Readers and Eaters* (2006) and Sandre Moore's *The Fairy Tale Cookbook: Fun Recipes for Families to Create and Eat Together* (2000). Yolen and her daughter Stemple correctly observe how much fairy tales are connected to food, such as Cinderella and pumpkins; they then provide appropriate recipes and intriguing marginalia relating to twenty traditional fairy tales. Moore's light-hearted, family-tested cookbook features recipes to accompany reading a broad range of children's literature, including fairy tales. She connects the texts with creative recipes such as "Green Eggs Hold the Ham," "Un-birthday Tarts," and the "Baby-Sitters Club Portable Energy Munchies."

4. Cookbooks That Focus on Healthy Living. A fourth category of children's literature-based cookbooks includes those with an intention to teach children either about cooking or eating nutritious foods. Karen Greene's *Once Upon a Recipe: Delicious, Healthy Foods for Kids of All Ages* (1987) encourages eating healthy foods. Greene may be heavy-handed about good nutrition, but she does understand cookbooks:

> Each page of this cookbook was created to stir a different dream. After all, the kitchen is as likely a landscape as any for bumping into fairy godmothers, for wish fulfillment, for seeing drawer after drawer of dreams come true.... In that spirit, *Once Upon A Recipe* is intended to bring parent and child together in the kitchen, mixing and giggling and baking and imagining. (6)

Greene is right to observe that kitchens are frequent settings for magical and transformational experiences in children's books, which may be a reason why children's literature-based cookbooks are popular.

Beatrix Potter's illustration of Peter Rabbit eating a carrot in Mr. Mac-Gregor's garden is the cover illustration to Arnold Dobrin's *Peter Rabbit's Natural Foods Cookbook* (1977). The book design of Dobrin's cookbook is small and square with liberal use of Potter's illustrations, replicating the format of Potter's original picture books. The intention seems to be to attract young readers as much as their parents who cook. The emphasis now is that Peter is eating healthy foods, specifically fruits and vegetables. Rabbit pie is noticeably absent in the recipes in Dobrin's book (although it is an important element in Potter's text), just as pork recipes are absent in Gram's *Babe's Country Cookbook*.

Both Dobrin's *Peter Rabbit's Natural Foods Cookbook* and Sara Paston-Williams's *Beatrix Potter's Country Cooking* (1991), a cookbook featuring lavish photographs, are published by Frederick Warne, Potter's original publisher. The association with Potter's publisher suggests the recipes are authorized. The well-researched and highly annotated *Beatrix Potter's Country Cooking* book is intended for older child readers and adults, particularly those interested in the English Lake District and its cooking styles. Paston-Williams includes a section on "Poultry and Game" that particularly focuses on the type of game Potter's husband, William Heelis, may have hunted. She includes two recipes for rabbit: "Rabbit Casserole with Cheese and Herb Dumplings" and "Old English Rabbit Pie." Though these recipes might disturb some readers, they are in keeping with Potter's comment "It does not do to be sentimental on a farm" (Paston-Williams 46).

5. Cookbooks That Successfully Enhance the Original. The final category of children's literature-based cookbooks encompasses those that enhance the original narrative. Usually they also are intended to teach children more about the texts, often by providing a historical context or sometimes by using recipes as supplements to imaginative ideas in the original. Examples of these cookbooks, which will be discussed, include Roald Dahl's cookbooks, Jean Craighead George's cookbooks, Chronicle Books' cookbooks based on *Star Wars* and Nickelodeon television shows, cookbooks based on American Girls books, and Barbara M. Walker's *The Little House Cookbook: Frontier Foods from Laura Ingalls Wilder's Classic Stories* (1979).

Lucy M. Long writes in "Culinary Tourism" that "participating in foodways implies the full spectrum of activities surrounding food" (23). Culinary tourism, she suggests, does not always require travel to destinations; it may be accomplished through reading cookbooks. Literary culinary tourism can be experienced through reading cookbooks linked to literature. Although Long acknowledges the sometimes derogatory aspect of "culinary tourism," she emphasizes how it widens readers' worlds (45). Similarly, though some cookbooks linked to children's literature may have drawbacks, the best are able to deepen readers' understanding of the texts.

The Roald Dahl cookbooks that use his children's books as an inspiration fit appropriately into category five. Dahl's stories reveal an author obsessed with food. Consider some of his books' titles: *Charlie and the Chocolate Factory* (1964), *James and the Giant Peach* (1961), and *Rhyme Stew* (1990). At first, cookbooks based on Dahl's books may seem odd. Yet, he and his collaborators clearly understand how to attract budding child cooks through creative titles, adventurous recipes, and clear directions for food that is surprisingly edible (although sometimes a little gross to look at!). Dahl and his wife Felicity were encouraged to "write a book for children, based on the many wonderful and varied foods that appear in his books" (*Revolting Recipes* 7). Before he died, Dahl assembled a "listing of every food from Willy Wonka's Nutty Crunch Surprise to the mount of mysterious spare ribs consumed by Hansel and Gretel in *Rhyme Stew* (*Revolting Recipes* 7). After his death, Felicity Dahl along with Josie Fison compiled the recipes that embody the spirit of Dahl's books into two cookbooks, which were illustrated by Quentin Blake: *Roald Dahl's Revolting Recipes* (1994) and *Roald Dahl's Even More Revolting Recipes* (2001). Some of the cookbooks discussed are not quite intended for actual cooking, but recipes in the Dahl-inspired books clearly are. The directions and photographs are accessible to children.

What child wouldn't want to try to make an "Eatable Marshmallow Pillow," "Bird Pie" with edible 'bird legs' sticking out (made with puff pastry), or "Candy-Coated Pencils for Sucking in Class?" The results might look revolting, but that is part of their gross-out charm. Many are quite tasty as well. The recipes are examples of what Roland Barthes defined in his essay on "Ornamental Cookery" in *Mythologies* (1972) as proceeding "in two contradictory ways ... on the one hand fleeing from nature thanks to a kind of frenzied baroque (sticking shrimps in lemon, making a chicken look pink ...), and on the other, trying to reconstitute it through an incongruous artifice (strewing meringue mushrooms and holly leaves on a traditional log-shaped Christmas cake ...)" (79). The Dahl cookbooks are imaginative enough in their oddly ornamental recipes that they have merit as cookbooks even without the original text connection. For instance, "A Piece of Soil with Engine Oil" (*Even More* 40–41) may sound disgusting but is actually a delicious chocolate cake.

Culinary Scrapbook and DIY Sensibility

Having established these criteria, it is also helpful to understand these cookbooks' overall book design and the multiple audiences that develop through their reading. Many children's literature-based cookbooks have both a scrapbook and do-it-yourself (DIY) sensibility. They often feature collages of brief excerpts from the original text followed by a recipe. This, too, gives them a sense of a travel scrapbook created after the trip, another form of culinary tourism. Sometimes the collections are merely recipes introduced with a relatively tangential connection and would fit clearly into the first category. This can be as mundane as the introduction to "Maggie's Lemonade" from Diane Blain's *The Boxcar Children Cookbook* (1991): "The family all sat around the long table to eat lunch. Maggie had sent up a large basket of sandwiches and salad and pink lemonade with ice in it—*Mike's Mystery*" (Blain 14). A recipe for lemonade follows. The literary link for this series is, of course, with Gertrude Chandler Warner's series, but the cookbook, as exemplified by this recipe, does not particularly enhance the original text or in this case make the lemonade, which turns pink with red cherry juice, that unusual. The same is true of Georgeanne Brennan's *Green Eggs and Ham Cookbook* (2006). It features "Cat's Mac and Cheese," which is linked to a brief reference to macaroni that appears in Dr. Seuss's *The Cat's Quizzer* (1976). It is a rather complicated recipe which calls for making a roux and stuffing pasta, rather than the traditional, out-of-the-box style elbow macaroni cooked with cheese, which is familiar to most children (and time-strapped parents). The chief drawback with each of these cookbooks is how the cookbook authors and art editors reimagine, or reposition, excerpts from the original text and illustrations in trying to effectively match recipes; they frequently stretch so far that the connections seem tenuous. In the case of these two cookbooks, the creators seem to lack the imagination or creativity of the original authors. An intriguing concept would be for a Dr. Seuss cookbook that challenges the creativity and wit of the Dahl cookbooks. Another cookbook that begs to be written is an imaginative one based on the *Harry Potter* series; just what is in butter beer or chocolate frogs?

As Bower observes in *Community Cookbooks*, "We hope to contribute to the ways 'non-literary' texts can be read and valued. In turn, increasing awareness of the process at work in nonliterary texts may inform new readings of the literary" (14). By repositioning illustrations and adding recipes to augment the original text, many children's literary-linked cookbooks reposition the primary works. John Berger has written about how the meanings of images are altered when taken out of context. In *Ways of Seeing* (1972) Berger has noted, "The art of the past no longer exists as it once did. Its authority is lost. In its place there is a language of images. What matters now is who uses that language for what purpose" (33). Beatrix Potter's work has different implications when it is seen through a lens of encouraging healthy eating or through a food biography of an animal producer. Each of the Potter cookbooks we have found has a solid purpose without being dull; each could be intriguing for the right audience. Recipes, as Janet Floyd and Laurel Forster observe in *The Recipe Reader: Narratives-Contexts-Traditions* (2003), "engage the reader or cook in a 'conversation' about culture and history in which the recipe and its context provide part of the text and the reader imagines (or even eats) the rest" (2).

Gender-neutral Cooking and Children's Commercial Supersystems

The Roald Dahl cookbooks are among the most gender neutral of children's cookbooks. As they were both published within the last fifteen years, perhaps they reflect changing roles of men and women in the kitchen. A study by the Families and Work Institute, reported by *USA Today* in 2004, found that unlike Baby Boomer fathers, Generation X fathers are helping out more at home, although the amount of child care and household work of Generation X mothers has not correspondingly decreased (Elias 5D). The role of men in food preparation has expanded beyond that of barbecuing, or weekend pancake breakfasts, as popularized in many 1950s-era cookbooks. Thomas Adler, in "Making Pancakes on Sunday: The Male Cook in Family Tradition," notes how barbecue expanded men's cooking roles (46). However, Jessamyn Neuhaus, in a well-researched analysis of 1950s cookbooks, finds cookbooks from that era not as repressive as perhaps once considered; she writes, "Like a layered Jell-O salad, there's more than meets the eye" (547). Neuhaus also observes, "Cookbooks offer vivid examples of what we might appropriately term a cultural text: recipes are loaded with meaning particular to their time and place" (536). Nevertheless, most of the literary cookbooks we have found primarily are still directed to girls and women.

Donald J. Sobol's *Encyclopedia Brown* is a notable boys' series in that it does include a cookbook, *Encyclopedia Brown Takes the Cake!: A Cook and Case Book* (1983); Glenn Andrews wrote the recipes. In this book, Encyclopedia Brown solves cases and related recipes follow. Chapter 7, the "Case of the Overstuffed Piñata," is accompanied by recipes for "Refried Beans," "Mexican Meat Mixture," "Tostados, Tacos or Corn Shells." Encyclopedia Brown is capable as a cook and a detective within a community of people who appreciate cooking and eating. Theophano has described "cookbooks as communities" (11). Encyclopedia Brown's cookbook underscores a community element involved in cooking, but other books also emphasize recipes as a way to reflect the larger community of the stories' main characters.

Several recent cookbooks for children understand how contemporary cooking has become less gender based as well as how children's commercial supersystems influence the purchase of books that adults make for children. Cookbooks about children's television and films extend the brand of a text while introducing children to cooking techniques. Chronicle Books has published Robin Davis's *The Star Wars Cookbook: Wookiee Cookies and Other Galactic Recipes* (1998); Frankie Frankeny and Wesley Martin's *Star Wars Cookbook II: Darth Malt and More Galactic Recipes* (2000); and Nickelodeon's *A Nick Cookbook: Stir Squirt Sizzle* (2004), with recipes based on the Nickelodeon television channel shows for children. Unlike most of the cookbooks examined in this essay, the book design of these three anticipates how child cooks will actually use the books. They are spiral-bound so they will lay flat, the pages are plastic coated to resist spills, and most recipes are accompanied by enticing color photographs featuring characters from the original texts. They are part of a children's commercial supersystem, and they are all succeeding in their mission as children's cookbooks with thoughtfully created recipes that are both tasty and understandable for young cooks. Like the Dahl books, these media connected texts feature appealing illustrations and intriguing titles—"Yoda Soda," "Princess Leia Danish Dos," "Pasta Squidward," and "Green Slime Birthday Cake."

The Disney Company is skilled at connecting children's and parents' interest in cooking as part of marketing its media empire; it has published numerous cookbooks for a wide variety of audiences. Though Ira L. Meyer's *Disney Recipes: From Animation to Inspiration* (2003) is written for adult cooks, each recipe includes a short section called "What Children Can Do" to give parents ideas for family involvement. Disney's film *Ratatouille* (2007), directed by Brad Bird, capitalizes on an increasing interest in restaurants and food preparation by both children and adults. The cookbook related to the film *What's Cooking?: A Cookbook for Kids* (2007) has an introduction by the esteemed American Chef Thomas Keller, who was also a consultant to the animated film. Perhaps *Ratatouille* signals a new developing community of younger gastronomes entering kitchens and expensive restaurants because of the influence of film and literary texts. This trend was noted by Alexandra Zissu in her January 28, 2007, *New York Times* article about "the growing wave of parents obsessed with all things culinary who are indoctrinating their children to the ways of gastronomy" (1). She observed that it begins with pregnant mothers eating garlicky foods to expand their newborns' tastes and expands to children's cooking classes and sophisticated cooking toys "as pricey as some working adult versions" (Zissu 6). Zissu adds, "Many parents have noticed that their children have as much affection for cooking shows as for the Cartoon Network" (6).

Creating a Community of Readers and Cooks

Children's cookbooks create a community of child readers and adults assisting child cooks. Theophano addresses multiple senses of cookbook communities beginning with women in the seventeenth century exchanging receipts. The folklorist writes: "There is much to be learned from reading a cookbook besides how to prepare food—discovering the stories told in the spaces between the recipes or within the recipes themselves. For me, leafing through a cookbook is like peering through a kitchen window" (Theophano 6). For children, who have a more limited personal history, the creation of community may be more immediate through cookbooks. They are, in a way, consuming the characters' food and their lives through a literary-linked cookbook. By consuming characters' food, children have the opportunity to participate in their culture.

Multiple audiences can be extrapolated for these children's cookbooks. Although these are information and activity books rather than strictly literary narratives, their primary function is a continuation of preexisting narratives. Consequently, adult and child readers come to the cookbooks already somewhat familiar with the narrative and are usually looking for ways to extend their enjoyment of the texts. Almost every children's cookbook encourages, if not stipulates, adult guidance. Although they are marketed as children's cookbooks, they specifically court both children and adults.

The primary audience for children's literature-based cookbooks is often young readers. Yet, a significant audience also forms of adults who either read or use the books in conjunction with children or simply purchase them for themselves. *Alice in Wonderland* enthusiasts will be amused by Lyn Calder's *Walt Disney's Alice's Tea Party* (1992) and add it to their collection, although many may not intend to use the recipes. Cooks who are passionate about cookbooks are another audience for cookbooks with literary connections. Cookbook fans enjoy seeing how recipes are refashioned. Some also provide cultural and social histories of different geographical areas or periods of history. Finally, some of these books are intended for adults who may continue to be fans of a book, series, or author. Two books like this are Sara Paston-Williams's *Beatrix Potter's Country Cooking* and William Anderson's *The Laura*

Ingalls Wilder Country Cookbook (1995). Both may be seen by less ambitious cooks as beautiful coffee table-style books to be viewed, rather than cookbooks to help produce a recipe. These cookbooks go beyond the typical child–adult dual audience and reflect a more complicated intersection of audiences.

By connecting primary and related texts, these cookbooks begin to form a literary community. The books' information and narratives complement each other. An underlying assumption is that the reader is now part of a community that is expanding upon the original texts. Perhaps this is a reason there are so many cookbooks for series books: a cookbook seems a natural extension for the community of readers.

Reflecting and Expanding on Original Narratives

As embedded discourses, Leonardi writes that cookbooks linked to literary texts present texts as constantly mirroring one another. The weaker of these cookbooks cannot stand alone and fit into our second category, Text Extensions; their primary charm is how they embellish the original. They are the literary equivalent of Hamburger Helper™, which helps extend the original for a second helping. If children are not already readers of the *Anne of Green Gables* series, it is hard to imagine why they would want to read the related cookbook. Perhaps somewhat better is Virginia H. Ellison's *The Pooh Cook Book* (1969), which shares the charm of A. A. Milne's text and Ernest Shephard's drawings. In addition, cooks who want honey recipes will find *The Pooh Cook Book* a good resource, as Ellison acknowledges referring to an American Honey Institute publication. Each recipe has a quotation from a Pooh book, and Ellison notes that rather than being intimately connected with the text, it allows the reader to "play a game of Guessing-which-Chapter-the-Quotation-Comes-From" (14), which is typical of this sort of cookbook.

The chief goal of many children's literature-based cookbooks is using food and recipes as a vehicle to make history come alive through an understanding of historical time periods. In "Toward a Psychosociology of Contemporary Food Consumption" Barthes notes, "One could say that an entire 'world' (social environment) is present in and signified by food" (23). These cookbooks combine food preparation information with preexisting literature, in an attempt to provide "instruction and delight." Floyd and Forster observe that "the recipe, in its intertextuality, is also itself a narrative which can engage the reader or cook in a 'conversation' about culture and history in which the recipe and its context provide part of the text and the reader imagines (or even eats) the rest" (2). Barbara Walker's *The Little House Cookbook: Frontier Foods from Laura Ingalls Wilder's Classic Stories* (1979) is perhaps the best historical cookbook related to children's literature; it clearly falls into our fifth category of cookbooks that successfully enhance the original text. The *Little House* series has inspired at least four authors to create cookbooks connected to the books. Walker's detailed cookbook, in turn, seems to have been an important influence on the style and recipes in the American Girl cookbooks.

All the cookbooks based on the *Little House* series assist culinary tourists unfamiliar with the details of nineteenth-century American farming and pioneer life. As Neuhaus observes, "Studying the eating patterns from a particular era may offer insights into society not readily available in standard social or political history" (531). Walker is a writer and designer, not a professional cook, but her cookbook is thoroughly researched, well supported by an extensive biography, and written in a lyrical style that holds its own with the excerpts of Wilder's texts. The cookbook uses Garth Williams's illustrations and the design, particularly, is similar to the primary text. What makes Walker's book a model of a children's literary cookbooks is how hers is a supplementary text that supports and enhances the original texts. Before providing the recipe for "Raw Turnip Snacks," Walker writes about turnips:

> The Ingallses' experience shows why turnips were a popular farm crop. As root foods in the soil they could survive grasshopper attacks and prairie fires. With their dense flesh and thick skins they could be held in storage through the winter. . . . We urge those who are not moved by cooked turnips to try raw turnip slices as a snack, with or without salt. . . . Slicing takes a good sharp knife and a practiced hand. Low-calorie turnips are excellent snacks for modern people whose problem is too many, rather than too few, good things to eat. (115)

Walker not only shows why lowly turnips were important to pioneers but that they could also be a tasty snack for modern readers. Her chapter "Foods from the Woods, Wilds, and Waters" is a reminder of when hunting was a crucial occupation for people who did not have the option of purchasing precut meat wrapped in plastic and Styrofoam. Pa may not have been the cook, but his role in securing the raw products was as necessary as Ma preparing them. Walker's cookbook emphasizes the importance of the entire family's role in food preparation.

Jean Craighead George's cookbooks—*The Wild, Wild Cookbook: A Guide for Young Wild-Food Foragers* (1982), re-edited and shortened with a less age-related title as *Acorn Pancakes, Dandelion Salad and 33 Other Wild Recipes* (1995) more than ten years later—are not specifically linked to her books. However, the recipes seem similar to food Sam Gibley selected for himself in George's *My Side of the Mountain* (1959). Written much like Euell Gibbons's *Stalking the Wild Asparagus* (1962), but for children, George's text may inspire readers to forage in their backyard. Her cookbooks also may motivate child and adult readers to look at nature differently and perhaps eat more adventurously.

Another children's author-produced cookbook is P. L. Travers's *Mary Poppins in the Kitchen: A Cookery Book with a Story* (1975). Published (not by Disney) after the successful 1963 Disney film, this cookbook could fit into several of the categories. It does have a frame story of several chapters at the beginning, but it is clear that Travers wanted to write a cookbook: "I have given Mary Poppins many of the recipes I knew as a child" (back cover). Travers's cookbook is a glimpse into a historic time period and, for American readers, another culture. The book is also clearly an extension of an established character, and popular media brand name, in print.

Learning history through cooking can become a form of culinary tourism, which may, or may not, result in culinary imperialism. In children's cookbooks, most of the tourism is in history, sort of like a cookbook walk through Colonial Williamsburg or Plymouth Plantation. Introducing cultures through food can be a productive way to discuss an Other, but it may leave a contemporary reader feeling superior, or at least grateful for labor-saving devices and nutrition advances. As Neuhaus observes, "Cookbooks offer vivid examples of what we might appropriately term a cultural text: recipes are loaded with meaning particular to their time and place" (536).

The American Girls Collection cookbook series gives young culinary tourists the experience of foodways during the United States' history. The American Girls cookbooks—Polly Athan's *Molly's Cookbook* (1994), Athan, et al.'s *Felicity's Cookbook* (1994), and Terri Bruan's *Kirsten's Cookbook* (1994), among others—move close to culinary imperialism as the dolls and accessories have been critiqued for fostering a sense of consumerism, their high cost, and exclusive merchandising (Susina 133). These cookbooks are another American Girl collectible among the vast merchandise sold in catalogs and urban stores. Yet, the American Girl series has created its own sense of community among mothers and daughters. It is a world where shopping for new products is often as important as historical connections. Cookbooks are an obvious way to expand the existing American Girls brand, to extend the children's commercial supersystem. In that sense, many of these cookbooks are no different than toys, jewelry, software, accessories, and a multitude of other interconnected products. This is true whether they are American Girls or the similarly abundant Peter Rabbit consumables and collectibles, as Margaret Mackey critiques in *The Case of Peter Rabbit: Changing Conditions of Literature for Children*. For those who may not yet have made the recipes or want the cultural experience of seeing how historical cooking is treated by a professional chef, girls and their families can try out the foods based on recipes found in the American Girls cookbooks at the American Girl Place bistros in Chicago, New York, Los Angeles, Dallas, and Atlanta.

What happens to the young reader of these children's literary-linked cookbooks? Does cooking change the dynamic or power structure of the author and reader? Leonardi writes, "Like a narrative, a recipe is reproducible, and further, its hearers-readers-receivers are encouraged to reproduce it and, in reproducing it, to revise it and make it their own. Unlike the repetition of narrative, however, a recipe's reproducibility can have a literal result, the dish itself" (344). In a sense, by creating food, the child and adult readers become creators of new texts and recipes that reflect their interpretation and expand the original narrative.

By following a recipe to make the described food, the power of creativity shifts from the cookbook to the cook as creator/author. Marianna Mayer in *The Mother Goose Cookbook*: *Rhymes and Recipes for the Very Young* (1998) writes:

> That thrill of participating in the sensory world of the kitchen is not unlike the excitement of a child's first forays into the world of reading, which often begins with nursery rhymes and the homegrown wisdom of Mother Goose. Like any good book, cooking opens a child's imagination to a creative, challenging world that ultimately encourages independence. (8).

Because children are already familiar with the characters in these literary cookbooks, they may feel more comfortable about trying new recipes and foods. As Mayer acknowledges, these cookbooks ultimately expand children's perspectives, including that of their palate. It allows them to indirectly consume the book. By reproducing recipes that are connected to characters, readers can get the sense of becoming one with text. It is a form of literary cannibalism in which you become what you eat. I consume, therefore I am. A sense of power derives from using your imagination as a reader and a cook. These cookbooks are intended to stir that imagination.

Works Cited

Cookbooks

Anderson, William. *The Laura Ingalls Wilder Country Cookbook*. Photos Leslie A. Kelly. New York: Harper, 1995.

Athan, Polly. *Molly's Cookbook: A Peek at Dining in the Past with Meals You Can Make Today*. Middleton, WI: Pleasant, 1994.

Athan, Polly, et al. *Felicity's Cookbook: A Peek at Dining in the Past with Meals You Can Cook Today*. Middleton, WI: Pleasant, 1994.

Bayley, Monica. *The Wonderful Wizard of Oz Cook Book*. Illus. W. W. Denslow. New York: Macmillan, 1981.

Bjork, Christine. *Elliot's Extraordinary Cookbook*. Illus. Lena Andersen. Trans. Joan Lundin. Stockholm: R&S Books, 1990.

Blain, Diane. *The Boxcar Children Cookbook*. Morton Grove, IL: Albert Whitman, 1991.

Braun, Terri, et al. *Kirsten's Cookbook: A Peek at Dining in the Past with Meals You Can Cook Today*. Middleton, WI: Pleasant, 1994.

Brennan, Georgeanne. *Green Eggs and Ham Cookbook: Recipes Inspired by Dr. Seuss*. Photos Frankie Frankeny. New York: Random, 2006.

Calder, Lyn. *Walt Disney's Alice's Tea Party*. Illus. Jesse Clay. New York: Disney, 1992.

Cauley, Lorinda Bryan. *Pease-Porridge Hot: A Mother Goose Cookbook*. New York: Putnam, 1977.

Cefali, Leslie. *Cook-a-Book: Reading Activities for Grades Pre-K to 6*. 2nd ed. Fort Atkinson, WI: Highsmith, 1999.

Dahl, Felicity, and Josie Fison. *Roald Dahl's Revolting Recipes*. Illus. Quentin Blake. Photos Jan Baldwin. New York: Viking, 1994.

———. *Roald Dahl's Even More Revolting Recipes*. Illus. Quentin Blake. New York: Viking, 2001.

Davis, Robin. *The Star Wars Cookbook: Wookiee Cookies and Other Galactic Recipes*. San Francisco: Chronicle, 1998.

Dobrin, Arnold. *Peter Rabbit's Natural Foods Cookbook*. Illus. Beatrix Potter. New York: Warne, 1977.

Ellison, Virginia. *The Pooh Cook Book: Inspired by Winnie-the-Pooh and The House at Pooh Corner by A. A. Milne*. Illus. Ernest H. Shepard. New York: Dutton, 1969.

Frankeny, Frankie, and Wesley Martin. *The Star Wars Cookbook II: Darth Malt and More Galactic*. San Francisco: Chronicle, 2000.

George, Jean Craighead. *Acorn Pancakes, Dandelion Salad and 33 Other Wild Recipes*. Illus. Paul Mirocha. New York: Harper, 1995.

———. *The Wild, Wild Cookbook: A Guide for Young Wild-Food Foragers*. Illus. Walter Kessell. New York: Crowell, 1982.

Gram, Dewey. *Babe's Country Cookbook: 80 Completely Meat Free Recipes!* Photos Martin Jacobs. New York: GT, 1998.

Greene, Karen. *Once Upon a Recipe: Delicious, Healthy Foods for Kids of All Ages*. New Hope, PA: New Hope, 1987.

Hazelton, Nika. *Raggedy Ann and Andy's Cookbook*. Indianapolis: Bobbs-Merrill, 1975.

Hopkinson, Deborah. *Fannie in the Kitchen*. Illus. Nancy Carpenter. New York: Athenaeum, 2001.

Keene, Carolyn. *The Nancy Drew Cookbook: Clues to Good Cooking*. New York: Grosset, 1973.

Keller, Thomas. *What's Cooking?: A Cookbook for Kids (Ratatouille)*. New York: Disney, 2007.

Key, Sara, et al. *The Wizard of Oz Cookbook: Breakfast in Kansas, Dessert in Oz*. New York: Abbeville, 1993.

Macdonald, Kate. *The Anne of Green Gables Cookbook*. Illus. Barbara DiLella. Toronto: Oxford UP, 1985.

MacGregor, Carol. *The Storybook Cookbook*. Illus. Ray Cruz. Garden City, NY: Doubleday, 1967.

Mayer, Marianna. *The Mother Goose Cookbook: Rhymes and Recipes for the Very Young*. Illus. Carol Schwartz. New York: Morrow, 1998.

Meyer, Ira L. *Disney Recipes: From Animation to Inspiration*. New York: Disney, 2003.

Moore, Sandre. *The Fairy Tale Cookbook: Fun Recipes for Families to Create and Eat Together*. Nashville: Cumberland, 2000.

Nickelodeon. *A Nick Cookbook. Stir Squirt Sizzle*. San Francisco: Chronicle, 2004.

Numeroff, Laura. *Mouse Cookies & More: A Treasury*. Illus. Felicia Bond. New York: Harper, 2006.

Paston-Williams, Sara. *Beatrix Potter's Country Cooking*. London: Warne, 1991.

Penner, Lucille Recht. *The Little Women Book: Games, Recipes, Crafts, and Other Homemade Pleasures*. Illus. Diane deGroat. New York: Random, 1995.

Sobol, Donald J., with Glenn Andrews. *Encyclopedia Brown Takes the Cake!: A Cook and Case Book*. New York: Scholastic, 1983.

Stallworth, Lyn. *Wond'rous Fare: A Classic Children's Cookbook*. Chicago: Calico, 1988.

Travers, P. L. *Mary Poppins in the Kitchen: A Cookery Book with a Story*. Culinary Consultant Maurice Moore-Betty. Illus. Mary Shepard. New York: Harcourt, 1975.

Walker, Barbara M. *The Little House Cookbook: Frontier Foods from Laura Ingalls Wilder's Classic Stories*. Illus. Garth Williams. New York: Harper, 1979.

Waters, Alice. *Fanny at Chez Panisse: A Child's Restaurant Adventures With 46 Recipes*. Illus. Ann Arnold. New York: Harper, 1992.

Wilder, Laura Ingalls. *My Little House Cookbook*. Recipes Amy Cotler. Illus. Holly Jones. New York: Scholastic, 1996.

Wolfe, Linda. *The Literary Gourmet: Menus from Masterpieces*. New York: Simon, 1962.

Yolen, Jane, and Heidi E. Y. Stemple. *Fairy Tale Feasts: A Literary Cookbook for Young Readers and Eaters*. Illus. Philippe Beha. Northampton, MA: Crocodile, 2006.

Critical Sources

Adler, Thomas A. "Making Pancakes on Sunday: The Male Cook in Family Tradition." *Western Folklore* 40 (1981): 46.

Barthes, Roland. "Ornamental Cookery." *Mythologies*. Trans. Annette Lavers. New York: Hill, 1972. 78–80.

———. "Toward a Psychosociology of Contemporary Food Consumption." *Food and Culture: A Reader*. Ed. Carole Counihan and Penny van Esterik. New York: Routledge, 1997. 20–27.

Berger, John. *Ways of Seeing*. London: Penguin, 1972.

Bower, Anne L., ed. *Community Cookbooks: Stories, Histories and Recipes for Reading*. Amherst: U of Massachusetts P, 1997.

Elias, Marilyn. "The Family-first Generation: Young Workers Seek Flexibility; Men Share Child Care." *USA Today*. Dec. 13, 2004: 5D.

Floyd, Janet, and Laurel Forster, eds. *The Recipe Reader: Narratives-Contexts-Traditions*. Burlington, VT: Ashgate, 2003.

———. "The Recipe in its Cultural Contexts." *The Recipe Reader: Narratives-Contexts-Traditions*. Ed. Janet Floyd and Laurel Forster. Burlington, VT: Ashgate, 2003. 1–11.

Gopnik, Adam. "Cooked Books: Real Food from Fictional Recipes." *The New Yorker* 9 April 2006: 80–85.

Haber, Barbara. *From Hardtack to Home Fries: An Uncommon History of American Cooks & Meals*. New York: Putman, 2002.

Inness, Sherrie A., ed. "'Enchantment of Mixing Spoons': Cooking Lessons for Girls and Boys." *Kitchen Culture in America*. Ed. Sherri A. Inness. Philadelphia: U of Pennsylvania P, 2000. 119–138.

Kinder, Marsha. *Playing with Power in Movies, Television, and Video Games: From Muppet Babies to Teenage Mutant Ninja Turtles*. Berkeley: U of California Press, 1991.

Leonardi, Susan J. "Recipes for Reading: Summer Pasta, Lobster á la Riseholme, and Key Lime Pie." *PMLA* 104.3 (May 1989): 340–347.

Long, Lucy M. "Culinary Tourism: A Folklorist Perspective on Eating and Otherness." *Culinary Tourism*. Ed. Lucy M. Long. Lexington: UP of Kentucky, 2004. 20–50.

Mackey, Margaret. *The Case of Peter Rabbit: Changing Conditions of Literature for Children*. New York: Garland, 1998.

Neuhaus, Jessamyn. "The Way to a Man's Heart: Gender Roles, Domestic Ideology, and Cookbooks in the 1950s." *Journal of Social History* (Spring 1999): 529–555.

Sceats, Sarah. "Regulation and Creativity: The Use of Recipes in Contemporary Fiction." *The Recipe Reader: Narratives-Contexts-Traditions*. Ed. Janet Floyd and Laurel Foster. Burlington, VT: Ashgate, 2003. 169–186.

Susina, Jan. "American Girls Collection: Barbies with a Sense of History." *Children's Literature Association Quarterly* 24.3 (Fall 1999): 130–135.

Theophano, Janet. *Eat My Words: Reading Women's Lives through the Cookbooks They Wrote*. New York: Palgrave, 2002.

Vandergrift, Kay E. "Cookbooks Based on Children's Books. *Vandergrift's Children's Literature Page*. <http://www.scils.rutgers.edu/~kvander/ChildrenLit/cookbooks.html>. SCILS, Rutgers, 1996–2007.

Zissu, Alexandra. "These Kids Never Say 'Yech!'." *New York Times* 28 January 2007: Style Section 1, 6.

Part III
Girls, Mothers, Children

Chapter Three

Recipe for Reciprocity and Repression: The Politics of Cooking and Consumption in Girls' Coming-of-Age Literature

Holly Blackford

From the myth of Persephone to the Biblical Genesis, from the anorexic poetics of Christina Rossetti's 1862 *Goblin Market* to Margaret Atwood's 1969 *The Edible Woman*, food is symbolically linked with our conceptions of female sexuality, desire, and development. Mervyn Nicholson argues that eating has an inherent relationship to sexuality: "Food is to the individual what sex is to the species," because sex is the "means of species-reproduction—the method that a species uses to perpetuate itself. But eating is a means of self-reproduction: consuming food is what the individual does in order to reproduce himself. . . . Eating and life, for a truly individual identity, are inseparable" (37). But food is not merely a means of pleasure and an expression of individual or sexual desire if you identify most with those who have to cook it and clean it up. What if you're little Laura Ingalls, watching Ma heavily churn the butter and, laboriously by hand, mix sausages for the winter in *Little House in the Big Woods*? What if you're Jamaica Kincaid's Annie John, spending your early childhood following around your mother while she gardens, shops, and cooks? What if you're Tita, in Laura Esquivel's *Like Water for Chocolate*, sentenced to endlessly make the tortillas? What if you're "a little princess" in Frances Hodgson's Burnett's novel, suddenly at the mercy of a world of women and endlessly tormented with kitchen errands? What if you're an orphan who seeks a home at Green Gables, in a town admiring of kitchen prowess, and you find cooking incompatible with your romantic nature?

Foodchains of power are constructed and expressed by activities of food consumption and production. In women's writing for girls on the threshold

41

of womanhood, food is not as much a heterosexual matter as it is an inter-generational matter between mothers and daughters. Food lies at the center of socialization rituals for children, and in girls' novels young female protagonists are often apprenticed to mother figures that are engaged in cooking activities. Such novels typically emphasize cooking at the expense of eating, partaking in the politics by which girls learn to curtail their own desires and sacrifice for others. Cooking is a form of self-control and a way to prepare the female character for repressing inner needs, packaging the self and female body for the pleasure of others. However, cooking is also an aesthetic expression of the female self, a subtle expression of female desire that can take on a life of its own—as in the image of Laura Ingalls's grandmother's syrup boiling over as she outjigs a man, or Jo's "bread 'riz' enough when it runs over the pans" (Alcott 114)—and contradict the intended lesson in self-denial

Across cultures, cooking invokes both wonder and anxiety in daughterly imaginations because the language of fairy tale and myth speaks through food rituals in diverse novels of female development. In fairy tales, which Marina Warner argues are female traditions that signify intergenerational dynamics, we find what Eric S. Rabkin terms "the Eden Complex," in which the young make a Promethean stand against elders who control food and thus hold power. In this tradition, mother figures that cook food have omnipotent powers over the young; symbolically, they have the fire (the cookstove) that the young need to become strong and rival them. In mythological thought, cooking is a form of mediation between nature and society, life and death, heaven and earth. It is inherently magical. Women across cultures are often responsible for transforming "the raw" into "the cooked," categories of nature and culture that Claude Lévi-Strauss felt indicative of the very structure of civilization. Thus cooking is also a metaphor for the role of women in socializing ("cooking") children. As Sherrie Ortner claims in her classic article "Is Female to Male as Nature Is to Culture?" women across cultures are a synecdoche for untransformed nature, particularly the body, because they reproduce and care for the bodies of others, even the bodies of the dead. Like cooking, the female body, as Adrienne Rich argues, has been seen as a space of liminality between the thresholds of life and death, inviting ambivalent representations of it.

The symbol of the maternal body that cooks for and nourishes children, also literally feeding them from the body, is inseparable from women's role in Western domestic economy. In her work on the meaning of housekeeping in texts of the nineteenth century, Ann Romines says that with their housework, women beat back the chaos of nature, but because women are identified with nature, they are always beating back a part of themselves (12–13). Cooking is a form of self-discipline, but it is also a way women cross many important boundaries, between raw and cooked, self and other, outside and inside, nature and culture. Cooking is a means by which the female body becomes a divine object of sacrifice for family communion, but the magical, transformative properties of the cook are also regarded with daughters' suspicion.

Fairy-tale and myth traditions find expression in scenes of food production that sort mother figures into divine sacrificial objects and evil witches, categories that Melanie Klein thought endemic to infantile perspectives on mothers as part- rather than whole objects. Tellingly, this split between divine women who nurture through food and evil women who make food abject parallels the traditional, patriarchal dichotomy of women as either Madonnas or whores. Witches with bubbling cauldrons serve as cannibalistic inversions of mothers. Divine mothers nurture with edible gifts, calling upon the tradition of food as an object of transformation, often originating with gods (Nicholson 40–41). Ironically, however, both good and bad mothers are equally problematic to growing daughters who are struggling to develop a sense of self. I find Julia Kristeva's theory of the semiotic useful in interpreting why it is that both divine and evil mothers are problematic. In her theory, the world of the mother is associated with the pre-Symbolic realm—the realm of shared milk, tears, preverbal communication, gestural and bodily rhythms, play and communication without words, and smells and sounds. All of these things are potently present in scenes of mothers cooking. This realm of the semiotic threatens the daughter's self-mastery and thus must be rejected; it becomes a realm that is either a lost Eden of mother–daughter communion through food and delicious scent, as in *Little House in the Big Woods* (1932) and *Annie John* (1985), or a sinister realm run by evil mother figures, as in *A Little Princess* (1905), *Anne of Green Gables* (1908), *Like Water for Chocolate* (1989), and coming-of-age slave narratives such as Harriet Jacobs's *Incidents in the Life of a Slave Girl* (1861). Bruno Bettleheim articulates the developmental importance of splitting parents into good and evil. After all, it is harder for children to accept and express rage at a parent seen in a more complex manner. The tendency for parallel mother figures to torture and nurture with cooked food suggests that rage is being expressed in girls' novels: rage at rituals that ask girls to ingest the maternal body and internalize its role, as if it were their own inner desires.

Certainly stories such as Karen Cushman's *The Midwife's Apprentice* (1995) and Laura Esquivel's Mexican novel *Like Water for Chocolate* contain these fairy-tale elements and Promethean plots. In the former, Brat is locked into a relationship with Jane Sharp because she is fed by her, and her mission becomes how to steal what Jane hoards for midwifery. There are parallels between Cinderella and Tita in *Like Water for Chocolate*; both are oppressed youngest daughters who have to forever labor for their mothers. To accomplish her Promethean transformation of the cooking fire for her own purposes, Tita has various divine female influences that assist her in the kitchen. It is Nacha in particular who, when she dies, leaves Tita "as if her real mother had died" (48), and who cooks through Tita, especially in making the rose petal quail that Pedro says is "a dish for the gods!" (51). He falsely thinks himself the god when he really means the dish is from the gods—a gift from a divine fairy godmother.

The divine quality of the sacrificing, good mother is continuously explored in nineteenth-century novels for girls, such as Susan Warner's *The Wide, Wide World* and Louisa May Alcott's *Little Women*. The Edenic function of mother–daughter unity is expressed through shared meals. For example, before Ellen is thrown to the mercy of the wide, wide world, she communes with her mother over tea and toast, where she is also instructed in the value of worshiping the Savior. The divine lesson is a displacement authorizing the daughter's worship of the mother, and through the teapot the two become one:

> To make her mother's tea was Ellen's regular business. She treated it as a very grave affair, and loved it as one of the pleasantest in the course of the day. She used in the first place to make sure that the kettle really boiled; then she carefully poured some water into the teapot and rinsed it, both to make it clean and to make it hot; then she knew exactly how much tea to put into the tiny little tea-pot, which was just big enough to hold two cups of tea, and having poured a very little boiling water to it, she used to set it by the side of the fire while she made a slice of toast. How careful Ellen was about that toast! The bread must not be cut too thick, nor too thin; the fire must, if possible, burn clear and bright, and she herself held the bread on a fork, just at the right distance from the coals to get nicely browned without burning. When this was done to her satisfaction (and if the first piece failed she would take another), she filled up the little tea-pot from the boiling kettle, and proceeded to make a cup of tea. She knew, and was very careful to put in, just the quantity of milk and sugar that her mother liked; and then she used to carry the tea and toast on a little tray to her mother's side, and very often held it there for her while she eat [sic]. All this Ellen did with the zeal that love gives, and though the same thing was to be gone over every night of the year, she was never wearied. It was a real pleasure; she had the greatest satisfaction in seeing that the little her mother could eat was prepared for her in the nicest possible manner; she knew her hands made it taste better; her mother often said so. (13)

Ellen's careful attentions to the details of tea-making express love through object-relations. The reader notices that the teapot has the perfect amount of room for two cups of tea, just the amount for the two individuals who dissolve boundaries between them through such liquid intimacy. Ellen's work requires intimate knowledge of the mother's body, and that body's tastes and preferences are present in every morsel of food and drink. Ellen feeds her mother, who is dying and thus receiving a kind of sacrament. Both in this scene partake of the divine, the younger with both religious "zeal" and earthly "pleasure." This scene is radically contrasted with Ellen's first venture into the marketplace, where she is sent to obtain cloth, and where she quickly becomes overwhelmed, disoriented, and incapable. This is because the market is a place that divides women from "the hands and heart" that make everything taste better; this is a common trope that recurs throughout women's writing. Food made and shared between women in the home is the center of divine domestic ritual, whereas excursions into the market are dangerous and divide mother from daughter. Women's domestic novels that feature girls in apprenticeship roles evince a kind of sentimental Marxism by advancing the point that wholeness is only found when head and hand lovingly labor for another. The mother in this novel is literally perishing from a consumptive state, quite concretely a sacrificial object. The treatment of tea-making is a "very grave affair" indeed.

The mother of the March family in *Little Women* is similarly a divine influence and sacrificial object. There are many images connoting the divinity of the mother in the novel, images such as a portrait of the Madonna that Amy is allowed to worship despite the novel's overt Protestantism. The mother presides over the teapot and various food-based rituals, and her four daughters observe extensive preparations for Marmee's return home at teatime. As Romines and Carroll Smith-Rosenberg argue, the "female world of love and ritual" in nineteenth-century women's circles takes on sacrificial rites through ritualistic repetition of housework and shared meals. Marmee is a figure of sacrifice at home but also outside the home; she advocates giving away Christmas breakfast to a family in need, suggesting that female virtue lies in the ability of a woman to prepare food and parcel it/herself up for others. The very nature of divine female sacrifice becomes problematic for the daughters, who are receiving instruction in the divine nature of female self-denial.

By receiving the mother's sacrifice, daughters are cannibalizing the mother and identifying with her as an object of consumption. The magic of divine mothers is not reproducible by humankind daughters, who are quite imperfect. Shame hits Meg when she has her own household and her jelly simply will not jell, signifying her failure in kitchen magic. In a chapter titled "Experiments," Marmee and her handmaiden Hannah take a holiday and Jo, having just read *The Wide Wide World* as if to render it an impossible or undesirable ideal to emulate, cooks a disastrous dinner because she lacks the "something more" of the cook:

> Language cannot describe the anxieties, experiences, and exertions which Jo underwent that morning; and the dinner she served up became a standing joke. Fearing to ask any more advice, she did her best alone, and discovered that something more than energy and good-will is necessary to make a cook. She boiled the asparagus hard for an hour, and was grieved to find the heads cooked off, and the stalks harder than ever. The bread burnt black; for the salad dressing so aggravated her, that she let everything else go, til she had convinced herself that she could not make it fit to eat. The lobster was a scarlet mystery to her, but she hammered and poked, till it was unshelled, and its meager proportions concealed in a grove of lettuce-leaves. (115)

The isolation and violence of her passionate cooking—boiling heads off, burning bread, being aggravated by salad dressing, hammering and poking the lobster—expose the violence veiled by the ideology of "the joy" of womanly cooking, for female labor and rage are to be daintily "concealed in a grove of lettuce-leaves," the woman's reduction to "meager proportions" hidden with decorative fluff. As her meal is tasted by guests that include a spinster, a maternal surrogate who will report the fiasco to Marmee, Jo "turned scarlet" (115), a word not accidentally mirroring the "scarlet mystery" of the lobster whose rawness resists taming.

Jo, Meg, and Amy, with her disastrous luncheon in the chapter "Artistic Attempts," cannot cook because nineteenth-century matriarchs have a magic up to which daughters cannot measure. Similarly, when Laura is on her own in *The First Four Years*, she fails at correctly cooking beans and putting sugar in her pies. *Little Women* is similar to *Little House in the Big Woods* in its depiction of the good mother as a goddess, whose labors are never exposed as violent or messy. For example, Laura's mother hulls corn all day but still "looked pretty" and "never splashed one drop of water on her pretty dress" (220). As this is impossible, we can understand that these daughter-writers are actually worshipping beautiful mothers as goddesses of the harvest. Both autobiographical novelists write of main characters who covertly rebel against maternal magic because they do not wish to emulate a model of a divinely cooked female character.

Fairy tales overtly structure the novels of Frances Hodgson Burnett and the politics of her scenes of female nourishment. To be a princess, Sara Crewe of *A Little Princess* must learn to become cannibalized, and she can only learn this by encountering a primal scene of a mother baking for a child. Sara Crewe is most oppressed by the cook who should be a symbol for plenty but instead refuses Sara food and sends her out into the street, where Sara sees a vision of the good mother in the woman baking fresh hot buns in the oven. This "motherly" woman of the hot buns is a complex signifier of what Sara cannot have because she would not grow with such a mother—and she would not need men, after all—and because she has to completely deny herself and her hunger to earn back princess status and the father's love. After Sara gives up her buns to an even hungrier child on the street, *that* child gets adopted by the good mother, and thus the novel rejects this alternate solution of female community for its protagonist. Ironically, Sara in some sense conjures this mother–child adoption, suggesting that mother–child relations are dependent upon female hunger, dependent upon an older female body being cannibalized, which may be a symbol for the way in which coming-of-age displaces the elder generation. Burnett's *The Secret Garden* (1909) provides another example in which Mary's real mother is selfish and unnurturing, whereas Mary finds a divine maternal presence in the garden (where Colin's mother has died) and in an earth-mother, Mrs. Sowerby, who nourishes Mary through Dickon even though she can barely feed her own family. Colin's assertion that there is magic in the garden is quite true; a dead mother is, in fact, the most magical because the most divine. Mary grows plump on the love of goddesses.

Tellingly, coming-of-age slave narratives such as Harriet Jacobs's *Incidents in the Life of A Slave Girl* deploy this binary opposition between divine cooks and tormenting witches through contrasting slave mothers and slave mistresses. In the fictional Linda Brent's novelized account, Aunt Marthy (Linda Brent's grandmother) is a divine kitchen wonder, able to bake the town's most prized crackers and preserves, and always waiting with open arms and food for her grandchildren. Mrs. Flint, on the other hand, is a bad mother with similar powers in the kitchen. She is repeatedly shown wandering around the kitchen and obsessively counting and controlling rations. She knows exactly how many biscuits a cup of flour should make and ensures that the slaves are not taking any food beyond their allowance. She actually spits in any extra food, creating abject food; she locks women away from their nursing infants, disrupting and altering feeding rituals. In Linda's perspective, Mrs. Flint is far worse than Mr. Flint because she is a woman and supposed to be a protector, but she uses her semiotic powers to abuse. However, as I have argued elsewhere, the imagery of the kitchen actually links Mrs. Flint and the grandmother as two sides of female power, both of which prevent, in different ways, Linda's own strategies for escaping slavery.

To make the contrast between the divine mother and witch explicit, novels for girls contrast good "homemade" food with the dangerous food of the marketplace, where the protagonists' circumstances profoundly change. Obviously, Jacobs is contrasting the motherly food of Aunt Marthy with the corrupt food being fed to her by the slave market. *Goblin Market* maintains a similar theme of the bad food available in a patriarchal marketplace, contrasted with the wholesome world of the homemade and housekeeping, where Laura and Lizzie "should" stay and work, as argued by Deborah Ann Thompson: "'Goblin Market' thus dramatizes Victorian women's entrance into the marketplace of an inchoate capitalist industrialist economy, both as commodities and as purchasers of commodities" (97). The gate at which Lizzie scolds Laura "reifies the partition the poem sets up between female household and the male market" (97). A similar theme can be found in *Little Women* when Amy, overly concerned with marketing herself as a lady, endeavors to impress her artistic friends with a luncheon featuring lobster salad. Mr. March is supposed to buy the lobster but as he does not, Amy is forced to market—like Little Red Riding Hood, cloaked and armed with a basket—but her journey ends in shame as the basket is upset and "the lobster, in all its vulgar size and brilliancy, was revealed to the high-born eyes of a Tudor!" (262). Like her sister before her, Amy finds herself with "a face nearly as red as her fish" (262), a telling detail of who becomes "raw" or improperly cooked food in the public sphere. Ellen's first voyage into the wide world is a voyage to the marketplace where she becomes disoriented and needs to be rescued by a man. In *The Midwife's Apprentice*, Brat receives a mirror at the market; there, she is christened with a name when a man mistakenly calls her Alyce, which she thereafter calls herself. If cooking is a metaphor for preparing the female character and self, then the market is a metaphor for ways in which female value is reduced, commodified, and shamed by being bought and sold.

L. M. Montgomery's *Anne of Green Gables* plots an inverse trope of coming-of-age as removal from the marketplace and entry into the proper female sphere of the home. Anne is transformed from a commodity and laborer, circulating between homes for hire, into a good Victorian girl of hearth and home. The novel is rich with fairy-tale elements and female symbols; the terrain of cooking, clothing, flowers, and jewelry defines her struggle for acceptance by women, particularly Marilla and Rachel Lynde. Anne's apprenticeship occurs in two educational settings—school and kitchen, where in both cases she experiences a variety of tests of female scrutiny. In Jacobs's slave narrative and Burnett's *A Little Princess*, the lines between servitude and divine womanhood are clearly drawn; in *Anne* the line is slippery and unclear. Rachel and Marilla are not far removed from evil kitchen witches when we meet them; you might say they are kindred spirits of fairy-tale witches as they preside and discourse over a table laid out for Anne's arrival. It is clear from our introduction to them in the Green Gables kitchen that Anne's struggle for acceptance and love is a struggle against elder women who control the domestic sphere with their meals and homemade goods.

The reader gets a description of the table laid out on the eve of Anne's arrival from Mrs. Lynde's point of view. Mrs. Lynde carefully decodes the place settings on the table and shows us that an intricate kitchen language is one that Cavendish women are expected to speak, both fluently and swiftly:

> Mrs. Rachel, before she had fairly closed the door, had taken mental note of everything that was on that table. There were three plates laid, so that Marilla must be expecting some one home with Matthew to tea; but the dishes were every-day dishes and there was only crab-apple preserves and one kind of cake, so that the expected company could not be any particular company. Yet what of Matthew's white collar and the sorrel mare? Mrs. Rachel was getting fairly dizzy with this unusual mystery about quiet, unmysterious Green Gables. (56)

Not being able to decode such a table, and yet proficient in its language, makes a matron as dizzy as the market makes the young girl Ellen in *The Wide, Wide World*. Although they are supposedly expecting a boy, it is clear from this kitchen anticipation and fairy-tale allusion that this is a girl's story. In the passage above, there is a symbolic meaning in the fact that the kitchen spread jars against Matthew's attire. First, the views of Anne by Matthew, instantly wooed, and by the women, not so instantly wooed, will greatly differ, as will their female expectations of Anne. Second, the kitchen language is in itself quite distinct from the public world where the man has gone. It waits as Anne's place of trial, and it will unfold as a discourse quite distinct from the romantic language of nature that Anne speaks and that wins over Matthew. The scene is crucial because it suggests a terrain of exclusively female power in a novel veiling its roots in the slave (here, indentured servant) narrative.

The first thing Anne does, besides not be a boy, is to not eat, privileging her emotional state and melodramatic nature over unconditional acceptance of the elder women's judgment. Anne's detested nickname is Carrots, tellingly a raw food that it is Marilla's job to cook. It is sometimes unclear whether Marilla wishes Anne to pass her tests, as is often the case in elder women of fairy tales, who feel ambivalence about being displaced. Many of the mistakes Anne makes are actually Marilla's fault. Anne gets Diana drunk because Marilla has actually put the raspberry cordial elsewhere and placed her homemade wine in Anne's path. The detail that she makes her own wine suggests a divine test by a mother figure, the wine purposely placed in a path of temptation. A similar test occurs in Chapter 21 when Anne flavors the cake for Mr. and Mrs. Allen with anodyne liniment, poured into an old empty vanilla bottle by Marilla, who this time acknowledges her fault (213). When voicing her anxiety to Diana about making the cake, Anne evokes a prayer for divine assistance. She has a premonition that the cake will fail: "I dreamed last night that I was chased all around by a fearful goblin with a big layer cake for a head," possibly indicative of a suspicion about Marilla. Her conclusion—"I suppose I shall just have to trust to Providence and be careful to put in the flour" (210)—suggests that she unconsciously knows the "goblin" or "goddess" who rules her servitude will only relinquish power if a higher God intervenes in the "gift" of well-cooked food. Indeed, the meal is also significant because for the first time Anne usurps Marilla's divine right and decorates the table with flowers (122), winning her way by arguing that the minister paid Mrs. Barry's table a compliment, thus "not entirely guiltless of the wisdom of the serpent" (212) in her clear struggle with a divine ruler.

The ambivalence of older women toward younger is expressed by Little Red's sense that grandmother is also a wolf, by Linda Brent's closing lines of her slave narrative ("with those gloomy recollections [of slavery] come tender memories of my good old grandmother, like light, fleecy clouds floating over a dark and troubled sea" (201)), and by the famous slap of Janie by her grandmother in Zora Neale Hurston's *Their Eyes Were Watching God* (1937). Seeing Janie kissed and thus "the end of her childhood," "Nanny's head and face looked like the standing roots of some old tree that had been torn away by storm. Foundation of ancient power that no longer mattered" (12). The archetype of the ancient tree of life, located in both the elder woman's face and in the scene of Janie's famous awakening under the pear tree, parallels the first debate between Marilla and Anne about whether the tree in Green Gables is an object of awakening beauty (Anne's view) or a deliverer of wormy fruit (Marilla's view), signifying rising youth or declining powers of the goddess. These ambivalences express the inevitable arc of female development;

although "ancient power" oppresses Janie for awhile—she is effectively "sold" by her grandmother to a man—she, like Jacobs, successfully struggles to reclaim appetite and obtain her "Tea Cake." Anne, in contrast, appeases "ancient" female trees by identifying with them—hence, her deep love of trees. On the brink of academic recognition, Anne has already passed the tests that matter for girls of fairy-tale texts:

> Anne got the tea and made hot biscuits that were light and white enough to defy even Mrs. Rachel's criticism.
> "I must say Anne has turned out a real smart girl," admitted Mrs. Rachel. (280)

The matron defines "smart" as good cook. The blessing of this community queen conferred, there is little left for Anne to do except realize the effect of her accomplishment—as if her entrance into Queen's and her scholarship are merely afterthoughts of what a kitchen wiz can do. Most girls' novels differentiate the homemade and the market; the story of this servant girl up against two formidable and divine mother figures—not necessarily evil but also divine in the sense of fairy godmothers who give her puffed sleeves, etcetera—proves that for colonized subjects, home is indeed a tough marketplace. Serving herself as an object of Marilla's pride and successful mothering, and thus staying in Cavendish to secure Marilla's Green Gables with a more subtle and guilty sacrifice than Tita's for her mother, Anne becomes a cooked carrot and her romantic spirit, antithetical to doing things like remembering to cover puddings, lessens. But her meals bear the unmistakable mark of Anne's artistry as well.

Two young characters that are particularly preoccupied with the food artistry of their mothers, and who undergo shifts in the opening world of the marketplace, are Laura in Laura Ingalls Wilder's *Little House in the Big Woods* and Annie of Jamaica Kincaid's *Annie John*. Although the protagonists are the products of different eras and nations, the former American and the latter Caribbean, they share the mythical elements of food production and consumption that express coming-of-age in various cultures. Both Laura and Annie spend the bulk of early childhood watching their mothers prepare food, documenting this food preparation with images of the mother's laboring body, descriptions of the scents of the mother and home, and Edenic visions of mother–daughter connection, which will change once they begin to grow a little. In fact, both grow uncomfortable with the amount of labor expended by the mother, and both actually begin to view the mother as more than a part-object and cook, a view that then threatens their Edenic visions of mothers perpetually cooking for them. During crucial scenes, both suddenly no longer recognize their mothers, and they mistakenly believe it's the mother that has changed, and both also suddenly realize that their mothers are sexual creatures with relationships to their fathers that do not necessarily involve them. The sudden realization that mothers are actually more than mothers—and are thus cooking themselves for their families—are primal scenes that demand more complex visions of mothers. Yet although both novels gesture toward the need to grow beyond fairy tales, they ultimately fall short of doing so.

Scenes of cooking abound in *Little House in the Big Woods*, so much so that we could describe Laura's early childhood as a cannibalistic one. The mother's food preparations stimulate the appetites of Laura and Mary such that they burn their tongues on freshly roasted pig's tail and do not even care. The worlds of the young Laura and Mary are centered on the rich emblems of semiotic existence, the scents, tastes, seasonal time, and ritualistic repetitions of the mother's body engaged in domestic ritual. The girls cannot even eat everything the mother prepares because some of it is "too rich for little girls" (17). The hands of the mother are always spicing and molding, working at the food. Symbolically, "the fire in the cookstove never went out" (19) in Laura's early childhood. Even the girls' play space—the attic—is an Edenic "lovely place to play" because it is packed with food and scent, sensuously described: "The red peppers and onions dangled overhead. The hams and venison hung in their paper wrappings, and all the bunches of dried herbs, the spicy herbs for cooking and the bitter herbs for medicine, gave the place a dusty-spicy smell" (20). The theme of play amidst an abundance of food, as well as the unlikely concordance between play and housework, is similar to *Little Women*. The girls in *Little House* find food production aesthetic and playful, as shown when they turn the pig's bladder into a balloon or when Ma makes pancake men for each child at Christmas; awe-inspired, "Mary and Laura ate theirs slowly in little bits, first the arms and legs and then the middle, saving the head for last" (79–80). All the girls eat their men this way, but Peter "ate the head off his man, right away" (79), a sign of disrespect for the mother's aesthetic production.

Prepared food in girls' novels like this one is paradoxically a sign of good mothering *and* a certain excess because it quickly becomes an aesthetic performance of the mother—even indicative of her pleasure. It is too excessive to be complete self-denial. Ma wishes her food to be more than functional; she goes to great lengths to make her food pretty. The butter churning, for example, requires immense preparation in itself, with little help from the daughters because of the weight of the churn, yet even further preparations to make the butter pretty. To make the butter yellow, Ma has to scrape a long carrot, heat it with milk, and squeeze the orange milk through a cloth bag, putting it into the churn. Interestingly, it is this aesthetic "extra" that stimulates discontent in both Mary and Laura: "Laura and Mary were allowed to eat the carrot after the milk had been squeezed out. Mary thought she ought to have the larger share because she was older, and Laura said she should have it because she was littler" (30). Throughout the novel, the mother's efforts at aesthetic "extras" trigger arguments between the girls. For example, Laura actually strikes Mary after Ma curls their hair and instructs them to ask their aunt whether she prefers yellow or brown curls. Similarly, Laura fights with her cousin Laura after watching her mother dress for the dance, where Ma wears her fashionable Eastern delaine, which has a pattern that Laura feels "looked like ripe strawberries" (128). It is telling that Laura projects an image of food onto her mother's finery. Like the mother's rich foods, Ma herself, when dressed, "looked so rich and fine that Laura was afraid to touch her" (142). Ma's body in this scene is reminiscent of the strawberry mold that Ma uses to beautify her butter, which makes the girls "breathless" as "the golden little butterpats, each with its strawberry on the top, dropped on to the plate" (33).

Ma's high aesthetic tastes hint to Laura that Ma, although divine, is actually more than an object of consumption for her family, and particularly for her children. This more complex vision of Ma reaches its climax in a market scene. It is in a shop where the girls get food that Laura, for the first time, sees a vision of her parents' affection for one another. Charles wants Ma to buy an apron, which Ma feels is not necessary, and he playfully says that she must or he will select a hideous pattern for her. Ma laughs and agrees. The scene thus features the romantic relationship between the parents and the aesthetics of cooking (an apron that Ma does not need), which expands Laura's vision of her mother to include being a consumer rather than just an object of consumption. Laura's response is quite dramatic. Laura becomes greedy; she puts so many rocks in her pocket that her pocket rips out, an equivalent, in this novel, to losing control over the bladder. The action gets her reprimanded for being greedy, but it does its office; the mother quickly comes over to see if the dress can be saved, and Laura has her mother to herself once more. But the scene has forever divided Laura from her mother, just as the candy gifted by the storekeeper distinguishes Laura and Mary. The rest of the *Little House* series will develop Laura's preference for Pa over Ma.

Glimpses of Ma's complexity threaten and destabilize Laura's "once upon a time" early childhood, quite similarly to the way in which Annie John's childhood is destabilized by the slow recognition that her mother is a woman and not just a meal. Annie John describes her mother as a powerful and erotic presence on her early consciousness; mother and daughter buy their fresh fish together, select fresh herbs from the garden, wash sheets and lay them out in the sunshine, and even bathe together in specially prepared fragrant baths, similar to the ones that Tita prepares for her mother but depicted as erotic and beautiful. Annie is completely identified with her mother and her local dishes:

> When we got home, my mother started to prepare our lunch (pumpkin soup with droppers, banana fritters with salt fish stewed in antroba and tomatoes, fungie with salt fish stewed in antroba and tomatoes, or pepper pot, all depending on what my mother had found at market that day). As my mother went about from pot to pot, stirring one, adding something to the other, I was ever in her wake. As she dipped into a pot

of boiling something or other to taste for correct seasoning, she would give me a taste of it also, asking me what I thought. Not that she really wanted to know what I thought, for she had told me many times that my taste buds were not quite developed yet, but it was just to include me in everything. (17)

The purpose of the cooking is inclusion and mother–daughter communion. Recognition that the mother exists beyond the world of the child ushers in Annie's adolescence and subsequent hostility. In fact, the first sign that the child is growing is that Annie forgets to pick up fish for her mother's cooking because she has been attending a child funeral in secret; thus it is death to childhood to not be included in her mother's cooking rituals.

In one very early scene that marks Annie's disillusionment with her mother, she returns home early from school and finds her mother and father having sex. She proceeds to loudly set the table, both to let them know she is home but also as a hopeful gesture towards the meal preparations, a terrain upon which mother is hers and only hers, just like Laura wins back her mother when she rips her pocket. The rest of *Annie John* develops further disruptions in mother–child communion, as, in Annie's view, the mother rejects the daughter because she is growing older. In reality, it is not clear who rejects whom; the novel suggests that daughters' points of view are limited. For example, one of the climactic scenes occurs when her mother denies that a meal she has prepared is breadfruit:

> My mother brought me my lunch. I could tell that it was the much hated breadfruit. My mother said not at all, it was a new kind of rice imported from Belgium, and not breadfruit, mashed and forced through a ricer, as I thought. She went back to talking to my father. My father could hardly get a few words out of his mouth before she was a jellyfish of laughter. I sat there, putting my food in my mouth. I could not believe that she couldn't see how miserable I was and so reach out a hand to comfort me and caress my cheek, the way she usually did when she sensed that something was amiss with me. I could not believe how she laughed at everything he said, and how bitter it made me feel to see how much she liked him. I ate my meal. The more I ate of it, the more I was sure that it was breadfruit. When I finished, my mother got up to remove my plate. As she started out the door, I said, "Tell me, really, the name of the thing I just ate."
>
> My mother said "you just ate some breadfruit. I made it look like rice so that you would eat it. It's very good for you, filled with lots of vitamins." As she said this, she laughed. She was standing half inside the door, half outside. Her body was in the shade of our house, but her head was in the sun. When she laughed, her mouth opened to show off big, shiny, sharp white teeth. It was as if my mother had suddenly turned into a crocodile. (83–84)

Annie is increasingly disidentified with the mother just as Laura is (throughout the series); we see that what is really going on in this scene is that Annie is fiercely jealous of her father. She discovers that she is not always first in her mother's affections, not the sole possessor of this individual called her mother, and not always in touch with the recipe. She is not in control of the communion, and she is angry that her mother is not omnipotent (not a goddess) and cannot tell that Annie is in need of comfort. Speech further disrupts the once-semiotic realm. The subsequent feeling is that her mother is not a cook but a cannibal. For a woman to express a self less than divine is cannibalistic, when one cannot grow beyond fairy tale.

Like in *Little House*, the final climax in *Annie John* occurs when the mother sees Annie at the marketplace and believes her to be flirting. The market separates mother–daughter forever. *Little House* and *Annie John* are similar because both Ingalls and Kincaid are reclaiming historical and national pasts as much as personal ones, and both are mourning a time when women were "purely" domestic and the center of a homemade economy—when women were objects of consumption more than consumers. Both novels move towards realism while maintaining the fairy-tale elements that give mythical power to female coming-of-age tales. Both shy away from fully recognizing that the categories of divine goddess and crocodile or witch might be aspects of the same woman, most fully hinted at in *Annie John*. But Annie evinces unreasonable hostility and rage at her mother for not being entirely one or the other; Annie simply cannot understand that it is not her mother that has changed, but her own point of view. Viewing the complexity of a mother is part of child development, but it is a difficult rite of passage. I always have difficulty convincing my classes that we are supposed to suspect Annie's perspectives. So perhaps Melanie Klein is right, and that it is just tremendously difficult to view the mother as a whole object—as neither cook nor crocodile. Doing so, after all, would mean that we begin to make reparations for the infantile phantasies of mothers as part-objects that, apparently, we all had as infants at the breast.

Works Cited

Alcott, Louisa May. *Little Women*. 1868. New York: Penguin, 1989.

Atwood, Margaret. *The Edible Woman*. New York: Knopf, 1998.

Bettleheim, Bruno. *The Uses of Enchantment: The Meaning and Importance of Fairy Tales*. New York: Vintage, 1989.

Blackford, Holly. "Figures of Orality: The Master, The Mistress, The Slave Mother in Harriet Jacobs's *Incidents in the Life of A Slave Girl: Written by Herself*." *Papers on Language and Literature* 37.3 (2001): 314–336.

Burnett, Frances Hodgson. *A Little Princess*. 1905. New York: Harper, 1963.

———. *The Secret Garden*. 1909. New York: Harper, 1987.

Cushman, Karen. *The Midwife's Apprentice*. New York: Harper, 1995.

Esquivel, Laura. *Like Water for Chocolate*. Trans. Carol Christensen and Thomas Christensen. New York: Doubleday, 1992.

Hurston, Zora Neale. *Their Eyes Were Watching God*. 1939. New York: Harper, 1998.

Jacobs, Harriet. *Incidents in the Life of a Slave Girl: Written by Herself.* 1861. Ed. Jean Yellin. Cambridge, MA: Harvard UP, 1987.

Kincaid, Jamaica. *Annie John.* New York: Farrar, 1985.

Klein, Melanie. *Love, Guilt and Reparation: And Other Works 1921–1945. The Writings of Melanie Klein, Volume 1.* New York: Free P, 2002.

Kristeva, Julia. *Revolution in Poetic Language.* Ed. Leon S. Roudiez. Trans. Margaret Waller. New York: Columbia UP, 1984.

Lévi-Strauss, Claude. *The Raw and the Cooked.* New York: Harper, 1969.

Montgomery, Lucy Maud. *Anne of Green Gables.* 1908. Ed. Cecily Devereaux. Peterborough, ON: Broadview, 2004.

Nicholson, Mervyn. "Food and Power: Homer, Carroll, Atwood and Others." *Mosaic* 20.3 (1987): 37–55.

Ortner, Sherry. *Making Gender: The Politics and Erotics of Culture.* Boston: Beacon, 1996.

Rabkin, Eric S. "Eat and Grow Strong: The Super-Natural Power of Forbidden Fruit." *Violence, Utopia, and the Kingdom of God: Fantasy and Ideology in the Bible.* Ed. George Aichele and Tina Pippin. New York: Routledge, 1998. 8–23.

Rich, Adrienne. *Of Woman Born: Motherhood as Experience and Institution.* New York: Norton, 1986.

Romines, Ann. *The Home Plot: Women, Writing and Domestic Ritual.* Amherst: U of Massachusetts P, 1992.

Rossetti, Christina. *Goblin Market and Other Poems.* New York: Dover, 1994.

Smith-Rosenberg, Carroll. "The Female World of Love and Ritual: Relations between Women in Nineteenth-century America." *Signs* 1 (1975): 1–29.

Thompson, Deborah Ann. "Anorexia as a Lived Trope: Christina Rossetti's 'Goblin Market.'" *Mosaic* 24.3/4 (1991): 89–106.

Warner, Marina. *From Beast to Blonde: On Fairy Tales and Their Tellers.* New York: Farrar, 1995.

Warner, Susan. *The Wide, Wide World.* 1850. New York: Feminist, 1987.

Wilder, Laura Ingalls. *The First Four Years.* New York: Harper, 1971.

———. *Little House in the Big Woods.* 1932. New York: Scholastic, 1963.

Chapter Four

The Apple of Her Eye:
The Mothering Ideology Fed by
Best-selling Trade Picture Books

Lisa Rowe Fraustino

Nancy Chodorow in her influential 1978 text *The Reproduction of Mothering* explains: "Women in their domestic role . . . reproduce themselves as mothers, emotionally and psychologically, in the next generation" (209). The significant role of children's books in the reproduction of patriarchal mothering, although obvious to most children's literature scholars, remains unquestioned by the millions of book buyers and readers who make momism a perpetual best seller. A quick search on Amazon.com will demonstrate the prolific appeal of what *Horn Book* editor Roger Sutton calls "I-Love-Baby-and-Baby-Loves-Me books" produced by and for adults, to be shared with precious young children (228). These books, while making mothers feel good about themselves, also help shape the child's lifelong expectations of mythically "good" mothers.

In *The Myths of Motherhood: How Culture Reinvents the Good Mother*, Shari Thurer argues that traits of a "good" mother are not universal or instinctive: "The good mother is reinvented as each age or society defines her anew, in its own terms, according to its own mythology" (xv). Those seeking current definitions often turn to child-rearing manuals such as those by pediatrician Dr. Benjamin Spock, whose *Baby and Child Care* has sold more than 50 million copies in seven editions since its first publication in 1946—"making it second in sales only to the Bible" according to The Dr. Spock Company. In Thurer's words, Spock "constructs a 'good' mother who is ever present, all-providing, inexhaustibly patient and tactful, and who anticipates the child's every need. Mother has become baby's servant" (258). Carolyn Daniel, author of *Voracious Children: Who Eats Whom in Children's Literature*, points out that "part of the good mother paradigm is food provisioning. This suits patriarchal culture, it suits the state and capitalism, it suits authors of children's stories who need a shortcut to representing the mother, but it doesn't necessarily suit women" (114). In fact, says Evelyn Nakano Glenn, editor of *Mothering: Ideology, Experience, and Agency*, "a patriarchal ideology of mothering locks women into biological reproduction, and denies them identities and selfhood outside mothering" (9).

Obviously, large numbers of children's books include mothers as characters, and I have discussed elsewhere the reproduction of mothering ideology in mass-market series titles (Fraustino, "Berenstain"). The current essay will look closely at the all-time best-selling trade picture books thematically focused on mother–child relationships and examine how food is used, both literally and metaphorically, in the reproduction of patriarchal mothering ideology that assumes women need to be mothers, mothers need their children, and children need their mothers, locking women into a biologically determined social role that carries with it culturally determined expectations. The books under discussion here were culled from the most recent *Publishers Weekly* listing of "All-Time Bestselling Children's Books" (Roback) which lists picture book, middle-grade, and Young Adult titles that have sold over 750,000 in hardcover or one million in paperback in the United States, not counting book club or international sales.

The Tale of Peter Rabbit's Currant Buns: A Good Mother Does Nothing But

Second only to *The Poky Little Puppy*, we find *The Tale of Peter Rabbit* by Beatrix Potter at the top of the hardcover list, with sales of 9,380,274 since its publication in 1902 (Roback), and it continues to sell briskly after its 100-year anniversary despite being in the public domain and freely available online. Though the story's middle focuses exclusively on Peter's adventures, the beginning and ending provide a domestic frame that establishes the traditional mother–child relationship found in the majority of popular picture books. Peter's caring mother establishes the major dramatic question on page two: "'Now my dears,' said old Mrs. Rabbit one morning, 'you may go into the fields or down the lane, but don't go into Mr. McGregor's garden: your Father had an accident there; he was put in a pie by Mrs. McGregor."

Though shown in the story's first illustration the way nature made her, biologically accurate and unclothed, the anthropomorphized Mrs. Rabbit in the second scene represents the human Good Mother, becoming a charter member of the "cult of the apron" Alleen Pace Nilsen famously found in her landmark 1971 study of women in children's books. Just as her apron protects her clothing while she cooks and cleans for her little dears, old Mrs. Rabbit protects her children with wise words and warm jackets. The good girls, future mothers in training themselves, gather around her attentively while Peter, the naughty boy, turns away. In the next scene, as Mother buttons Peter's jacket—

the very jacket he'll later lose to Mr. McGregor's scarecrow—his mother says, "Now run along, and don't get into mischief. I am going out." Where she goes, of course, is to the baker's to buy bread and currant buns (definitely not rabbit food, as her lessons are for human consumption) while Peter's sisters gather blackberries. This is their own choice of activity, apparently, for the play of good little girls is practice for women's work—we can infer this by the baskets Mother hands out to them but not to Peter. His life as a male will take him out of the domestic sphere, on the adventures that will make a man of him. Even after death, Father sets the example that Peter will follow, as son defies Mother to enter the forbidden garden. Finally the story turns full circle back to the domestic sphere, with Mother "busy cooking." She puts Peter to bed with "camomile tea" for his stomachache and happily ends the story with good food for the good girls, "bread and milk and blackberries for supper," showing food as a tool of matriarchal power, reward or punishment. (Blackberries are sweeter than camomile, granted, yet as a good girl child I always envied Peter his being waited on in bed after his disobedience, lucky boy.)

In an influential 1972 study of sex-role socialization in picture books, Lenore J. Weitzman and others found women greatly underrepresented, and both men and women sex-stereotyped, as "men engage in a wide variety of occupations while women are presented only as wives and mothers" (1125). Like the majority of picture books, *The Tale of Peter Rabbit* shows the mother only as a mother, performing the duties deemed good under patriarchy, to the exclusion of other possible activities a woman might choose to suit herself—say, socialize with friends, play an instrument, read a book, or do work other than domestic labor. Mrs. Rabbit supports Weitzman's conclusion that "Loving, watching, and helping are among the few activities allowed to women in picture books" (1130). Though the females outnumber the males in *The Tale of Peter Rabbit*, a rare occurrence in classics, we can see that the girls also fit the passive mold, and Peter goes where the action is and gets the bulk of the attention.

The Giving Tree's Apples: A Good Mother Gives All

Those who write, illustrate, and publish picture books have come a long way towards correcting gender imbalances and widening the roles of women since the feminist scholarship of the 1970s; however, it is difficult to see any improvement based on the all-time best-selling list. Many older texts still sell briskly enough to remain in print in a competitive market. In fact, the next mother-defining picture book on our hardcover countdown, ranked at number 14 with 5,603,187 copies sold since its publication in 1964, continues to do so well in hardcover that it has never even been released in paperback (Roback). Shel Silverstein's *The Giving Tree* was named by *American Heritage* as the Most Overrated Classic Children's Book because, in the words of Ellen Handler Spitz, "It perpetuates a myth of the selfless, all-giving mother who exists only to be used and the image of a male child who can offer no reciprocity, express no gratitude, feel no empathy—an insatiable creature who encounters no limits for his demands" (46). Beginning with the cover image of the subtly personified tree dropping an apple to an expectant human child, the tree freely gives all she has to feed the desires of a boy who plays "king of the forest" and goes on to sell all the tree's apples for money, cut off her branches to build a house, and finally cut her trunk to make a boat; in fact, the tree stump is happy in the end because the boy, an old man now, comes back to sit on her.

Although many have read Silverstein's story as a parable with either a religious or an environmental theme, the self-sacrificing tree more logically can be read not as God's love or Mother Nature but as the culturally defined "good" mother of humans, an argument I have made in greater length elsewhere (Fraustino, "At the Core"). Every day the little boy plays with the tree, climbing up her trunk in an image suggestive of a small child clinging to his mother's leg, swinging from her branches the way a mother twirls a child in her arms. When the boy naps in her shade, her roots resemble a lap. As a young child, the boy loves the tree very much, but as he gets older he acts more out of self-love, as adolescents often do. He is even so callous as to carve "M. E. & Y. L." in the tree's trunk above "M. E. & T." Despite his abandonment, giving to the taking boy makes the tree happy; only after he lugs off her trunk for a boat is she "not really happy," and even then it is because she has nothing left to give the boy. It's quite a stretch to read a female gendered tree as a patriarchal God's self-sacrificial love of man, and the environment wouldn't be happy in the end to be turned into a stump. Only the mythologized "good" mother in our culture is defined by her giving completely and unconditionally like the Dr. Spockian "ever-present, all-providing, inexhaustibly patient and tactful" Giving Tree.

Carolyn Daniel has generalized about mothers in children's books, "The powerlessness and subordinated status of her socially assigned domestic role is acknowledged and accepted as a natural aspect of her gender" (104). Perhaps this is why so many people fail to see the problem with Silverstein's message despite decades of criticism, including Jackson and Dell's 1979 parody "The Other Giving Tree" and Strandburg and Livo's incisive 1986 article "*The Giving Tree* or There Is a Sucker Born Every Minute," among others. Shari Thurer's point, though not made regarding *The Giving Tree*, couldn't be more pertinent: "There is a glaring need to restore to mother her own presence, to understand that she is a person, not merely an object for her child, to recognize her subjectivity" (xii). People just don't realize this; they practice what Diekman and Murnen call "benevolent sexism," or "a tendency to endorse the traditional feminine ideal or to view women in idealized, overly romantic terms" (375).

Patriarchal gender patterns, present in many children's books as well as in other media, are deeply internalized in children by repeated exposure at an early age. In the case of *The Giving Tree*, young readers see that boys are allowed to go off and do what they want, unlike girls, who by gender affiliation are assigned the tree's rooted role, doling out apples. This is not to say that patriarchy is kind to the "taking boy." What happened to Y. L.? Where is the wife for whose home the tree sacrificed her limbs? Why is the boy alone in the end? *The Giving Tree* resolution shows that males who take physically from women and cannot give emotionally are unable to sustain satisfying relationships—hence wind up alone on a stump that is the equivalent of mother's grave. And she, the martyr mother who gave, gave, gave, can be equally blamed for allowing him to consume her. She feeds him patriarchal ideology along with her apples, her limbs, and her very trunk that he uses to build a boat, metaphorically returning to her womb and their umbilical feeding connection.

Are You My Mother?'s Worm: A Good Mother Is Biological—And, She Stays Home

P. D. Eastman's *Are You My Mother?*, published in 1960, has sold 4,135,762 copies in hardcover, ranking at number 24 (Roback). A mother bird leaves the nest to find food for her hatching chick, who then goes looking for her, asking every creature or machine he meets: "Are you my mother?" Tellingly, it never occurs to the little bird to ask, "Are you my father?" Don't some daddy birds share in the care of their hatchlings? This plot reflects the essentialist assumption that children require the nurturing of their mother—in fact, the very mother who incubated the egg. No substitute will do. This baby bird is born desperately wanting—because the dominant culture says it needs—its biological mother.

Not surprisingly, adoptive families feel some anxiety while reading this and other picture books sharing the Find-Mama trope, such as the one my own children read as part of their literature-based second-grade education, *Is Your Mama a Llama?*, written by Deborah Guarino and illustrated by Steven Kellogg (popular but not yet an all-time best seller). The little llama goes around asking all his friends the question, and they all answer in rhymed couplets describing their species. It's a cute way to recognize bats, cows, and kangaroos but not mothers who look different from their offspring. Authors and illustrators have responded with rewrites that show alternative family structures, including *A Mother for Choco?*, Keiko Kasza's revisioning of *Are You My Mother?* An abandoned bird sets off to find his mother, searching for one "just like me," as the dominant ideology dictates. However, in Mrs. Bear he finds an adoptive mother who looks different but meets Choco's needs for hugs, songs, and even other siblings who all look different—Hippy, Ally, and Piggy—reflecting the evolving ideology that a good mother is the person who provides primary caregiving. This includes apple pie for Choco.

Paradoxically, even as Eastman's mother bird pursues her culturally dictated role of feeding the child, she subliminally reveals mid-twentieth century society's wariness toward the working mother, especially a single one. The plot may be cute in an anthropomorphic sort of way, but the astute reader cannot help but note that the baby is in real physical danger because his mother chooses to leave him home with no supervision nor even the protective warnings that old Mrs.

Rabbit gives her older children when she goes for their currant buns. It's a long fall out of that tree, and out in the big world the bird talks to many strangers who, if not in the genetically altered fantasy world of a children's picture book, would be more likely to eat him or crush him than help a birdie out. What's more, as if the inherent danger of leaving latchkey kids home alone isn't enough to strike terror into a working mother's heart, now she has to worry about her kid *not knowing who she is* when she brings home the worm. What if he takes his first step without her there? What if he starts calling somebody else "Mommy?"

This very question provides the title and the text for a unique 2006 Find-Mama pop-up book with art by Maurice Sendak, scenario by Arthur Yorinks, and paper engineering by Matthew Reinhart (2006). Resembling a game of hide-and-seek or peek-a-boo, *Mommy?* both mocks and embeds many of our deeply held myths of motherhood found in the all-time best sellers. A Sendakian boy child enters a house of horrors and asks, "MOMMY?" In a parodic reversal of picture book expectations, we see an aproned mad scientist cooking up mutant creatures, not apple pie. Perhaps he is Daddy? The child proceeds through the house and tames a series of male monsters by sticking a pacifier in the vampire's mouth, removing the bolt from Franky's neck, unraveling the mummy, and pantsing the werewolf while a she-ghoul in red shoes points and laughs. She also points the way to the last page, outside in a cemetery, where the child finds his mother-mummy in a crypt, wired up to some mad scientist equipment powered by lightning. She exclaims with outstretched arms, "B-A-B-Y!", the only word other than "MOMMY?" in the text. So it's all about the primary bond between mother and baby. No male can substitute (as Mary Shelley's Dr. Frankenstein found). The house, metaphorically associated with the female body, is a house of horrors for someone negotiating masculinity— yet the fearless child is right at home here and conquers all the demons. The mother is beautiful, mysterious, monstrous, and has been waiting patiently with love, if indeed she is really alive, given her location. Perhaps she died in childbirth; but even if she lives, her prior life has ended. Now she is bound to her encrypted mothering role as signified by the umbilical-like cords that bind her. Metaphorically, then, any mommy under the myths of motherhood becomes a mummy, wrapped up in her domestic role.

Where the Wild Things Are's Hot Supper: Mother = Food = Love

Maurice Sendak's *Where the Wild Things Are*, the 1964 Caldecott Medalist, a best seller in both hardcover (number 63 and 1,972,147 copies) and paper (number 32 and 3,789,359 copies) (Roback), never shows the mother and only mentions her once, yet it is at its core about a mother–child relationship. Unlike the other best sellers under discussion, it deals with the psychological complexity of the primary bond from the child's perspective and steps away from modeling mythical good-mother behavior or feeding adult needs. Indeed, Mary Galbraith has argued that the story "breaks ground with its portrayal of a mother who is not coping serenely with her child" and "fails him in four ways": by failing to address his rage, by being the first to call him a name, by "[isolating] him without food," and by using food as a substitute for her own presence in the end (160). Galbraith claims, "My exposition of Max's mother's failures is not meant to fault her as a fictional character, nor to fault Maurice Sendak for portraying her in this way," for "one could argue that both mother and son are 'locked in' to their conflict by their isolation from human contact with family and community" (163). Max's mother is certainly no Giving Tree. She's human and real and reveals the ambivalence aptly expressed by Adrienne Rich in her 1976 groundbreaking text *Of Woman Born* (but almost never expressed in picture books): "My children cause me the most exquisite suffering of which I have any experience . . . the murderous alternation between bitter resentment and raw-edged nerves, and blissful gratification and tenderness" (21). Perhaps she's not a Good Mother, but she's likely a "good-enough" mother in the sense popularized by psychoanalyst and pediatrician D. W. Winnicott.

Like Beatrix Potter, Sendak uses a domestic frame to establish the major dramatic question, and food is part of both the main conflict and the resolution. Wolf-suited Max has hanged his bear, driven nails into the walls in what Spitz calls "a thinly disguised attack on" the mother represented by the house (*Inside* 127), chased the dog with a fork—"made mischief of one kind and another"—building to the only overt mention of Max's mother in the story:

> his mother called him "WILD THING!"
> and Max said "I'LL EAT YOU UP!"
> so he was sent to bed without eating anything.

Here we see a moment that epitomizes a central point that Dorothy Dinnerstein makes in *The Mermaid and the Minotaur*, in which she traces the psychoanalytic roots of patriarchal power to female-dominated childhood: "Woman is the will's first, overwhelming adversary. . . . In our first real contests of will, we find ourselves, more often than not, defeated" (166). Max must tame his wild ways to join the human world symbolized by the books he stands on to drive his nail with a civilized man's hammer, and his mother must discipline him. Mother is not all milk and honey; she enforces the social order through what Keeling and Pollard call "food's signifying regimes" (142).

Spitz reads Max's expression in the next picture as "resorting magically to a plan of triumphing over this 'bad' mother" who has deprived him of herself/food (129). Sendak himself has said that Max "discharges his anger against his mother" (*Caldecott* 151), and saying he'll eat her up does seem a violent threat: he'll consume her. However, when Max later leaves the wild things behind, and they cry: "Oh please don't go—we'll eat you up—we love you so!", the final phrase adds crucial information to understanding Max's state of mind. Perhaps Max believes "I'LL EAT YOU UP" means the same thing as "I LOVE YOU SO!" According to Anna Freud, "The image of food and the mother-image remain merged into one until the child is weaned from the breast" (111), so it is not surprising that a child as young as Max may still view his mother as an edible woman (presumably he loves the little terrier he chases with the fork, too?). Later, after Max tames the wild things and has had his fill of rumpus, he sends them "off to bed without their supper," for no apparent reason except being the wild things they are, and this reminds the reader that the whole adventure has really been about the conflict between Max and his mother. Now he is "lonely." The wild things of his imagination cannot substitute for where "someone loved him best of all," home with his mother. Despite their conflict, then, we know that Max knows his mother loves him best, as a culturally defined good mother should, as signified by the smell of "good things to eat" that leads him to his room

> where he found his supper waiting for him
> and it was still hot.

The food represents the mother and her love.

The Runaway Bunny's Carrot: Mothers Can't Exist Without Their Children

Another widely beloved classic picture book about mother–child relationships is Margaret Wise Brown's *The Runaway Bunny*, a best seller in three formats: number 104 as a hardcover board book with sales of 1,212,945; number 145 in hardcover with sales of 1,913,157; and in paperback number 188 with sales of 750,456 (Roback). Fans of the book see a "good mother" who loves her child so much that she wants to be with him all the time and protect him; however, she reveals herself as controlling more than caring when she says, "If you become a sailboat and sail away from me . . . I will become the wind and blow you where I want you to go." Perhaps she read *The Tale of Peter Rabbit* and fears that her son will get into mischief if she lets him go off by himself. Perhaps she feels rejected or abandoned by his desire to run away, despite that being a normal childhood expression of independence as well as a ploy for affection. This mother's attachment is so strong that she will become anything, go anywhere, to prevent her son's leaving her, "For you are my little bunny," she tells him, as if he is her possession.

Though Roni Natov notes that "clearly the mother is not ready to let her child go into nature" (68), she views the story structure as "mirroring the affirmation of self for the baby rabbit and also for the mother, in a bond of true reciprocity" (66). I disagree. Certainly such an opportunity exists; this is a moment, as Natov says, of "rapprochement" (66), in which, as psychoanalytic theorist Jessica Benjamin describes it, "a conflict emerges between the infant's grandiose aspirations and the perceived reality of her or his limitations and dependency" (134). However, the bunny mother fails to hold up her end of the deal, here. According to Benjamin:

> If the mother is unable both to set a clear boundary for the child and to recognize the child's intentions and will, to insist on her own separateness and respect that of the child, the child does not really 'get' that the mother is also a person, a subject in her own right. Instead, the child continues to see her as all-powerful, either omnipotently controlling or engulfingly weak. (135)

The weak Giving Tree mother becomes engulfed. Max successfully negotiates mutuality through fantasy. The bunny mother overwhelms. After we see images of her stalking her runaway bunny everywhere, from the mountains to the seas and across tightropes, we see them pictured in the *Good Night Moon* room rocking chair, staring each other down. When I was a sentimental young mother myself, I used to read that illustration as a loving gaze, but now I see the powerless little bunny coming to the realization that there's no escape from his omnipotent mother's control. Indeed, the page turn reveals his sense of defeat in the battle of wills identified by Dinnerstein. "'Shucks,' said the bunny, 'I might just as well stay where I am and be your little bunny.'"

Though they may seem very different from each other, the smother bunny mother can be seen as the alter ego of the giving tree mother. Both act out of fear of losing their sons to the world beyond home. The giving tree mother, created from the (sub)consciousness of a male author, allows the boy to go off on his own but gives him whatever she can to keep him coming back to her—hence her unhappiness when she has nothing left to give. The taking boy gets all the benefits of being babied and loses none of the privileges of adulthood. The bunny mother, from the (sub)consciousness of a female author, controls aggressively rather than passively. She's not going to sacrifice her own life to keep her son; she's simply never going to let him leave her. Though its admirers say that *The Runaway Bunny* reinforces a young child's need to know that Mommy loves him unconditionally and will take care of him even when he's not making it easy, this book goes beyond the child's healthy developmental needs into the realm of the mother's unhealthy neediness for the child. Her final words, "Have a carrot," remind us of the earlier image of her using the bunny's stereotypical favorite food to fish him out of the creek when he tries to swim away, her fishing line cast like an attempt to reconnect the umbilical cord (this last an observation for which I thank Hollins student Claudia Pearson). I can't help but picture that carrot with a hook inside it, a symbol of attachment, signifying the harm hidden within an ideology that defines woman as mother. If she loses her child, she loses her very identity.

Love You Forever's Suckling Embrace: A Mother Always Has a Baby Around

If you're a fan of the popular television series *Friends*, you may have seen Joey read what is perhaps the most psychologically questionable best seller to Emma on her first birthday, to Rachel's sentimental delight and Phoebe's scrunch-nosed comment, "That book sucks." *Love You Forever*, written by Robert Munsch and illustrated by Sheila McGraw, has sold over 18 million copies internationally, so its appeal isn't limited to the 1,049,000 hardcover buyers (ranking number 128) and the whopping 6,970,000 paperback copies (ranking number 4) in the United States in well over 60 printings. This, the most recently published book about mothers on the all-time best-selling list, has also outsold both *The Runaway Bunny* and *The Giving Tree*, suggesting that classic status and tradition have less to do with the rankings than how strongly the themes connect with the mother market in popular culture (indeed, all four of the Harry Potter books then in print had already neared the top of both hard and soft lists). Munsch's story begins with a mother holding her new baby in nursing position as she rocks and sings:

> I'll love you forever,
> I'll like you for always,
> As long as I'm living
> my baby you'll be

He grows older—age two, nine, teenage—and at night while he's sleeping, the ever-loving mother creeps into his room to cradle him in her arms and sing the refrain. Even after he is a grown man, the elderly mother drives across town with her ladder, climbs into her son's room, and sings the same lullaby, embodying the woman whose identity is determined by biological production, who is supposed to receive her greatest satisfaction from motherhood. This story offers us the giving-tree-chase-the-bunny mother combined. Mommy lets her boy have his independence by day, but by night, when he's sleeping, she reverts him to that infant who depended on her for everything. It is that baby once a part of her body that she loves forever—not necessarily the boy who grows up and says bad words in front of grandma.

It may be reassuring to be told your mother will love you forever, but how many kids always want to be her suckling babe? On his official Web site, author Robert Munsch says that he wrote *Love You Forever* "as a memorial for two stillborn babies we had in 1979 and 1980"—an adult, grief-centered motive far from the normal developmental concerns of a child audience. In the end, when the grown son holds his dying mother on his lap and sings the song, we see an embodiment of the adult desire to have children who will take care of us in our old age. As Lucy Rollin has pointed out, this image "might be seen as a hint that the mother who shares this book with her child expects the same treatment—rather a large burden to place on a child who has trouble foreseeing his own growth much less his parents' aging" (108). One antidote to *Love You Forever* is Todd Parr's *The Mommy Book*, in which mommies do all sorts of different things, some conventional ("Some mommies drive minivans"), some unconventional ("Some mommies drive motorcycles"). Some cook at home, some order pizza—because we can't have a mommy book without feeding the kids. However: "All mommies like to watch you sleep!" Parr's model mommy, though, has the sense to watch from the door.

The Apple of Her Eye and Other Conclusions

Collectively, what ideology do these best sellers feed us? Interestingly, none of the authors were/are mothers themselves; hence, representations of mothers in best-selling picture books about mothering come from somewhere other than mothering experience. Else Holmelund Minarik had a daughter who was the inspiration for her *Little Bear* storybooks in Ursula Nordstrom's "I Can Read" series, with illustrations by Maurice Sendak. Though not a picture book, *Little Bear* ranks 205 on the paperback best-selling list with sales of 1,585,832 (Roback) and is worth noting here. On the back of my 1985 paperback version, the copy reads in large letters, "Mother Bear is always there." Wearing an apron, by the way. On the cover of *Little Bear*, she holds him on her lap and they share an adoring gaze. All four stories center on Mother taking good care of Little Bear, including making him a surprise birthday cake because "I never did forget your birthday, and I never will." Another story ends with lunch, and then a nap, "For you are my little bear, and I know it," echoing the runaway bunny's mother with a big difference: Mother Bear is reassuring the child that she hasn't forgotten the day she gave birth to him, not claiming ownership. Minarik's Mother Bear does fit Dr. Spock's good-mother job description and lacks human frailties, but she doesn't go to extremes. Minarik's mother seems sane and responsible possibly because of the author's lived experience.

In all of the other best-selling books discussed here, except for *Where the Wild Things Are*, instead of depicting a real-life mother who sometimes gets angry, who sometimes resents the demands of children, who has interests beyond the child, "Motherhood is utterly sentimentalized" (Thurer xii). *Love You Forever*, published after the second wave of feminism had influenced children's publishing, does allow the mother some ambivalence—"Sometimes his mother would say, '*This kid is driving me CRAZY!*' and "Sometimes his mother wanted to sell him to the *zoo!*"—but the humorous, tongue-in-cheek tone gives no hint of bitter resentment or raw-edged nerves. In fact, judging the book by its cover, we can read the boy's bad behaviors as oh-so-cute. His mother can't show honest ambivalence because society's myth demands what Thurer calls "the mother who is always loving, selfless, tranquil; the one who finds passionate fulfillment in every detail of child rearing" (xii).

In contrast, Liz Rosenberg's 1993 *Monster Mama*, with illustrations by Stephen Gammell, shows a mother whose "bad moods terrified the neighborhood. Still, she had the sweetest touch in the world when Patrick Edward ran a fever." This mother teaches her son to be "fearless, like her," and to take care of himself out in the world. One day on his way "to pick out something lovely for dessert," bullies surround him, eat his dessert, and insult his mother. He roars, "YOU LEAVE MY MOTHER OUT OF THIS!"; his mother comes running, and she gets that situation under control with some tough love and a "strawberry tea cake with French whipped cream on top." After the sweet love-food, the story ends with the same comforting message as most picture books with Mama in the title: "No matter where you go, or what you do, I will be there. Because I am your mother, even if I am a monster—and I love you." It's a terrific honest book and, alas, currently out of print. Popular culture prefers stumps and old ladies with ladders strapped to their cars.

Two of the best-selling books discussed, *The Tale of Peter Rabbit* and *Are You My Mother?*, suggest a woman working outside of the home, and that labor is the provision of food for her child. "The prevailing mythology does concede that some mothers have to work outside the home," says Thurer, "but it classifies such an endeavor as a necessary evil. The really good mother is a full-time mother" (xi). Although anthropomorphized birds and bunnies could allow readers of various ethnicities to place themselves into the subject positions of the protagonists, the values and the full-time mothering lifestyle depicted in the best sellers are clearly mainstream, white, and middle-class. The lower-income bunnies would be leaving their own little bunnies with their grammabunnies in order to care for upper-class bunnies and put the currant buns on the table. White, middle-class values of momism even inscribe the more recent *Big Momma Makes the World* by Phyllis Root, illustrated by Helen Oxenbury, published in 2002 and winner of the Boston Globe-Horn Book Award. I first heard the text read aloud, and the Southern American voice sounds enough like African American Vernacular English that it surprised me to see Momma not painted as a person of color. She's a single mom, baby on her hip, doing the work of God, complete with light and dark, water and earth, and all the creatures, but:

> Making a world was a lot of work,
> what with the laundry piling up
> and the dishes needing doing.

She also makes cookies. It seems no matter what else a woman does, domesticity defines her.

The Giving Tree, The Runaway Bunny, and *Love You Forever* are all about how incredibly much the mother loves the child, as if that is her only role in life. The mother–child relationship is intense, one-on-one, all-consuming. There's no career for the woman, no interest in nondomestic activities, and this is even the case for the best book of the bunch, *Where the Wild Things Are.* Except for the dead dad and the silent sisters in *The Tale of Peter Rabbit,* we see no fathers or siblings around to share the mother's love—nor share in the labor of child rearing, for that matter. Mom has no friends. Her child is her primary love interest. We certainly never see comical naked cartoon parents chasing each other around the bed in answer to the question "Why do Mummy and Daddy lock me out of their bedroom?" as United Kingdom children get to in Babette Cole's 2003 *Mummy Never Told Me*, a very funny book that peels back many layers of mothering myths (I discovered the book in Taiwan, as European taboos are not available in the United States.)

Aproned Old Mrs. Rabbit, too, shows that it is the mother's job to raise the children—teach them, protect them, feed them—and fathers can just as well be baked into a pie. Of course, the absence of fathers in best-selling books does a disservice to real-life parents of both genders. As Anderson and Hamilton found in a study of 200 prominent picture books, "Fathers were significantly under-represented, and they were presented as unaffectionate and indolent in terms of feeding, carrying babies, and talking with children. Mother made most of the contact with children, and expressed emotion more often than did the fathers" (149). The cultural script is slowly changing, and fathers are now granted a spot on the best-seller list with Sam McBratney's 1995 blockbuster, *Guess How Much I Love You*, with the board book version ranked number 56 and sales of 2,199,550 and the hardcover number 74 and 1,630,908 (Roback). Here we learn that the father's love is the biggest of all.

A book that does represent a range of ethnic and gender diversity through multiple images of animal families is the 1998 *What Daddies Do Best/What Mommies Do Best*, written by Laura Numeroff and illustrated by Lynn Mun-singer. This clever reversible book can be read from either end, one side show-ing mommies with children and the other showing daddies doing the exact same activities, but differently. Unfortunately, in a few spots this book does allow Daddy to one-up Mommy, as when he pushes the child to ride a bike without training wheels or, more pertinent to our present topic, makes a big-ger, more perfect birthday cake (and thanks go to Eastern Connecticut State University senior seminar student Susan O'Neil for noticing this).

Perhaps most significant, these books are all about boys, each the apple of his mother's eye. To find a best-selling mother–child relationship book that features a daughter we have to scroll all the way down to number 324 on the paperback list (Roback) to Robert McCloskey's *Blueberries for Sal*, first pub-lished in 1948. Sal, in fact, could be misread as male with her androgynous appearance and name; and her alter ego, Little Bear, is male. The opening illustration shows Sal in the kitchen training for her domestic future as she helps her mother can blueberries. "Then we will have food for the winter," her mother explains. Meanwhile, Little Bear has come with his mother to "eat lots of berries and grow big and fat. We must store up food for the long, cold winter." When Sal and Little Bear each get lost and go mother hunting, they encounter "a mother crow and her children" (eating berries, of course), "a mother partridge and her children" (eating berries, of course), all sending the message that mothering and feeding are a natural pairing.

The fact that virtually all of the best-selling individual trade picture books about mother–child relationships focus exclusively on a boy-child reflects the stereotype of male superiority. Mothers had logical reasons to prefer sons in the days before women's suffrage, when a son provided the hand that rocked the cradle with a connection to patriarchal power that she might not be able to achieve through her husband. As Marjorie DeVault has pointed out, "the ideal family that most people try to construct is built on women's service for men," and "caring is typically done in ways that reinforce men's entitlement and women's subservience" (13). Hence the very roots of the patriarchal order are found in *The Giving Tree* and the other books discussed here. Not only do images of food and their significations reinforce outmoded cultural myths of motherhood for the adults who read these books to their children; they also serve as the earliest training manuals for a girl's future position of ever-present, all-providing, and inexhaustibly patient mother—for by focusing on mother–son relationships, they place the girl in the gendered subject position of mother rather than child.

If the parent's objective is to show through literature that a mother means love, there are books available that do so without sacrificing the self or smothering the child. I particularly like *Mama, Do You Love Me?* by Barbara M. Joosse, illustrated by Barbara Lavallee, published in 1991. It follows a similar narrative pattern as *The Runaway Bunny*, with the child issuing challenges to test the mother's love, but with responses that allow the child independence and agency. In response to impossible answers the mother gives to the limits of her love—"more than the whale loves his spout" and "till the stars turn to fish in the sky"—the child challenges her with realistic limits, asking: "Mama, what if I carried our eggs—our ptarmigan eggs!—and I tried to be careful, and I tried to walk slowly, but I fell and the eggs broke?" Because eggs function both as food necessary for their survival and as metaphor of their mother–daughter bond, this question strikes to the heart of their relationship. The mother responds: "Then I would be sorry. But still, I would love you." With each new question the child escalates her challenges: "What if I put salmon in your parka" . . . "threw water at our lamp" . . . "ran away" . . . "stayed away and sang with the wolves," and the mother responds in kind: "Then I would be angry" . . . "very angry" . . . "worried" . . . "sad," and through it all:

> I will love you,
> forever and for always,
> because you are
> my Dear One.

This ending echoes the refrain of *Love You Forever* but doesn't stagnate at still-born love. Unlike most mother–child books, this one features a daughter and also deviates from the overrepresented white, middle-class family model. A widely popular book that remains in print in various formats, I hope it will supplant some weaker mother stories in the next *Publishers Weekly* best-selling list.

The physical act of reading to a child on the lap mimics the position of nursing, giving the experience a nurturing quality, with the book substituting for the mother's milk, its contents feeding the mind, filling it with images and messages that either transmit or subvert the dominant ideology. When the book happens to be about the mother–child relationship, the metaphor of maternal feeding becomes doubly potent. In ways both overt and subliminal, images of food in popular children's picture books reconstruct a cultural myth of the "good" mother and ultimately serve to help reproduce her generation after generation, perpetuating a definition that I would argue needs a major revision to suit contemporary women and their families.

Works Cited

Anderson, David A., and Mykol Hamilton. "Gender Role Stereotyping of Parents in Children's Picture Books: The Invisible Father." *Sex Roles* 52.3/4 (2005): 145–151.

Benjamin, Jessica. "The Omnipotent Mother: A Psychoanalytic Study of Fantasy and Reality." *Representations of Motherhood*. Ed. Donna Bassin, et al. New Haven, CT: Yale UP, 1994. 129–146.

Brown, Margaret Wise. *The Runaway Bunny*. 1942. New York: Harper, 1972.

Chodorow, Nancy J. *The Reproduction of Mothering: Psychoanalysis and the Sociology of Gender With a New Preface*. 1978. Los Angeles: U of California P, 1999.

Cole, Babette. *Mummy Never Told Me*. London: Red Fox, 2003.

Daniel, Carolyn. *Voracious Children: Who Eats Whom in Children's Literature*. New York: Routledge, 2006.

DeVault, Marjorie L. *Feeding the Family: The Social Organization of Caring as Gendered Work*. Chicago: U of Chicago P, 1991.

Diekman, Amanda B., and Sarah K. Murnen. "Learning to Be Little Women and Little Men: The Inequitable Gender Equality of Nonsexist Children's Literature.' *Sex Roles* 50.5/6 (2004): 373–385.

Dinnerstein, Dorothy. *The Mermaid and the Minotaur: Sexual Arrangements and Human Malaise*. 1976. New York: Other P, 1999.

"Dr. Benjamin Spock, 1903–1998." 2004. The Dr. Spock Company. 1 June 2004. <http://www.drspock.com>.

Eastman, P. D. *Are You My Mother?* New York: Random House, 1960.

Fraustino, Lisa Rowe. "At the Core of *The Giving Tree*'s Signifying Apples." *Food for Thought*. Ed. Annette Magid. London: Cambridge Scholars, in press.

———. "The Berenstain Bears and the Reproduction of Mothering." *The Lion and the Unicorn* 31.3 (2007): 250–263.

Freud, Anna. "The Psychoanalytic Study of Infantile Feeding Disturbances." *Food and Culture: A Reader*. Ed. Carole Counihan and Penny Van Esterik. New York: Routledge, 1997. 107–116.

Galbraith, Mary. "Where Mother Isn't." *Paunch* (1999): 160–165.

Glenn, Evelyn Nakano, et al., eds. *Mothering: Ideology, Experience, and Agency*. New York: Routledge, 1994.

Guarino, Deborah. *Is Your Mama a Llama?* New York: Scholastic, 1989.

Jackson, Jacqueline, and Carol Dell. "The Other Giving Tree." *Language Arts* 56.4(1979): 427–429.

Joosse, Barbara M. *Mama, Do You Love Me?* San Francisco: Chronicle, 1991.

Kasza, Keiko. *A Mother for Choco*. New York: Putnam, 1992.

Keeling, Kara, and Scott Pollard. "Power, Food, and Eating in Maurice Sendak and Henrik Drescher: *Where the Wild Things Are, In the Night Kitchen*, and *The Boy Who Ate Around*." *Children's Literature in Education* 30.2 (1999): 127–143.

McBratney, Sam. *Guess How Much I Love You?* Cambridge, MA: Candlewick, 1995.

McCloskey, Robert. *Blueberries for Sal*. 1948. New York: Puffin, 1976.

Minarik, Else Holmelund. *Little Bear*. 1957. New York: Harper, 1985.

Munsch, Robert. *Love You Forever*. Toronto/Buffalo: Firefly, 1986.

———. *The Official Robert Munsch Website*. 2004. Bob Munsch Eng. Ltd. 29 May 2004. <http://www.robertmunsch.com>.

Natov, Roni. *The Poetics of Childhood*. New York: Routledge, 2002.

Nilsen, Alleen Pace. "Women in Children's Literature." *College English* 32.8 (1971): 918–926.

Numeroff, Laura. *What Daddies Do Best/What Mommies Do Best*. New York: Simon & Schuster, 1998.

Parr, Todd. *The Mommy Book*. Boston: Little, 2002.

Potter, Beatrix. *The Tale of Peter Rabbit*. 1902. New York: Warne, 2002.

Rich, Adrienne. *Of Woman Born: Motherhood as Experience and Institution*. 1976. New York: Norton, 1995.

Roback, Diane, and Jason Britton, eds. Comp. Debbie Hochman Turvey. "All-Time Bestselling Children's Books." *Publishers Weekly* 17 Dec 2001: 24–32. EBSCO. Eastern CT State U Lib. 21 Jan 2004 <http://www.epnet.com.csulib.ctstateu.edu>.

Rollin, Lucy. "Good-Enough Mother Hubbard." *Psychoanalytic Responses to Children's Literature*. Ed. Lucy Rollin and Mark I. West. Jefferson, NC: McFarland, 1999. 97–110.

Root, Phyllis. *Big Momma Makes the World*. Cambridge, MA: Candlewick, 2002.

Rosenberg, Liz. *Monster Mama*. New York: Philomel, 1993.

Sendak, Maurice. *Caldecott & Co.: Notes on Books & Pictures*. New York: Farrar, 1988.

———, et al. *Mommy?* New York: Scholastic, 2006.

———. *Where the Wild Things Are*. New York: Harper, 1963.

Silverstein, Shel. *The Giving Tree*. 1964. New York: Harper, 1992.

Spitz, Ellen Handler. *Inside Picture Books*. New Haven: Yale UP, 1999.

———. "Overrated and Underrated: Classic Children's Book." *American Heritage* 50 (1999): 46.

Strandburg, Walter L., and Norma J. Livo. "*The Giving Tree* or There Is a Sucker Born Every Minute." *Children's Literature in Education* 17.1 (1986): 17–24.

Sutton, Roger. "Guess How Much I Love You, Catcher in the Rye." *The Horn Book* 80. 3 (May/June 2004): 228–229.

Thurer, Shari L. *The Myths of Motherhood: How Culture Reinvents the Good Mother*. New York: Penguin, 1994.

Weitzman, Lenore J., et al. "Sex-Role Socialization in Picture Books for Preschool Children." *American Journal of Sociology* 77.6 (1972): 1125–1150.

Part IV

Food and the Body

Chapter Five
Nancy Drew and the "F" Word

Leona W. Fisher

When *The Nancy Drew Cookbook* appeared in its first printing in 1973, Harriet Stratemeyer Adams, self-styled "Carolyn Keene" and head of the Stratemeyer Syndicate that produced the series, discovered that the recipe for "Italian Salsa di Pomodoro (Tomato Sauce)" lacked the tomatoes (138).[1] Copies were quickly recalled and the second printing corrected the error. But Adams was still severely disappointed on another level, as she complained to her publisher:

> I had planned to give copies to many friends, but am too ashamed of the first edition to do so. . . . [With the exception of the professional editing] From every other angle the book is a disaster and unworthy of being a companion to the NANCY DREW series. The fault rests with the Art Department [at Grosset and Dunlap] and the layout person. From the beginning I was disappointed with the picture situation. I did not want sticks of butter or disproportionate milk cartons but sketches with some originality and cute quips, some of which we supplied but they were brushed off. (Letter from Adams to Harold Roth, 28 March 1973, Box 39, Stratemeyer Syndicate Records, New York Public Library)[2]

She subsequently repeated her complaints to the Art Department itself: "Having been promised . . . that the pictures would be original and whimsical . . . , it was an added shock to see the cook book with mundane flour sifters and egg boxes which any third grader could have drawn" (Letter from Adams to Kay Ward, 25 April 1973, Box 41, SSR-NYPL). Clearly she wanted "her" heroine to be paid the domestic compliment of an artistic kitchen.

Others were also disappointed, and not for aesthetic reasons. The (Oregon) *Daily News'* review of the book, by Georgia Smith, for instance, showed disappointment that the book undercut Nancy's appeal as a strong role model: "Ironically, Nancy's had a modest following among feminists up 'til now. . . . Nancy has proven herself no slouch in the liberation department. . . . Now a girl like that doesn't usually mess around with pudding. Even 'Mystery Corn Pudding'" (2 August 1973, Box 32, SSR-NYPL). A bookseller in Charlotte, North Carolina also worried that "we may be relegating the famous girl detective to the kitchen," though he conceded that the book is "a cute idea" and is selling well (Letter from Eric Svenson to Stratemeyer Syndicate, 30 April 1973, Box 32, SSR-NYPL). Feminist writer Bobbie Ann Mason first expressed her horror at the concept in 1975:

> But why a cookbook? Why, at a time when Nancy's skills should have broadened to include mechanics, computer programming, electronic counter-surveillance, and space travel—why a cookbook? . . . I might have expected *Nancy's Guide to Sports* or *Nancy's Guide to Self-Reliance* or some ecological handbook. Or, better, a *Guide to Sleuthing* from this wonder-girl gumshoe with the magnifying glass eternally poised over a footprint. . . .
>
> If the cookbook had come out when I was twelve, I would have felt horribly betrayed. Now I feel it confirms my assessment of the series and provides a convenient postscript. This is what Nancy is really all about. Here is proof of the pudding, so to speak, for Nancy is liberated from the kitchen but she hasn't abandoned it. . . . Nancy digs being dainty, and domesticity is, after all, still where it's at for a girl. (129–130)

At the very least, use of the word "cute" by two very different critics would seem to bode ill for the book, if not for Nancy herself, whose attitude towards both food and life is never "cute" under any circumstances. In any case, however attractive the idea commercially (and children's cookbooks based on fictional characters and series were becoming popular in the 1970s), the recipes contained therein bear little relationship to the actual food that has appeared in the series.[3] With the exception of the breakfast menu, which includes such edibles as "Chief McGinnis's Waffles" and "Ski Jump Hot Chocolate," the recipes seem designed only to advertise the novels and not to represent accurately the foods served within the books. They are therefore named arbitrarily after characters or titles and, as an extensive reading of the books confirms, nothing remotely resembling "Bungalow Mystery Salad" (44), containing "yellow or red bananas" and ginger ale, or "Hidden Staircase Biscuits" (45), containing maraschino cherry juice, has ever been served by either Hannah Gruen or (we hope) anyone else in fact or fiction.

Yet food has been a central presence in Nancy Drew novels since the 1930s and continues to play various roles. If we examine the place of food and eating in these books in relation to the extreme reactions implied above in the responses to the cookbook—what we might call "tea party coziness" (Mason 127) and consumerism, in Adams's case, versus feminist independence and agency, on the other critics' parts—some rather complex and illuminating discoveries emerge.[4] Although I agree with critics such as Mason and Lee Zacharias (1027) that eating may serve as "a luscious sex substitute" (Mason 127) for preteens, I will also argue, beyond that obvious Freudianism, that food functions in the series in ways that are both imbricated with other themes and issues, and productively contradictory. Most obviously, as a marker of class, food persists throughout the series' eight decades as a signifier of the protagonists' privileged status and ability to consume at will, and also serving as a moral marker of both genteel poverty and criminality. At the level of discourse and plot, cooking and eating (stopping at those endless tearooms, breaking for idyllic picnic lunches packed by the maternal Hannah, even learning to cook gourmet food at glamorous culinary resorts) provide repetitive ritual, domestic comfort, and needed breaks from the car chases and cliff-hanging action, as well as offering opportunities for strategic eavesdropping or for intimate communication among the three chums (Nancy, Bess, and George). And finally, in terms of characterization, the three sleuths' individual relationships to food fundamentally construct and ground their characters and personalities. Nancy's healthy appetite and occasional forgetfulness about eating when she is in the throes of a mystery, George's "boyish" indifference to food and willingness to torment Bess about her eating and diets, and Bess's eternal "hunger" and worries about her weight—all establish their varied relationships to themselves as subjects as well as to the world; in this regard it is Bess particularly who represents the texts' central and conflicted ideology.

In relation to each topic (class/privilege, discursive structure, characterization/subject position), if we explore the changes across the decades—for example, from the Depression-era excess and the "cholesterol-rich" (Caprio 25) 1950s to the ethnic and yuppie 1980s; from being waited on by servants to the post-1959 revisions' more egalitarian portrayal of kitchen chores; from Bess's obsession with ice cream sundaes to her "boy-craziness" and her expanded consumerism/consumption as a shopper; and so on—we can begin to see the centrality of this trope to the larger project of the books as a whole: the construction of "typical" (albeit idealized) twentieth-century upper-middle-class girlhood. Each of the three topics intersects with the others and, as could be predicted in the depiction of a quasi-feminist hero who cooks and washes dishes as well as chases criminals, performs multiple contradictory moves that have enabled girl readers to negotiate among the possible meanings. Readers of the series across the decades confirm that they are relieved, for example, to learn that Bess struggles with her weight and that she is less than "perfect" in her own (and, frequently, her cousin George's) estimation.[5] Still others attest to the inspiration they received from voyeuristic participation in all those adjective-heavy tea party and picnic menus, drawing inspiration for what Peter Stoneley (borrowing from Richard Ohmann) calls "upscale emulation" (93) from the unattainable lifestyle that Nancy and her circle enjoy.

Food as Signifier of Class Status

In terms of class issues, food—its procurement, "production," and consumption—both changes and remains the same across the decades that the series has existed, following cultural as well as economic conditions. As Diane McGee demonstrates in *Writing the Meal: Dinner in the Fiction of Early Twentieth-Century Women Writers*, "The culture determines what is eaten, by whom, when, and under what circumstances" (12).[6] In the first few books from the early 1930s, food predictably does not dominate, but instead is relegated to subordinate clauses ("After dinner," "When they had finished luncheon," etc.) or exists behind the closed doors of the kitchen; after the serving of a meal, we are told simply that "Hannah, the maid . . . retired" (*The Secret of the Old Clock* 1930, 3).[7] Yet as Peter Stoneley points out in relation to girls' series in general, one experiences "the unremitting presence of the imperatives of class" (93) even in these simple linguistic turns. Nancy occasionally "helped clear away the breakfast dishes" (*The Mystery at Lilac Inn* 1931, 112) but customarily remains removed from food production, gracious, and grateful. In these early versions of the texts, Nancy is also likely to "*tell* Hannah, the housekeeper, to prepare sandwiches" (*The Secret of Red Gate Farm* 1931, 19; emphasis added), and in the 1961 revision she "*asked*" her to do so (13; emphasis added). Throughout the early series Hannah "obligingly packed one of her famous picnic lunches" (*Diary* 1932, 3) and "served a delightful luncheon" (54), and the girls typically stay out of the kitchen unless Hannah is ill or absent. When the girls are visiting others, cooks are frequently Black and obsequious, for example in *The Password to Larkspur Lane* (1933), in which Nancy's friend, Helen Corning, describes her servant as "'a peach, and anything we might want to eat, she'll prepare for us'" (122). Sure enough, "The luxury of breakfast in bed was accorded Helen and Nancy by the genial black cook, and over cocoa, rolls, and fluffy scrambled eggs, Nancy pondered over what use to make of the day" (140). Similarly, in the 1936 version of *The Mystery of the Ivory Charm*, the small Indian prince whom they rescue from being kidnapped joins the girls in a picnic and Bess delights in being waited on: "'It's nice having someone do all the work,' Bess sighed blissfully. 'If Coya lived at our house I'd be spoiled soon'" (43). Order and luxury, comfort and abundance—upper-class privileges—constitute a foundational aspect of the girls' lives, making it unnecessary for them to lift a finger, and ironically so, at a time when much of the country was scrambling for subsistence.[8]

During this decade the manner in which food is consumed, as well as its presence or absence, designates the class status as well as the morality of a character—in a conflation of manners and morals more Victorian than modern. Thus, Jacob Aborn, Laura's supposed guardian in *The Hidden Staircase*, "gulped his tea in one swallow [and] crumbled his cake upon the table cloth" (1930, 38), marking himself as lower class and an impostor long before he is formally exposed as a villain. In contrast, the deserving poor or fallen gentlefolk (a popular trope in these Great Depression books), whose wealth and status will ultimately be restored by Nancy, seldom have enough to eat, as in *The Clue in the Diary*, in which the family of the suspected criminal eat only eggs (1932, 64), so that Nancy becomes their domestic savior by buying and preparing a "feast" for the mother and child (73) with characteristic noblesse oblige. There is never an issue of money, as Nancy always has sufficient funds to buy any food that is needed to supplement Hannah's provisions or a character's larder. Through these and dozens of other examples, and as Peter Stoneley writes of girls' series in general, "the reader joins the leisure class in a community of taste, for she too has learned to recognise who is and who is not 'our sort'" (96).

In the 1940s wartime texts there is somewhat less mention of food, perhaps in deference to rationing, although the girls usually manage to fit in three meals a day, and by the 1950s, elaborate menus have generally reappeared, as well as a focus on sweets and "hot cocoa," and Bess-as-Betty Crocker often ventures into the kitchen to bake her calorie-laden desserts (especially chocolate cakes) or cheese soufflés. Most of the egregious class references have disappeared by this time, along with the ethnic and racial specificity and insensitivity that characterized the earlier books. By this time Hannah is fully integrated into the family and eats with Nancy and her father, and the girls often help Hannah to cook or clean up. When they are guests, they also take their turns at preparation; the Black servant is also omitted from the 1966 revision of *The Password to Larkspur Lane* as "The girls dressed quickly and helped their hostess [Mrs. Corning, Helen's mother] prepare a dinner of steak, potatoes, green beans, and watermelon. Afterward, they insisted upon tidying the kitchen without her assistance" (82). Food tends to appear in these revisions only when it has some direct relevance to the mystery's plot, and there are many fewer cases of stopping at tearooms or quaint roadside inns for "luncheon."

From the 1960s onward an entirely new emphasis appears on ethnic and regional cuisines, including appropriately trendy descriptions of Chinese, African, French, even Scottish meals, depending on the mystery's characters and locale. It is therefore possible to track changes in attitudes towards race, class, ethnicity, and physical health—as well as an escalating globalization—through the changing references to food. In *The Mystery of the Fire Dragon* (1961), set in both New York and Hong Kong, Nancy's "Aunt Eloise and the girls ordered Peking duck and bean sprouts which were to follow birds'-nest soup" (104); later in Hong Kong, Ned orders "A little sweet-and-sour pork, beef fried in oyster sauce, bamboo shoots, rice, and almond tea," a feast which Nancy says "sounds like a Chinese Thanksgiving dinner" (158). *The Thirteenth Pearl* (1979), which takes place in Japan and retains many of the Syndicate's earlier attitudes towards persons of Asian descent (typically called "Asiatics"), offers an elaborate description of sushi and green tea (41); *The Emerald-Eyed Cat Mystery* (1984), partially set in San Francisco's Chinatown, refers to "honeyed spareribs, followed by a delectable soup, and finally, the specialty of the house, Peking duck" (30). Even in New York, the dishes take on an ethnic flavor: "Nancy bit into a crusty slice [of pizza] topped with sausage, roasted red peppers, creamy mozzarella cheese, and fresh basil" (*The Riddle of the Ruby Gazelle* 1997, 16); bagels and cream cheese (25) as well as Nathan's hot dogs (72) are also a requirement of the ambience. As with the technical and geographical information that Harriet Adams insisted must be accurate, the references to food would seem to be part of the educational mission of the books, insuring that American girls would be aware of the range of "authentic" dining possibilities around the world. There is, however, very little attention paid to those who produce the dishes and no real discussion of how they taste, with the texts relying on adjectives like "delectable" and "creamy" to summarize the experience.

Even with the increasing sophistication, "comfort" foods do not disappear: hot cocoa dominates and continues to solidify new bonds of friendship or to mark a late-night discussion of developments in the mystery, and Hannah's famous bouillon serves to restore circulation after exposure to the elements and console Nancy after she has been conked on the head or tied, gagged, and locked in a closet or rat-infested cellar (as happens at least once per book). Cocoa is closely followed by chocolate layer cake and chocolate sundaes as a staple in the diet (at least until recently, when designer muffins and "energy bars" appear to have taken over).[9] These luxury foods certainly differentiate the sleuths from the large numbers of working-class (and even some middle-class) persons who could not afford such fare during the Depression nor ever imagine frequenting tearooms or having a maid.

As in most middle-class households before the 1990s, the Drew family and its intimate associates do eat three meals a day (two of them customarily as a family unit), come hell or high water (and there is plenty of both in Nancy's adventurous life). If we were to calculate the caloric intake, given the descriptions, we would have to conclude that the girls take in between 4,000 and 6,000 calories a day, enough to sustain a professional athlete. Pancakes and sandwiches are always consumed in multiples, and until the 1980s, nearly every lunch and dinner is accompanied by a rich homemade dessert. As with Nancy's designer clothes (particularly as illustrated by Russell Tandy in the 1930s), the conspicuous consumption of expensive and abundant food contributes to the wish-fulfillment fantasy of the series and demonstrates the class politics of the Stratemeyer Syndicate's ideology. From the meat-and-potatoes-centered menus that represent prosperity in the Depression 1930s, to the solid postwar "American" feasts that signal patriotism and complacency in the 1940s and 1950s, to the ethnic variety of the 1960s to 1980s, and finally, to the split between youth food (especially pizza) and the gourmet cuisine of the "cooking-school" texts (see my discussion below), the books' menus illustrate unselfconscious entitlement.

Food as Discursive Structure

In *The Secret of Shadow Ranch* (1931), the fifth of the series and the first book in which George and Bess appear, the setting is a ranch, and food figures prominently for the first time. All three girls are equally enthusiastic about the "hot biscuits, chicken sizzling in butter, and fragrant coffee" (31), suggesting healthy appetites on all of their parts, but by the 1965 revision Bess is described as "slightly plump" (1), and George condescendingly tells her, "'Eating is really a very fattening hobby, dear cousin'" (138). Once Bess and George enter the picture as Nancy's stalwart "chums," pursuing the culprit is almost always accompanied by appropriate breaks for "luncheon," snacks, and dinner—no matter how urgent the chase; very few of the books seem to forget this orderly normative routine. Menus change but continue to occupy an important place in the structure of the mystery's solution. Even the books that do not describe menus are sprinkled with such phrases as "Nancy finished her breakfast" (*The Secret of the Old Clock*, 1959 rev., 20), "after luncheon," and "when they had finished their dinner," as if to reassure the reader that the routine of life continues in the midst of the mystery. Nancy may forget to call home, but she almost never refuses a request by George or usually Bess to stop for a bite. Sometimes these breaks in the action serve only to release tension, but often the stops for food enable Nancy to eavesdrop on a crucial conversation or to observe an action that furthers the mystery or helps to solve it—so that they become part of the structural web of the novel. At times she even volunteers to work as a waitress in order to facilitate her sleuthing, such as in *The Sign of the Twisted Candles* (1932).

The texts that actually plot food as setting for the mystery clearly confirm the privileged attitudes that dominate the books, but they also solidify the girls' relationship and involve them in a common pursuit beyond detecting (as do their athletic activities, particularly in the early books). The three books in this category begin in 1988 with #21 in The Nancy Drew Files subseries, *Recipe for Murder* (1988) and continue with #117 and #174 in the main series, *Mystery on the Menu* (1993) and *A Taste of Danger* (2003). In all three, the trio of sleuths attends a culinary workshop away from home and discovers that danger, like food, follows Nancy wherever she goes. The food jokes center on Bess, but the activities of learning to prepare and cook food involve all of them and are clearly meant to draw in the reader as well. Thus, in *Recipe for Murder*, Bess declares that "All I want to do is eat" (2) and demands to know if the cooking school has a pastry class, and George retorts, "Pastry class. Didn't you just start a new diet?" (4). The text even includes instructions on how to make a white sauce (32) and is laced with references to éclairs and cordon bleu, and the solution to the mystery hinges on Bess's discovery that the proportions for certain recipes are all wrong (113). In *Mystery on the Menu* (1993), Bess once again signs up for the pastry class, this time at the Wolfe Culinary Institute in Putney Grove, New York, and the mystery hinges on the stealing of recipes from competitors, but the text also includes references to petit fours, orange and arugula salad, "pizzas topped with goat cheese, ham, and pineapple" (131), Triple-Chocolate Mousse Torte (150), and a Mississippi Mud Pie contest (146). Finally, in *A Taste of Danger* (2003), set in Gourmet Getaway, the Berkshires, Hannah actually goes with the girls, and Bess is distracted by a "five-foot-ten hunk, with blond hair and lashes to die for" (20), overtly conflating her desires for food and flirtation. But the plot also includes learning about truffles (as Bess puts it, "mushrooms dug up by pigs in France" [50]), as well as how to dress pheasants, and what to do with "cabbage, figs, and apricots" (94). These texts all make explicit what the remainder of the series (over 200 books at this point) implies repeatedly: that food is at the heart of the comradeship, structure of desire, and construction of American girlhood reinforced throughout the Nancy Drew books. The great writer about food M. F. K. Fisher has summarized the case for this conjunction in her 1976 classic, *The Art of Eating*:

> It seems to me that our three basic needs, for food and security and love, are so mixed and mingled and entwined that we cannot straightly think of one without the others. So it happens that when I write of hunger, I am really writing about love and hunger for it, and warmth and the love of it and the hunger for it . . . and then the warmth and richness and fine reality of hunger satisfied . . . and it is all one. (Fisher 353 qtd. in Chernin 97)

If we add to this desire for warmth and love the desire for a privileged life that exceeds our own realistic expectations, then the series bountifully rewards its "romantic" readers.

Food as Signifier of Character

All three girls are partially revealed by their relationships to food, but Bess, as the "plump" member of the trio who is always "starved" or "famished," comes to represent a particularly relevant piece of twentieth-century "girl history" and sociology: a search for power and selfhood that is intimately related to food. Using Judith Rodin's famous term, Bess's relation to women's "normative obsession" (Rodin qtd. in Brumberg 122) with food and eating positions her as the defining member of the trio with regard to body image, self-definition, consumerism, and, ultimately, sexuality and feminism. It is clear to many critics that "female authority and female appetite emerge as related issues" and that there is "the dual association of the mouth with both eating and speaking" (Heller and Moran 3, 2). Finally, cooking itself can be seen as both an oppressive activity for women and a source of power and pleasure (Heller and Moran 8).[10] Given the complexity of this imbricated set of considerations and contradictions, it is possible to conclude that Bess is more complex and significant than she has seemed to be throughout the decades of her presence in the series.

As feminist critics have demonstrated, it is likely that an excessive focus on food will manifest itself in a concern for display or appearance—even to the point of an eating disorder (as is hinted about Bess, with her fondness for near-binges). Bess is almost as addicted to shopping as to food, sometimes even describing her purchases in terms of implicit culinary metaphors. For instance, as early as *The Clue of the Leaning Chimney* (1949), she gushes to Nancy: "I bought two dresses. . . . They're positively *yummy*" (40; emphasis added); a later description implicitly conflates the language of fashion with that of food when the narrator describes Bess as "looking very cute in a pale-pink taffeta" and whispering excitedly to Nancy, "Did you see the *luscious* layer cake on the dining-room table?" (57; emphasis added). On a single page in *The Triple Hoax* (1979) Bess first states, "Now that we've averted a disaster, I'd like to look at dresses," then declares "that she could not go much longer without food" (107). If we remember that from the beginning of her appearances in the books she has been known for her "taste" and that in 1946 she had been unable to resist buying fake French perfume from a "gypsy" woman who turned out to be a fraud (*The Mystery of the Tolling Bell* 9), then it should be clear that Bess's appetites and her desires for beauty and love are deeply entwined. *The Case of the Vanishing Veil* (1988), set in Boston, makes explicit the differences among the girls' priorities, as George makes a list of "places she wanted to see in Boston. Bess makes a shopping list . . . [and] Nancy . . . a list of suspects and clues" (29–30). Bess also predictably catches the bouquet at the wedding they are attending.

To complicate the discussion, her representation affirms and reaffirms Bess's constantly failed effort at control, often associated with eating disorders, as well as her unrealistic view of her weight (since five extra pounds hardly constitute being overweight or even "plump," except in a thin-obsessed culture)—and Bess does participate fully in the trio's adventures despite her "feminine" personality and persistent squeamishness (two other traits that the texts associate with her dimpled "plumpness").[11] Although Joan Jacobs Brumberg in *The Body Project* labels her (and a similar character in the Grace Harlow series) as the archetypal "fat character who served as a humorous foil to the well-liked, smart protagonist, who was always slim" (99), Bess's fans will not recognize her in this description: she may be humorous at times, but she is not ridiculous, nor is she "fat" by any definition—medical or aesthetic. In fact, her earliest appearance, in *The Secret of Shadow Ranch* (1931), stresses that she is "romantic" (15) and "noted for always doing the correct thing at the correct time. Though she lacked the dash and vivacity of her cousin [George], she was better looking and dressed with more care and taste" (4). Although she is the first to announce "I'm about starved" (38) when they go horseback riding, and later, "I'm hungry enough to eat a fried rock" (146), the text does not describe her as "plump" or overweight. She also exhibits the first signs of contradictory impulses towards her own eating, verified only by her gratuitously harsh cousin:

> "I'm getting fatter every day of my life," Bess complained as she munched a sandwich. "This is my third."
> "Fifth you mean," George corrected her brutally. (78)

The Secret of Red Gate Farm (1931) also does not initially describe her as overweight, although Bess herself once again complains, "'I'm too plump to rush along like this,'" and George "muttered brutally," "'It's good for you'" (3). Developing this theme, the author later has George use the second sense of my titular F word for the second time in the series, "You're fat enough as it is," and the narrator repeats the adverb "brutally" (43). This is also the text that describes Bess as consuming seven pancakes (75), and by 1932 she is called "Plump Bess" by the narrator as she once again eats five sandwiches while declaring defensively, "I don't claim to be on a diet" (*The Clue in the Diary* 2). Yet the narrator still describes Bess as "pretty and lady-like and sedate" (2), in contrast to George's rambunctious athleticism, whereas the 1962 revision tones down and condenses both aspects of Bess's body and character with "The slightly plump, pretty girl reached for a third sandwich" (1), omitting Bess's reference to a diet. The early series was obviously still struggling with how to differentiate the three girls and had not yet settled on Bess's (or George's) characterization.

In the next book, *Nancy's Mysterious Letter* (1932), however, Bess is already "dieting" and breaking her diet, so that "'Cocoa and sweet cakes are off my list, but only after this afternoon. Then I'll start all over again'" (5)—defining her as vacillating in her will power. She now has developed "plump curves" (29), though these are omitted from the 1968 revision, which calls her simply "blond and slightly overweight," with newly acquired "deep dimples" (2). In the 1934 *The Clue of the Broken Locket*, Bess's characterization has settled in: she is "a very pretty blonde, inclined to be overweight" and "very feminine" (5), even though there are few references to food. In the 1965 revision's completely changed plot, there are constant references to food, and Bess becomes "the culinary expert" (110), as the girls interrupt their sleuthing to devour meal after meal. By *The Message in the Hollow Oak* (1935), Bess has acquired "luxurious locks" (6), but there are no references to her weight, and it is Nancy who claims that she must "hurry home, . . . I promised Hannah I'd bake a chocolate cake for luncheon" (24); in the 1972 revision, Bess is once again "slightly plump" with "delightful dimples" (3) as she "moaned": "'Oh, my diet!'" (96). Later when the girls discover that their food is gone, Bess explicitly articulates her persistent dilemma with appetite as beyond her control:

> Bess sat down on the ground, disconsolate.
> "Oh, don't be silly!" George chided her cousin. "It wouldn't hurt you to go without a meal."

"You're a good one to talk," Bess replied. "You eat all you want and stay slim. I can't help it if I get hungry." (129)

Several of the late 1930s books do not mention food, and the 1940 *The Mystery of the Brass Bound Trunk*, set on board ship and in Argentina, has only a brief mention of seasickness that turns out to be poisoning and Bess's later comment: "'Oh, dear' . . . 'I've eaten too much again. I'll never get thin in this country with its rich foods'" (156). The postwar books reintroduce a focus on food, dieting, and Bess's plumpness. In *The Mystery of the Tolling Bell* (1946), for example, there are whole pages devoted to descriptions of food, as well as references to Bess's figure and George's teasing (softened to "blunt"); George even includes her own envy of Nancy's metabolism in the following exchange:

> "Maybe I ought to diet!" [said Bess]
> "You certainly should," said George bluntly, glancing at her cousin's plump figure. "But I guess I shouldn't say anything. I wish I were slim like you, Nancy." (2)

The late 1940s and the 1950s further stressed Bess's femininity and self-indulgence—even her implicit construction as a sex object within the rules of normative heterosexuality. Thus the 1953 *The Clue of the Velvet Mask* calls Bess "a plump, jolly girl" who enjoys dressing as a "southern belle" and George disguises herself as a "boy" for a masquerade (6); the 1969 revision calls her only "slightly plump" and softens George's cross-dressing to a "pageboy" (6).[12] All of these feminizing touches stand in stark contrast to Nancy Drew author Mildred Wirt Benson's strong descriptions of all three girls in the novels of the 1930s. For example, *The Clue in the Diary* (1932) even has Nancy make reference to George's "brawn" as the result of time "spent in the gym" and "the amount of food you eat" (173); she also states unequivocally, "Three capable, muscular, brainy girls such as we are shouldn't need any help" (174).

But the 1950s were the era of the "feminine mystique" (Friedan) and of what Jungian critic Betsy Caprio has termed "Two-Dimensional Nancy" (174–175), noting that "1959, the year of the first Nancy Drew revisions, was also the year the Barbie Doll was born" (22).[13] In 1956, *The Hidden Window Mystery* states that Bess "was very feminine and wore frilly dresses. She was blond and slightly overweight because of her fondness for rich food" (9); there are no changes in this description in the 1975 revision.[14] Similarly, the 1966 revision of *The Password to Larkspur Lane* describes Bess as "blond, pretty, and somewhat plump" (74) as she declares, "'I don't know which is harder: to keep *on* a diet or keep *in* a secret'" (75). Along with the increased references to her plumpness this new focus on Bess's "giggle" continues somewhat inexplicably into the more progressive 1960s and even the feminist 1970s and beyond, establishing Bess's superficiality and "girliness" in contrast to her two friends. In fact, the ghostwriters' standard presentation of Bess starts to conflate her two insatiable desires more overtly in the 1970s and 1980s: "Blond-haired Bess was bubbly and easygoing, and always on the look-out for two things: a good diet and a great date. So far she hadn't found either. She was constantly trying to lose five pounds, and she fell in and out of love every other month" (*Secrets Can Kill* 3).[15] This more explicit boy-craziness, particularly in the Nancy Drew Files, brings together Bess's hunger for food, interest in fashion, and focus on romance in a way that had been foreshadowed throughout the series, with hints about Bess's sexualized characterization as early as her first appearance:

> "I hope we meet some nice men," Bess put in.
> "So do I, for your sake," George teased. "Your trip will be a failure if you don't capture the heart of at least one handsome cowbay [sic]." (*The Secret of Shadow Ranch* 1931, 108).

At this point in our discussion we are therefore compelled to consider yet another "F" word, at least in its sublimated child-version, in the suggestion of Bess's sexual "hunger."

Whichever representation dominates in a given decade, Bess persistently occupies a vexed position in relation to eating (as well as cooking, shopping, gender, and sexuality), and it is never entirely clear whether the Syndicate intended her to be a negative or positive role model for the prepubescent girls who read the books. Certainly the ambiguous definitions of words and concepts like "taste" and "appetite" would suggest a metonymic relationship between food and a character who exhibits extravagant desires. Were readers to take seriously Bess's obsessions with going on a diet and losing five pounds or were they to desire her voluptuous body? Were they to identify with her timidity or to focus on her participation in the adventures and her willingness to relinquish her plans for slimming whenever a chocolate layer cake popped into view? Was she to provide a subject position for the readers who could not match Nancy in brains or George in brawn but who nonetheless wanted to identify with the adventure? Did she provide a complement to George's neat style of dress and tomboyish athleticism so that the two of them together could begin to approximate Nancy's multifaceted personality or was she meant to be a strong alternative personality in her own right? Because it is clear in the literature of the twentieth century that eating disorders and relationships to food have to do with gender, choice, and self-empowerment, at the very least it is arguable that Bess's continual assertions of her position constitute a form of self-definition and control over her environment (which, given her friendship with Nancy, is arguably a terrifying one). As Lilian Furst writes in the introduction to *Disorderly Eaters: Texts in Self-Empowerment*, "eating, like noneating, is a tool for power both over oneself and over one's surroundings" (Furst and Graham 4).

In confirmation of this mixed message and conflicted ideology, when a new illustrator for the Syndicate in the 1950s inadvertently drew Nancy's hair as reddish or "titian," Harriet Adams decided to let the mistake stand because the hair color differentiation made it possible to distinguish her from Bess. Whereas Russell Tandy's 1930s Carole Lombard-like Nancy was superbly svelte, by the 1950s there was a general understanding that Nancy should become a bit younger and less sophisticated—more like the bobby-soxer to whom she was supposed to appeal—hence very much the same size as Bess. Yet Adams also advised the Art Department to "Have Nancy's hair cover a little more of her cheek to make her face slimmer" (Letter from Harriet Adams to Jane Ayers, Grosset and Dunlap Art Department, 5 September 1973, Box 41, SSR-NYPL), obviously concerned that her heroine represent the American post-Twiggy ideal of the early 1970s (or the earlier one of the girl who could never be "too thin or too rich"). Of all the illustrations (both cover and internal) I have examined, only one, for the revised version of *The Scarlet Slipper Mystery* (1974: 43) presents Bess as even slightly different in size from her two friends; in this black-and-white drawing she is dressed in a dark leotard in order to teach a ballet class, and she may actually be a size eight rather than a four or six like Nancy and George. Yet thirty-six pages later she is described, perhaps for the hundredth time, as "the plump girl" (79). She certainly could not offer a convincing subject position for a young reader struggling with obesity.

*   *   *

Though food and eating may not represent a conscious ideology in the books, I do believe that the complex working out of this trope in relation to weight, class, domesticity, desire, sexuality, and power illustrates both the books' inherent and enduring classism and gender conservatism and, in the case of Bess at least, a reassurance to readers of all eras that, in Susie Orbach's famous phrase, "fat is a feminist issue" (1978). Following Orbach's advice to her clients and readers, Bess does assert her desires and take her pleasures seriously; she may be preoccupied with her weight but she is not rendered helpless by it.[16]

As to the various F words implied by my title: F is for *food*, of course; it is also, therefore, for *fat* (or, in this case, plump), with its connotations of plenitude and class privilege—and of potential eating disorders. But, as we have seen, with their submerged but reappearing sense of agency and subjectivity, the Nancy Drew books also imply that F is for *feminism* (as well as, perhaps paradoxically, *femininity*, although Third Wave feminists would perhaps not see the contradiction). The only F word not literally signified within the terms of my argument, therefore, is the expected vulgar one, although it is also clear that Bess functions as the primary sexual signifier from the beginning. But after all, it is George, the slim and athletic chum, not Bess, who lays all rumors to rest about her potential lesbianism by apparently being the first of the trio to lose her virginity to a boyfriend—in the fifth Nancy Drew on Campus, for older readers: *Secret Rules* (1996, 7).

The new Nancy Drew: Girl Detective series (narrated in the first person by Nancy), which began in March 2004, erases all references to diets, overweight, and overeating in reference to Bess, although she is described in *False Notes* (2004) as "pleasantly plump" (23). Nancy as narrator simply tells us: "If you looked up the word girl in the dictionary, you'd find Bess's picture there to illustrate it. She's pretty, blond, and curvy in all the right places, with dimples in both cheeks and a wardrobe full of flowery dresses" (7). Bess has also (implausibly) become a mechanical wizard who can repair any broken apparatus that crosses her path, although she has not given up her love for shopping, further complicating the subject position that she offers readers. As Nancy puts it, "Bess lives for fashion and boys. Or at least that's what you would think if you didn't bother to get to know Bess well. Underneath her girly exterior beats the heart of a die-hard mechanic. She's never met an engine she didn't like" (*Action!* 22). As we see in this passage, interpretation is no longer being left to the reader as Bess's contradictions are embraced and her character explained by the book's point-of-view.

And food? It persists, if in different cultural manifestations befitting the new times. George's stay-at-home mother has become a caterer, the girls eat power bars and "protein smoothies" to keep them going, and the vandalizing of a neighbor's zucchini patch provides the subplot for the first book (*Without a Trace* 2004). The girls have, of course, retained (or regained) their virginity, and the F word has lost both its ambiguity and its richness.

Notes

1 A shorter version of this chapter was read at the 2004 MLA Conference in Philadelphia on the panel on "Food in Children's Literature," organized by Kara Keeling and Scott Pollard, 28 December 2004. It is also important to note, for those not familiar with the Nancy Drew books, that all books attributed to "Carolyn Keene" have been ghostwritten and that the first fifty-six books, published by Grosset and Dunlap, were the productions of the Stratemeyer Syndicate, whose founder, Edward Stratemeyer, conceived of the series and outlined the first three novels published in 1930. Subsequent books in the main series and its spin-offs, from 1979 onward, are published by Simon and Schuster.

2 The Stratemeyer Syndicate Records, New York Public Library, will subsequently be identified in the text as SSR-NYPL and by box number.

3 See "Comfort Food: The Nancy Drew Cookbook" Web site.

4 It is interesting that recent books on Nancy Drew, such as those by Melanie Rehak and Ilana Nash, do not address the topic of food beyond a casual mention, although Rehak points out Bess's "boy-crazy qualities" as early

as *The Secret of Shadow Ranch* (143) and quotes the same passage I do from *Secrets Can Kill* about "a good diet and a great date" (301); she also notes that in the later books marketed for older readers, boyfriends take precedence over food: "Gone were the chaste picnics" (302). Nash calls Bess "an overweight sensualist" who "loves the pleasures offered by food, physical comfort, and (chaste) flirtations with handsome boys. These proclivities limit her physical endurance and her willingness to take risks" (39).

5 As Rehak states it, echoing many earlier critics, "if you were not as perfect as Nancy, surely you were at least interesting enough to be like—and thus to be—one of the closest chums of the queen bee" (142).

6 McGee quotes from Roland Barthes's "Toward a Psychosociology of Contemporary Food Consumption" and grounds much of her analysis on Barthes's semiotic reading of the meal as a text: "One could say that an entire 'world' (social environment) is present in and signified by food" (Barthes 170 qtd. in McGee 2001: 10).

7 All Nancy Drew books will hereafter be cited followed by dates if not included in the text; revisions of the original fifty-six books will be cited by dates followed by "rev."

8 It is also worth noting that although Nancy is clearly upper-middle-class, Bess and George do not have famous lawyer-fathers or blue roadsters or Hannah Gruens. They are partaking in Nancy's patrician lifestyle (and freedom) because of their friendship.

9 See the new Nancy Drew: Girl Detective series that began with three "breeders" (a publisher's term for the initial trial books of a series) in 2004.

10 Heller and Moran cite several other critics but paraphrase them and fold their ideas into their synthetic introduction.

11 As Nancy says in Bess's defense in the 1965 version of *The Clue of the Broken Locket* (and elsewhere), "Bess always worries about the possibility of running into danger, but she's one of the world's best sports when the necessity arises" (4). Even the early text *The Secret of Shadow Ranch* states authoritatively, "Yet, for all her good-natured complaining, Bess Marvin had stood the ordeal better than either Alice or George" (93).

12 This is presumably a response to increasing homophobia, manifested also in the softening of George's "boyish" tendencies throughout that decade and beyond.

13 Caprio continues: "The Nancy of this time is not unlike Barbie and, also, she is akin to the vapid, baby-doll movie heroines of the 1950s and early 1960s (Tammy, Gidget, et al.) [.] All reflect the regression in the status of women during the decades after World War II" (22).

14 Implicitly extending the Barbie era, Caprio concludes her Era Three: Two Dimensional Nancy with #56, *The Thirteenth Pearl*, the last book published by Grosset and Dunlap in 1979; the continuing depictions of Bess as frivolous and feminine would therefore support her description of the Syndicate's ideology during these years.

15 Plunkett-Powell detects a "new personality" in a 1989 book in a spin-off series: "In Nancy Drew Files Case #36, *Over the Edge* (1989), Bess's new personality is summarized well: 'Bess could be in an arctic iceberg and still manage to find a cute guy. She has a two-track mind—boys and food'" (94). She also claims, however, that "This transition started as early as 1946, when Bess is described as a 'plump, jolly girl' absolutely obsessed with her looks" (93). It should be clear that I do not share this view of Bess: she delights in food, boys, and shopping, and she refers constantly to those "five pounds" and her diets, but she is far from "obsessed with her looks. "Nor is this personality "new," as we have seen. There is more of what M. F. K. Fisher would call "pleasure" than neurosis in Bess's attitudes.

16 Given Bess's periodic, but by no means constant, claims that she is "famished" or "starved," as well as her communal rather than secretive approach to eating, there is evidence that she does in fact follow the distinction that Orbach makes between "mouth hunger," related to obsession, and "stomach hunger," which signals a healthy attitude towards food (118).

Works Cited

Barthes, Roland. "Toward a Psychosociology of Contemporary Food Consumption." Trans. Elborg Forster. *Annales. E.S.C.* 16 (Sept-Oct 1961): 977–986. Rpt. in *Food and Drink in History*. Eds. Robert Forster Forster and Orest Ranum. Baltimore: Johns Hopkins UP, 1979. 166–174.

Brumberg, Joan Jacobs. *The Body Project: An Intimate History of American Girls*. New York: Vintage, 1997.

Caprio, Betsy. *The Mystery of Nancy Drew: Girl Sleuth on the Couch*. Trabuco Canyon: Source, 1992.

Chernin, Kim. *The Hungry Self*. New York: Harper, 1986.

"Comfort Food: The Nancy Drew Cookbook." *NancyDrewSleuth*. 25 Feb. 2001. <http://www.nancydrewsleuth.com/cbfood.html>.

Fisher, M. F. K. *The Art of Eating*. New York: Vintage, 1976.

Friedan, Betty. *The Feminine Mystique*. 1963. Intro. Anna Quindlen. New York: Norton, 2001.

Furst, Lilian R., and Peter W. Graham, eds. *Disorderly Eaters: Texts in Self-Empowerment*. University Park: Pennsylvania State UP, 1992.

Heller, Tamar, and Patricia Moran, eds. *Scenes of the Apple: Food and the Female Body in Nineteenth- and Twentieth-Century Women's Writing*. Albany, NY: SUNY UP, 2003.

Keene, Carolyn. *Action!* Nancy Drew: Girl Detective. New York: Simon, 2004.

———. *The Case of the Vanishing Veil*. New York: Simon, 1988.

———. *The Clue in the Diary*. New York: Grosset, 1932, rev. 1962.

———. *The Clue of the Broken Locket*. New York: Grosset, 1934, rev.1965.

———. *The Clue of the Leaning Chimney*. New York: Grosset, 1949.

———. *The Clue of the Velvet Mask*. New York: Grosset, 1953, rev.1969.

———. *The Emerald-Eyed Cat Mystery*. New York: Simon, 1984.

———. *False Notes*. Nancy Drew: Girl Detective. New York: Simon, 2004.

———. *The Hidden Staircase*. New York: Grosset, 1930.

———. *The Hidden Window Mystery*. New York: Grosset, 1956, rev. 1975.

———. *The Message in the Hollow Oak*. New York: Grosset, 1935, rev. 1972.

———. *The Mystery at Lilac Inn*. New York: Grosset, 1930, rev. 1961.

———. *The Mystery of the Brass Bound Trunk*. New York: Grosset, 1940.

———. *The Mystery of the Fire Dragon*. New York: Grosset, 1961.

———. *The Mystery of the Ivory Charm*. New York: Grosset, 1936, rev. 1974.

———. *The Mystery of the Tolling Bell*. New York: Grosset, 1946.

———. *Mystery on the Menu*. New York: Simon, 1993.

———. *The Nancy Drew Cookbook: Clues to Good Cooking*. New York: Grosset, 1973.

———. *Nancy's Mysterious Letter*. New York: Grosset, 1932, rev. 1968.

———. *Over the Edge*. Nancy Drew Files. New York: Simon, 1989.

———. *The Password to Larkspur Lane*. New York: Grosset, 1932, rev. 1966.

———. *Recipe for Murder*. Nancy Drew Files. New York: Simon, 1988.

———. *The Riddle of the Ruby Gazelle*. New York: Simon, 1997.

———. *The Scarlet Slipper Mystery*. New York: Grosset, 1954, rev. 1974.

———. *The Secret at Shadow Ranch*. New York: Grosset, 1931.

———. *The Secret of Red Gate Farm*. New York: Grosset, 1931, rev. 1961.

———. *The Secret of Shadow Ranch*. New York: Grosset, 1931, rev. 1965.

———. *The Secret of the Old Clock*. New York: Grosset, 1930, rev. 1959.

———. *Secret Rules*. Nancy Drew on Campus. New York: Simon, 1996.

———. *Secrets Can Kill*. Nancy Drew Files. New York: Simon, 1986.

———. *The Sign of the Twisted Candles*. New York: Grosset, 1932.

———. *A Taste of Danger*. New York: Simon, 2003.

———. *The Thirteenth Pearl*. New York: Grosset, 1979.

———. *The Triple Hoax*. New York: Simon, 1979.

———. *Without a Trace*. Nancy Drew: Girl Detective. New York: Simon, 2004.

Mason, Bobbie Ann. *The Girl Sleuth*. 1975. Athens: U of Georgia P, 1995.

McGee, Diane. *Writing the Meal: Dinner in the Fiction of Early Twentieth-Century Women Writers*. Toronto: U of Toronto P, 2001.

Nash, Ilana. *American Sweethearts: Teenage Girls in Twentieth-Century Popular Culture*. Bloomington: Indiana UP, 2006.

Ohmann, Richard. *Selling Culture: Magazines, Markets, and Class at the Turn of the Century*. London: Verso, 1996.

Orbach, Susie. *Fat is a Feminist Issue: A Self-Help Guide for Compulsive Eaters*. 1978. New York: Berkley, 1979.

Plunkett-Powell, Karen. *The Nancy Drew Scrapbook*. New York: St. Martin's, 1993.

Rehak, Melanie. *Girl Sleuth: Nancy Drew and the Women Who Created Her*. Orlando: Harcourt, 2005.

Stoneley, Peter. *Consumerism and American Girls' Literature, 1860–1940*. Cambridge, UK: Cambridge UP, 2003.

Stratemeyer Syndicate Records, 1832–1984. Manuscripts and Archives Division, New York Public Library.

Zacharias, Lee. "Nancy Drew, Ballbuster." *Journal of Popular Culture* 9.4 (1976): 1027–1038.

Chapter Six
To Eat and Be Eaten in Nineteenth-Century Children's Literature

Jacqueline M. Labbe

For my soul's and body's food,
I will take what does me good.
Spite of folk's or sages' cry,
Take what does me good will I.

(**William Allingham, "[For My Soul's and Body's Good]"**)

Throughout the nineteenth century, food was a contentious issue. Whether it was the dining etiquette newly demanded by an increasingly prosperous middle class, or the outrage occasioned by the scandal of food adulteration, or the moralities attached to eating too much or too little or the right stuff or the wrong stuff, eating, appetite, and digestion occupied many minds.[1] The children's literature of the period uses the motif frequently: children eat, often sweet things, and often against the wishes of those who bring them up. For the middle and upper classes, for whom the next meal was a certainty and the question was, rather, how many courses it might consist of, children's appetites received regulation that those of adults often did not; as Carolyn Daniel describes it, "the austerity of the traditional nursery upbringing, a child-rearing regime much influenced by Puritan discourses ... recommended an extremely bland and restricted diet for children," a reality that is complemented, in children's literature, by "fictional feasting: copious quantities of rich, sweet, and ... fat-laden foods ... served to children who seem to have huge appetites" (11, 2). Children thus read or were read texts wherein their own privations were overturned. And yet, as Daniel points out, although appetites may have been satiated in literature, moral codes nonetheless mandated punishment: hence Carroll's Alice and her misadventures with food and drink, Rossetti's trio of girls for whom eating is rendered impossible, Kingsley's water-baby Tom whose greed physically deforms him, and Ewing's little "MacGreedy" whose attempts to eat the "delicious" almond at the core of a Christmas cracker comfit require him to "suck his way" through "a large amount of white lead . . . white paint and chalk."[2] Allingham's motto, above, is perhaps necessarily vague on "what does me good."

But Allingham is also clear that "what does me good" might not match the lore offered by "folk" and "sages," the authorities, both domestic and worldly, who regulate the eating habits of dependents. The Puritan discourses mentioned by Daniel, possibly more accurately described as Evangelical, regarded venial sins such as gluttony, sloth and greed as the precursors to mortal sins, a direct route made plain in a text like Mary Martha Sherwood's *The Fairchild Family*, where childish squabbling, for instance, prompts the notorious gibbet scene.[3] Under this rubric, eating too much—or sometimes wanting to eat at all—stands as a marker of the child's inherent viciousness, the residue of Original Sin that only the most loving and attentive of parents could purge their children of through, as Daniel phrases it, austerity. And so, children's stories feature children who eat, rightly and wrongly: whether in the didactic tales popular in the early nineteenth century, or in the fantasies that developed in reaction to the perceived restrictions of didacticism. Shadowing the paradigm of the "voracious," sinful child, however, is the Romantic ideal of the innocent, natural, pure and uncorrupted representative of one's happier and uncomplicated past.[4] This model child teaches rather than being taught; his or her purity is put to the service of those degraded by life, cleansing and rehabilitating them. In the world of the Victorian novel, this is Dickens's Little Nell or MacDonald's Diamond, adaptations of Sherwood's Charles Trueman whose "happy death" inspires those around him to live more godly lives (219 *passim*). But this child serves another function as well. If the vicious, greedy child is partly defined as one who eats, then the pure, uncorrupted child is not the noneater but rather the eaten. The good child is, in Allingham's phrase, "what does me good."

In this essay I will explore several children's texts wherein children are eaten. In a culture where food is regularly adulterated, what could be more pure for the system than a child? The Eucharistic climax of Rossetti's "Goblin Market" allows the pure sister Lizzie to heal the fallen sister Laura's moral wounds when she exclaims

"Come and kiss me.
Never mind my bruises,
Hug me, kiss me, suck my juices
Squeezed from goblin fruits for you,

Goblin pulp and goblin dew.
Eat me, drink me, love me;
Laura, make much of me;
For your sake I have braved the glen
And had to do with goblin merchant men." (ll. 465–474)

Rossetti's poem conflates Lizzie's body with what has been slathered on it: goblin pulp and goblin dew merge with Lizzie herself even as the invitations to eat and drink are themselves predicated on the separation of pulp, dew, and body. Nonetheless, Rossetti's language insists on the physical consuming of Lizzie for the decontamination of Laura. Likewise, in Catherine Sinclair's *Holiday House* (1839), Harry and his sister Laura invite their friends for tea only to find that they have forgotten the small detail of supplying food. To right this wrong, Harry imagines a drastic solution: "Harry felt so unspeakably wretched, that, if some kind fairy could only have turned him into a Norwich bun at the moment, he would gladly have consented to be cut in pieces, that his ravenous guests might be satisfied" (19). Harry's lament shows his conviction that "duty" and "politeness" are paramount; unlike the plum pudding in *Through the Looking-Glass*, he willingly would offer himself to the knife in order to "satisfy" his guests. Although lacking the religious overtones of Rossetti's text, Harry's imagined self-sacrifice resonates with a goodness that places the satisfaction of others above the preservation of the self. At the same time, Harry offers himself figuratively in atonement for his lack of hospitality, a kind of self-inflicted punishment that, he anticipates, would satisfy his guests both corporeally and morally. Eating the good child, then, is "good for me" and good for (in this case) him: moral imperatives are placated and the ingestion of purity benefits eater and eaten.

But Harry's desire to be eaten also suggests a complication in the eater/eaten, bad/good paradigm, because it occurs in a text wherein punishment is a running theme. It is one thing for the pure child to offer itself as food for others; it is another when the child is coerced into doing so. Harry and his sister Laura spend most of the first half of *Holiday House* on the receiving end of an enthusiastic regime of corporal punishment by the aptly named Mrs. Crabtree, who operates within the system of "spare the rod, spoil the child." For Mrs. Crabtree, her charges bear the Evangelically derived taint of sin and require her vigilance and her cat-o-nine-tails. If the good child can be persuaded that to be eaten is its best fate, can the same be said of the bad child? In other words, if the Romantic ideal of the pure child offers unadulterated food for the soul, does the Evangelical anti-ideal of the sinful child open the possibility that the best punishment for sin is also to be eaten? The greedy, slothful, gluttonous child functions as the adulterated child in a Romantic paradigm; consumed by impure eaters, the sinful child, in an ironic reversal of purification, is incorporated by the embodiment of its own system.

The real-world scandal of food adulteration resonates within these texts. From about the 1830s to the 1880s—a period coinciding with the so-called "golden age of children's literature" during which the texts under discussion were published—all manner of food was regularly contaminated by producers eager to increase their profits and magnify their yields: "most of the commonest foods, drinks and condiments . . . contain[ed] various adulterants for adding weight and bulk, imparting smell and taste and other properties" (Kassim 9).[5] Alum in bread was one of the most widespread additions, and one of the most benign, in that it did not actually poison the consumer; far more threatening was the strychnine in beer, the lead chromate in mustard, the copper carbonate and bisulphate of mercury in confectionery. Although in 1860 an Act for Preventing the Adulteration of Articles of Food and Drink was passed, it had little effect, relying as it did mainly on voluntary efforts to reduce unhealthy additives. MacGreedy's experience with the Christmas cracker comfit, all white lead and paint, reflects a reality not substantially changed by 1870, when Ewing published her story. The scandal was, however, a public one, especially as the decades wore on; the question of purity that occupied those concerned with public welfare applied equally well to food, childhood, and morality. The adulterated child, in other words, merely reifies an endemic social contamination, while simultaneously operating as a solution—or at least a scapegoat—for those in need of cleansing.

The pure child of the Romantic tradition, then, who welcomes being eaten as a Christ-like act of mercy, is shadowed by the impure, adulterated child, who needs to be eaten for his (usually) own good. When ingestion and punishment cooperate, what had mitigated impurity now reifies it. Even as the good child purifies or at least rewards its eater, the bad child, in being eaten, consolidates its badness. When their eaters are giants, the enormity of the badness of the sinful child takes on a physical shape. Even though the Evangelical worldview accepted the unavoidability of the sinful child, it also made plain the difficulty of eradicating sin: the reason the Fairchild children are subjected to trips to gibbets and other deathly scenes is exactly to reinforce for them the magnitude of their potential for wickedness and to argue for the need for constant self-surveillance. Mrs. Crabtree's cat-o-nine-tails is another example of this, as is her grumble that she "must do her duty, and make [Harry and Laura] good children, though she were to flay them alive first" (21). Likewise, the Romantic desire for uncorrupted childhood innocence means that the adulterated child is a monstrous one, its defect gigantic. The giant, then, is the only eater capable of ingesting the bad child, the punishment suiting the crime. As Timothy Morton phrases it, "you eat what you are": "food can substantiate empirical reality" (265). When a giant eats a bad child, his corporeal desires and the child's corporeal monstrousness coincide; that the child is represented as a delicacy for the epicurean giant emphasizes the immensity of its sin. The giant treats the bad child as a luxury, a lip-smacking treat; he cultivates the child, encouraging its moral laxity while also taking advantage of it. In this formulation, only the child bad enough to be eaten is good enough to eat.

When thinking about hungry giants, it is important to note that the most familiar, he who lives at the top of the beanstalk, is more interested in Eng-lish*men*: "be he live or be he dead, I'll grind his bones to make my bread." The *frisson* represented by this giant operates at a remove from the child Jack, whose native naiveté or cunning, depending on which version of the story is being read, allows him to best the giant, run off with his treasures, and do the killing, if not the eating. When Harry and Laura's Uncle David, in *Holiday House*, narrates his "Nonsensical Story about Giants and Fairies," he brings his rapt audience right to the threshold of the danger the story outlines. Keeping in mind Harry's earlier desire to serve himself to his ravenous guests, it is telling that immediately preceding Uncle David's story, Harry has found himself hanging out of a top-story window, and calls to his sister, "I have behaved very ill, and deserve the worst that can happen. If I do break my head, it will save Mrs. Crabtree the trouble of breaking it for me, after I come down" (73). In reaction to his adventure, and upon wishing he could do nothing all day like a "grown-up man," Harry, along with Laura, begs Uncle David for a story "about very bad boys, and giants, and fairies" (73, 74). Acquiescing, Uncle David begins a "wonderful story ... about liking to be idle or busy, and [Harry and Laura] must find out the moral for [them]selves" (74). Thus, although the story is "nonsensical," it is simultaneously full of meaning, with an immanent moral the children are challenged to discover.

Ostensibly, the story opposes the attractions of the fairy Do-nothing and the fairy Teach-all. Both invite "a very idle, greedy, naughty boy," Master No-book, to visit, and he chooses Castle Needless, where delicate and luxurious food is in abundance and "we never think of exerting ourselves for anything" (75). The fairy Do-nothing lives next door to the giant Snap-'em-up, whose favorite food is "little boys, as fat as possible, fried in crumbs of bread, with plenty of pepper and salt" (76). Once ensconced at Castle Needless, Master No-book finds his idleness less pleasant than he expected, but having "been fed for a week, and ... as fat already as a prize ox," his tempting appearance ("a large, fat, overgrown boy, as round as a dumpling, lying on a bed of roses") causes the giant to pick him up, take him home, and present him to his cook for preparation.[6]

> On reaching home, the giant immediately hung Master No-book by the hair of his head, on a prodigious hook in the larder, having first taken some large lumps of nasty suet, forcing them down his throat to make him still fatter, and then stirring the fire, that he might be almost melted with heat, to make his liver grow larger. On a shelf quite near, Master No-book perceived the dead bodies of six other boys, whom he remembered to have seen fattening in the fairy Do-nothing's garden, while he recollected how some of them had rejoiced at the thoughts of leading a long, useless, idle life, with no one to please but themselves. (77)

Clearly, these are spoiled, bad children, the perfect fodder for a giant. Uncle David's details, which align Master No-book with a force-fed goose, emphasize the delectable quality of the bad child: his alimentary purity emblematizes his moral adulteration. On the brink of being eaten, the boy "began at last to reflect seriously upon his former ways" (77) and gazes with longing out the window at the fairy Teach-all's industriously happy group. After a battle provoked by the giant's attempt to seize some of these good boys to add to his dish of "scolloped children," he and the fairy Do-nothing are vanquished and killed, Master No-book is rescued and rehabilitated by the fairy Teach-all, and Harry resolves to "take care not to be found hanging any day, on a hook in the larder!" (78, 79).

Uncle David's story is not hard to decipher, but just in case its whimsy has misled some readers, Sinclair allows the children's grandmother, Lady Harriet, to conclude the chapter by describing the "progress of a wise and a foolish man, to see which Harry and [Laura] would prefer copying" (80). With the example, and the threat, of Master No-book before them, their choice is clear. In order to be good Romantic children, pure and choice, they reject the image of the slothful, gluttonous Master No-book. After this chapter, the tone of *Holiday House* darkens precipitously; the "nonsensical story" effectively concludes the first half of the book, which has focused on the children's heedlessness and frolics, as well as their constant punishment at the hands of Mrs. Crabtree. Culminating with the threat, not merely of death, but of being eaten to satisfy the appetite of a giant avatar, their carelessness receives increasingly harsh body blows, until they are subdued entirely by the death of their beloved older brother Frank, a perfect boy both in Romantic and Evangelical terms, whose body is eaten away by illness. Frank, like Rossetti's Lizzie, functions as a sacrifice; "God Himself has laid His hand upon us," and Laura and Harry at last learn to be sober.[7] As Harry observed after Uncle David's story, Frank "must have spent a month with the good fairy" (79), but the immunity this grants him from falling victim to Snap-'em-up simply preserves him as future nourishment for his siblings, even if only figuratively.

Sinclair's text merges the Evangelical preoccupation with the native sinfulness of the child with a Romantic conviction of the natural purity of the child. Harry and Laura are made to associate their behavior with that of Master No-book ("Laura and I still belong to the No-book family" [79]) and to experience, vicariously, the danger this signals, whereas Frank from the first, "by the blessing of God," walks "the narrow path that leadeth to eternal life" (10). By inserting a ravenous giant in her story, Sinclair also anticipates the Victorian preference for fantasy rather than didactic reality in texts for children. "Uncle David's Nonsensical Story" successfully combines fairy-tale and didactic elements, and by turning the bad child into a giant's preferred delicacy Sinclair literalizes the idea that "food [stands] as a metaphor for human behavior" (Daniel 25). When Master No-book *becomes* food, he stands as nothing more than a physical representation of his sinful behavior. In George MacDonald's "The Giant's Heart," the didactic is subsumed within the fantastic; Evangelicalism itself, though still active, has largely given way culturally to a High Church/Low Church Anglican split, and the Romantic ideology of childhood has overtaken the Evangelical fear of childhood sin. The adulterated child, however, suffers from the same unhealthy added ingredients: sloth, gluttony, greed. "The Giant's Heart" first appeared as a chapter in MacDonald's novel for adults, *Adela Cathcart*, where it is narrated to a mixed group of children, some eager, some jaded, by Adela's uncle, who is concerned for her moral development. Before the story begins, the narrating uncle makes plain the link between the bad child and foodstuffs, mentioning a "priggish imp, with a face as round as [a] plum pudding"; only a few sentences later this "fat-faced boy" reacts to the opening description of the

> "wicked giant . . . who used to catch little children and plant them in his garden. . . . He liked greedy boys best that ate plum pudding till they felt as if their belts were too tight."
>
> Here the fat-faced boy stuck both his hands inside his belt. (317)

Defined by his comparison to a pudding, the boy serves as a visible example of the children the giant likes best.

MacDonald, unconventional in his doctrine but committed to the idea that sin exists almost physically,[8] creates a giant who "likes greedy boys best" but who also, according to his wife, "is fond of little children, particularly little girls . . . so fond of them that he eats them up" (319).[9] The wife thus introduces a new strand to the bad giant/bad child plot. Within the giant's moral universe, eating a child is an expression of love, albeit gustatory, but according to the giant's wife it reflects well on him; as she contends, her husband "is a very good man" (319). By acting on his fondness, the giant proves his goodness—his fitness—as a giant man in a giant world, while also demonstrating his authenticity as a giant in a fictional world. MacDonald implicitly allows two models of behavior and morality to overlap, as the giant proves his goodness by being bad (eating children) and also, for his wife at least, proving his goodness by being good (eating children). The giant seems to be, in other words, both an agent of his own moral system and an instrument of the text's. By fulfilling his function as an eater of bad children, he verifies his goodness in a paradox that remains unresolved.

Along with fleshing out its giant's character, MacDonald's text goes even further than Sinclair's in its representation of adulterated children: readers see

> . . . a row of little boys, about a dozen, with very fat faces and goggle eyes, sitting before the fire, and staring stupidly into it.
>
> . . . .
>
> [The giant] strode up to the wretched children. Now, what made them very wretched indeed was, that they knew if they could only keep from eating, and grow thin, the giant would dislike them, and turn them out to find their way home; but notwithstanding this, so greedy were they,

> that they ate as much as ever they could hold. The giantess, who fed them, comforted herself with thinking that they were not real boys and girls, but only little pigs pretending to be boys and girls. (320)

MacDonald makes it plain that gluttony dehumanizes these children, whereas restraint and self-control (growing thin) would reanimate their humanity.[10] As little pigs in disguise, they are fit food for the giant, who only eats what suits, and soothes, him: "If it were not for a bite of a radish now and then, I never could bear [the responsibility of looking after his heart]" (323). The giant, who "grew little children in his garden instead of radishes" (316), conflates the two, just as his wife does when she identifies the children as pigs. This reinforces the badness of the child even more than Sinclair's version did, as her lazy boys are nonetheless always human boys: Master No-book may be fattened *like* a goose, but the goose exists only by implication, contained within the image for gastronomically aware readers. As pseudo-radishes and masquerading pigs, however, MacDonald's bad children are barely children at all, their core substance almost entirely given over to corruption.

MacDonald drives this point home when he allows one "dough-faced boy" to be boiled for lying to the giant only to be "throw[n . . .] out with the ladle" by the giantess "as if he had been a black-beetle that had tumbled in and had had the worst of it" (321).[11] Whether pudding-faced or dough-faced, these children have become food; they are what they eat. MacDonald inserts morality into the act of eating: children who have lost sight of their purity are merely vegetables or animals or pastry, so stupid they can barely count themselves. If we follow the lead of a giant spider, who explains that he "eat[s] nothing but what is mischievous or useless" (332), then we see, once again, that the bad child has forsaken its identity *as* child. When the narrator is wrapping up his tale he chastises a girl who plans to tell the story to "Amy" and make her scream: "'No, no; you mustn't be unkind,' said I; 'else you will never help little children against wicked giants. The giants will eat you too, then'" (337). By rejecting her duty to look after those smaller and more helpless than her—by acting against her "kind"—the girl risks making herself appetizing to hungry giants. Her enigmatic reply, "'Oh! I know what you mean. You can't frighten me,'" shows how far she has already traveled from the realms of good childhood (337). In fact, as an "elder gir[l], who promised fair to reach before long the summit of uncompromising womanhood" (337–338), she represents another form of adulteration: the *adult*-erated child. The narrator betrays his discomfort with a being who, unlike a bad child, cannot be controlled either through narrative or through ingestion. She makes him "feel very small," perhaps like a child, in danger himself from a giant (338).[12]

It is, perhaps, telling that though the good child may be the best food, it is the bad children who actually end up as culinary delights. More than simply delicious treats for immoral giants, however, they function, through their tempting yet unwholesome fatness, to neutralize sin through incorporating and thus eliminating it. When bad giants eat bad children, the bad child delights no one but his eater, who in consuming purges him. "Goblin Market" and its Eucharistic narrative, on the other hand, show what can be done with the image of the body meant to be eaten and yet not consumed. Rossetti writes a new Christ with Lizzie, one who can sacrifice herself and yet live to tell the tale to her children. The absolute Romantic ideal, Lizzie embodies a self-aware purity that allows her to use her body to transform the poison of the goblins' fruit into its own antidote. "Who eateth of thee hungers not / ... / Fed at Thy table, we are filled": ingesting the purity of the good child is a totemic activity, one that allows the child to feed the needs of the faithful while maintaining its own subjective integrity.[13] In a complementary way, the bad child, spoiled and adulterated, must be eaten, digested, incorporated as part of a greater wickedness.

When food transmutes from nourishment for the child's body to a metonym for the child's body, eating is less about satisfying corporeal needs than about symbolizing moral needs. In the texts under discussion here, food acts to trope forms of childish corruption; when the texts figure painful punishment and children themselves in terms of food, they combine bodily sensations like satiety and self-flagellation. Thus, Harry offers himself in place of an absent cake as its best and most suitable substitute; Lizzie allows her body to act as a kind of melting pot for the juices that will sate and redeem Laura; Master No-Book is rescued in the nick of time from his indolent acquiescence in his own destruction; and the greedy boys in "The Giant's Heart" are helpless to control their own gluttony. Whether pure and purifying or adulterated, the children in these texts give the playfulness of "I'm going to eat you up" a new and darker meaning. In moving from the pure child whose ingestion cleanses and overcomes sin to the bad child whose ingestion is required to combat and punish sin, I am not meaning to institute a contradiction, however. Rather, I wish to suggest that the trope of the eaten child is itself contradictory. If the child is innocent, it "does me good." If the child is corrupted and adulterated, it "does me good." What changes is the nature of "me" and, concomitantly, the effect on the child. Moral salvation or merely digestion—"for bodily or mental food,/ Use whatever does you good" (Allingham, "[For bodily or mental food]"). In the end, it is not about the consumed, but the eater.

Notes:

1 See, for instance, Meir, Stern, and Daniel. Subsequent references to these texts will be made in the body of the essay.

2 See Lewis Carroll, *Alice in Wonderland* (1865); Christina Rossetti, *Speaking Likenesses* (1870); Charles Kingsley, *The Water-Babies* (1863); Juliana Horatia Ewing, "Christmas Crackers" (1870), in Auerbach and Knoepflmacher 161.

3 When the Fairchild children allow a disagreement to become an argument, their father tells them the story of two brothers, whose dispute led one to kill the other. To drive home the lesson, he takes the children to view the

murderous brother's body, still on display, although badly decomposed, on a gibbet near the site of his crime. For most readers, this episode epitomizes the book's Evangelical hostility to children. Closer readers, however, note Sherwood's use of fairy-tale imagery in the gibbet chapter, as well as the Fairchild parents' frequent expressions of love for their children.

4   "Voracious," of course, is Daniel's word; see p. 12 and *passim*. She also notes that "the tenets of Romanticism and Puritanism persist and coexist" (12). It is on the implications of "*who eats whom*" (12) that our approaches diverge.

5   See also Wohl 50 *passim*.

6   The fairy Do-nothing operates in collusion with the giant, calling her garden his "preserve" and hoping to be invited to dinner when the "dainty morsel" Master No-book is served up (76, 77).

7   As I argue in "Doctrine, Suffering and the Morality of Death in Didactic Children's Fiction," they had learned this already; the final lesson is an unnecessary one. See 454–456.

8   See, for instance, the *Princess* books, where goblins have adapted to a life without the sun/Son (*The Princess and the Goblin*) and where human venality manifests itself bestially just under the skin (*The Princess and Curdie*).

9   If greedy boys = bad boys, the giant's favorite food, do girls, culturally constructed as pure, compete for yumminess? This is the only time girls are mentioned as potential food. It may simply reflect that the Giant's wife is addressing a little girl at the time.

10 When, towards the end of the story, the giant attempts to keep back a child after freeing the others, and excuses himself because "he was the thinnest of the lot" (336), MacDonald adds hypocrisy to the giant's various moral failings. The reference to thinness also bears comparison with Master No-Book's fattening. Where he is force-fed, the boys in MacDonald's story gorge themselves, a willing self-sacrifice eased by the bodily pleasures their greed contributes to. One is reminded of Hansel, who, with Gretel's help, outwits the witch attempting to fatten him up by offering her a chicken bone to feel for plumpness rather than his own finger. Hansel, it would seem, is neither bad enough *nor* good enough to eat.

11 As it happens, the boy is punished unfairly; when asked by the giant where the story's two protagonists are hiding, he answers truthfully that they are in the broom, but the resourceful children "catch hold of the bristles" and save themselves (321). The giant's precipitousness illustrates his own moral blindness, which is further emphasized by his decision to "wear nothing but white stockings on Sunday" (318).

12 Luckily, the narrator, and female children as well, are redeemed by a "darling little blue-eyed girl," who says, "'Thank you, dear Mr. Smith. I will be good. It was a very nice story. If I was a man, I would kill all the wicked people in the world. But I am only a little girl, you know; so I can only be

good'" (338). Although this reassures the narrator that there is at least "one good woman," it also shows how well she has learned the tale's lesson: the sinful deserve to be killed.

13 Frank's death in *Holiday House* stands outside this paradigm, because he should not have died; his is an unnecessary sacrifice that props up a conflicted narrative. The quotation is from "Bread Enough and to Spare," by Horatius Bonar, *The Song of the New Creation* (1872), ll. 11, 21.

Works Cited

Allingham, William. *Blackberries*. London: Reeves, 1890.

Auerbach, Nina, and U. C. Knoepflmacher, eds. *Forbidden Journeys: Fairy Tales and Fantasies by Victorian Women Writers*. Chicago: U of Chicago P, 1992.

Daniel, Carolyn. *Voracious Children: Who Eats Whom in Children's Literature*. New York: Routledge, 2006.

Kassim, Lozah. "The Co-Operative Movement and Food Adulteration in the Nineteenth Century." *Manchester Region History Review* 15 (2001): 9–18.

Labbe, Jacqueline M. "Doctrine, Suffering and the Morality of Death in Didactic Children's Fiction." *British Journal of Eighteenth-Century Studies* 29 (2006): 445–459.

MacDonald, George. *Adela Cathcart*. 1864. Whitethorn, CA: Johannesen, 1994.

Meir, Natalie Kapetanios. "'A fashionable dinner is arranged as follows': Victorian Dining Taxonomies." *Victorian Literature and Culture* 33 (2005): 133–148.

Morton, Timothy. "Let Them Eat Romanticism: Materialism, Ideology, and Diet Studies." *Cultures of Taste/Theories of Appetite: Eating Romanticism*. Ed. Timothy Morton. New York: Palgrave, 2004. 257–276.

Rossetti, Christina. *Goblin Market*. New York: Dover, 1983.

Sherwood, Mrs [Mary Martha]. *The History of the Fairchild Family or, the Child's Manual: Being a Collection of Stories Calculated to Shew the Importance and Effects of a Religious Education*. Part one 1818. New York: Garland, 1977.

Sinclair, Catherine. *Holiday House*. 1839. *Masterworks of Children's Literature*. Ed. Robert Lee Wolff. Vol. 5, Part I. New York: Stonehill, 1985.

Stern, Rebecca F. "Adulteration Detected: Food and Fraud in Christina Rossetti's 'Goblin Market.'" *Nineteenth-Century Literature* 57 (2003): 477–511.

Wohl, A. S. *Endangered Lives: Public Health in Victorian Britain*. Cambridge, MA: Harvard UP, 1983.

Chapter Seven
"Voracious Appetites": The Construction of "Fatness" in the Boy Hero in English Children's Literature

Jean Webb

Obesity is an escalating problem in Western culture and is a particularly worrying phenomenon in childhood, as it leads to associated diseases, limited projected life span, and a poor quality of life for children who are overweight. Being overweight impacts on child subjects not only physically but also psychologically, because the children may well be teased, bullied, and marginalized as being different and perceived as ineffectual members of their peer group who do not conform to the cultural norm. Negative characteristics are popularly associated with being overweight, such as being lazy, slovenly, cowardly, untrustworthy, self-indulgent, and unintelligent. As Marcia Glessner, John Hoover, and Lisa Hazlett point out, body image is an integral factor in contemporary media-driven Western culture (Glessner, et al. 116). Adolescent culture has a strong desire to conform to the idealized peer group model and body shape. Those who do not achieve this aspiration suffer both from the maltreatment executed on them by their peers and also from that which they inflict upon themselves through poor self-image and low self-esteem. Overweight children therefore become the victims of others and of themselves. The intention of this discussion is to trace the roots of the negative representation of the overweight child, to go back beyond contemporary media representation and to trace the literary depictions in English texts of the overweight child. The position taken here is that the negative representation of the fat child is a cultural construction which has been unchallenged and unquestioned and has thus permeated and become embedded in the consciousness of Western society.

There are two driving factors in the cultural construction of the overweight figure, that of morality and that of cultural desire to produce the culturally approved model of the subject. The moral impetus in English culture is sited in the teachings of the Church. The notion of the Seven Sins were "distinctly categorized" (Moseley 150) in the work of the Greek theologian, Evagrius of Pontus, AD 345–399, who identified eight sins that were modified to seven in the late sixth century by Pope Gregory the Great. As C. W. D. R. Moseley states:

> The Seven Sins which, if there is no repentance, lead to the death of the soul, are pride, covetousness, lust, envy, gluttony, anger and sloth. . . . .
>
> All are seen as being related to one another, and all, in essence, are a denial of one's creaturely relationship to God, a rejection of his gifts, and, as a result, by asserting the supreme importance of one's own self and will, a denial of one's proper relationship to fellow human beings and to the rest of God's creation. The root of the sins is *cupiditas*, which may indeed be translated as "covetousness," . . . the desire to have things one's own way. (Moseley 150)

References to sin are frequent within the litany of the Church of England *Book of Common Prayer* (1662), although there is no direct naming of the Seven Sins per se.

> From all blindness of heart;
> from pride, vain-glory, and hypocrisy;
> from envy, hatred, and malice, and all uncharitableness,
> **good Lord, deliver us.**
> From fornication, and all other deadly sin;
> and from all the deceits of the world, the flesh, and the devil,
> **good Lord, deliver us.** (*The Book of Common Prayer* 25)

Self-indulgence in food, which comes under the sin of gluttony, is implicit here in deceits of the flesh, which can be linked with worldly desire, uncharitableness, envy, and malice. The negative focus therefore is upon the self rather than external responsibilities, demands, and loyalties. The "desire to have things one's own way" militates against the desires of the Church. Where Church and State are integrally linked, as in England certainly until the end of the nineteenth century, then the moral teachings of the Church have a direct impact upon the construction of the ideal English subject. Morality and the construction of the patriotic subject were combined with models of physicality in writing for children in the work of writers who were involved with the Muscular Christianity movement, which was linked with Christian Socialism.

In 1848 a group met to discuss how they could prevent revolution by tackling the social problems of the working classes; they came to be known as Christian Socialists. This group included the clergyman and writer Charles Kingsley and

Thomas Hughes, the author of *Tom Brown's Schooldays* (1857). From this nexus developed the movement known as Muscular Christianity, which emphasized masculinity and healthy living. The phrase "Muscular Christianity" probably first appeared in an 1857 English review of Charles Kingsley's novel *Two Years Ago* (1857). One year later, the same phrase was used to describe Thomas Hughes's highly influential novel *Tom Brown's School Days*, about life at Rugby Public School (in American terms a private, non-State-run school). *Tom Brown's School Days* was an inspiration for the English boy's adventure story, which was based upon and disseminated values of imperialism. The characteristics of the boy hero, epitomized by Tom Brown, had been identified two years earlier by Charles Kingsley in his dedication prefacing *Westward Ho!* (1855). Kingsley addressed The Rajah Sir James Brooke, K. C .B., and George Augustus Selwyn, Bishop of New Zealand, who represented imperialism and the Church. Kingsley nominated the values he admired and revered in these figureheads, which he traced back to an idealized essence of Englishness embodied in Elizabethan times. The dedication reads as follows:

> That type of English virtue, at once manful and godly, practical and enthusiastic, prudent and self-sacrificing, which he [Kingsley] has tried to depict in these pages, they have exhibited in a form even purer and more heroic than that in which he has drest it, and than that in which it was exhibited by the worthies whom Elizabeth, without distinction of rank or age, gathered round her in the ever glorious wars of her great reign. (Kingsley Dedication)

Kingsley is representing an essence of English manliness which he would want his young readers to espouse, that is being manful, godly, practical, enthusiastic, prudent, self-sacrificing, moving across class barriers, and dedicated to the furtherance of English interests through war. Furthermore this hero is athletic and sporty, and one would deduce not overweight. These are the very characteristics depicted in Hughes's *Tom Brown* combined with Tom's bravery on the rugby field, despite not being the largest or the oldest of players; his protection of the weak in the way that he cared for his sickly (and effeminized) young friend; and the courage he showed in fighting off the bullies. Tom would go on to be a bastion of the Empire.

G. A. Henty's boy heroes were cast in the same ideological and physical mold. Henty had travelled widely as one of the first war correspondents. His novels reflect his knowledge both geographically and historically, with titles such as *With Clive in India: or the Beginnings of an Empire* (1884) and *With Buller in Natal: or, a Born Leader* (1900). Henty was known as "the Boy's Historian"; his stories were widely read across the British Empire and colonies and also included in school syllabi and reading programs. Charlie Marryat, the hero of *With Clive in India: or the Beginnings of an Empire*, is described as follows:

> He was slight in build, but his schoolfellows knew that Charlie Marryat's muscles were as firm and as hard as any boy in the school. In all sports requiring activity and endurance rather than weight and strength he was always conspicuous. Not one in the school could compete with him in long-distance running. He was a capital swimmer and one of the best boxers in the school. He had a reputation for being a leader in every mischievous prank; but he was honourable and manly, would scorn to shelter himself under the semblance of a lie, and was a prime favourite with his masters as well as his schoolfellows. (Henty 1)

These adventure stories are still published and popular in America today, continuing the dissemination of this idealized heroic model. Embedded in the novels of, for example, Charles Kingsley, G. A. Henty, R. M. Ballantyne, and others, is a model of heroism which drew directly upon Muscular Christianity and the fit sporting young hero who was usually not physically large.

The connection between food, eating, and morality was also included by Charles Kingsley in his moral fairy tale "for a land baby," *The Water Babies* (1863). As a member of the clergy, Charles Kingsley would also be well aware of teaching against the dangers of the temptations of the Seven Sins, the sixth of which was gluttony. Kingsley includes a warning episode in *The Water Babies*. Tom, the focal character, is sorely tempted by the sweets kept in the cupboard of the fairy Mrs. Bedonebyasyoudid. By engaging in the pleasures of overindulgence Tom risks rejection from her soft warm lap, where he loves to luxuriate in her attentions:

> Now you may fancy that Tom was quite good, when he had everything that he could want or wish; but you would be very much mistaken. Being quite comfortable is a very good thing; but it does not always make people good. Indeed it sometimes makes them naughty, as it has made the people in America; and as it made the people in the Bible who waxed fat and kicked like horses overfed and underworked. And I am very sorry to say that this happened to little Tom. For he grew so fond of the sea-bull's eyes and sea-lollipops, that his foolish little head could think of nothing else: and he was always longing for more, and wondering when the strange lady would come again and give him some, and what she would give him, and how much, and whether she would give him more than others. And he thought of nothing but lollipops by day and dreamt of nothing else by night . . . (Kingsley 115–116)

The passage continues with the scene of Tom succumbing to temptation, which is described as a frenzy of guilty secret and stealthy gorging:

> And then he would only eat one, and he did; and then he would only eat two, and then three, and so on; and then he was terrified lest she should

come and catch him, and began gobbling them down so fast that he did not taste them, or have any pleasure in them; and then he felt sick, and would have only one more; and then only one more again; and so on till he had eaten them all up. (Kingsley 116)

Kingsley makes a direct link between morality and gluttony as part of Tom's journey of moral education from being an ignorant and un-Christian boy chimney sweep, to a water baby, and finally emerging as a Great Man of Science to take his place in the formation of the British Empire through industry and application.

The literary model of heroism thus constructed through these texts is culturally central to the "project" of Empire. By implication the antithetical characters (i.e. those who cannot rise to such heroism) are physically limited, and thus a "space" was created for those characters who were not physically proficient and athletic to be stereotyped with a range of negative personality traits. The "Muscular Christian" model of heroism dominantly continued—and does so today—setting up oppositional stereotypes. The most well-known one in English children's literature is the character Billy Bunter, who centrally filled the space left in opposition to the Muscular hero. Billy Bunter of *The Greyfriars School Stories* was created by Charles Hunter under the nom de plume of Frank Richards ("Billy Bunter"). Billy Bunter appeared in 1908 in stories about Greyfriars School in the Magnet paper, which was principally for boys. Richards also wrote thirty-eight books featuring Bunter between 1947 and 1965. Furthermore, during the 1950s and early 1960s the BBC produced a television series where Bunter was played by the actor Gerald Campion. Although featured as the central protagonist, Billy Bunter is a "hero" with antiheroic qualities who is set up as a comic character and is the butt of jokes. He is decidedly overweight, greedy, a spy, lazy, and cowardly. In all, he demonstrates negative qualities in opposition to the ideal qualities of the Muscular Christian hero. Bunter is not very intelligent, surviving by cunning; he is in the remedial class and is described as "the fat owl of the Remove." *Tom Brown's Schooldays* provides a model for the Bunter stories, as it is set in a public school, where there is a good deal of focus on the interaction between the boys. Bob Cherry is the attractive, handsome proficient hero of Greyfriars, a leader and sportsman; Bunter is clearly an exaggerated negative distortion of such. The audience/reader is "invited" to focus on his physicality as the source and manifestation of his unattractive and negative traits. The illustrations for the Magnet paper and Bunter books were faithfully portrayed by Gerald Campion, the actor who played the eponymous fat antihero in the television series. Physically Bunter is obviously overweight; this is emphasized by his tightly fitting clothing and checked trousers, which accentuate the curved nature of his body. Bunter's trousers also stand out against the style of the more somber school uniform of the period worn by his schoolfellows. It is notable that Bunter's food choices are unhealthy, sweet, highly calorific foods, as with the sticky buns which he so lovingly devours in great quantities. Food becomes sexualized because Bunter is often portrayed with an almost lascivious, sly expression as he is about to consume that which he loves. Iced buns themselves are almost sexual objects, sweet, soft, moist, and fulsome in the mouth. Amoral overtones are added to his greed as Bunter will be the one engaging in quasi-criminal acts such as "stealing" the last bun. In accord with the nature of his eating habits, the depiction of Bunter is effeminized with the emphasis being placed on his overly coiffured hair, the curls more befitting of a girl than an aspiring hero in the ideal mode of Muscular Christianity. In short, his food choices are in accord with the demasculinization of the obese figure. Bunter could certainly not be imagined leading the fray to fight for king and country.

As this historical review develops, the complexity of attitudes towards the overweight, fat child become ever more apparent. The characters considered thus far are exemplars, constructed as being fat as an outward symbol of their dysfunctional personality, negative values, and general unlikeableness. Philosophically the roots lie in the construction of the male child as one fit to take on the moral and spiritual values of the dominant culture to continue to run and expand the British Empire. Pragmatically, the coming generation of British Imperialists and colonizers would ideally be physically fit, strong and able to defeat the enemies of Empire and survive in inclement climates and situations. The model constructed therefore has no identification of fatness in relation to the child figure per se: it is a device, part of a cultural strategy. There is no questioning as to why the child should be thus physically configured. The implicit assumption is that this physical manifestation is how the child is and that it is linked with personality rather than being a physical condition, or the physical manifestation of psychological unhappiness on the part of the child, or that to be larger than other children is "normal" or acceptable but culturally negative.

William Golding, writing in the aftermath of World War II, was challenging the values and mores of a culture that had fought two wars employing those very values which had underpinned imperialism. He was writing from the perspective of a culture which was endeavoring to reconstruct itself, to create a new Britishness in the knowledge of the collapsing Empire, and the paucity of life after the war, when the phrase "we had won the war, but lost the peace" came readily to the minds of many. Golding's allegorical novel, *Lord of the Flies* (1954), is a critique of such values. A party of schoolboys is cast-away upon an uninhabited island following an airplane crash. One group, who are from a public school and are members of the choir, "go native." Golding organizes this disintegration around athleticism, body size, and food. Ralph, the athletic hero, who stands against such savagery, parallels his nineteenth-century heroic forerunners. The description of Ralph echoes that of Henty's Charlie Marryat from seventy years earlier:

He was old enough, twelve years and a few months, to have lost the prominent tummy of childhood; and not yet old enough for adolescence to have made him awkward. You could see now that he might make a boxer, as far as width and heaviness of shoulders went, but there was a mildness about his mouth and eyes that proclaimed no devil. (Golding 10)

The character of Ralph exudes a confidence which is especially attractive to Piggy, the fat boy, who "attaches" himself to Ralph. The real name of the fat boy is not revealed; he is prepared to take any name other than the nickname "Piggy" by which he is tormentingly known throughout the story:

"I don't care what they call me," he said confidentially, "so long as they don't call me what they used to call me at school."
Ralph was faintly interested.
"What was that?"
The fat boy glanced over his shoulder, then leaned towards Ralph.
He whispered.
"They used to call me 'Piggy.'"
Ralph shrieked with laughter. He jumped up.
"Piggy! Piggy!"
Ralph danced out into the hot air of the beach and then returned as a fighter-plane with wings swept back, and machine-gunned Piggy. (Golding 11)

Ralph will become the friend of Piggy and the respected hero of the book; however, even he indulges in this tormenting behavior. Here Piggy is the target of Ralph's play-fighting and the future victim of the savage choirboys. Ralph's machine-gunning is a shadow play of the war which has recently ended, a war which was directed at the helpless and those who were different from the Aryan "norm." It is thus "acceptable" that the fat boy becomes the target, a norm of boyish behavior. It is also logical that the fat boy is the victim in the allegorical scheme of Golding's work; as he has no real name, he is both anonymous and universal: an Every Fat Boy.

Piggy's use of language also denotes that he is from a working-class background, somewhat underprivileged. The public school boys are thus victimizing the lower classes when they torment Piggy. He cannot compete with them linguistically or physically. Interestingly, swimming is an activity which is highlighted. Ralph is an athletic and fluent swimmer, a very different case from that of Piggy.

Ralph did a surface dive and swam under water with his eyes open; . . . He turned over holding his nose, and a golden light danced and shattered just over his face. Piggy was looking determined and began to take off his shorts. Presently he was palely and fatly naked. He tiptoed down the sandy side of the pool, and sat there up to his neck in water smiling proudly at Ralph.

"Aren't you going to swim?"

Piggy shook his head.

"I can't swim. I wasn't allowed. My asthma—"

"Sucks to your ass-mar!"

Piggy bore this with a sort of humble patience.

"You can't half swim well." (Golding 13)

Piggy has learned to be humble as a way of dealing with his "deficiencies." Overweight, physically inept; poor eyesight; an asthma sufferer; orphaned and looked after by his aunt; educationally and socially limited yet conscientious and thoughtful, Piggy is at the butt end of this society of upper-middle-class privileged boys. Piggy does not portray any of the negative moral and personal attributes displayed by Billy Bunter. Bunter's unattractive and despicable behavior affords him a protection against what would otherwise be the dominant fellows in his peer group. Bunter manages to be both victim and subversive antihero, whereas poor Piggy is a victim who earns the sympathy of the reader, and of Ralph. The suggested source of his weight problem is that his aunt gives him as many sweets as he can eat from the shop which she runs. Although her action is a contributory factor it is viewed sympathetically, because this is a symbol of caring for this rather sad and pathetic figure. The reference to sweet eating is also associated with home and civilization. Golding melds together the island landscape with food and the child subjects, thus demonstrating and developing a division between civilization and disintegration of controlled behavior.

A natural primeval need is for food. On landing on the island the boys forage for and gorge on fruit in the forest: "The heat of the tropics, the descent, the search for food and now the sweaty march along the beach had given them the complexion of newly washed plums" (19). Newly estranged from civilization, these boys are naturalized into the landscape by association with the fruits found wild on the island. In contrast, Ralph, who defends civilized behavior, associates fond memories of home with the landscape: "There was a jumble of the usual squareness, with one great block sitting out in the lagoon. Sea birds were nesting there. 'Like icing,' said Ralph, 'on a pink cake'" (25). In the context of the island, home (England) becomes the exotic, symbolized by Ralph's image of sumptuous, extravagant processed food. Whereas he would initially wish for the comfort of sweet cake, the other boys, followers of Jack, have a desire for meat. Under Jack's direction they hunt down a pig. Their first attempt at killing is portrayed in a frenzy, that of the pig and Jack's uncontrolled violence, which stops short of slaughter, "because of the enormity of cutting into living flesh; because of the unbearable blood" (Golding 30). This incident leads to the realization for the need for organization, rules and a system of leadership symbolized by the holding of the conch. Thus the opposition between Jack and Ralph is established. Jack represents the primeval, the "going native"; Ralph is representative of maintaining and holding on to civilization. Although the boys can survive on fruits, they have a craving for pig meat. On his following attempts, Jack tracks the pig and the very description blends him into the landscape, for he is "streaked with brown earth" (Golding 47). On returning from the kill, Jack and his followers vividly and excitedly describe the hunt, interspersed with their chanting: *"Kill the pig. Cut her throat. Spill her blood"* (Golding 66). They have lost all sense of the need to escape from the island, for they abandon the signal fire for the thrill of the chase and the kill. Later the chant is taken up when the boys under Jack engage in a manic and terrifying dance. The descent into cultural chaos circulates about the hunting of pigs, a poignant echo in relation to the fat boy's nickname. A boy is substituted for the pig and the chant becomes *"Kill the beast. Cut his throat. Spill his blood"* (Golding 145). Any semblance of cultured controlled behavior has dissolved, for they have reverted to a primeval savagery and blood-lust which does not stop at murder, first of Simon and later of Piggy.

Golding's novel is a controlled downward spiral, exposing savagery beneath the surface of civilization. The resultant savagery of the boys and "going native" is plausible, for their education, designed to make them fit rulers and administrators of the British Empire, has furnished them with the behavior and attitudes which enable them to be a colonizing dominant force. They accept being directed; they work as a team under the leadership of Jack; they have a sense of group power, which becomes akin to a cult, displaying the negative dark side of the ideological drivers that enabled the achievement of imperialistic dominance. Power always requires a victim, and here the fat child symbolizes the weaknesses that would militate against the success of empire.

The negative stereotyping of the fat child continues throughout the twentieth century right up to contemporary times, for example with Edmund in C. S. Lewis's *The Lion, the Witch and the Wardrobe* (1950). Although Edmund is not described as being overweight, he does have a fixation about food; for example when Lucy suggests that they rescue the Faun he remarks, "A lot we could do! . . . [W]hen we haven't even got anything to eat!" (Lewis 59). Edmund's preoccupation with food and his greed are his fatal flaws, for he is so tempted by the Turkish delight offered by the White Witch that he is prepared to betray his family, and by implication his patriotic values. Edmund is overtaken by greed, forgetting his manners and any sense of protecting his family and friends during what was actually an interrogation by the White Witch:

> While he was eating, the Queen kept asking him questions. At first Edmund tried to remember that it is rude to speak with one's mouth full, but soon he forgot about this and only thought of trying to shovel down as much Turkish Delight as he could, and the more he ate the more he wanted to eat, and he never asked himself why the Queen should be so inquisitive. (Lewis 39)

Roald Dahl's Augustus Gloop in *Charlie and the Chocolate Factory* (1967) also succumbs to the temptations of sweet foods, in his case chocolate. Augustus is rather cruelly described as follows in terms of the food he loves. He was:

> ... a nine year-old boy who was so enormously fat he looked as though he had been blown up with a powerful pump. Great flabby folds of fat bulged out from every part of his body, and his face was like a monstrous ball of dough with two small greedy currant eyes peering out upon the world. (Dahl 34)

His overindulgent mother enthusiastically comments that: "Eating is his hobby you know, you know. That's all he's interested in. But still, that's better than being a hooligan and shooting off zip guns and things like that in his spare time. Isn't it? And what I always say is, he wouldn't go on eating like he does unless he needed nourishment, would he?" (Dahl 34). Augustus is another character whose physical indulgence is punished as moral failing by the treatment meted out to him by Mr. Wonka (i.e. Dahl) in his chocolate factory, the site of social retribution for all that Dahl dislikes. Mrs. Gloop reveals, through her extended celebration of her son, that she is in fact confounded by his habits, as she tries to find excuses for her son's eating problem, rather than seek out the underlying reasons for his extreme behavior. Augustus's moral flaw is greed, the sixth sin of gluttony. Similarly, Dudley Dursley in J. K. Rowling's *Harry Potter and the Philosopher's Stone* (1997), Harry's human cousin, is overweight, badly behaved, and spoilt by his parents: a thoroughly unpleasant person all told.

The commonality between Edmund, Augustus Gloop, and Dudley Dursley is that each has an adult enabler. The Witch inveigles Edmund into betrayal through tempting him with food, and the parents of Augustus and Dudley lack the appropriate attitudes in parenting, as demonstrated by overindulging their children, giving in to their greedy desires. The parental lack of the exercise of discipline and social and moral training are symbolized by the child's greed. The authors, in each case, use food as a device to expose the moral weaknesses of the children, which are compounded in the cases of Gloop and Dursley by their being portrayed as overweight. These have been only a few examples of the negative portrayal of overweight and overindulged children. None of the texts, with the exception of Golding's *Lord of the Flies*, really attempt to enter the interior world of the child. However, attitudes are changing in books of the late twentieth and early twenty-first century.

Catherine Forde's *Fat Boy Swim* (2003) represents what I would describe as a "new wave" of books which have fat characters. *Fat Boy Swim* follows from, for example, *Staying Fat for Sarah Byrnes* by Chris Crutcher (1993), in presenting an overweight adolescent boy for whom body size is a big problem. Teenage Jimmy, the protagonist of *Fat Boy Swim*, is tall, very overweight, and lacks confidence. He is bullied by both his peer group and his teachers and eats excessively to comfort himself. The novel enters into the interiority of Jimmy's experience, the psychological battles he has with himself:

> He was just fat.
> Lardy.
> Ginormous.
> Clinically obese . . .
>
> "Don't start that again," Jimmy warned himself aloud, but it was tough. As soon as he got thinking about it, he had a fight on his hands to stop his mind from scrolling down the litany of names for fat he'd been called over the years. Must be hundreds of them. Maybe thousands.
>
> "Just words. Ignore them. Switch off. Walk away."
>
> Aunt Pol had taught Jimmy many years ago, and to a certain extent, he had learned to follow her advice. He shrugged off insults. Sticks and stones and all that.
>
> But inside, deep inside, it blooming hurt. Every time. Inside, Jimmy didn't feel like Smelly Kelly, Fat Boy Fat. Of course not. He was just—a teenager. Normal in every way. Apart from his size. (Forde 21)

The novel explores various areas of his life, for example at school, at home, and in the wider community, eventually enabling Jimmy to confront his own fears and inadequacies and thus appreciating what he does well. Jimmy learns to overcome his fear of water and discovers that he is a very good swimmer. This is a central turning point in the reconstruction of the hero figure in the twenty-first century. Here is an overweight protagonist who is physically proficient; in fact he excels. Furthermore, his successes are within a competitive sporting context. The overbearing image of the nineteenth-century hero is being balanced by the positive portrayal of fatness and confronting the problem. *Fat Boy Swim* is not an irresponsible celebration of the overweight hero, for there are the associated health problems and discomfort associated with the physical condition which cannot be denied, plus the psychological and social misery he experiences through being obese. For example, Jimmy is asthmatic, a condition exacerbated by his weight; moreover, the summer weather produces feelings of "suffocating under his own sticky weight" (Forde 4). Socially Jimmy is an outcast. At school he dreads the football field because the game exposes his physical ineptitude. Jimmy consequently suffers the jibes of both children and teachers: the sports master makes the rest of the class wait until Jimmy has showered, commenting, "You'll all be dismissed when he's nice and clean for his mammy" (Forde 11). The sneering remark infantilizes the adolescent boy, drawing attention to him and exacerbating is overall lack of confidence, which in turn leads to bouts of excessive comfort eating.

"GI Joe's words churned like ingredients boiling in a stewpot. They burned. They hurt. Gnawed Jimmy like hunger" (Forde 72). Forde expresses the depth of Jimmy's hurt by using analogies to food and hunger, for this is how he translates his emotional pain and unhappiness into a tangibility to then be salved by overeating. "Reaching under his bed, he withdrew his stash of emergency rations. Unwrapped a multipack of Mars bars, settled back on the bed . . ." (Forde 72). The eating experience is described in quasi-erotic language to capture the emotional compensation of the indulgence: "His mouth filled with soft sweet flavours: toffee, mallow, creamy milk chocolate. They coated his teeth and his tongue, plastering the arch of his palate. Jimmy allowed himself a little sigh. That's better, he told himself. You needed that" (Forde 73). Forde realistically tempers the indulgence and the central unhappiness of the lad by recording the battle Jimmy has with his conscience. "*Stop it. Look what you are doing to yourself,* a voice in his head implored" (Forde 73). This is not an easy battle of conscience against a self-destructive will, for the excess and indulgence increases with a certain negative gusto:

> Jimmy unwrapped another Mars bar. Noisily. He stuffed it whole into his mouth making loud mashing noises, pulping the chocolate. Chomping down so he wouldn't hear his nagging voice of reason.
> *Stop. You're making yourself ill. You have to stop.*
> I've had a rotten day, Jimmy justified himself. (Forde 73)

Jimmy's "mother" also has difficulties in facing up to his problems, yet she and Aunt Pol do not discuss the matter. Mum follows medical requirements insofar as taking him to the hospital, but she is unable to confront her own guilt about his weight.

> Mum wouldn't even have scales in the house. She never mentioned his weight, even on Obesity Clinic Days.
> "We've got hospital today," she'd say, making sure she shredded any new diet sheets the consultants gave Jimmy the minute she got home. *"How . . . are you . . . expected . . . to live . . . on this rabbit food?"* (Forde 68)

Her denial reflects her own feelings of guilt and a sense of failure in raising her adopted son (as the novel later reveals) as a healthy person combined with feelings of love expressed through indulgence in "proper" food as opposed to seemingly insubstantial yet healthy salads fit for "rabbits." As with the parents of Augustus Gloop and Dudley Dursley in the lighter and more humorous works of Dahl and Rowling, Jimmy's caretakers have the tendency to overindulge and spoil. Both Mum and Aunt Pol have to face their responsibility and dislike of his behavior and resultant condition.

> When Aunt Pol spoke her voice was minute. "I just wish he was—you know—normal. I mean he's pathetic. Bingeing because he's so flipping miserable. No pals . . ."

"I hope you're not suggesting it's my fault—" Mum's voice quavered in indignation.

"—You know I'm not saying that," Aunt Pol interrupted. "I know what you've done and I'm grateful. It's just that I look at Jimmy and it cracks me up inside. He's enormous and we're letting him get that way." (Forde 78)

Pol uses the language which neither they nor Jimmy wish to hear; "fat," "obese," "gross" are the words she finally has to use to shock herself, Mum, and Jimmy into confronting his problem. Forde does, however, present a pragmatic solution to solving a physical problem while demonstrating the effort and will power required. Interestingly, the activity of swimming and the associated prowess achieved by succeeding competitively are factors in Chris Crutcher's *Staying Fat for Sarah Byrnes*, for again this is a young very overweight focalizer who has a very poor self-image and changes his life positively through swimming. The choice made by the authors to nominate swimming as an activity which literally and metaphorically reshapes these obese characters is a realistic decision allied to the very nature of the exercise itself. Interestingly, prowess with swimming has also been a notable feature of the "traditional" construction of the hero, as discussed previously. Through the protagonists' success at swimming, Crutcher and Forde present possible achievement and applause for the young readers who may also be fat and who may realizably translate this example into their own life practice, without necessarily having to win trophies and championship races. Being overweight is thus presented as a physical problem for which there are pragmatic solutions.

Catherine Forde also translates the matter of food from being a negative into a positive factor in Jimmy's life. He is a very good cook but hides away his talents for fear of ridicule because of the negative association between his social persona and food. Food, cooking, and eating are therefore presented in the text as "normal" and to be enjoyed when undertaken with reason. They are not presented as the cause of Jimmy's problem. His irrational indulgence is instead revealed as a part of his "natural" mode of antisocial, self-destructive behavior.

The structure of the text approaches adolescent overweight as a problem to be solved. The key factors that contribute to the condition of child obesity—that is, overeating, an unhealthy diet, and lack of exercise—are dealt with pragmatically: they are presented as problems to which there are solutions which are achievable both within the fictional text and in real life. Forde, however, goes much further than a pragmatic approach, for she presents obesity as a manifestation of both social and physical factors, raising the "chicken and egg question" of whether the root cause of obesity is physical or social circumstances. As an adolescent, Jimmy is highly self-conscious, that is, conscious of his own sense of identity. As an adolescent, Jimmy is also highly conscious of what his peers and social groupings outside the family think of him. His identity is formulated by others through negative association with his body size, the construction placed upon him, and it thus becomes the identity which supplants and suffocates his own. His true capabilities and his suppressed identity emerge with success, as outlined above; however, the deeper plot of the novel is that of the revelation of the true identities of the key adults who surround Jimmy: his widowed mother, his young and lively Aunt Pol, and the priest who is also the school sports coach.

Aunt Pol and Jimmy have a close and good relationship in which they share a love of food. The positive relationships Jimmy has with his mother and Aunt Pol provide a safe household for him away from the outside worlds of school and the local community where he is bullied and pushed very hard by the sports coach "GI Joe"—behavior which in itself is on the edge of bullying. Jimmy's dead father is presented as a somewhat grim and disapproving figure, for example, in the family photographs where Jimmy is a babe in arms, held by Pol. The male substitute for the dead father becomes GI Joe, the priest and sports coach. He adopts the cause of getting Jimmy to get fitter, learn to swim, and then swim competitively. This is a tough relationship for Jimmy, for this unasked for mentor takes the initially rather reluctant Jimmy through a highly demanding regime towards fitness. It emerges through their developing relationship that GI Joe has run a sanctuary for deprived children in Africa, where he felt he was able to make a positive difference despite the extreme circumstances. Throughout, the reader senses that, although a priest, he is dislocated and unhappy with himself. At the end of the novel he returns to Africa and sends a photograph of himself elated, and fulfilled, surrounded by happy children. The implication here is that GI Joe was also on a quest for emotional and personal fulfillment: to discover his role and emotional identity.

Similarly, the revelation of the plot revolves around the discovery of true identity. Jimmy's discovery is that the roles of mother and aunt are reversed, for Aunt Pol is in fact Jimmy's mother, the boy being the product of a teenage pregnancy with an absent father. The explanation of the disapproving attitude of Jimmy's dead surrogate father thus becomes clear. Pol faces up to her responsibilities of motherhood and is prepared to accept her denied identity. Jimmy traces his father, who was himself a good swimmer and also a large man. The elements of the plot thus come together in a set of conclusions which suggest that the crux of the problem is the question of identity, of facing truths.

Genetically Jimmy is large bodied, as is Eric, the overweight protagonist in *Staying Fat for Sarah Byrnes*. Eric's mother tries to ease matters for her obese son:

> She looked up and smiled. "You look a lot better than your dad," she said. "He was compulsive, ate all the time. You're big and solid. That's different."
>
> "Big and solid as twelve pounds of mashed potatoes in an eight-pound bag," I said. "If you dressed me up in an orange-and-red sweater, you could ride me around the world in eighty days." (Crutcher 2)

Both Jimmy and Eric have a negative sense of self for which food is compensation, but which only adds to their problem. The question for each is how they live with their physicality in a positive sense. Both novels are *Bildungsromans*, novels of self-discovery and development not only for the adolescent focalizer but also for the adult characters. The implication suggested by Forde is that the negative social construction of obesity exacerbates the problem for the overweight child. The psychological roots of his need to overeat emanate from a lack of self-worth resulting from the negative social responses he experiences, a lack of self-understanding per se, and a lack of dealing with his natural body size, the combination of which override his true nature. The revelation and acceptance of the true identities and roles of the adults close to Jimmy means that the family can now develop in an honest manner with a sense of integrity. Forde presents the problem of adolescent obesity as a symptom of underlying problems which are socially generated and are also incorporated into the boy's problematic relationship with himself and society. The suggestion is that the adult and the culturally constructed worlds create the circumstances whereby a potentially obese child becomes so. Chicken or egg—which comes first? Is the child overweight and then society exacerbates the problem, or do social circumstances trigger the behavior which produces obesity? Forde's answer is holistic and moral: there is potential to produce the unhappy, unhealthy, and overweight adolescent in a society that lacks honesty, and cultural mores and behavior exacerbate the situation in a potentially vulnerable child. She also gives hope in the provision of a pragmatic and positive solution.

Chris Crutcher portrays a similarly holistic social philosophy in *Staying Fat for Sarah Byrnes* but extends the notion of the stigma of obesity to alliance with other physically damaged conditions. Sarah Byrnes has been dreadfully abused by her father, one result of which is to leave her face terribly scarred. The overly large and retiring Eric and the small and feisty Sarah, who fights her way through life, become friends and find that they have an aptitude for writing. Sarah bolsters Eric and forces him to face the adversities of his social world with courage, and Eric finally confronts the maladapted and vicious Mr. Byrnes, in addition to "defeating" those other adolescent bullies who have made Eric's life miserable. As with Forde's novel, in addition to success at swimming, the adolescent male hero also has another talent: for Jimmy it was cooking, for Eric, writing. Their lives have the potential to expand positively as their waistlines recede healthily. In both novels, the roots of the problems which these adolescents face lie within society. Physicality can be controlled when there is a stronger sense of social harmony and caring, when a sense of order has been restored.

Louis Sachar's *Holes* takes the discussion of the overweight adolescent boy further into the interrogation of social problems where the protagonist, Stanley, is accused of deviant behavior and sent to a detention center. In fact, he is the victim of a series of incidental factors which lead to his being unjustly sentenced to hard labor for a theft which he did not commit.

Stanley's occupation in the center is to dig holes in an area of desert, a severe and physically punishing sentence. While in the center, where the boys are badly treated, he teaches another lad, Zero, to read. When Zero absconds, Stanley finally saves him from death in the desert. Stanley has a great sense of humanity, even though he is not the brightest of lads. He works hard at his tasks, loses weight because of the extreme exercise, and becomes a physically strong young man, transformed from an overweight, overly large adolescent destined to be a social dropout and loser. The truth of the circumstances, which led him to be sentenced to time in the center, is finally discovered, and Stanley begins a new and positive pathway in life.

The shift denoted in these texts is important, for Sachar, Crutcher, and Forde are writing the obese adolescent as a hero who transforms himself by effort; they are writing, as it were, the *Bildungsroman* of weight loss. Sachar and Crutcher are American authors; Catherine Forde's story is set in Scotland. Interestingly, there is therefore no nationally based reason for these authors to adopt the English cultural model of the hero. Their texts revolve around the moral and social problems experienced by their characters while addressing the ever-increasing problem of the obese adolescent, which has moved beyond national boundaries but is deep-seated within Western lifestyles, diet, and eating behavior.

Obesity is a condition of Western culture which has shifted in cultural importance from the nineteenth century to the present day. The nineteenth-century negative depiction of the overweight child in English children's literature as the victimized subject acted as an opposition to emphasize and magnify the positive qualities of the boy hero. The compound construction of the negative and positive aspects of maleness in association with body size acted as an agent of cultural imperialism. Paradoxically, obesity was employed as part of a "positive" philosophical and cultural determination. The "demonization" of the overweight child became absorbed into cultural "habit" as an acceptable stereotypical representation of morally negative and culturally threatening behavior. That construct still persists. However, in contemporary society, where obesity itself is a problem that threatens the future of Western culture with its projected burden on health care systems and the efficiency and productivity of capitalist society, authors have begun to take the approach towards the reconstruction of the hero within a social context: the overweight adolescent is, as it were, being recon"figured." Where writers go now with this worrying and pressing situation of obesity in the younger generations will be food for thought and provide plenty of words to chew over.

Note: I wish to thank my colleague and friend, Dr. Derek Peters, Research Co-ordinator in Sports Science at the University of Worcester, for asking me the seemingly simple question: "Can you see any connections between obesity and children's literature?", without which this study would not have been generated.

Works Cited

"Billy Bunter of Greyfriars School." *Whirligig: 1950s British Television Nostalgia.* 20 July 2008 <http://www.whirligig-tv.co.uk/tv/children/bunter/bunter.htm>.

Book of Common Prayer, The. Cambridge: Cambridge UP. 1662 version.

Crutcher, Chris. *Staying Fat for Sarah Byrnes.* New York: Bantam, 1993.

Dahl, Roald. *Charlie and the Chocolate Factory.* 1964. Harmondsworth, UK: Puffin, 1967.

Forde, Catherine. *Fat Boy Swim.* London: Egmont Children's Books, 2003.

Glessner, Marcia M., John H. Hoover, and Lisa A. Hazlett. "The Portrayal of Overweight in Adolescent Fiction." *Reclaiming Children and Youth* 15:2 Summer (2006): 116–123.

Golding, William. *Lord of the Flies.* 1954. London: Penguin, 1960.

Henty, G. A. *With Clive in India: or the Beginnings of an Empire.* 1884. Rahway, NJ: Mershon, 1900.

———. *With Buller in Natal: or, a Born Leader.* New York: Scribner, 1900.

Hughes, Thomas. *Tom Brown's Schooldays.* 1857. Oxford: Oxford UP, 1989.

Kingsley, Charles. *The Water Babies.* 1863. Oxford: Oxford UP, 1995.

———. *Westward Ho!* 1855. New York: Scribner, 1992.

Lewis, C. S. *The Lion, the Witch and the Wardrobe.* New York: Macmillan,1950.

Moseley, C. W. D. R. . *Chaucer: The Pardoner's Tale.* London: Penguin, 1987.

Rowling, J. K. *Harry Potter and the Philosopher's Stone.* London: Bloomsbury, 1997.

Sachar, Louis. *Holes.* New York: Foster, 1998.

Part V
Global/Multicultural/ Postcolonial Food

Chapter Eight

"The Eaters of Everything": Etiquettes of Empire in Kipling's Narratives of Imperial Boys

Winnie Chan

Bard of the British Empire, refuser of both a knighthood and the British Poet Laureateship, "the most complete man of genius" Henry James had ever known, the youngest recipient ever of the Nobel Prize in literature, pariah of syllabus-makers throughout the English-speaking world: of all the things Rudyard Kipling might be called, "gastronome" does not exactly leap to mind. Yet Kipling's description of an enormous bowl "as big as thy head" and "full of hot rice" skillfully extorted from a muttering old crone who adds "good, steaming vegetable curry, clap[s] a fried cake atop, and a morsel of clarified butter on the cake, [and then] dab[s] a lump of sour tamarind conserve at the side" is worthy of any Zagat-wielding, *sous-vide*-ing, Sub-Zero-refrigerating "foodie." Such an enthusiast would doubtless join Kipling's young hero in "look[ing] at the load lovingly" (Kipling, *Kim* 62). Nor is this gastronomic rhapsody an aberration within Kipling's *oeuvre*, let alone *Kim*, a novel that abounds with "beautiful meals" (66). In his quest for an identity that reconciles his Indian sensibilities with his British imperial destiny, Kimball O'Hara literally eats his way along the Grand Trunk Road, "a flap of soft, greasy Mussalman bread" here, "cakes all warm and well scented with *hing* [asafoetida], curds and sugar [sic]" there (69, 244).

Clearly, food plays a conspicuous role in *Kim*, Kipling's last novel set in India, an allegory of the British Empire just as the sun was threatening to set on it, inscribed onto a *Bildungsroman* about a boy's adventures navigating the increasingly tortuous divide between colonizer and the colonized. Orphaned and left in the care of a "half-caste" opium addict, Kim can hardly help following his stomach, because "Sometimes there was food in the house, more often there was not, and then Kim went out again to eat with his native friends" (44, 51). From the inside out, eating with these "native friends" transforms Kim into "the Little Friend of all the World" (51). Muslim or Hindu, Brahmin or Buddhist, Kim understands the vagaries of gastronomic ritual. His versatile appetites play no small part in his virtuosity at the cultural cross-dressing that makes him such a valuable player in "the Great Game" of imperial espionage. It is thus fitting that in this game, whose object is to snuff out insurrections among a bewildering variety of natives, fellow players in Her Majesty's service recognize each other through a "test-sentence" that quibbles over the preparation of *tarkeean*, "the well-loved word" for a vegetable curry (231, 247).

If Kim's success as an instrument of empire is predicated on his ability to eat everything, however, the same cannot be said of Mowgli, the feral young hero of *The Jungle Books* (1894, 1895), published six and seven years earlier. In them, the grey apes are ostracized from jungle society for flouting the Law of the Jungle, the gravity of their transgressions needing no further elaboration than that they are "the eaters of everything" (25). Moreover, the infant Mowgli's introduction into jungle society begins in a debate over whether or not, and by which denizens of the jungle, he may be eaten. There is a time and a place for the eating of everything, both works suggest. Like *Kim*, *The Jungle Books* are (as S. P. Mohanty, Jenny Sharpe, and Patrick Brantlinger, among other critics, have observed) allegories of empire that seek specifically to revise the narrative of the India Mutiny of 1857–1858. Mowgli's and Kim's negotiations of gastronomic convention make a provocative index to the nature of this revision, vividly imagined for consumption back home at the imperial center, where gastronomic conventions were undergoing constant revision and refinement.

If, some seventy years earlier, the French lawyer Jean-Anthelme Brillat-Savarin could claim, "*Dis-moi ce que tu manges, et je te dirai ce que tu es*" ("Tell me what you eat, and I will tell you what you are"), then late-Victorian domestic discourse sought ways to establish "what" one was by not only what was eaten, but also when, where, with whom, how much, and with what utensils and accompaniments. Their ostentatious, imperious precision notwithstanding, these household guides frequently contradicted each other, not to mention themselves. In spite of the complications further introduced by contact with Britain's far-flung colonies, this discourse promoted the assumption that Britons everywhere would set the standard for civilized behavior, beginning at the table.

As revealed in its gastronomic explorations, *Kim*'s allegory of empire revises, by refining, the allegory elaborated in *The Jungle Books*. Where the unrestrained consumptions of the grey apes in *The Jungle Books* demonstrate the notorious "muddle" of India for boys at home in Britain, Kim's consumptions evince mastery of the Other. What sets Kim's "eating of everything" apart from that of the grey apes is that he regulates his consumptions by the etiquettes of his colonized hosts. Kim's orientalism thus enacts an ideal etiquette of Empire. For good reason does Robert Baden-Powell, in establishing the rules of *Scouting for Boys*, cite Kim as "well worth reading," because it demonstrates "what valuable work a boy scout could do for his country if he were sufficiently trained and sufficiently intelligent" (19). At the same time that these children's stories defined for at least a generation of British readers the increasingly troubled relation between themselves and the imperial periphery, *The Jungle Books* and *Kim* number among Kipling's most enduring, least controversial work.

Domesticating empire, they share an unlikely project with Victorian domestic discourse. Between metropole and periphery, cookery books proliferated in both directions, keeping Angels in the House and aspiring *memsahibs* alike apprised of increasingly complicated standards of civil behavior that reified anxieties about an empire that, as the Cambridge historian J. R. Seeley famously phrased it, had expanded "in a fit of absence of mind" (8). An eloquent champion of Britain's imperialist project, Seeley was by no means alone in the scramble to make sense of pursuing empire for the sake of empire. Coinciding with such instances of national reflection, many of these mass-produced late-Victorian cookery books vacillated between taking advantage of the Empire's bounty by incorporating far-flung ingredients and techniques or preserving authentically English (or at least European) gastronomic practices. In nurseries throughout Britain and its empire, boys were socialized by women who themselves were socialized by a domestic discourse that emphasized ever more intricate rules for civilized behavior. Exhibiting the public face of private life, the dining room evolved into a masculine space, the stage upon which men enacted the rules cookery books and household guides dictated to women, as Judith Flanders demonstrates in her exposé *Inside the Victorian Home* (254; see also 269–281). Late-Victorian domestic discourse thus throws into intriguing relief scenes of eating in Kipling's beloved tales about boys for boys. Suffused with lessons about the rules and rituals of eating, these adventures of what Don Randall terms "imperial boys" seek to codify and reinforce an etiquette of Empire whose administration had become increasingly volatile.

Here it is worth remembering that the so-called Mutiny in India had erupted over an extreme variation on etiquette, which arose from gastronomic scruples governed by religion and caste. The new Enfield rifle, it was rumored, used cartridges that were greased with pork and beef fat and were thus unclean to the Muslim and Hindu troops who had to bite the ends off the cartridges before using them. Moreover, the lore surrounding the insurgency holds that it spread via chapattis, unleavened flatbreads that struck fear into the Anglo-Indian settlers. Indeed, the "mutiny narratives" that became such a sensation in Britain seldom fail to mention "a mysterious affair about some chupatties" (Coopland 70). By the *fin de siècle*, when Kipling published his allegories of the event for children, the Mutiny was old, yet still-disturbing news, along with the distinctions between gastronomic scruples that had become a shorthand for India's inscrutability. The action of *Kim* takes place in the 1880s, when the insurrections would have been within the memories of its characters but not its young readers. The same might be said of *The Jungle Books*, which, on confusing occasion, exempt the Englishman from the jungle's laws. In "Her Majesty's Servants," the last story from the first *Jungle Book* and one that does not mention Mowgli, an Englishman's eating habits make him an object of fear. Fluent in "beast talk" (136), Dick Cunliffe makes a neat analogy to Mowgli. But where Mowgli "obey[s] faithfully" the Law that he "must never kill or eat any cattle young or old" (10), Dick is held to no such scruples. In fact, he is unaware of them. Exempt from the Law of the Jungle while enforcing Her Majesty's laws there, he stands in for the English. A frightened bullock reveals "What's the matter with white men?" Almost epiphanically does Dick realize, "We eat beef—a thing that no cattle-driver [that is, a *native* cattle driver] touches—and of course the cattle do not like it" (138). It is likely, however, that Kipling's young reader at home in Britain would not have found the bullock's disclosure to be the revelation it is to Dick Cunliffe.

By then, India's tortuous etiquettes were far-famed and longstanding. Yet, as late as 1891, three years before the first *Jungle Book* appeared, Mrs. Grace Johnson still saw fit to instruct would-be *memsahibs* in the bewildering varieties of Indian eating habits:

> [I]t must be also remembered that the mode of cookery varies in India according to the castes or religions. For instance, a Hindoo will live on vegetables, rice, wheat, pease, ghee, fruit, milk, &c., &c., while a Mussulman uses meat freely. The Anglo-Indian style is a modification, and partly added to by French and Italian methods, so as to please the European palate. (Johnson n.p.)

At the same time that she suggests that the visitor should take for granted that Indian food would be adapted to a European palate (not to mention her inaccurate observation about Muslims), Johnson nonetheless encourages awareness of local distinctions, which she neither ridicules nor dismisses, and which were by no means new. In fact, British contact with India had had a long history of stimulating debate over the moral dimensions of European eating habits. Until the seventeenth century, it was commonly assumed that herbivorous humans had not existed since before the fall of Adam and Eve, when God gave them dominion over the beasts. Tristram Stuart's recent, sprawling cultural history of vegetarianism reveals how contact with India shocked European travelers into "a crisis in conscience," because their own carnivorous diets seemed to deny them the moral superiority they had always assumed over the world's benighted peoples (xx).

Despite indications of sophistication in India, it was nonetheless still commonly accepted that India was "great, grey, formless" (142)—a muddle—as

Figure 8.1 "Our Cook Room" and "Our Burra Khana," plates 34 and 23, respectively, in George Francklin Atkinson, *Curry and Rice (on Forty Plates)* (1858). Note the contrasts in setting and lighting, as well as the distance between the "plates" within the volume.

even Kipling puts it in *Kim*. In *The Jungle Books*, as Don Randall argues, the "anarchic community" of the grey apes makes them analogous to Indian "village society" (76). Their indiscriminate eating habits indicate just how far beyond the pale of jungle society they are. Their manners are as chaotic as their diet. As *memsahibs'* "companions" and cookery books multiplied, they promoted generalizations about Indian diets that confirmed the perception of India as muddle. Even as settlers generalized regional dishes and adapted them to placate British palates, the variety of culinary and gastronomic habits of this colony was assumed to be, and popularized as, an index to a disordered, essentially Indian character. *The Wife's Help to Indian Cookery* (1888) typifies this conflation. Its author, W. H. Dawe, an Allahabad tax collector, seems to have needed no greater claim to culinary authority than having "had the advantage of intercourse with those best experienced in the subject" in the form of "several Anglo-Indian families." Prefaced by the assertion that "Nothing is so Lovely in Woman as her Study of the Household," the volume numbers among the more bizarre performances in what was often an already irrationally xenophobic genre. A chapter titled "Wifie's Help" avers,

> It cannot be denied that eating and drinking is far from being observed as an art in India. Dinners are disfigured by a useless proportion, an absurd piling together of dishes, and no single guest ever makes an acquaintance with more than half the good things offered to him. It may, no doubt, be urged on the other side that it is well to provide a variety from which a judicious selection may be made; but amid an excessive variety the will is puzzled and the judgment confused. (Dawe 2)

Dawe subscribes to a facile trope. For him, the "useless proportion," "absurdity," and "excess" of the Indian palate are indicative of a "puzzled" and "confused" society.

Immediately after the Mutiny, the contrasting assumptions about India underlying Johnson's and Dawe's guides to women setting up households there had already collided in one contradictory volume: George Francklin Atkinson's *Curry and Rice (on Forty Plates) or the Ingredients of Social Life at "Our Station" in India*. Written and illustrated by Atkinson, a captain in the Bengal Engineers, and dedicated to William Makepeace Thackeray, the volume belongs to a Victorian genre that packaged picturesque Indian life for consumption by Britons at home. Figuring the entire subcontinent as an exotic yet familiar banquet of comestibles, the title alone invites just this sort of domestic consumption, as the volume goes on, rather tediously, to elaborate a conceit that puns on the lithograph plates and highly seasoned life they supposedly picture. Numerous personages including Major Garlic, Judge Turmeric, and Lord Coriander maintain order over "Our Station" at "Kabob," an order made urgently relevant by the volume's publication date, 1858, which coincides with the post-Mutiny transfer of control over the subcontinent to the Crown.

As if to promote this illusion of order, *Curry and Rice* constructs the English dinner as somehow baffling to the natives whose culture and cuisine are humorously offered up as "ours" to readers at home. The colonials' meals are prepared by native cooks in "Our Cook Room" (34), depicted as a dark, primitive space far removed from "the scenes of spotless purity" that surely characterize "our kitchens" at home.[1] (See Figure 8.1.) Despite this contrast, and fortunately for the transplanted English diner, no trace of either "our" cook room or the "Eastern Soyers" who toil within remains at the site of consumption. In "Our Burra Khana," "literally a grand feed" (23), only the lithograph's exotic title and the attendants it pictures indicate that the grand feed is taking place anywhere but in an English dining room. (See Figure 8.1.) As Atkinson's narrator boasts, the native cook "can and does, with equal facility, dress a dinner in a tented field," providing for the *sahib* "the certainty of as excellent a dinner as ever graced his table in the land of the West" (34). Allowed no identity except for an ancillary association with food, the Indian becomes an invisible instrument for reproducing England in India. This transformation analogously bears out Anne McClintock's argument that the Victorian cult of domesticity effaced the working-class woman, on whose labor the illusion of the leisurely middle-class housewife depended (163–173). In *Curry and Rice*, Indian men replace working-class women on the invisible margin.

Visible Indians, by contrast, are baffled by the mysteries of English cuisine. To those consuming *Curry and Rice* at home, "Our Nuwab" (nabob) must have cut a comfortingly ridiculous figure. Despite his "taste for English sports and pastimes," this Brahmin can never master the vagaries of English tastes, let alone table manners. At his table,

> Lobsters and "tart fruits" commingle, while truffled sausages and sugared almonds share mutually the same dish. . . . the table slaves of his highness are not adepts at Christian cookery, and trifling irregularities greet the senses. The salad indicates the presence of cod-liver oil, and we have faint suspicions that "Day and Martin" [a popular brand of shoe blacking] has been introduced as a sauce. (Atkinson 29)

"The table slaves of his highness" would do well to consult the "Eastern Soyers" of "Our Cook Room." As this culinary disparity suggests, what eludes the Brahmin is readily available to Atkinson's implied "us," the Englishman abroad.

Such characterizations throw into bold (if not spicy) relief *The Jungle Books'* condemnation of "the eaters of everything," whose indiscriminate eating is analogous to the chaos that so many Anglo-Indian settlers associated with India after the Mutiny. It is, after all, the lame and regally named tiger Shere Khan who introduces Mowgli to the Seeoni wolf pack, claiming the right to eat "the man cub." Even more unthinkable than "our" Nuwab's use of Day and Martin's shoe blacking as a sauce, Shere Khan's obscene appetites, like those of the grey apes, ostracize him from jungle society. Unable to hunt honorably, Shere Khan hunts and eats cattle, the first beast that Mowgli "faithfully" learns to spare, not least because of its Hindu associations. More-over, the tastes of the "lame butcher" (6) suggest his degeneracy, confirming the "true" lore "that man-eaters become mangy, and lose their teeth" (3). By contrast, the bear Baloo "can come and go where he pleases because he eats only nuts and roots and honey" (8). Baloo's privilege within jungle society is a direct consequence of his gastronomic conduct. Those who observe rules rule. As W. W. Robson observes in his introduction to the Oxford edition, Kipling's young readers would have recognized in the gastronomically disci-plined Baloo an English "schoolmaste[r] in animal costume" (xviii). Just as Kim's eating of India acquaints him so intimately with the subcontinent that his Buddhist *lama* exclaims, "no white man knows this land as thou knowest" (129), so Mowgli's principal means of initiation into the Law of the Jungle occurs by way of his stomach: "And he grew and grew strong as a boy must grow who does not know he is learning any lessons, and who has nothing in the world to think of except things to eat" (10).

Despite their loose arrangement—as a collection of short stories inter-spersed with verse, and intermittently unified by the motif of Mowgli's adventures—*The Jungle Books* do cohere remarkably in their emphasis on gas-tronomic rules and distinctions. Given this recurrent motif, it should come as no surprise that one of the poems, significantly titled "The Law of the Jungle," should emphasize the rules of eating:

> Remember the Wolf is a hunter—go forth and get food of thine own.
> * * *
> The Kill of the Pack is the meat of the Pack. Ye must eat where it lies;
> And no one may carry away of that meat to his lair, or he dies.
> The kill of the Wolf is the meat of the Wolf. He may do what he will.
> But, till he has given permission, the Pack may not eat of that Kill. (166–167)

Nothing could be more foreign—or familiar—to the Victorian interior.

Decades before Mowgli and Kim began to captivate British boys by laying down the Law, their mothers and grandmothers had experienced an obsessive refinement of the rules governing the conduct of a middle-class home. As Eliz-abeth Driver has shown in her exhaustive catalogue of cookery books, recipes and table manners had never before attracted the scrutiny they would among the late Victorians. In these publications, etiquette becomes a synonym for civilized behavior and a metonym for civilization itself. Authored primarily by what Sarah Stickney Ellis had celebrated as "the women of England," whether Angels in Victorian houses or *memsahibs* abroad, cookery books codified the etiquette worthy of a great civilization. Because of them, perhaps, do the Brit-ish remain the exemplar of civilized behavior. Even the most modest British house can do its part. Despite its modest size and its ostensibly modest subject,

Jessie Conrad's *Handbook of Cookery for a Small House* manages pronouncements of magisterial proportions. Quotidian "heroism" involving "simple but scrupulous care in all the processes in making food ready for consumption" would, in her system, defeat the "evil" represented by "the smell of cooking" (Conrad 1–2, vii–viii). In edicts reminiscent of the Old Testament, the imperious little volume commands, among other things, that

> No saucepan should be allowed of course to boil over.
> No frying pan should ever be put on the fire without the butter or lard being first placed in it, and that not before the pan is required for use.
> No joint should be placed in the oven so high as to allow the fat to splutter against the roof of the oven.
> No joint should be baked in a tin which is too small for it.
> No vegetables should be cooked without a sufficient amount of water in the saucepan and no green vegetables should be cooked with the lid on.
> No frying pan while in use should be allowed to remain on the fire with only the fat in it. A piece of whatever you are frying, bacon, fish, fritters should be left in till another piece is placed in the fat.
> The pan must be removed directly finished with. (2)

And so on. Conrad's handbook is notable not for its commandments or their hyperbole, but for its preface. Jessie Conrad was married to Joseph Conrad, whose *Heart of Darkness* numbers among the master narratives of Empire. Undeservedly forgotten, Joseph Conrad's curious preface to his wife's cookery book declares cookery books "the only product of the human mind altogether above suspicion," and "the inhabitants of the little houses . . . the arbiters of the nation's destiny" (vii–viii).

That the Conrads agreed on this of all matters is not surprising. Jessie Conrad's hyperbole belonged to what, by 1923, was a familiar idiom in domestic discourse. Those unfamiliar with Victorian cookery books may be surprised at the range of conduct they encompass, as well as the nationalistic—even militaristic—tone adopted by the most popular examples. Much depended upon dinner, after all. For all her grand plans regarding Borrioboola-Gha and her ability to "see nothing nearer than Africa," Mrs. Jellyby's inability to get dinner to the table either cooked or on time in Charles Dickens's *Bleak House* speaks volumes about her philanthropic projects for "the Dark Continent." In fact, Dickens's readers in 1853 would have instantly recognized in her dismal skills at household management a satire of Great Britain on the eve of the New Imperialism, which in the last quarter of the century would culminate in the infamous Scramble for Africa. Such moments of political upheaval stimulate national reflection, whose rhetoric influences the most ordinary varieties of personal behavior. Following the 1857 Mutiny, a proliferation of cookery books formed a united front of disciplined domesticity among the rising middle classes. Perhaps not coincidentally, these remain institutions of

British domesticity. The 1865 edition of Eliza Acton's *Modern Cookery for Private Families* (1845) exhorts "the Young Housekeepers of England" to perfect their skills in order to feed the men "to whose indefatigable industry we are mainly indebted for our advancement in science, in art, in literature, and in general civilization," whereas Isabella Beeton's opening salvo in her 1861 *Book of Household Management* famously likens "the mistress of the house" to "the commander of an army" (Acton viii; Beeton 1).

Extending Edward Said's observations in *Culture and Imperialism* about novels as vehicles for imperialist ideology, late-Victorian children's adventures and their mothers' cookery books make a potent fusion for promoting this ideology to an Empire in its waning stages. Kipling's young readers delighted in his wholesomely violent adventures, but their mothers had already experienced an extensive indoctrination in the rules of eating. Condemning the excesses of the grey apes and Shere Khan, *The Jungle Books* resonate with Alexis Soyer's celebrated exhortations to thrift, as well as Maria Rundell's earlier injunctions against "excessive luxury, such as essence of ham, and that wasteful expenditure of large quantities of meat for gravy, which so greatly contributes to keep up the price, and is no less injurious to abstain" (Rundell n.p.; Soyer 5).

Both converge on what Lord Baden-Powell called "the home-front," on which British manhood was socialized in service of the Empire. It is perhaps worth noting, then, that Kipling invented Mowgli's and Kim's gastronomic initiations while he was struggling to set up a household for his young family. Despite his early fame and success, the collapse of the Oriental Banking Company cut short the Kiplings' honeymoon and forced them to improvise domesticity among the American bride's family at Bliss Cottage in Brattleboro, Vermont, an unlikely place for the composition of *The Jungle Books*. The refinements of their etiquettes in *Kim* were made among Kipling's family in Torquay, Devonshire, where the young family fled after a sensationally publicized and litigated quarrel with his in-laws. The same years saw annual holidays in Cape Town, South Africa, as well as the births of two daughters and a son. All the while, as he would claim in his posthumous memoir, *Something of Myself*, "at the back of my head there was an uneasiness, based on things that men were telling me about affairs outside England" (Kipling 86). Whether they occurred in South Africa or India, those affairs inevitably returned to England, even if Kipling himself did not. Though occurring on the other side of the globe, the India Mutiny provoked anxieties that traveled far and lasted long, reaching into the intimate corners of late-Victorian life in cookery and writing for children, both relatively new forms of publication that reflected Britain's turn inward as its national interests expanded ever outward. These intersect in unlikely ways in Kipling's narratives of imperial boys, allegories of empire by the Bard of Empire.

Notes

1   George Francklin Atkinson, *Curry and Rice (on Forty Plates), or the Ingredients of Social Life at "Our Station" in India* (London: John B. Day, 1858). New Delhi's Asian Educational Services issued a facsimile in 1999. Because the volume is unpaginated, further references to it will indicate the plate numbers and their accompanying text.

Works Cited

Acton, Eliza. *Modern Cookery for Private Families, Reduced to a System of Easy Practice in a Series of Carefully Tested Receipts, in which the Principles of Baron Liebig and Other Eminent Writers Have been as Much as Possible Applied and Explained.* London: Longman, 1865.

Atkinson, George Francklin. *Curry and Rice (on Forty Plates), or the Ingredients of Social Life at "Our Station" in India.* 1858. London: Day. Facsimile, New Delhi: Asian Educational Services, 1999.

Baden-Powell, Robert. *Scouting for Boys.* 1908. Mineola, NY: Dover, 2007.

Beeton, Isabella. *Mrs. Beeton's Book of Household Management.* London: Beeton, 1861.

Brantlinger, Patrick. *Rule of Darkness.* Ithaca, NY: Cornell UP, 1988.

Conrad, Jessie. *A Handbook of Cookery for a Small House.* London: Heinemann, 1923.

Coopland, Rebecca M. *A Lady's Escape from Gwalior and Life in the Fort of Agra during the Mutinies of 1857.* London: Smith, 1857.

Dawe, W. H. *The Wife's Help to Indian Cookery: Being a Practical Manual for Housekeepers.* London: Elliot Stock, 1888.

Driver, Elizabeth. *A Bibliography of Cookery Books Published in Britain, 1875–1914.* London: Prospect, 1989.

Ellis, Sarah Stickney. *The Women of England: Their Social Duties and Domestic Habits, by Mrs Ellis.* London: Fisher, 1845.

Flanders, Judith. *Inside the Victorian Home: A Portrait of Domestic Life in Victorian England.* 2003. New York: Norton, 2004.

Johnson, Grace. *Anglo-Indian and Oriental Cookery by Mrs. Grace Johnson.* London: Allen, 1891.

Kipling, Rudyard. *The Jungle Books.* 1894–1895. Ed. W. W. Robson. Oxford: Oxford UP, 1987.

———. *Kim.* 1901. Ed. Edward Said. London: Penguin, 1987.

———. *Something of Myself for Friends Known and Unknown.* 1937. Ed. Thomas Pinney. Cambridge, UK: Cambridge UP, 1990.

McClintock, Anne. *Imperial Leather: Race, Gender, and Sexuality in the Colonial Conquest.* New York: Routledge, 1995.

Mohanty, S. P. "Kipling's Children and the Colour Line," *Race and Class* 31 (1989): 21–40.

Randall, Don. *Kipling's Imperial Boy: Adolescence and Cultural Hybridity.* New York: Palgrave, 2000.

Rundell, Maria. "Advertisement," *Domestic Cookery for the Use of Private Families.* 1807. Halifax, Can.: Milner, 1860.

Said, Edward. *Culture and Imperialism.* New York: Knopf, 1993.

Seeley, Sir John Robert. *The Expansion of England: Two Courses of Lectures.* Boston: Roberts, 1883.

Sharpe, Jenny. *Allegories of Empire: The Figure of Woman in the Colonial Text.* Minneapolis: U of Minnesota P, 1993.

Soyer, Alexis Benoît. *A Shilling Cookery for the People, Embracing an Entirely New System of Plain Cookery, and Domestic Economy.* London: Routledge, 1854.

Stuart, Tristram. *The Bloodless Revolution: A Cultural History of Vegetarianism from 1600 to Modern Times.* 2006. New York: Norton, 2007.

Chapter Nine
Eating Different, Looking Different: Food in Asian American Childhood

Lan Dong

Tell me what you eat and I will tell you who you are.
— Jean Anthelme Brillat-Savarin (3)

If you are what you eat, then what am I?

—Geeta Kothari (91)

1933, San Francisco, California: 11-year-old Jade Snow Wong began to take charge of grocery shopping and to help with the cooking of three meals a day for her family of three adults and three young children. Every weekday, after she came home from American day school and before she went to Christian Chinese evening school, Jade Snow would use the daily budget of fifty cents to purchase a small chicken, three bunches of Chinese greens, three whole Rex soles or sand dabs, and about a half pound of pork (Wong 54).

1942, Manzanar, California: 7-year-old Jeanne Wakatsuki was horrified when she saw that in her newly received army mess kit the syrup from a scoop of canned apricots was seeping through her little mound of overcooked steamed rice served beside canned Vienna sausage and string beans (Houston and Houston 20). After her mother jabbed her in the back, Jeanne was not able to complain or protest, yet this scene would linger in her memory for a long time.

As the memoirs above suggest, children's literature as well as literary texts about childhood are frequently "filled with food-related images, notions, and values: hospitality, gluttony, celebration, tradition, appetite, obesity" (Katz 192). These two scenarios are examples in which Chinese and Japanese American children have come to terms with their ethnic identity through food consumption as well as through cooking and dining customs. When the authors, Jade Snow Wong and Jeanne Wakatsuki Houston, later revisit their respective girlhoods in writing, the images of particular food and mealtime practices stand out in their memories.

Martin Manalansan points out that "food has long been considered a vehicle for remembrance, as Proust and his madeleines have shown us" (362). Recollecting the shock of seeing the pink, shiny, and fishy-smelling canned tuna that is so different from her schoolmates' tuna sandwiches, Geeta Kothari confesses her childhood resentment towards her immigrant parents because they fail to provide "the clues to proper behavior: what to eat and how to eat it" (92). What her parents lack, of course, is the "clues to proper behavior" in America. Whenever the family visits relatives back in New Delhi and Bombay, her parents know all the rules about food and eating. Echoing Kothari's childhood anecdote, Anita Mannur recollects that the "Indianized" spicy yellow tuna fish sandwiches that her mother made for her school lunches, though initially surprising her, later become her comfort food and mark a "particular food-mediated racial tension" ("Introduction" 210). Furthermore, essays collected in the 2004 special issue of *Massachusetts Review—Food Matters* (45.3) imagine how "food consolidates ethnic identity" (Mannur, "Introduction" 215). In terms of Asian American food customs, writings that appeared in the 2006 special issue of *Amerasia Journal—Asian Americans on Meat versus Rice* (32.2), whose title takes a cue from Samuel Gompers and Herman Gutstadt's 1908 publication, "Meat vs. Rice: American Manhood Against Asiatic Cooliehood," explore the cultural and political meanings of food within and outside of Asian American communities.

Exploring further this scholarly lead on food and ethnic identity, the following discussion examines how American-born children of Asian descent understand their identity and bicultural heritage through the culinary habits that they adopt in childhood from their families. In particular, it explores how food functions as a complex signifier in representing Chinese and Japanese American identity through analyzing two memoirs about girlhood told from the child narrators' points of view: Jade Snow Wong's *Fifth Chinese Daughter* (1950) and Jeanne Wakatsuki Houston and James D. Houston's *Farewell to Manzanar: A True Story of Japanese American Experience during and after the World War II Internment* (1973).

Jade Snow Wong's autobiography, told as a third-person narrative in order to conform to the Chinese tradition, records the first twenty-four years of the author's life. Born and raised in a Christian Chinese immigrant family in San Francisco's Chinatown from the 1920s to the 1940s, the narrator, Jade Snow, displays little confusion about her identity in her recollection. From early childhood, Jade Snow primarily defines who she is through her home

Proustian Madeleine: expression used to describe smell, tastes, sounds or any sensations reminding you of childhood.

Marcel Proust.

rearing, which follows traditional Chinese culture: she is the fifth Chinese daughter born in America to immigrant parents. In particular, Chinese food and food-related activities filter through Jade Snow's narrative about her girlhood and young adulthood. They serve as important symbols that mark her ethnic identity, whether Jade Snow lives at home or in American households. Because she takes care of the daily meals for the whole family at a young age, her childhood is centered, between classes, in the Chinatown grocery shops and in her parents' kitchen. Food and proper food preparation appear to be significant ways of fulfilling Jade Snow's duty as a filial and well-behaved Chinese American daughter. When, as a teenager, she moves out of her parents' house to pursue her college education, her ability to entertain her American acquaintances with homemade Chinese food proves to be an important means by which she establishes her social life beyond the confines of the Chinese American community.

Even though college education and housekeeping jobs provide the opportunity for Jade Snow to live outside Chinatown and see more of "American society," the culinary practices that she acquired in girlhood remain consistent along with her self-identification as an American-born Chinese daughter. Therefore, it is not surprising that in the young narrator's understanding, food—including the ways of cooking, serving, and eating—is embedded with cultural meanings and her personal identity. As the author points out in her introduction to the 1989 reprinted edition: "food, family, and endurance (in that order) characterize Chinese consciousness" (Wong viii). Thus, in this autobiography, the narrator Jade Snow's Chinese heritage is portrayed particularly through the meticulous description of Chinese food, food preparation, and food-related activities.

Fifth Chinese Daughter covers a time span of the author's life from girlhood to young adulthood with a consistent narrative about specific food that symbolizes her Chinese identity, but Jeanne Wakatsuki Houston's memoir, *Farewell to Manzanar*, focuses on one particular time period—the three and a half years that her family spent in the internment camp during World War II—as well as its far-reaching influences on her childhood, her whole life, and her kin. The main character, Jeanne, relates her narrative from a girl's perspective. The change in the Wakatsukis' family life is embodied by the altered mealtime practices before, during, and after the internment. More specifically, as a child in the Manzanar relocation camp, Jeanne has noted how much the changes of food and dining patterns modify her family relationships and her own identity. Living in a predominantly white neighborhood and being the only "oriental" student in her class, Jeanne does not really identify herself as Japanese American in the pre-internment years. When she is put, for an extended time, in an isolated Japanese American community at Manzanar, surrounded by barbed-wire fence and guard towers, she is forced to reconsider who she is.

On a psychological level, "food and language are the cultural traits humans learn first, and the ones that they change with the greatest reluctance. . . . the food they ate as children forever defines familiarity and comfort" (Gabaccia 6). As one of the victims of wartime hysteria and paranoia during World War II, young Jeanne loses access to the familiar comfort food that she was accustomed to in Manzanar. Homemade Japanese dishes that her mother used to prepare turn into strange combinations such as steamed rice with sweets. The whole family sitting together around the big dining table and cozily enjoying dinner is replaced by members scattered to different places. Once the family unit falls apart, it is hard to return to the nice old times. The Wakatsukis never resume the way of eating together as one family even after the evacuation ends shortly after the war is over; neither are the closeness and intimacy among family members restored. When Manzanar is closed, some older siblings already have moved to the East Coast. The rest of the family has to start from scratch.

When Jeanne started working on this memoir with her husband, James D. Houston, they set as their mission to tell people that "what actually went on inside . . . [was] a good deal more than day-to-day life inside the compound" (Houston and Houston ix–x). Jeanne's retrospective observations of her childhood in Manzanar use food as an important signifier for the young narrator to realize her Japanese American identity as an individual and to represent Japanese American internment experience as a community member.

Just as the bagel has become "an icon of urban, northeastern eating, a key ingredient of the multi-ethnic mix . . . known as 'New York deli'" in the twentieth century (Gabaccia 3), rice routinely plays a crucial role in indicating Asian identity. Since the early nineteenth century, Asian Americans have been connected with their foodways in literary and other popular discourses in the United States (Mannur, "Asian-American Food-Scapes" 3). In particular, rice as the staple food in many countries in Asia as well as Asian American communities continues to serve as a core metaphor for Asian American identity. In both *Fifth Chinese Daughter* and *Farewell to Manzanar*, rice is the central metaphor by which Jade Snow and Jeanne absorb their respective cultural heritages and become aware of their ethnic identities. When Jade Snow is still in grade school, she already has attained the key value of rice in her family's daily diet. Using her mother's words, Jade Snow tells the reader: at all times get the rice on the stove first, because if the rice is cooked well, "the other accompaniments are secondary. But if the rice is underdone or improperly cooked, the most delicious meat or vegetables cannot make up for it. The reputation of a good cook begins with good rice" (Wong 57). Not only does rice always receive first attention in her family when it comes to meal preparation, but cooking rice is so essential that her father stands 6-year-old Jade Snow on a stool at the kitchen sink and teaches her the skills and steps for making "faultless rice" (Wong 57), despite the fact that her mother usually takes care of the household chores. Because of the crucial position rice holds in the Wong family, purchasing rice is never part of Jade Snow's daily shopping routine. Rather, it is such an important household matter that it requires the talent of both her parents.

In her recollection, Jade Snow gives a lengthy description of how her parents purchase the right kind of rice in bulk, imported from China after careful comparison and selection of the rice dealer's samples, how she learns to measure the correct amount for each meal, as well as how to properly wash and cook rice. Even as a young child, Jade Snow gains the knowledge that "the principal accomplishments or requirements of any Chinese female" is washing the rice appropriately (Wong 57). She depicts the procedure:

> It was first dampened with a little water, then rubbed for a while with both hands (if you were a child like Jade Snow) or with one hand (if you were a grownup). White starch would come off the rice and bleed into the water. You rinsed after the thorough first rubbing of about a hundred strokes. Then rub, scrub, and rinse again. Rub, scrub, and rinse again. Then rinse, rinse, rinse. Three scrubbings; six rinsings; these were the minimum treatments. When the water came out clear, the rice had been thoroughly cleansed. (Wong 58)

Such careful treatment that involves multiple rubbing, scrubbing, and rinsing is just one step in preparing the rice correctly in the Wong household. Resulting from an equally cautious and delicate cooking process in a pot with a tightly fitting lid, the ideal rice would end up as tender, smooth, snowy, fluffy, and separate morsels within half an hour (Wong 58). This formula for flawless rice is only part of the comprehensive cooking ritual that Jade Snow has to learn, practice, and internalize in everyday life at a young age and carries on into her adulthood. When she moves out of her parents' house for work and education in her teenage years, homemade Chinese foods and her ability to cook them continue to function as significant symbols of her Chinese heritage and a way to introduce Chinese culture to her non-Chinese social connections and activities. Later on, when Jade Snow starts to raise her own family, she usually helps her own children with their homework in the kitchen while cooking and is proud of the fact that all her sons and daughters are "able to create delicious innovations at the wok" (Wong viii).

Food, as Rüdiger Kunow contends, always functions as a representation: it "not only feeds but also organizes us"; "the making, taking, and disposing of aliments are socially and culturally inflected" (151). If the knowledge of shopping for the right kinds of groceries and cooking skills that Jade Snow obtained in childhood are part of her Chinese training at home during her preteen years, they turn out to be helpful tools in establishing her social life outside Chinatown later on. After finishing a two-year education at a junior college in San Francisco, Jade Snow has the privilege of going to the prestigious Mills College in Oakland, California, with a full scholarship and a work-study position. She lives in and maintains the undergraduate dean's house in order to defray her living expenses. During her coming of age, Chinese cuisine evolves as an important element for Jade Snow's social connections, even though she has to miss the experience of living in a residential hall on campus. In the dean's Kapioani house, she prepares for her college friends a delicious homemade meal of steamed rice, egg foo young with ham and celery, and tomato beef. During summer vacation, the dean asks her to cook a Chinese dinner for a world-famous United States string quartet. With the whole-hearted support from her family, the dishes served as buffet—sweet-and-sour pineapple pork, bean sprouts with beef served with cooked rice, and Chinese melon soup—make a splash among the musicians. Such social occasions lead to Jade Snow's further contemplation of the different aspects of Chinese culture and her unique identity as a Chinese American daughter. Living away from home gives Jade Snow an opportunity to review her Chinese education and home rearing from a distance and also provides a comparative framework for the reader to see the differences as well as similarities between Eastern and Western cultures. Introducing Chinese food to non-Chinese acquaintance outside the Chinatown community with success indicates the possibility of combining Chinese-ness and American-ness in her own identity without creating tension or conflict. The co-existence of the narrator's bi-cultural heritage is an important message in Wong's memoir and is partly responsible for its appeal to the readers.

If Jade Snow's narrative contains a fairly consistent image of Chinese cuisine in her life within and outside the Wongs' family house in San Francisco's Chinatown, Jeanne Wakatsuki Houston's story in *Farewell to Manzanar* sheds more light on the change of food and dining practice for the Wakatsukis in the 1940s. Before the FBI took away her father in December of 1941 shortly after Pearl Harbor, the Wakatsukis live in a big frame house in Ocean Park near Santa Monica and are the only Japanese family in the neighborhood. For the first few years of her life, Jeanne is not fully aware of her Japanese identity and actually develops a fear of "Oriental faces" (Houston and Houston 10–11). She refers to the Japanese American children living down in Terminal Island as tough and mean "ghetto kids" (Houston and Houston 12) and does not associate herself with them. For Jeanne, the Island full of Japanese American residents is "as foreign as India or Arabia would have been" before the evacuation (Houston and Houston 11). The transition from a Caucasian neighborhood to the internment camp in Manzanar comes to mean something different for Jeanne as well as for her mother and elder siblings. Given their problematic positions as prisoners without charges or trials, the adults feel insulted and challenged. All are forced to endure the harsh living conditions in the camp. But to the little girl, the most dramatic change is mealtime. The young narrator tells the reader:

> [before the internment,] mealtime had always been the center of our family scene. In the camp, and afterward, I would often recall with deep yearning the old round wooden table in our dining room in Ocean Park, the biggest piece of furniture we owned, large enough to seat twelve or

thirteen of us at once. A tall row of elegant, lathe-turned spindles separated this table from the kitchen, allowing talk to pass from one room
to the other. Dinners were always noisy, and they were always abundant
with great pots of boiled rice, platters of home-grown vegetables, fish
Papa caught. (Houston and Houston 35)

That this family of thirteen—a grandmother, parents, and ten children (some
already married)—dines together on Japanese cuisine is probably the stron-
gest symbol of family unity that Jeanne, as the youngest child, is able to decipher before the internment. Right after the family is relocated to Manzanar,
she realizes that what to eat and how to eat it have changed dramatically.

The first meal in the Manzanar internment camp shocks 7-year-old Jeanne,
as well as other Japanese Americans present in the mess hall, mainly because
of the way rice is served. In her book, *Voracious Children: Who Eats Whom in
Children's Literature* (2006), Carolyn Daniel reiterates Brillat-Savarin's well-
known statement, as shown in the first epigraph, that "certain foods impart
certain qualities to the eater, that is, you are (or you become) what you eat"
(25). Even though Jeanne is only seven at the time and has never identified
herself as "oriental" before Pearl Harbor, she acquires the knowledge about
food and food serving through everyday consumption in her family life. The
Japanese food served at family gatherings is the indicator that marks her "family's history and difference" (Dong 146). The combination of canned fruit in
syrup poured over rice, as Jeanne explains, might look like an appealing dessert to the Caucasian servers. But Japanese eat rice only with salty or savory
foods, never with sweet things (Houston and Houston 20). Such a mixture as
apricot-rice violates the rules of serving and eating rice for people of Japanese
heritage, and there is no question of it becoming an inedible mess for the
new Manzanar residents in 1942. If "rice has been a dominant metaphor of
the Japanese," as Ohnuki-Tierney has proposed (4–5), then the inappropri-
ately served rice symbolizes the uprooted status of Wakatsuki family and their
Japanese American community.

In actuality, cooking their own meals is out of the question in Manzanar;
there is neither enough room nor the necessary furniture for the family to
dine together. Although there is always enough food to eat in the camp no
matter what is served, people have to stand outside the mess halls in lines in
the biting winter wind or scorching summer sun to get their meals. Shortly
after their arrival, Jeanne, her siblings, mother, and grandmother start to dine
in different places: some eat in the mess halls, some with friends, and others
in their cramped barracks. "Eating is symbolically associated with the most
deeply felt human experiences, and thus expresses things that are sometimes
difficult to articulate in everyday language" (Farb and Armelagos 111). Not
only do Jeanne's parents lose control of what kind of food they eat and how
it is served, but they also cannot hold the family together at mealtime any
longer. A couple of years after the internment began, sociologists noticed the

changes to the Japanese American families and consequently made recommendations for family members to dine together again, but it was too late. "Most people resented this," including Jeanne; "they griped and grumbled" (Houston and Houston 37). The young generations had started to integrate into American foodways and American culture. Later, they are the first batch to leave the camp and to relocate in the East Coast and Midwest when job opportunities open up. During her stay in Manzanar, Jeanne is too young to understand and to articulate the loss of family integrity symbolized by food and dining habits. Nor is she able to comprehend its profound influence on the family structure and the relationships among its members. At the time, Jeanne is a young girl who cares more about the joy in eating in groups with her peers than about the collapse of the integrated family unit. It is not until she reflects as an adult on the internment experience and its aftermath that she yearns for the family "dignity and filial strength" (Houston and Houston 37) embodied by particular food and dining customs that never recover, even many years after the war.

To the question "what is food?" Roland Barthes responds: "[i]t is not only a collection of products that can be used for statistical or nutritional studies. It is also, and at the same time, a system of communication, a body of images, a protocol of usages, situations, and behavior" (21). For the young narrator Jade Snow, food as a communication system, a protocol, and an embodiment of her Chinese identity is consumed on different levels. On the everyday level, her usual school-day breakfast is not cereal, milk, orange juice, toast, pancake, or omelet. Instead, it often includes "fresh-cooked rice, boiled salt fish sprinkled with peanut oil and shredded ginger root, soup with mustard greens, and steamed preserved duck eggs with chopped pork" (Wong 18). In Jade Snow's world, food is not only an important part of people's daily life but also a key element in community activities and celebration in which the group communicates, bonds, and exchanges gifts and blessings with each other. On the level of festival occasions, the act of serving special food at particular events such as the Chinese New Year, Jade's younger brother's birth announcement and full-month feast, as well as her Fourth Older Sister's wedding, integrates various elements of Chinese tradition into her childhood.

Compared to the Wongs' daily routine of steamed marinated chicken (sometimes squabs or salt fish), fried sole with chopped ginger root, greens cooked in soup stock made from sliced pork, and the essential bowls of steamed rice, the seven-day Chinese New Year (usually in February) is blessed with some luxury and specialty foods. It is a time to celebrate the fruitful and blessed past year, to welcome a prosperous coming year, and to relax after working all year. Food, social activities, and entertainment consist of visiting, firecrackers, the lion dance, and gifts—including good-luck packets of money for the children. Household decorations as well as sweetmeats (like candied melon, coconut, kumquats, and lichee nuts) and red melon seeds, a common New Year's treat for visitors, all bear the quality of being propitious because "they meant life, new life, a fruitful life, and a sweet life" (Wong 39). Besides the extra bountiful New Year's dinner with her father's special lichee chicken, a huge roast duck, and a variety of other carefully prepared dishes, Jade Snow and her siblings also enjoy the delicious tidbits exchanged between households in the Chinatown community: sweet puddings (brown sugar, special flour, red dates, and sesame seeds), salty puddings (ground-root flour, fat pork, chopped baby shrimps, mushrooms, red ginger, and parsley), deep-fried dumplings (filled with ground soybeans and rolled in sesame seeds), and tiny turnovers (chopped roast pork, bamboo shoots, spices, and chewy, translucent paste) (Wong 40). All these tasty accompaniments, as the young narrator states, make her feel lucky to be born in the Chinese heritage.

After her younger brother "Forgiveness from Heaven" is born, Jade Snow's family distribute, to their relatives and friends, paper bags filled with the customary delicious announcements, including red eggs, sections of chicken, and slices of pickled white ginger root. The guests who call on her mother are served special pigs' feet vinegar (Wong 25). When the newborn is one month old, the family hosts a big feast with numerous visitors, too many for young Jade Snow to count. Ducks, chickens, squabs, pork, and beef, all cooked with "appropriate spices, seasonings and vegetables," are served side by side with "[l]aughter, excitement, and anticipation (Wong 26). Such a celebration, especially the particular food served, proves to have long-lasting influence on Jade Snow's understanding of Chinese tradition. As a young girl, she may not have the vocabulary to write down the social occasion, but food certainly leaves a mark in her memory. Thereafter whenever there is the smell of the specially prepared pigs-feet vinegar in Chinatown, Jade Snow knows immediately somebody is holding a celebration for a newborn.

If the image of Chinatown and the food it offers in Jade Snow's girlhood remains consistent and indicates her Chinese identity in *Fifth Chinese Daughter*, the food-related prewar social events presented in Jeanne Wakatsuki Houston's *Farewell to Manzanar* embody a nostalgic past that often is in sharp contrast to the present in Manzanar. Even though Jeanne's remembrance focuses mainly on wartime, one single event captures the years prior to the internment and stands out in the young girl's narrative: the silver wedding anniversary that the family celebrates in 1940. Besides the silver gifts her parents receive from guests on that day, then lose during the internment, Jeanne particularly remembers the food served buffet style "in glistening abundance—chicken teriyaki, pickled vegetables, egg rolls, cucumber and abalone salad, the seaweed-wrapped rice balls called sushi, shrimp, prawns, fresh lobster, and finally, taking up what seemed like half the tablecloth, a great gleaming roast pig with a bright red apple in its mouth" (Houston and Houston 57). At that time, the family structure is clear and simple: her father always leads the way. Jeanne presents to the reader in great detail how Papa, a well-dressed fellow and captain of the Wakatsukis, carves the roast pig that indicates the beginning of the feast:

> [H]e lifted a huge butcher's cleaver, and while Goosey and Blackie . . .
> held each side of a long cutting board beneath its neck, Papa chopped
> the head off in two swift, crunching strokes. . . . Three more strokes and
> Papa had the animal split—two sides of roast pork steaming from within.
> With serious face and a high-held, final flick he split each side in half,
> quartering the pig. . . . [A]s he wiped his hands he said imperiously to his
> sons, "Cut it up. You girls, bring the platters here. Everybody wants to
> eat." (Houston and Houston 58)

Following his detention at Fort Lincoln in Bismarck, North Dakota, as a prisoner of war, the patriarchal Papa unfortunately never resumes his position or his character. After he joins the family in Manzanar, he would brew rice wine or canned syrupy fruit brandy and then sip it until he was "blind drunk" (Houston and Houston 65). "Alcoholic" was probably not part of young Jeanne's vocabulary at that time, but Papa's abuse of food and his drinking problem angers her and triggers the family's further breakdown.

According to Adam Gopnik's categorization, Jade Snow Wong belongs to the group of writers "who present on the page not just the result but the whole process—not just what people eat but how they make it, exactly how much garlic is chopped, and how, and when it is placed in the pan" (80). She includes detailed cooking instructions for many of the dishes in her memoir. Moreover, she also suggests possible substitutes in preparing certain dishes and explains to the reader that there is bountiful space in Chinese culinary practice for imagination and personal preferences once a person learns the basic principles.

A huge success right after its publication in 1950, *Fifth Chinese Daughter* not only incurred readers and critics' enthusiasm, but it also caught the attention of the US State Department. The State Department published translations of Jade Snow Wong's book in a number of languages and dialects in Asia and sponsored a four-month tour in 1953 for her to speak to a variety of Asian audiences. This national reception to her work might be related to the positive image that Wong's writing presents about her being an American-born daughter growing up in Chinatown and trained in traditional Chinese customs at home by her rather strict parents and by the Christian Chinese school. After all, this 24-year-old fifth daughter of the Wongs manages to finish college with neither financial support from her family nor loans and to become an up-and-coming pottery artist and enamellist as the book closes.

Compared to the consistent image portrayed in Wong's girlhood recollections in which Chinese food is at the center of her family's and her personal life, the Houstons' memoir leaves the reader to consider what power food has in shaping and changing people's lives. In *Fifth Chinese Daughter*, traditional food is portrayed as being consumed not only on a daily basis and at festive occasions but also as an introduction to Chinese culture to the young narrator's non-Chinese friends. By contrast, in reflections of her girlhood, the narrator of *Farewell to Manzanar* chooses the particular vehicle of food and food serving to articulate the far-reaching, dramatic influence of the internment on her family and her identity. It is the loss of her family's culinary traditions that leads to the breakup of the Wakatsukis' family, whose members head in different directions and, in the process, find their own ways within the context of the internment camp. It is the change of food and dining patterns that forces Jeanne to reconsider her Japanese American identity. Nonetheless, no matter the different roles that food practices take within these two memoirs—whether as a central activity or as a catalyst for uprootedness and change—the Asian American culinary world remains a potent image in the narrators' memories of their girlhoods.

Works Cited

Asian Americans on Meat versus Rice. Spec. issue of *Amerasia Journal* 32.2 (2006).

Barthes, Roland. "Toward a Psychosociology of Contemporary Food Consumption." *Food and Culture: A Reader.* Ed. Carole Counihan and Penny Van Esterik. New York: Routledge, 1997. 20–27.

Brillat-Savarin, Jean Anthelme. *The Physiology of Taste, or Meditations on Transcendental Gastronomy.* 1825. New York: Dover, 1960.

Daniel, Carolyn. *Voracious Children: Who Eats Whom in Children's Literature.* New York: Routledge, 2006.

Dong, Lan. "Turning Japanese, Turning Japanese American: David Mura's *Memoirs of a Sansei.*" *The AnaChronisT* 10 (2004): 143–152.

Farb, Peter, and George Armelagos. *Consuming Passions: The Anthropology of Eating.* Boston: Houghton, 1980.

Food Matters. Spec. issue of *Massachusetts Review* 45.3 (Autumn 2004).

Gabaccia, Donna R. *We Are What We Eat: Ethnic Food and the Making of Americans.* Cambridge, MA: Harvard UP, 1998.

Gopnik, Adam. "Cooked Books: Real Food from Fictional Recipes." *The New Yorker* 9 April 2007: 80–85.

Houston, Jeanne Wakatsuki, and James D. Houston. *Farewell to Manzanar: A True Story of Japanese-American Experience During and After the World War II Internment.* New York: Dell, 1973.

Katz, Wendy R. "Some Uses of Food in Children's Literature." *Children's Literature in Education* 11.4 (1980): 192–199.

Kothari, Geeta. "If You Are What You Eat, Then What Am I?" *The Best American Essays 2000.* Ed. Alan P. Lightman and Robert Atwan. Boston: Houghton, 2000. 91–100.

Kunow, Rüdiger. "Eating Indian(s): Food, Representation, and the Indian Diaspora in the United States." *Eating Culture: The Poetics and Politics of Food.* Ed. Tobias Döring, Markus Heide, and Susanne Mühleisen. Heidelberg, Ger.: Universitätsverlag, 2003. 151–175.

Manalansan, Martin F., IV. "Prairie*scapes*: Mapping Food, Loss, and Longing." *Food Matters.* Spec. issue of *Massachusetts Review* 45.3 (Fall 2004): 361–365.

Mannur, Anita. "Introduction." *Food Matters.* Spec. issue of *Massachusetts Review* 45.3 (Fall 2004): 209–216.

———. "Asian-American Food-Scapes." *Amerasia Journal* 32.2 (2006): 1–5.

Ohnuki-Tierney, Emiko. *Rice as Self: Japanese Identities through Time.* Princeton: Princeton UP, 1993.

Wong, Jade Snow. *Fifth Chinese Daughter.* 1945. Seattle: U of Washington P, 1989.

Chapter Ten

The Potato Eaters: Food Collection in Irish Famine Literature for Children

Karen Hill McNamara

The single most powerful signifier of Irish identity is food. Or, more specifically, lack of food. No other Western country has been so defined, so culturally impacted, and so radically changed from one "food centric" event: the Great Irish Famine of the mid-1800s, also known as the Potato Famine, The Great Hunger, or in Irish, *An Gorta Mor.* The physical and emotional dependence on food is clearly authenticated through contemporary children's literature portraying this catastrophic period. The narratives reveal the horrors of the Great Famine, the relentless hunger, and the quest for food, through the eyes of courageous children determined to survive. These historical novels for children and young adults illustrate the strength and fortitude of these heroes, thus constructing a strong, proud national identity for the Irish and Irish Americans.

In 1845, there were more than eight million people in Ireland, the vast majority of native Irish subsisting almost exclusively on potatoes. Incredibly, the average man consumed seventy potatoes per day, and over fifty years, one man could eat a million potatoes (Feirtear 6–7)! This dependence on a single food had devastating consequences when a catastrophic blight destroyed much of the potato harvests of 1845, 1846, 1848, and 1849. Over this period, an estimated one to one and a half million people died of starvation and disease, and another two million were forced to immigrate to new worlds, mainly to the United States, Britain, Canada, and Australia. Irish Famine historian and scholar Christine Kinealy described the Great Famine as "one of the most lethal famines in modern history, accounting for a loss of 25 percent of the population in Ireland over a period of six years" (2). In fact, sixteen decades have passed since the start of the Great Famine, and yet Ireland's population has never recovered. Ireland remains the only country in Europe with a current population (four million) smaller than it was in 1845 (Ireland). Historians, economists, sociologists, educators, journalists, and politicians have debated the varied and controversial causes for the Irish Famine, but all agree that it is a defining event in Irish history. The consequences of the Great Famine changed more than the course of Irish history; the resulting Irish diaspora affected the shape of world history, especially that of America. There are nearly one hundred million people around the globe who claim some Irish ancestry and, as reported in the 2000 US Federal Census, over thirty million of these are Americans, many of whom are in the United States today as a result of the Famine. The impact of the Great Famine is critical to understanding modern Irish and American history.

Despite the significance of the Great Famine, it has inspired relatively little fictional writing, especially in the domain of juvenile literature.[1] The absence of children's novels in Ireland that sought to educate young people about the Great Famine and its ramifications is ironic, for Ireland is a nation with a world-renowned literary reputation and a passion for history. Recently, many scholars have been addressing this "silence" that seems to have surrounded the Famine.[2] The pathos of suffering and the psychological legacy of diaspora associated with the catastrophe appear to have had long-term consequences on the psyches of Irish and Irish emigrants. The children's novelists I interviewed spoke vehemently about the silence and the Famine's effect on Irish culture.[3] Shame and survival guilt are at the core of this issue. Feelings of deep shame that are associated with being perceived as passive victims, or feelings of guilt that are associated with being perceived as ruthless survivors, have contributed to the sounds of silence. I believe that this ideology influenced children's authors and publishers, resulting in a paucity of books available on the topic for children. Since the commemoration of the 150th anniversary of the Irish Famine in the mid-1990s, the topic has received a dramatic increase in media, literary, and scholarly attention. School systems, reacting to this new public awareness, have started addressing the Great Famine, and today it is taught in every school district in Ireland and is included in many American school curriculums as well. This change has also been reflected in children's literature, as authors from around the world have begun to reconstruct history by producing quality children's literature that depicts this historic and traumatic event.

In the interests of clarity, the following list provides a brief survey of the twenty-four children's and young adult fictional Irish Famine texts I will be discussing in this essay. The novels are presented in alphabetical order by author name; the author's nationality is noted, as are any related sequels.

The Search of Mary Katherine Mulloy by Carole Bolton (American)
The Potato Eaters by Karen Branson (American)
The Haunting of Kildoran Abbey by Eve Bunting (Irish-American)
Rachel LeMoyne by Eileen Charbonneau (American)
Under the Hawthorn Tree by Marita Conlon-McKenna (Irish)
   * *Wildflower Girl*
   * *Fields of Home*
Now, Ameriky by Betty Sue Cummings (American)
So Far from Home by Barry Denenberg (American)
Nory Ryan's Song by Patricia Reilly Giff (Irish-American)
   * *Maggie's Door*
   * *Water Street*
The Famine Secret by Cora Harrison (Irish)
Katie's Wish by Barbara Shook Hazen (Irish-American)
The Grave by James Heneghan (Canadian)
The Hungry Wind by Soinbhe Lally (Irish)
Red Bird of Ireland by Sondra Gordon Langford (American)
The Coldest Winter by Elizabeth Lutzeier (English)
   * *Bound for America*
Knockabeg: A Famine Tale by Mary E. Lyons (Irish-American)
Mary-Anne's Famine by Colette McCormack (Irish)
   * *After the Famine*
Famine by Arthur McKeown (Irish) Dublin
Twist of Gold by Michael Morpurgo (English)
The Irish Dresser: The Story of Hope during The Great Hunger (An Gorta Mor, 1845–1850) by Cynthia G. Neale (American)
A Voyage from Ireland: Fiona McGilray's Story by Clare Pastore (American)
Black Harvest by Ann Pilling (English)
Annie Quinn in America by Mical Schneider (American)
Boston! Boston! by Michael Smith (New Zealander)
How I Survived the Irish Famine by Laura Wilson (English)

Children's writers have imaginatively represented the Irish Famine, bringing the event to life in a way that traditional textbooks cannot. Young people, rarely represented in history books, are the main protagonists in juvenile fiction. Famine novels help young readers understand the greatest crisis in Irish history by personifying it through fictional characters that they can empathize with, thus making the readers connect and identify with the history of the Great Hunger.

The Famine is typically viewed though the eyes of a poor, Irish-Catholic child who is orphaned or has at least one parent dead. The main theme in each of these books is essentially one of survival, escaping starvation and disease, with the storylines often following predictable patterns. Although some novels present the Famine from a slightly nontraditional angle and may insert unique twists and turns in the plot, overall there is a remarkable consistency in the way the catastrophe is portrayed.

Most books introduce the Famine at the start of the narrative, typically with the stench of the rotting potatoes in the field of a small farm, the desperate attempts to salvage any unspoiled potatoes, and the ultimate resignation that blight has occurred. The reader vicariously witnesses the vast hunger the youngster, frequently female, and her family experience as they seek to survive. Most tales contain the historically accurate portrayal of the cruelty meted out to the peasants by the merciless and predatory landlords. Eviction scenes show the suffering and deprivation of thousands who were callously evicted from their homes by English soldiers. Inevitably, the story includes the tumbling of a poor widow's cottage. With their homes demolished, leaving the main character and her family destitute, the quest for food and work begins. There are depictions of wretched laborers working for a pittance and the contemptuous export of corn and cattle from Ireland while the poor starve.

Death is omnipresent. These are not cheery tales, as they deal with cruelty and hardship, and are heart wrenching at times. The young hero often loses her parents and a baby sister to starvation or Famine fever, caused by lack of food. Yet, despite how desperate the situation may appear during the plot, the key to survival is usually found in the predictable escape from Ireland. There is the journey to the docks, usually on foot, where the protagonist has a series of encounters with the starving along the road. Eventually the young woman reaches the docks and makes the horrendous passage to North America in a "coffin ship." These narratives offer the Irish immigrant a fresh start, and the story is able to conclude on a happy or at least hopeful note.

Historical records report that during the potato blight the starving peasants gathered food through any means possible in order to preserve life at all costs. Oftentimes this battle against constant hunger involved drastic measures, many of which are depicted in the children's books. What follows is an examination of the historically accurate representations of food collection that authors have portrayed in books for young readers.

Mouths Stained Green

Consider *Nory Ryan's Song* (2000), the most popular children's Irish Famine novel in North America. Written by two-time Newbery Honor-winner Patricia Reilly Giff, a descendant of Famine immigrants, this ALA Notable Book has been widely distributed in the United States and has sold numerous copies. Giff has written two sequels, *Maggie's Door* (2003) and *Water Street* (2006). In Giff's first Famine story, 12-year-old Nory notices people with "circles of green around their mouths," and when she determines what they are eating she and her younger brother, Patch, immediately join them, "sucking on the blades of grass" (90). Later on in the story Nory observes that "even the grass was sparse because people had pulled up huge clumps to suck on" (110).

The children in *Under the Hawthorn Tree* (1990) by Marita Conlon-McKenna also "chewed grass" (107), and young Kate, in Barbara Shook Hazen's picture book *Katie's Wish,* gathers grass to stretch her "meager meals," but more often this action is witnessed or heard about second hand. In Barry Denenberg's *So Far from Home: The Diary of Mary Driscoll, an Irish Mill Girl* (1997), part of the "Dear America" series, Mary records in her journal seeing a "beggar woman" who "was covered only by a filthy sack and her mouth was stained green from eating grass" (Denenberg 13). In *How I Survived the Irish Famine* (2001) Mary O'Flynn writes that she found two children searching in the dung heap for cabbage stalks and observes that the boy's "mouth was stained green from eating grass" (Wilson 19). In Arthur McKeown's *Famine* (1997), Maggie overhears a fellow ship passenger report, "I saw an old man lying dead in a ditch with bits of grass sticking out of his mouth" (30).

Carole Bolton's novel, *The Search of Mary Katherine Mulloy,* which was published in the United States in 1974 and has the distinction of being the first Irish Famine children's novel published, notes: "We ate nettles; we begged food; sometimes we stole it" (62). In despair, the poor stalked through farmers' fields digging for edible roots and gathering weeds. A passage in *The Coldest Winter* (1991) by British author Elizabeth Lutzeier observes: "He had found some nettles as well, growing in the ruins, and he put them in the pot with some water ... the nettles were bitter and they didn't fill you up, but Eamon wasn't used to eating a full meal any longer" (32). Children's literature portrays how the lack of food became so acute during the crisis that the hungry and desperate people were willing to eat almost anything in an effort to survive. "They chewed on dandelion leaves to fool their stomachs into thinking they were getting a good meal" (Lutzeier 5). The depiction of lips green from eating grass and other weeds is a powerful image in Famine folklore and children's literature.

Bleeding the Cows

As the Irish grew hungrier, they would seek out cows and bleed them, using the blood, rich in iron and protein, for nourishment. These graphic descriptions frequent juvenile Famine novels, as the following passages indicate: "But there are no potatoes, and people are draining blood from the cattle and mixing it with a bit of meal to stay alive" (95–96), in American author Mical Schneider's *Annie Quinn in America* (2001); "A man from Corofin told me his cattle died of weakness because people were coming at night and drawing pints of blood out of them" (16), in Irish writer Cora Harrison's *The Famine Secret* (1998); and "Michael took blood from one of Major Lloyd's cow tonight. He cut the beast's skin, drew a quart of blood and brought it home in a bowl. Mother baked it into a cake. I was glad of it, for we had nothing but nettle soup for five days" (20–21), in British author Laura Wilson's *How I Survived the Irish Famine* (2001).

It is interesting to note that American authors sometimes play to modern sensibilities and present their protagonists reacting to the bleeding with disdain. For example, Mary E. Lyon's character, Eamon, is upset, "his rolling stomach" alerting the reader to how he feels about this practice (45). In *A Voyage From Ireland in 1849* (2001), part of the "Journey to America" series, written by American Clare Pastore, the system of bleeding cows is introduced to the reader and the protagonist at the same time. "Fiona watched in wonder, and a little bit of disgust, as a man made a small cut on the cow's neck. He collected blood in a cup that Ma had brought, and then handed it back to her. Mary was wide-eyed in fascination" (20). A few pages later the reader discovers along with Fiona the reason for this act:

> "Patrick?" she asked quietly. "What was that man doing to our cow today?"
>
> "He was a bleeder, Fiona," Patrick explained. "He knows just how to cut an animal so its blood can be drawn, but it will not suffer at all. Ma . . ."
>
> He stopped a moment and looked down at the ground. Then he took a deep breath and finished quickly, "Ma put the blood in the cabbage water for extra nourishment."
>
> Fiona was so weak, and so hungry, that she didn't even let herself think for a moment what was in her meal that night. (22)

American author, Cynthia G. Neale, has her character, Nora, echo Fiona's sentiments in *The Irish Dresser* (2004). "I'm so hungry, even the thought of drinking blood does not sicken me or anyone standing around watching this strange procedure. I think that the hunger must be making us all crazy in Ireland" (56). From the examples shown above, it seems to me that authors from the United States make the assumption that the hero, and by extension, the American child reader, would share the notion that bleeding cows is unsavory and only used as a measure of last resort.

The writing by Irish author Maria Conlon-McKenna in *Under the Hawthorn Tree*, however, is historically realistic as the protagonists are quite familiar with bleeding cows and see nothing odd about this. Michael tells his sister Eily, "I heard Father tell us stories often enough about times before the potatoes failed and he and his father bled the landlord's cattle" (129). This attitude is more in line with the realities of Ireland in the 1840s, and the novel provides accurate details of how the cow is bled:

> He was patting the cow on the neck and rubbing his hand down her front and side to find a vein. His father had told him that if you hit the main vein by mistake, the animal would bleed to death in a few minutes. He searched around until he found a likely one. Eily passed him the blade.

He made a nick in the finer skin under the neck, but nothing happened. He deepened the cut and a droplet or two of blood appeared. The cow lowed and rolled her frightened eyes. (129)

Conlon-McKenna, cognizant that her young Irish audience is familiar with black (blood) pudding, presents the reaction to bleeding cattle with cultural authenticity, and Eily and Michael, different from Fiona and Nora, are not squeamish about this meal and "swallowed it quickly" (132). *Under the Hawthorn Tree* (1990), a groundbreaking narrative, was the first Irish Famine book published for children in Ireland, 140 years after the catastrophe, and marked the beginning of the Irish exploring the subject for its young people. When I interviewed Conlon-McKenna in Dublin she recounted that book surprised Irish publishers by becoming the most commercially successful Irish novel for children, winning countless international awards and resulting in two sequels (Conlon-McKenna 2001). Conlon-McKenna has created "Children of the Famine" trilogy that includes *Wildflower Girl* (1991) and *Fields of Home* (1996).

Eating Dogs

In addition to bleeding cows and eating grass, several novelists include the killing and eating of unconventional animals in the battle against starvation. The overwhelming hunger reduced people to eating mice, rabbits, badgers, birds, and even horses, donkeys, cats, and dogs (Bartoletti 94). There are a number of points to be made about the treatment of dogs in the Famine stories. Although a main character is not shown consuming a dog, the practice is often referenced in the children's literature. In *The Search of Mary Katherine Mulloy,* the reader is informed about "reports of people eating rats and dogs and other things that people do not ordinarily eat" (48). In *How I Survived the Irish Famine,* Mary writes in her journal that a neighboring family "had eaten the dog the day before" (21).

Another title, *Black Harvest* (1983) written by British author Ann Pilling, similarly comments, "When the seed potatoes had been eaten there would have been nothing left, though some people killed their dogs and ate them, and others ate rats" (174). When I interviewed Pilling in Oxford she explained that she was commissioned to write a ghost story, and decided to use a horrible event in history in order to have the tale rooted in reality. The Irish Famine was "more chilling" than anything Pilling could invent (Pilling 2001). Part horror story, part time-slip, *Black Harvest* is the tale of three modern-day English children who are vacationing in the Irish countryside and become possessed by ghosts who died during the Famine. The children take on the suffering of the starving family. Well-received when first published, *Black Harvest* remains in print, is now considered a "Collins Modern Classic," and has the distinction of being the longest-selling Irish Famine narrative for children.

Some authors note the scarcity of the dogs in the countryside and offer reasons for this. In *So Far From Home,* Barry Denenberg includes Mary recording in her diary, "No dogs bark in the night—for they are either dead or too weak to cry out" (9) Another novel includes, "I had noticed that there did not seem to be too many dogs about. Those that were ... often banded together into packs and became wild" (Bolton 49). Also consider Eve Bunting, the prolific Irish-American author of over 240 books for children and a Caldecott Medal winner. One of Bunting's first children's novels, *The Haunting of Kildoran Abbey* (1978), has a character remark, "I haven't seen hide nor hair of a dog in all the county this twelve-month," and her friend laments about his dog, "We had to turn him out to fend for himself awhile back, when the hunger got so bad. We hear tell he's turned wild now" (16). Bunting's novel is an adventure tale that centers around eight homeless and orphaned Irish youths in 1847. Columb and Finn Mullen, 15-year-old twins, are the leaders of a group who band together to feed a starving village by capturing a barge filled with food en route to England.

During the Great Famine, dogs were loathed and feared. In *Annie Quinn in America* the destitute in the ditches are described as "no more than piles of rags," who "swatted weakly at the wild dogs that sniffed and prowled among them" (Schneider 25). Frail and debilitated, many Irish were unable to bury their dead properly, and ravenous dogs turned scavengers, sniffing out shallow graves and eating the diseased corpses. References of this are made in the children's novels, such as in *Boston! Boston!:* "They laid his body in a ditch, as the cemetery was full, and covered it with stones to keep the dogs of the city from digging it up" (Smith 103). In *Red Bird of Ireland,* Aderyn eerily notes, "There were dogs running here and there carrying what looked like bones in their mouths. What kind of bones? I hadn't the stomach to look" (Langford 132). In fact, in *Under the Hawthorn Tree* an entire chapter, "The Dogs" is devoted to an attack on the children by vicious dogs.

> ... in a flash the collie had pulled itself up on its forelegs. She pushed it off, but it sank its jaws into her arm and started to drag the limb back and forth as if trying to pull the bone from its socket. Peggy was screaming with pain. (Conlon-McKenna 96)

Peggy, her skin torn and bleeding, is rescued when her brother Michael strikes the dog so violently that the animal collapses dead. The chapter is heart wrenching and concludes with Michael relieved that he saved his sister but despondent over his action. "Michael sat on the stone wall, his head in his hands. 'I don't like killing things, Eily,' he murmured" (99).

Some novelists place contemporary or suburban notions of dogs as pets which could be considered anachronistic in a book set during the mid-1840s during the Great Famine. In Arthur McKeown's easy-reader-format novel, *Famine,* little Maggie is distraught when she leaves behind her dog, Sal, in

Belfast before they board a ship to America. Perhaps McKeown inserts this age-appropriate and modern-day anecdote because children relate to literature according to their own experiences. A child today may be better able to empathize with the sacrifices made in emigrating from their home in Ireland with this inclusion.

Unorthodox measures, such as people eating everything from dogs and grass, to the bleeding of cows, to foraging for unconventional food such as nettles and seaweed, are distinctive images in Famine novels and demonstrate to young readers the scale of the tragedy and the ends to which the Irish were driven. Young readers are likely to remember the vivid characterizations of the starving peasants, images that illustrate the severe lack of food:

> They all had the same look. The cheeks are sunken, the eyes wide and staring, with deep circles underneath, the lips narrow and tight, and in some the skin had a yellow tinge. Hunger and sickness had changed these people. How they were like ghosts. (Conlon-McKenna 80)

Betty Sue Cummings illustrates the victims in *Now, Ameriky* (1979): "Her husband sat unmoving, thin to the point of death, defeated in mind and body. A little boy lay on a small pallet, staring with cloudy, patient eyes, his half-naked body bloated with hunger" (17). Horrifying images are also conveyed in Canadian James Heneghan's time-slip novel *The Grave*: "Little kids sat on the roadside in a silent stupor, every rib starkly visible, no hair on their heads but thick downy hair on their faces that made them look like monkeys" (107). Carole Bolton similarly writes,

> Nora wasted away that spring. She reminded me of Egyptian mummies that I had heard about, for her skin hung over her bones like dry, wrinkled paper, and her face was that of a skull. Hunger had given Sally and Joe the look of two little monkeys. (48)

The narration in *Red Bird of Ireland* (1983) by American Sondra Gordon Langford is especially heart wrenching:

> I passed a young woman sitting against a rock. She held her tiny baby against her breast. "Drink, little one, drink," she was crooning. But the baby was beyond drinking or crying or breathing. She sang to it and bent her head over it as if it were still alive. (Langford 132)

These explicit passages illustrate the traumatic atmosphere that permeates some of these novels. The authors consistently use graphic descriptions of the appalling conditions that the Irish suffered, suggesting the authors were united in reconstructing children as capable of understanding and dealing with such tragedy. Several decades ago unsettling truths were often revised, avoided, or softened. Today's writers appear to share a common ideology regarding what children should be exposed to, that history should no longer be sugar-coated, and the importance of depicting past events authentically. It is necessary to note that the horror is not gratuitous; the increased frankness is presented to cultivate children's knowledge of this crucial event in Irish history.

Even picture books, intended for the younger reader, such as *Katie's Wish* (2002), illustrated by Caldecott Medal winner Emily Arnold McCully, realistically describe the famished children. "I've seen bloated bellies and babies too weak to blink," Katie overhears a neighbor report (Hazen). These disturbing details are documented in contemporary accounts. Haunting and harrowing, brutal consequences of this mid-nineteenth century calamity are presented to young readers of Irish Famine literature.

Young Heroes

These are survival stories. The resourcefulness and inner courage necessitated in escaping starvation and fever under horrendous circumstances lie at the center of these novels. Whereas adult Famine literature is often told in terms of passive victimization or resistance, children's Famine literature centers on the will to survive incredible hardships. The main characters are consistently courageous, spirited, quick-witted, and independent. Determined to create new and better worlds for themselves, these young heroes learn to endure and to seize every chance for survival. It is my argument that the traits and qualities of these protagonists represent "Irishness" to readers.

Take, for example, American Susan Campbell Bartoletti's *Black Potatoes* (2001), which was awarded the coveted Robert F. Sibert Award for the most distinguished informational book for children published in 2001. This 160-page text examines the events of the Famine and the experiences of ordinary people living in that time. When I interviewed Bartoletti in Pennsylvania, she explained that she intentionally avoided highlighting the victimization and instead focused on heroism.

> What are the heroic acts? If we look at searching in fields for turnip tops and edible weeds, that is a heroic act. Yes, you are a victim, but you are also a hero because you are struggling to survive and help your family survive. (Bartoletti 2002)

This attitude is a familiar one, and several of the authors I interviewed share a distinct ideological purpose to present heroism in the body of texts they have written for children. When I spoke with Conlon-McKenna, she expressed a view similar to Bartoletti's, noting that the central theme in *Under the Hawthorn Tree* is that these children have made up their minds to survive. "They're not going to be beaten; they're not going to lie down and

die," Conlon-McKenna told me (2001). A passage from the novel illustrates
this theme:

> Michael and Eily decided that they must get Peggy and themselves strong
> enough again for the rest of the journey. It was their only chance. The
> next few days were spent hunting for food. They had to keep the fire going
> also. They had finished the blood. Michael went searching at night and
> had been lucky enough to catch a rat and a hedgehog. They had lost their
> squeamishness by now and knew that all that mattered was their survival.
> Nettles were plentiful, and every ripened berry was also picked. (133)

Novels about the Great Famine allow readers to vicariously experience the
devastating effects that famine, poverty, and homelessness can have on people—as well as provide an understanding of human resilience. The authors
are consciously reconstructing history in a way that gives agency to the child
protagonist and by extension to the readers. Children, who are beginning to
form their own values and principles, can learn from the bravery and hope
of the protagonists who persevered against the odds. I believe these stories
allow young readers today to relate to these Irish protagonists as heroes,
thus counteracting potential guilt and shame that may have plagued the
generations before them.

Why Didn't the Irish Just Fish?

Consider this personal memory relating to this guilt and shame theme that
I am trying to convey. I have vague recollections of my social studies teacher
remarking how it was ludicrous that the Irish never fished the seas, implying that they were responsible for starving. This sentiment is not unique, and
some of my American contemporaries had similar recollections that the Irish
were too lazy, too stupid to save themselves. "It is difficult at first to understand why the Irish people, thousands of whom lived near the coast, did not
fish," Cecil Woodham-Smith acknowledged in the groundbreaking text, *The
Great Hunger: Ireland 1845–1849* (1962), the first mainstream factual account
on the Irish Famine (298). Certainly it is unflattering for a nation to perceive
itself as passive victims.

Contemporary Irish children's literature has changed this misconception.
Embedded in numerous narratives are the various reasons explaining why
Ireland, an island surrounded by water, failed to take advantage of its mari-
time wealth. Many novels educate children by portraying their characters taking risks by fishing illegally. American author Eileen Carbonneau informs her
readers about the laws in Ireland during the 1840s in her young adult romance
novel, *Rachel LeMoyne* (1998). Rachel observes the manor home as a "place
of crystal chandeliers, oil paintings, majestic trees, and a trout-filled river in

which the poor might be killed for fishing" (65). The disparity between the English landlords and the Irish peasants is clearly shown.

Nearly every novel shows families combing the shore for edible food, such as *The Hungry Wind* (1997), by Irish author Soinbhe Lally:

> Each day the women and girls went to the rocks to gather seaweed and shellfish. At one end of the strand there were stretches of muddy sand, encrusted with acres of mussels, but they were not allowed to pick those. For fear that hunger would tempt them the landlord's agent, Mister Hamilton, sent his men to warn tenants that the mussel beds were not included in their shore rights. (14)

In *Nory Ryan's Song*, Nory and her family live along the west coast of Ireland, and her neighbors fish for a living. Disaster hits when their landlord, Lord Cunningham, confiscates their currach:

> The currach was gone too, gone to pay for the Mallons' rent from last year. Gone, not even for Cunningham to use. "What would he want with the sea, and the cold, and the aching hard work?" Liam had said. "What would he want with the danger?"
>
> Devlin [the landlord's agent] had locked it up with chains on the pier in the harbor. It would be there, with the tar on the canvas drying and cracking, until great holes appeared and the currach wasted away. It wouldn't be the first time. There were others there, waiting for the owners to pay the rent they owed and get them back, but that never happened. (69)

Many fishermen, thinking the blight would be short lived, had pawned or sold their tackle and nets. A passage from *Knockabeg: A Famine Tale* (2001), a fantasy novel written by Irish American Mary E. Lyons, illustrates this theme as well: "The shillings go to Lord Armitage Shank for his bloody rent! Many families have even sold their hide canoes and fishing nets to pay the fee" (5). Lyons also penned a nonfiction book for children, *Feed the Children First: Irish Memories of the Great Hunger* (2002), which is a compelling collection of first-person accounts of the Irish Famine, interwoven with period photos and sketches.

Several books explain that the coastal dwellers who might have hoped for food from the sea found that weather conditions made it impossible to risk going out in curraghs or that the starving peasants were too weakened by hunger to handle their boats. Other novels note that scarcity of fish and that beaches and rocks were quickly stripped of whatever food they held. "Dad caught an occasional fish, but the lake was soon fished out" (Bolton 30). These examples certainly do not correlate laziness with Irishness. Instead, the books educate young readers by illustrating the varied and complex circumstances surrounding the fishing problem, such as fishermen being forced to sell their gear to buy food for their families and fishing rights belonging to the English landlords.

The Potato Eaters

The notion that the Irish peasants were somehow responsible for the consequences of the Famine due to their reliance on the potato as their principle food source is corrected in the children's books. Readers are shown how the Irish land system helped create this dependence and that the landless laborers grew cash crops, such as wheat, solely to pay the rent. This is exemplified in Karen Branson's *The Potato Eaters* (1979):

> "Once we did grow other things, Maureen," Ma said. "Cabbages, turnips, marrow, as well as potatoes. We even hoped to own a cow one day. But then the land-rents were raised, not just ours, but everyone's. More land had to be planted in oats, more time spent working towards the rent. Praties don't need much tending; sure you've seen how a small bed will yield a dozen fine pecks with hardly even a nod from your da." (14)

In addition, Eve Bunting educates her young readers with the following:

> The tenant farmers, like our father, grow potatoes to feed their families. The other crops are grown to pay the landlord for the rent, and he sells them in England.... [I]f you don't pay your rent, in money or crops, you're put out of your house. Then you just die faster, that's all. You starve in a field or a hole in the ground. (62)

Shame, which may have been associated with passive victimization, has now been replaced by an accurate historical understanding of this issue. Children's literature of the Irish Famine, nonexistent during my childhood, sheds a new light on complicated issues and educates children by weaving historical information throughout the narrative.

"He took the soup"

Adults may recall the phrase, "he took the soup" or the insulting term, *souper*. These expressions are still heard today and were coined during the Irish Famine when anti-Catholic zealots would provide free soup to the destitute villagers if they first agreed to renounce their religion. So strong was the Catholic faith in Ireland during this time that some Irish starved to death rather than converting to Protestantism. Those that did turn apostate and partake in the soup were called soupers, and the disdainful stigma often marked their families for generations. *Souperism*, the nickname for this proselytization aspect of evangelical Protestant missions, is more frequent in Famine folklore than in historical research. Souperism did occur, but the extent was greatly exaggerated. However, it created tremendous tension where it did exist, resulting in long-lasting and bitter memories that have been passed down from generation to generation.

Though not a universal motif in the children's Irish Famine narratives, souperism is mentioned in several works. Interestingly, the reaction by the main characters is usually one of ambivalence, and vague attention is given to the religious pressure. For example, in *Under the Hawthorn Tree*, Eily, Michael, and Peggy sleep outside a soup kitchen in order to be the first in line the next day.

> During the night an old man shook them and told them to be on their way, as the heathens would try to convert them in the morning and if they took another mug of soup they may as well take the Queen's shilling. The children were puzzled, but simply ignored him (81–82).

The children were offered stew the following day and were not asked to renounce their faith. Certainly no guilt or shame is associated with the old man's remark, and the story moves forward without additional comment.

Souperism is also mentioned in passing in Heneghan's *The Grave* where the teenage protagonist, Tom Mullen, is confused when he is labeled as a souper:

> We joined a lineup for soup and had to take it inside and listen to a sermon from a bad-tempered minister named Nangle who went on and on about popery and sin and other stuff I didn't understand. As we came out, a bunch of old biddies were standing in the street yelling at us, calling us Soupers. I was too tired to ask Hannah what the fuss was about. (103)

Tom appears too famished and fatigued to be concerned about derogatory comments from onlookers, and no conversion of faith in exchange for food occurs in the novel.

In *Mary-Anne's Famine* (1994), written by Irish author Colette McCormack, the soup kitchens are accepted, and the local priest even encourages his parishioners to partake in the charity. Mary-Anne records in her journal:

> The soup kitchens are near us and we must make use of them. Father O'Rourke tells us never to mind that the people who give out the soup are not of our religion, to live is the important thing. Some people turn from being Catholics so they will get more soup and other help. We drink the soup but it is not very good. (16–17)

In *Red Bird of Ireland,* Aderyn hears about the evangelical Protestants second hand, and the story line is sympathetic to Famine victims who succumb to souperism:

> "We saw something else by the wharf, Father Domhnaill," said Seamas. "There was a little house from which some well-dressed people were offering soup to the poor who stood around. There were many poor and hungry, but no one would eat. A man told me that, in order to get that soup, you have to blaspheme the Blessed Virgin and the Holy Catholic Church. Can that be true?"
>
> "I'm afraid so," said Uncle Domhnaill. "I've been told, by priest and others, that there is food being given out, all over Ireland, to those who will abjure their Catholic faith. Some poor souls are so hungry that they do turn from their faith in order to get some food. Those who do so are well cared for, afterward. I don't judge a starving person who does what he feels he must in order to stay alive, or keep his family alive. I pray for him. God in heaven will be his judge, not I." (Langford 147–148)

Collectively, there is a lack of any serious religious tension in children's literature of the Famine, and it is interesting to note that souperism is not referenced again during the narratives. These passages show compassion to the starving people who took the soup. The characters are not ostracized or made to feel blameworthy in any way. Although the practice of souperism was not widespread, where it did occur it still remains an emotive part of the oral culture of the Famine, and guilt and anger are still in the mindset of some Irish and Irish Americans today. Children's literature, however, appears to play a pivotal role in dissipating this souperism friction. Perhaps a more confident Irish identity results from this new understanding and awareness. The protagonists, with whom the young readers identify, are heroes, surviving by any means they can, whether it is accepting soup from people of a different religion, fishing illegally on the landlord's land, eating grass, or bleeding cows.

Conclusion

One of the great ironies of the Famine years is the abundance of food in the midst of terrible want. Large quantities of grain and livestock were exported from Ireland while the poor starved. Children's novels address this horrifying historical fact, thus revealing the root causes of famines, which include the reality that politics often prevents the distribution of food to the victims. For example:

We had to have something to eat. Something more than water with roots and leaves Anna had saved. We had to have real food. Anna spoke without opening her eyes. "They are starving to death in their houses," she said. "Yes," I told her, a tap of pain in my forehead. "We would have had enough," she said, "even without the potatoes, if the English had left us the animals, the grain." (Giff 118)

Amarta Sen, the 1998 Nobel laureate economist, has argued that modern famines are not about food but a lack of will in its distribution. "A major problem with food aid is that much of it never reaches the starving" (qtd. in O'Grada 47). Readers should be aware that the extremes of famine and poverty during the 1840s are still pervasive in Africa and other parts of the world.

Scholars continue to debate the complex causes and consequences of this tragic and inflammatory episode in European history, and writers of children's books vary in the degree to which political aspects of the event are presented. Novelists often suffuse politics with philosophy, sometimes to poignant effect. Laura Wilson has Mary reflect, "You need food in your belly before you can have feelings in your heart or thoughts in your head" (25). Mary E. Lyons's narrator muses, "Who amongst us can measure the pain of starvation? The hungry are too weak to tell it. The well-fed are too comfortable to imagine it" (49). Historical fiction often reflects present ideologies and values, thus understanding the human impact of the Irish Famine can help young readers sympathize with today's world hunger issues. Children's novels depicting the Great Famine provide linkages between the past and the present. Youngsters, who often identify with the characters in the storyline, relate to the perseverance of these protagonists and believe that they too can learn to handle difficult situations. Reading about the Great Hunger gives Irish and Irish American children a deeper historical understanding of the role food played in their ancestral homeland, thus constructing new definitions of Irishness and a richer cultural identity.

Notes:

1   I have compiled a comprehensive bibliography of historical fiction written for children and young adults depicting the Great Irish Famine. Every imaginative story written in English expressly for young readers and rooted in the events of the Famine met the criteria for the study. The qualifying works were published in the United States, Ireland, England, Canada, Scotland, and New Zealand. The bibliography is the most expansive to date, ranging in format from picture books to young adult novels and in style from stories set in Famine-torn Ireland to those that utilize the Famine as a springboard for a tale of immigration to America. Although there has been prolific literary output on other historical events

for children, there have only been 42 historical fiction books published on the Irish Famine (McNamara 21–31).

2. See the works by Tim Pat Coogan, Tom Hayden, and Christine Kinealy.

3. Avi, Susan Campbell Bartoletti, Susan Brocker, Eve Bunting, Eileen Charbonneau, Marita Conlon-McKenna, Malachy Doyle, Carol Drinkwater, Marie-Louise Fitzpatrick, Patricia Reilly Giff, Cora Harrison, Barbara Shook Hazen, James Heneghan, Lynn Kositsky, Soinbhe Lally, Elisabeth Lutzeier, Mary E. Lyons, Yvonne MacGrory, Colette McCormack, Arthur McKeown, Michael Morpurgo, Janet Nolan, Clare Pastore, Norah Perez, Ann Pilling, David Ross, Mical Schneider, Joyce A. Stengel, Laura Wilson.

Works Cited

Bartoletti, Susan Campbell. *Black Potatoes*. Boston: Houghton, 2001.
———. Personal interview. 13 June 2002.
Bolton, Carole. *The Search of Mary Katherine Mulloy*. New York: Nelson, 1974.
Branson, Karen. *The Potato Eaters*. New York: Nelson, 1979.
Bunting, Eve. *The Haunting of Kildoran Abbey*. New York: Warne, 1978.
Charbonneau, Eileen. *Rachel Le Moyne*. New York: Doherty, 1998.
Conlon-McKenna, Marita. Personal interview. 21 August 2001.
———. *Fields of Home*. Dublin: O'Brien, 1996.
———. *Under the Hawthorn Tree*. New York: Holiday, 1990.
———. *Wildflower Girl*. Dublin: O'Brien, 1991.
Coogan, Tim. *Wherever Green Is Worn: The Story of the Irish Diasporoa*. London: Arrow, 2002.
Cummings, Betty Sue. *Now, Ameriky*. New York: Atheneum, 1979.
Denenberg, Barry. *So Far from Home: The Diary of Mary Driscoll, an Irish Mill Girl (Dear America)*. New York: Scholastic, 1997.
Feirtear Pierce, and Gail Seekamp. *The Irish Famine*. Dublin: Blackwater, 1999.
Giff, Patricia Reilly. *Maggie's Door*. New York: Lamb, 2003.
———. *Nory Ryan's Song*. New York: Delacorte, 2000.
———. *Water Street*. New York: Lamb, 2006.
Harrison, Cora. *The Famine Secret*. Dublin: Wolfhound, 1998.
Hayden, Tom, ed. *Irish Hunger, Personal Reflections on the Legacy of the Famine*. Boulder, CO: Roberts Rinehart, 1997.
———. *Irish on the Inside*. New York: Verso, 2001.
Hazen, Barbara Shook. *Katie's Wish*. Ill. Emily Arnold McCully. New York: Dial, 2002.
Heneghan, James. *The Grave*. New York: Foster, 2000.
"Ireland." *Country Reports*. July 2007. 17 October 2007. <http://www.countryreports.org/country.aspx?countryid=118&countryName=Ireland>.
Kinealy, Christine. "The Famine Killed Everything: Living with the Memory of the Great Hunger." *Ireland's Great Hunger*. Eds. David A. Valone and Christine Kinealy. Lanham, MD: UP of America, 2002. 1–40.
Lally, Soinbhe. *The Hungry Wind*. Dublin: Poolbeg, 1997.
Langford, Sondra Gordon. *Red Bird of Ireland*. New York: Atheneum, 1983.
Lutzeier, Elizabeth. *The Coldest Winter*. London: Oxford UP, 1991.
———. *Bound for America*. London: Oxford UP, 2000.
Lyons, Mary E. *Feed the Children First: Irish Memories of the Great Hunger*. New York: Atheneum, 2002.
———. *Knockabeg: A Famine Tale*. Boston: Houghton, 2001.
McCormack, Colette. *Mary-Anne's Famine*. Cork, Ire.: Attic, 1994.
———. *After the Famine*. Dublin: Attic, 1995.
McKeown, Arthur. *Famine*. Dublin: Poolbeg, 1997.
McNamara, Karen Hill. "Children's Literature of the Great Irish Famine: An Annotated Bibliography." *Foilsiu: An Interdisciplinary Journal of Irish Studies* 3.1 (2003): 21–31.
Morpurgo, Michael. *Twist of Gold*. London: Kaye, 1983.

Neale, Cynthia G. *The Irish Dresser: The Story of Hope During The Great Hunger (An Gorta Mor, 1845–1850)*. Shippensburg, PA: White Mane Kids, 2004.

O'Grada, Cormac. *Black '47 and Beyond: The Great Irish Famine in History, Economy, and Memory*. Princeton: Princeton UP, 1999.

Pastore, Clare. *A Voyage from Ireland: Fiona McGilray's Story*. New York: Berkley Jam, 2001.

Pilling, Ann. *Black Harvest*. London: Armada, 1983.

———. Personal Interview, 5 July 2001.

Schneider, Mical. *Annie Quinn in America*. Minneapolis: Lerner, 2001.

Smith, Michael. *Boston! Boston!* Dublin: Poolbeg, 1997.

Wilson, Laura. *How I Survived the Irish Famine: The Journal of Mary O'Flynn*. New York: Harper, 2001.

Woodham-Smith, Cecil. *The Great Hunger: Ireland 1845–1849*. London: Penguin, 1962.

Chapter Eleven

The Keys to the Kitchen:
Cooking and Latina Power in Latin(o)
American Children's Stories

Genny Ballard

Food, cooking, and the rituals that surround them in Latino and Latin American children's literature reflect gender roles, cultural identity, and power structures inherent in family dynamics. In some recent Latin(o) American children's literature, being able to cook and acquire food for the family represents the acquisition of power for female characters. In this chapter I examine the acquisition of knowledge regarding food and cooking as a right of passage for young women in contemporary children's stories from three different cultural groups: rural Cuba, the United States/Mexican border, and Chicanos in the United States. Each of these children's stories focuses on the relationships between girls and older female mentors as represented through food and food preparation. In Senel Paz's *Las hermanas* (1993), the daughters have to learn to cook and acquire food for the family in their mother's absence, and in Gary Soto's *Too Many Tamales* (1993), a girl feels that learning to cook tamales makes her more mature. In Gloria Anzaldúa's *Prietita and the Ghost Woman/Prietita y la Llorona* (1995), a child needs to learn how to use herbs to heal her mother.

In all three books, girls form special bonds with older women who teach them to cook, and in each case the cooking serves a substantial purpose. The relationships that the young characters develop with their older mentors around food will be explored in order to elucidate their impact on the children's development. In the case of the characters in *Las hermanas*, it is the grandmother who teaches them to cook traditional Cuban dishes; in *Too*

Many Tamales the mother teaches the young girl how to cook tamales; and in *Prietita and the Ghost Woman,* the title character has two mythical mentors: a *curandera,* or medicine woman, and a crying ghost woman.

In Senel Paz's picture book *Las hermanas* (1993), two young Cuban girls learn to feed the family in their mother's absence. Food in this story is featured prominently—mostly in its scarcity. The setting for the story is important as it refers to a Cuban food rationing program during the "Special Period" of the 1990s—a time of great economic constraint that followed the collapse of the Soviet Union (Pérez 424). By learning to cook and acquire food on a limited budget, the girls in the story mature and gain authority in their family.

In Gary Soto's *Too Many Tamales* (1993), text and illustrations show that the young female protagonist, Maria, feels cooking tamales and helping her mother in the kitchen mean she is a grown-up. Maria borrows her mother's diamond ring without asking so that she will feel even more grown-up. When she fears that she lost her mother's ring in the dough while making tamales, she makes her cousins eat all of the tamales to try to find the ring, which her mother had on her finger all along. Maria, who is upset by the whole incident, can only calm herself down by cooking.

In a third story, Gloria Anzaldúa's picture book *Prietita and the Ghost Woman/Prietita y la Llorona* (1995), Prietita spends time with a local healer learning how to cook natural remedies. When she hears that her mother's illness has returned, she trespasses onto the dangerous King Ranch in Texas to try to find rue, an ingredient in the remedy for her mother's ailment. Soon she gets lost in the forest where the mythical crying woman, *La Llorona,* appears and guides her to the plant and then out of the woods. It is then that the healer feels that Prietita is mature enough to learn to cook remedies herself.

In each of these stories, it is through their relationship to food and the mentorship of their mothers and elders that the young female characters become empowered. The girls in each book gain power in three different ways, with the common thread being their increased knowledge of food preparation. Among these three stories the best example is found in Senel Paz's award-winning Spanish-language picture book *Las hermanas,* which prominently features two sisters who learn to prepare and acquire food while their mother lives and works in La Habana, the country's capital. The girls come of age in their mother's absence, taking care of their little brother, who narrates the story, and learning to cook from their blind grandmother.

In *Las hermanas,* the little brother informs us that the sisters are not ashamed to ask the grocery store owner for one more week of credit, and that they lie to bill collectors and, to win him over, make food and coffee for the man who brings the electric bill. The girls are the ones who know how much food to borrow from the neighbors and how much food to lend when the neighbors need it. Quickly we discover information about the migrant mother, the girls' sexual maturation, food and social identity, and the extended family.

The setting for *Las hermanas* is an unnamed town a great distance from La Habana, Cuba. The first line of the story informs the reader of the mother's absence: "*En cuanto su madre se fue a trabajar para La Habana . . .*" [When their mother went to work in La Habana . . .] (Paz 7). We know the distance is great because the mother lives and works in the capital and is unable to return home at night to stay with her children. Indeed, the absent mother is one of the story's principal themes, as it is a theme of many classic children's stories (including *Cinderella, Snow White, The Little Mermaid, Beauty and the Beast*), but the migrant mother is a twist on the old theme. In *Las hermanas* the mother is living but absent from the home; therefore, these children, unlike children in classical tales, await their mother's return. The thought of her underlies many of their actions, as evidenced by references to her throughout the book.

Several scenes reveal information that allows the reader to formulate an opinion about the mother–daughter relationship in the story. Sometimes the sisters publicly place the blame on their mother for not sending enough money to pay for food. "*Le explican al bodeguero que mamá mandará todo el dinero la semana que viene*" [They explain to the grocer that mamá will send him all of the money next week] (13). The sisters consider themselves responsible for the bills, but they still have their mother to blame when there is not enough money. This section of the book furtively refers to a distinct feature of Cuban culture: food rationing. A *bodega* is a food store set up to distribute the rations, available to a family unit, as indicated by their *libreta*, or food book. Since 1962, Cuba has had a food rationing program that allows families to purchase a specific amount of food per month (Zimbalist 412). So without much explanation, the author lets the reader know that the young girls have to learn how to live with food rationing as well as how to cook and purchase food with very little money.

The sisters have obviously established a pattern of telling creditors that their mother is away in the capital. However, the man who comes to collect the electric bill does not care. "*Al que cobra la luz sí que no le importa el cuento que mamá está en la Habana*" [The one who collects the electric bill does not care that mamá is in Habana] (15). This statement has many layers: it shows that the bill collector has heard the story so many times that he no longer cares and that the story about their mother is no longer sufficient for him, as it was for the grocer. As a result, for the electric company man, the sisters embellish their story. The boy completes his sentence by stating: "*pero las hermanas le guardan café fuerte y cuando llega se ponen tan simpáticas y abuela está tan enferma y yo estoy tan enfermo que entre los dos hemos tomado diez pesos de medicina*" [but the sisters save some strong coffee for him and when he comes they act so sweet and grandmother is so sick and I am so sick that between the two of us we have taken ten pounds of medicine] (15). This scene is a progression from the previous scene, which took place in the store. Though the grocer accepted their mother as the culprit, the electric bill collector does not, and so the girls must use other means to appease him, including coffee, kindness, and exaggerated excuses. This scene shows some independence on the girls' part; now they know they cannot simply rely on their mother to pay the bill, nor can they rely on the story of their mother to appease the collector. They are forced to rely on themselves, their wits, and a little bit of flirtation served up with strong coffee.

It is through food and cooking that the girls change their position within the family structure. It is also important that food marks cultural identity in this story because the foods that they learn to cook from their grandmother are Cuban; the girls learn to cook *sofrito*, rice, and *natilla de chocolate*. Food and cooking symbolize the change in the sisters from girls to adolescents. Cooking is, in fact, the first of the chores mentioned among the new things the sisters do now that their mother has left: "*Cocinan, lavan, planchan*" [They cook, they wash, they iron] (7). There is a great difference between the way adults and children relate to food in this book. Adults buy and prepare the food, and children consume the food. But here, the girls, who are becoming adults, are the ones who purchase and prepare the food, and even eat last: "*Nos sirven primero a abuela y a mí*" [First, they serve grandmother and me] (9). This order shows respect and maturity on their part; by serving the grandmother and little boy first, the sisters are showing deference to them. Further growth and maturity is revealed when the boy indicates that his sisters no longer fight over who will be allowed to scrape and eat the crusty rice from the bottom of the pan. "*Ya no lloran por ponerse la mejor bata ni comerse las raspas del arroz*" [Now they do not whine to put on the best dresses or to eat the crusty rice at the bottom of the pan] (9). In many Central American and Caribbean countries where rice is a staple, some people prefer the hard rice at the bottom of the pan, so giving this up would be a sacrifice for the girls.

Food also connects the girls to their grandmother, their history, and their Cuban identity because the food they learn to cook is Cuban. In the story, the grandmother helps them with their cooking. "*Ella a veces les cuenta alguna historia y les explica cómo se hace el sofrito y lo difícil que es que el arroz salga bien, ni duro ni en pelotas*" [She sometimes tells them stories and she explains how to make *sofrito* and how difficult it is to get the rice to come out right, not dry or clumpy] (11). Not only is rice a staple in Cuba, but sofrito is a common Cuban food; made with onions, green peppers, and garlic cooked into a paste, *sofrito* is used as flavoring in many meals. It would not be uncommon for families to have *sofrito* prepared in order to have it on hand to use every day. By learning to make *sofrito* and rice, the girls remain closely connected to their roots.

Early in the story, the boy refers to neighbors borrowing salt or onions, making reference to the girls' generosity, saying "*saben cuánto deben dar si son las vecinas las que no tienen cebollas o sal*" [they know how much to give the neighbors when they do not have enough onions or salt] (9). This shows that the girls have obtained the knowledge expected of those who are in charge of households. It also marks a pattern that has been established in their family—of sharing food with others. Perhaps their mother shared, so they know they must share even while she is gone, despite being in difficult straits. Their changing relationship towards food and cooking marks the girls' passage into adulthood. Using food to connect with their neighbors, learning to cook, manipulating the electric bill collector with food and care, and serving their brother and their grandmother first are all signs of maturity, and ways of demonstrating their ability to run the home in their mother's absence.

Near the story's end, one final reference to the absent mother serves as a bridge to understanding the adolescent sisters' sexual maturation. Here, the little boy describes what he sees when he walks in on his sisters: "*Un día entré de repente y las sorprendí delante del espejo, con los zapatos de tacones de mamá y los labios pintados:asustadas, se echaron a reír*" [One day I walked in and surprised them in front of the mirror, with mom's high heels and lipstick on, they began to laugh] (25). The illustration on this page shows the little boy entering his mother's room. The girls are in front of the mirror, wearing high heels and putting on makeup. In *The Pleasures of Children's Literature*, Perry Nodelman and Mavis Reimer write that illustrations are "less important as a source of aesthetic delight than as a source of information about a story" (278). All of the previous illustrations that reference the mother portray her absence in relation to their need for her: to cook, clean, take care of the boy and the grandmother, and pay the bills. The illustration provides new information as it shows the girls transforming in physical appearance from children to adults, thus becoming their own mother. From the illustration, however, we can see that the boy is unhappy about his sisters' usurping his mother's things. It is a logical extension to believe, then, that the boy rejects his sisters as a substitute for his mother—an interpretation he confirms at story's end.

The mother–daughter relationship is fraught with tensions as the girls seek to replace their mother in the home. The transformation of girls into mother occurs in subtle ways throughout the book. One way is through signs of their sexual maturation. Even though he comments on their seemingly strange actions, it is obvious he cannot understand what is happening to them. The book refers variously to the development of the girls into adults. Early in the story we read a list of the things the girls no longer do: "*no se juntan con las demás niñas a bailar la suiza porque rompen los zapatos, no juegan con los varones*" [they do not get together with the other girls to jump rope because it ruins their shoes, they do not play with boys] (Paz 9). This statement implies that the girls used to play with boys when they were younger, and now they do not. Later there is another reference to the girls' new attraction to boys: "*y cuando llega del trabajo el hijo de Felamida a uno le cae mucha risa, y si pasa en bicicleta el muchacho de la carnicería se dan pellizcos por los rincones*" [and when Felamida's son comes in from work one of them laughs a lot, and if the butcher's delivery boy passes on bicycle they pinch each other in the corners] (23). The clearest example of the sisters' sexual maturation is the difference in the flirtatious way they treat the bill collector. When he comes to the house, they give him coffee and act sweetly instead of paying the bill (15). The illustration on this page shows one of the girls blushing and the other locked in eye contact with the bill collector.

One dichotomy related to family structures in this story is the difference between children and adults. Here, their little brother represents childhood, the mother represents adulthood, and the sisters become the bridge between the two. The illustrations support the idea that the girls are maturing in the course of the story because the girls appear to be very young in the illustrations: one wears braids, and they both wear hair bows. If, in fact, they are very young, then their maturation can be seen as premature, precipitated by their mother's absence.

The girls' relationship with their grandmother is one of mutual care: they feed her, administer her medicine, and take her outside to "*coger fresco al patio*" [get fresh air on the patio] (Paz 7). The grandmother, on the other hand, is the only character who has a connection to the family's past and tradition. She tells the girls stories and allows them to rummage through the attic and admire her old treasures, even though this makes her nervous: "*De todos modos, abuela tiembla cuando las oye sacando de su baúl los vasos floreados que le regaló el abuelo el día de la boda, los platos que le trajo en el primer aniversario, la máquina de moler carne que se la compró antes de casados*" [In any case, grandmother trembles when she hears them taking out of her chest the flowered vases that grandfather gave her on their wedding day, the dishes he brought her on their first anniversary, the meat grinder he bought her before they were married] (17).

One particular passage tells of how the grandmother gives her engagement ring and earrings to the sisters "*con el encargo que nunca las pierdan, pues esa sortijita fue de su abuela y las dormilonas ni sabe a qué vieja por ahí para atrás pertenecieron, y ambas cosas están nuevecitas*" [with the order never to lose them, because that ring was her grandmother's, and the earrings, no one even knows who they used to belong to way back when, and both of them look like new] (19). The boy, without judgment, makes these comments. Although alluding to a past that was more affluent, he provides no commentary on the current situation. The grandmother's role in the story—as matriarch of the family—therefore connects the girls to their past: the history of their family and the history of their country. She supports tradition, teaches the girls, and encourages them in their new roles within the family.

In *Las hermanas*, the children must endure poverty, sometimes borrowing food and frequently lacking money to pay bills. Taking this into account, the items their grandmother saves in her chest and gives to the girls may appear frivolous, but they are the children's last connection to their past and to their late grandfather. The anecdotes the grandmother tells allude to better times in the family: perhaps the family was more stable before the Revolution. However, the story makes no mention of the Castro regime, the Revolution, or politics. Young child readers may have no context for questioning why the family situation has changed, but older, more informed readers may understand the reasons for the current economic status of the family.

Food as a marker of Cuban identity is one of the central themes of this story, and the characters' relationship to food tells us much about them. Food marks cultural identity in this story because the sisters learn to cook Cuban foods, and this helps foment their relationship with their grandmother. It is while they are caring for her that she tells them how to cook. The shortage of food in the household may be exacerbated by the economic situation in Cuba at the time of publication of the story. And most importantly, the girls learn how to endear themselves to people through food, and they care for the family by learning to borrow, buy, and prepare food. Cooking in this story is a marker of maturity: an idea that is shared by Maria, the protagonist of *Too Many Tamales*.

Gary Soto is the author of several stories that feature Chicano children growing up in the United States, the most notable of which, *Baseball in April* (1990), was voted ALA's Best Book for Young Adults. In Soto's picture book *Too Many Tamales*, the protagonist, Maria, acts like a "grown-up" as she helps her mother cook Christmas tamales. While learning from her mother how to make tamales, she slips her mother's ring on just for a moment, but when she checks again later the ring is gone.

Compared to Paz's story, set in Cuba's Special Period, this narrative tells quite a different tale regarding food supply: there is scarcity in the lives of the Cuban children in *Las hermanas*, but there is abundance in the lives of the Americans in *Too Many Tamales*. The sisters in *Las hermanas* are barely getting enough food, yet the family in *Too Many Tamales* is able to make a second batch of tamales when the children eat the first two dozen. Illustrations further reinforce this point; in *Las hermanas* the boy and the grandmother are pictured eating first, and the sisters wait to eat a small simple dinner (Paz 8), but in *Too Many Tamales* Maria and her cousin stand before a plate heaping full of tamales too big to fit on one page (Soto 14–15). On the next page, the children start to eat all of the tamales, and "their stomachs were stretched till they hurt, but the cousins kept eating until only one tamale remained on the plate" (16). Maria orders the other children to eat until it hurts, providing a stark contrast to the sisters in *Las hermanas*, who have to learn to negotiate to get enough food just to feed themselves and their brother and grandmother.

As in *Las hermanas*, the illustrations help tell the story in *Too Many Tamales*, which is beautifully illustrated by Ed Martinez. Abundance is but one aspect of the story, which is conveyed in seventeen full color oil paintings, including many close-ups that trace Maria's emotions as she transitions from joyful to happy to panicked to despondent and back to content. Another sign of abundance, seen both in the story and the illustrations, is when the family comes in with armloads of gifts to add to the piles already under the Christmas tree.

Also, as in *Las hermanas*, preparation of food is, again, a mark of maturity. For Maria it is important to appear grown-up, and to her the two most obvious symbols of maturity are jewelry and the ability to cook. The narrator says of Maria in the beginning of the story, "She was acting grown-up now, helping her mother make tamales. Their hands were sticky with masa" (2); and subsequently, "She felt grown-up now wearing her mother's apron. Her mom had even let her wear lipstick and perfume. If only I could wear mom's ring, she thought to herself" (3). Maria obviously longs to be grown-up and learning to cook is one of the steps in this maturation process.

Maria appears to be a leader among her cousins. When all of her cousins arrive, Maria, who appears to be an only child, takes all of the other children up to her room. The text says that "Maria grabbed Dolores by the arm and took her upstairs to play, with the other cousins tagging along after them" (11). In the illustrations it appears that Dolores is an older cousin, Teresa is a younger cousin, and Danny is the youngest. Dolores may be the biggest, but Maria is in charge; it is she who devises the plan to find the lost ring and tells the other cousins, even Dolores, to eat all of the tamales. "Eat them" she commands, once all of the cousins stand before the heaping pile of tamales (15).

The illustration on this page is particularly revealing. In it the children stand behind the tamales looking over them. The tamales are painted in the foreground, making each look enormous. Nodelman and Reimer refer to this technique in illustrations as *overlap*. They say that artists' use of overlapping suggests particular relationships between the objects they depict. The placement of the oversized tamales in the foreground means that they are to be read as a difficult challenge. *Focus,* another technique that Nodelman and Reimer discuss, is also used in this illustration. They assert that "viewers focus on private feelings" when the illustration is of a close-up of the characters' faces (Nodelman and Reimer 291). Through the facial expressions of the children we can sense their dread of the task before them. Perhaps it is because Maria helped cook the tamales that she feels more empowered to force the cousins to eat them all. As the children make their way through the giant plate of tamales, their resilience wanes until Maria pushes them on: "keep eating, Maria scolded" (16). The illustration on this page shows Maria standing in front of all of the other children raising a finger at them as the other children obey with pained looks. After the problem of the lost ring is resolved, the story ends the way it begins—with Maria's hands in the masa. Ironically, in Spanish, "manos en la masa" or "hands in the dough" can be translated into the idiomatic expression we use in English "caught red handed." Maria certainly was caught with her manos en la masa!

Cooking tamales is one of the only indications that Maria is from a Chicano family. The other allusions to her culture are the names of the characters (Rosa, Teresa, Danny, Dolores) and the illustrations containing corn husks, manteca, and masa, all tamale ingredients. According to Alice Guadalupe Tapp, tamales date back in Mexican and Central American history to pre-Columbian times, to as early as 5,000 BCE, when it is believed that the need for portable food during wartime brought about their invention (1–2). Today tamales are still a popular food for daily consumption in Mexico and Central America. But in the United States, because of the preparation involved, they are more commonly cooked for celebrations by Chicanos just as they are in *Too Many Tamales*. According to Jeffery Pilcher, in *¡Qué vivan los tamales!*, his study of food and Mexican identity, the tamale was always a food used for celebrations, even dating back to pre-Hispanic times. It was only through the technological innovations in the twentieth century that they became popular as a lunch food, often sold by street vendors. Fossilized cornhusks found near the pyramid of the Sun and Moon at Teotihuacán may date tamale consumption as far back as 250 BCE-750 CE. Pilcher calls tamales the "hallmark of festive banquets" (Pilcher 11).

Soto's use of this iconic Mexican food, the tamale, is rich. In his story the tamale becomes an objective correlative for Maria, whose emotions can be traced through the presence and abundance of tamales. This idea is most apparent near the end of the story when the ring is found on her mother's finger, yet Maria is still not completely relieved. It is only once she starts to make more tamales that she is able to relax. Maria admits to her mother that she and her cousins ate all of the tamales. She feels sick and wants to cry, but once she begins to cook a new batch of tamales she starts to feel better. "And when Maria put her hands back into the bowl of masa, the leftover tear was gone" (30). Thus she is only finally relieved when she begins cooking again. Maria feels stronger and more in control when she is cooking.

The ability to cook takes on a different meaning in *Prietita and the Ghost Woman,* in which Gloria Anzaldúa (1942–2004), Chicana feminist, poet, scholar, and activist, tells the story of a young girl who asks a traditional healer for help when her mother falls ill. In this bilingual picture book, the young female protagonist, Prietita, wants to learn how to cook potions from Doña Lola the *curandera*, or the traditional healer, of her town. The character of the *curandera* is a frequently used trope among Latina writers in their depictions of the border.

At the beginning of the story, Prietita is planting herbs at the healer's house when her little sister comes to tell her that their mother is very ill. The healer suggests a potion made with rue, but says she has none of the plant left to make it. She tells Prietita that the King Ranch is the best place to get the rue plant but warns how dangerous it is to trespass on that farm. Prietita goes anyway in search of the rue (an herb sometimes used as an antispasmodic) and is magically helped by friendly animals through the dangerous forest, where "they shoot trespassers" (6). Suddenly she is frightened by the haunting voice of the legendary *Llorona*, who steals children when they wander alone near the water. Instead of kidnapping her, this incarnation of the *Llorona* guides Prietita to the rue plant and then flies her to safety on the other side of the fence, where her family awaits.

In "Tradition and Mythology: Signatures of Landscape in Chicana Literature," Tey Rebolledo discusses the tendency of Chicana writers such as Anzaldúa to use cultural icons such as *La Malinche* and *La Llorona* as well as *curanderas* and *brujas*. Rebolledo interprets their use as a reclaiming and reinterpretation of myth and legend that provide a mythohistorical context. In her essay collection *Nepantla: Essays from the Land in the Middle*, Pat Mora refers to herself as a *poeta curandera* (15). There are many connections between Mora and Anzaldúa's work, and this could be another. Perhaps Anzaldúa's curandera is also to be read as a poet whose words are herbs she uses to heal. Pat Mora, like Anzaldúa, also talks in her *Nepantla* about how important it is that the *curanderas* pass down their work. In "Poet as Curandera," Mora says: "learned wisdom, ritual, solutions springing from the land. All are essential to *curanderas*, who listen to voices from the past and the present, who evolve from their culture" (15). So if we see the *curandera* symbolically, either as poet or other purveyor of Latino culture, then her relationship with the young Prietita becomes more significant.

If we apply this idea here, then the *curandera*, who has knowledge of the earth, is passing it along to Prietita so that she can continue the healing work. For Prietita to be a healer, she needs to have the knowledge of the land and what remedies it can provide. Perhaps this strong female character, the *curandera*, is meant to be seen symbolically as a purveyor of Latino culture. Prietita is meant to learn specifically how to use herbs to heal but then also learn to value her heritage and pass it along. So while the girls in the other books learn from their mothers and grandmothers, Prietita learns from the *curandera* so that she can save her mother and perhaps save her culture.

The *Llorona*, or crying woman, is perhaps the most notable character of Latin American folklore. There are several variations of the *Llorona* story, which is usually propagated as a cautionary tale by parents who warn their children not to walk alone. Most *Llorona* tales tell of a beautiful young woman who is abandoned by her husband, who leaves her for another woman. In most versions of the story, the mother drowns her children to save them from a life of poverty. According to legend, the repentant *Llorona* can be heard crying near bodies of water, waiting to find lost children to replace her own dead ones.

The author Gloria Anzaldúa said that she heard the *Llorona* tale many times as a child, and that as a child, like all of her peers, she was afraid. She writes that even then, though, she wondered if there was another side to the *Llorona*. She takes this same search for deeper meaning into her approach to food in the story. She says that the *curanderas* or healers know things about food and its healing powers, and she hopes that children will "look beneath the surface of what things seem to be in order to find the truths that may be hidden" (from postscript). It is a goal of her protagonist to gain the knowledge of how to use plants to heal. The use of the figure of the *Llorona* is not the most familiar one to readers but it is the one that Anzaldúa has used before. Ana Carbonell discusses the way Anzaldúa and other Chicana writers have transformed and modernized the traditional legend of the *Llorona*:

> Within folkloric literature on the La Llorona legend, La Llorona emerges as both a figure of maternal betrayal and maternal resistance. While she is most often imagined as a destructive figure, contemporary Chicana writers Helena Maria Viramontes and Sandra Cisneros, by constructing defiant Llorona heroines in their respective short stories, "The Cariboo Cafe" and "Woman Hollering Creek," have propagated and vitalized the set of tales about maternal resistance. Viramontes and Cisneros do not explicitly invoke La Llorona's pre-conquest antecedents in their writings, yet they make implicit references to pre-conquest figures, and their Llorona heroines undergo a transformative process that strikingly resembles the process described by Anzaldúa in her "Coatlicue State." (Carbonell 54)

It is this transformed *Llorona* that we are introduced to in *Prietita y la Llorona*. The *Llorona* here is a positive figure, a maternal and helpful guide that assists Prietita in her quest. Anzaldúa has purposefully transformed the notion of this character, as she has many others from the *Cihuacoatl in Borderlands/La Frontera*, who goes from destroyer to earth mother and, in another of her poems, the *curandera* that changes from witch to healer, and the *Llorona* converts from murderer to guide.

In the town of the story, the *curandera* obviously has a position of power because Prietita's family uses the healer for curing their medical ailments.

Prietita hopes to one day have the knowledge of home remedies that the healer has, and so she spends time with her mentor the healer trying to learn about the medicinal uses of plants and other foods. From the illustrations by Christina Gonzalez, it is obvious that the kitchen of the healer serves as both a place for food preparation and a laboratory for making natural medicines (6). The walls are full of herbs and vegetables hanging to dry, and the illustration is bordered by plates, bowls, and fruits. There are herbs, aloe, garlic, and chili peppers hanging along the wall behind the kitchen table. The illustrations on this page give the message that food is both for nourishment as well as healing.

When Prietita returns from the forest with the rue, she gives it to the healer, who is impressed by her bravery. As a reward, the healer promises to teach her to make the remedy: "'Tomorrow, I'll show you how to prepare the healing remedio for your mother,' said Doña Lola. 'I am proud of you. You have grown up this night'" (29). She must prove herself by showing bravery and maturity in order to earn the respect of the healer and the right to learn to prepare the remedy. Soon she will be able to fulfill her goal of using food to heal.

All of the child protagonists in the three picture books, *Las hermanas, Too Many Tamales,* and *Prietita and the Ghost Woman,* have different relationships to food, but they do have one thing in common: gaining knowledge of food and its preparation gives them more authority. They have either learned to cook, to buy food, or to make home remedies, and have gained strength through doing so. With their grandmother's guidance, the sisters in *Las hermanas* transition into adulthood to take their mother's place as providers of food. Maria, in *Too Many Tamales,* pushes her cousins to eat the tamales that she has just made in order to find her mother's ring, and then she is only consoled by the act of cooking with her mother to replace the tamales she made her cousins eat. Prietita crosses into the dangerous King Ranch to get the life-saving herb for her mother and thereby earns the respect of the healer who will teach her to prepare the remedy. Through their relationships with their elder female mentors, girl characters learn more about food and its preparation, gaining control and self-confidence while strengthening their bonds with their mothers and grandmothers and carrying on the traditions of their culture.

Works Cited

Anzaldúa, Gloria. *Prietita and the Ghost Woman.* Ill. Christina Gonzalez. San Francisco: Children's Book P, 1995.

―――. *Borderlands/La Frontera: The New Mestiza.* San Francisco: Spinsters/Aunt Lute, 1987.

Carbonell, Ana María. "From Llorona to Gritona: Coatlicue in Feminist Tales by Viramontes and Cisneros." *Religion, Myth and Ritual.* Spec. issue of *MELUS* 24.2 (Summer 1999): 53–74.

Mora, Pat. *Nepantla: Essays from the Land in the Middle.* U of New Mexico P, 1993.

Nodelman, Perry, and Mavis Reimer. *The Pleasures of Children's Literature.* 3rd ed. Boston: Allyn, 2003.

Paz, Senel. *Las hermanas.* Mexico City: CIDCLI, 1993.

Pérez, Louis A. *Cuba between Reform & Revolution.* 2nd ed. Oxford: Oxford UP, 1995.

Pilcher, Jeffery M. *¡Que vivan los tamales! Food and the Making of Mexican Identity.* Albuquerque: U of New Mexico P, 1998.

Rebolledo, Tey Diana. "Tradition and Mythology: Signatures of Landscape in Chicana Literature." *The Desert is No Lady: Southwestern Landscapes in Women's Writing and Art.* Ed. Vera Norwood and Janice J. Monk. New Haven: Yale UP, 1987. 96–124.

Soto, Gary. *Too Many Tamales.* Ill. Ed Martinez. New York: Putnam, 1993.

Tapp, Alice Guadalupe. *Tamales 101: A Beginner's Guide to Making Tamales.* Berkeley, CA: Ten Speed, 2002.

Zimbalist, Andrew. "Teetering on the Brink: Cuba's Current Economic and Political Crisis." *Journal of Latin American Studies* 24.2 (May 1992): 407–418.

Chapter Twelve

Sugar or Spice?
The Flavor of Gender Self-Identity in an
Example of Brazilian Children's Literature

Richard Vernon

The tradition of children's literature of twentieth-century Brazil differs significantly from most English-language children's literature. As Kimberly Reynolds states, and others have pointed out, "children's literature is more concerned with shaping its readers' attitudes than most" (ix). And indeed most children's stories of Western cultures for centuries have sought to make use of children's impressionability in order to instill values of societal conformity—demonstrating examples that reward compliance and punish dissidence. Brazil's children's literature, however, was conceived and formed in a comparatively repressive society often manipulated by dictatorial powers such that many of the most popular writers for young people have emphasized analysis of societal and governmental dictates over simple conformation. A second important difference, and arguably the source of the first, is the presence of a single guiding omnipresent influence, that of the declared father of Brazilian children's literature, Monteiro Lobato. Ana Maria Bohrer's *A menina açucarada* (The Sugar-coated Girl) is an intriguing, fairly contemporary, and in many ways typical, example of Brazilian children's literature. The story reveals the cultural complexities and difficulties children face in deciding not to conform and demonstrates the far-reaching influence of Lobato, who began a trend in the 1920s to which there are now beginning to appear some parallels in English language children's literature.

In 1997 José Roberto Whitaker Penteado published a study on the enduring nature of the influence of Monteiro Lobato in which he provides evidence that between 50 and 75% of those who occupied leadership positions in Brazilian society in the 1980s and 90s had read Lobato, and more than half of those considered themselves significantly influenced by this reading (205). An occasional victim of the Vargas regime,[1] Lobato, through his fictional characters, advocated independent thought, feminism, individual freedom mixed with national pride, and the scrutiny of cultural tradition. Though his influence is widespread among prominent Brazilians, it has been greatest perhaps among subsequent writers of Brazilian children's literature. During the violent and repressive Brazilian military dictatorship that began in 1964 and lasted more than twenty years, a group of Brazilian writers discovered that children's literature, as an area that largely escaped the eyes of the political censors, constituted a medium through which they could impart freethinking political views of critical thinking, individual freedom, social justice, and resistance to authority. Many of these writers, such as Ana Maria Machado, Lygia Bojunga, and Ruth Rocha, inspired by Monteiro Lobato, became and continue to be commercially and critically successful, even in the current relatively democratic regime of tolerance. One of the most prolific of these, Ana Maria Machado, has published more than 96 books for children, won the Hans Christian Andersen Medal in 2000, and been inducted into the Brazilian Academy of Letters.

Bohrer's *A menina açucarada*, published in 1994 by FTD, and in the *Primeiras Histórias* series (a series in which Machado also has 46 titles), is a contemporary example of this tradition of children's literature that advocates resistance to traditional authority and refusal to conform to prescribed societal roles. Despite winning the João de Barro award, a Brazilian national award for children's literature, with her first book *Memórias de uma gatinha impressora* (Memoirs of a Publishing Cat) in 1976, Bohrer is considerably less famous and prolific than those authors mentioned above and has only published seven books for young readers. In this way, she perhaps demonstrates that the trends begun by Lobato extend far beyond the giants of contemporary Brazilian children's literature. Bohrer readily acknowledges the mark of Lobato's work on her own, and that of her contemporaries, but states that it is an influence of principle rather than technique. She explains that he taught them the importance of maintaining freedom of thought even in the face of difficult and oppressive realities (Bohrer, "Respostas"). This freedom of thought is demonstrated and embraced by Manoela, the protagonist in the story here examined, as is the potential cost, or negative consequences, of fearlessly acting upon such notions. Manoela lives, like Lobato's characters, in an environment free from fear of the punishments dreamed up by adults. Lobato's characters, like Manoela, live in a setting in which the only consequences to one's actions are the natural ones. Manoela makes her own decisions without fear and happily pays the price.

A menina açucarada equates food with social and gender identity and shows how one little girl is successful in determining her own "flavor." It tells the story of 5-year-old Manoela who lives among very affectionate family and friends. Manoela is chubby and pink and is a described as *"gostosa"* (delicious) and also as a perfectly ripe papaya. Manoela is tired of the pinches, hugs, and kisses her family showers on her and that leave her skin sticky, her hair messy, and her clothes crumpled. Her upcoming fifth birthday party is a source of worry to her as she anticipates the affection-fest that is sure to ensue with so many friends and family present. Her worries are justified, and when Manoela descends the stair to greet her party guests everyone begins to kiss her. On this day, however, it is as if Manoela were covered in sugar. Her guests comment on her remarkably sweet flavor and sugary taste. No one, not even the family dog, can resist her and, in a bizarre turn, the kisses turn to licks, as the guests smother her as if she were a lollipop, exclaiming that the girl is pure sugar. Once again Manoela's clothes are crumpled, her skin sticky, and her hair a mess. When her mother discovers her state, she sends her back to her room to change her clothes. On the way to her room she passes through the kitchen where she gets a terrific idea, one of the kind "*que até podem mudar a vida de uma menina*" (that can even change the life of a little girl). She picks up a bottle of hot pepper sauce and carries it to her room. She changes her clothes, combs her hair, and then covers herself with the pepper sauce. She returns to her guests very calmly—"*calmissimamente.*" When the guests see her descend the stairs, they again press about her and resume their previous licking.

We read that those who had not yet tasted her delicious sugar flavor wanted to, and those who had wanted to again. The hot sauce soon has everyone in tears, crying for water as the smoke ascends from their mouths.

As they drink the water the sound of the fires in their bellies being extinguished is heard. The adults consider Manoela's trick a terrible outrage and highly impertinent. Manoela's young male cousins, on the other hand, are very impressed, calling her resolute, ingenious, and courageous. The party continues

Figure 12.1. Bohrer, Ana Maria. *A meninia açucarada.* Editora FTD, São Paulo, 1994. Illustration on pages 14–15. Permission for use granted by Cláudia Helena Lacerda Cernohorsky.

with the cake, gifts, etcetera. When the time comes for the guests to leave, everyone is satisfied with simply waving their goodbyes from a distance to Manoela rather than giving her the highly traditional goodbye kiss. Cousin Bombinha comments that he won't kiss her because she now has a terrible taste.

Although this story deals more with flavor than food per se, in many ways the two are inseparable. As Pasi Falk, in his work on modern taste preferences, states, "The mouth acts both as an organ of *sensory* and sensual experience and of *censorship*: either you swallow it up or spit it out" (79). Manoela with her pleasing taste is accepted, sought after and repeatedly "consumed." We are told she is a member of a family who loves kisses and in fact has the surname of Beijoquim, a play on the Portuguese word *beijoqueiro*, meaning someone who is fond of kissing. Her assigned familial role is to receive kisses—to be the object of her family and friends' affection. As their name implies, kissing for this family is a necessity, and kissing Manoela is a pressing need almost to the point of biological drive, manifested through "sugar" consumption. Sugar is manifestly connected to the notion of nutritive subsistence. In his defense of sugar, Strong insists "we cannot think without the idea of sweetness, any more than our bodily chemistry can work without the fact of it" (qtd. in Falk 73). And Paul Rozin points out that the preference for sweets may be more biological than cultural:

Figure 12.2. Bohrer, Ana Maria. *A meninia açucarada.* Editora FTD, São Paulo, 1994. Illustration on page 17. Permission for use granted by Cláudia Helena Lacerda Cernohorsky.

Our species, and many other mammalian generalist or omnivore species, have an innate preference for sweet substances. . . . This taste bias presumably has its adaptive basis in the fact that sweet taste is characteristic of energy sources (sugars). . . . Furthermore, since the biology of the system is "the sweeter the better," individual discoveries that enhance the sweetness of available foods would be incorporated into the technology of the culture. . . . Both the refining of sugar (with the associated agricultural and sociopolitical developments) . . . and the development of artificial sweeteners are so motivated. (228)

We read that Manoela's family and friends like to kiss her and think that she likes to be kissed. They take no notice of the faces she makes, or her physical efforts to escape the affection. On the day of her party, when the simple kisses evolve into licks, marking a progression in the steps to complete consumption, her role as submissive female "object" of affection becomes closer to that of consumable. Her dislike of this position represents her fear of identity loss—an identity consumed by her friends and family.

The idea that you are what you eat, exemplified to the extreme in the popularly held belief regarding anthropophagy (that the eater obtains the qualities of the eaten), is given the status almost of cultural universal by Otto Fenichel:

The ideas of eating an object or being eaten by an object remain the ways in which any reunion with objects is thought of unconsciously. The magical communion of "becoming the same substance," either by eating the same food or by mixing the respective bloods, and the magical belief that a person becomes similar to the object he has eaten are based on this fact. (63)

As Falk reminds us, "This is the situation psychoanalysis defines as the 'oral stage' where the 'oral introjection' is simultaneously the executive of the 'primary identification' . . ." (74). It is the method of primary identification for the child, but as Fenichel's words imply, on some level the oral introjection remains an important part of adult identity as well. How many parents express their affection for their very young children verbally with terms such as "you're so yummy I could gobble you up," or similar language that expresses a desire to consume, or to dissolve and integrate their children, or what they perceive as childlike qualities, into themselves?

The source of the adult longing to incorporate the qualities of children is given a plausible rationalization in Kimberly Reynolds' explanation of the social construct of childhood from the late nineteenth century to the close of the twentieth. She demonstrates how the middle-class insecurity, caused by extreme social and political changes at the end of the nineteenth century, such as challenges to "Christianity, patriarchy, and British imperialism," contributed heavily to a new cult of childhood and a very different image of childhood than had been held in Britain in previous eras. Childhood became a golden age of innocence, security, and redemption (16). The works of children's literature of the time, most of which are still considered classics and are popular in many languages and cultures, glorify childhood or reveal the adult fantasy of returning to or prolonging it—*Peter Pan*, the stories of Francis Hodgson Burnett, and the tales of Oscar Wilde, such as *The Selfish Giant*, being some of the more salient examples. Reynolds emphasizes that such literature evinces more an adult preoccupation with and nostalgia for childhood rather than any desire on the part of children to maintain their youth, pointing out that most children are quite willing to hasten their maturity. She emphasizes that the appearance of the theme of containing time and/or "the effects of maturity" appeared first in adult literature such as H. G. Wells's *The Time Machine*, Henry James's *What Maisie Knew*, and of course Oscar Wilde's *The Picture of Dorian Gray* (17).

If the idea "of eating an object" is the way "in which any reunion with objects is thought of unconsciously," as Fenichel notes, and oral introjection is the "the executive of the 'primary identification'" of the earliest stage of childhood, as Falk observes, then it is not difficult to read Manoela's friends and family's treatment of her, and indeed all adult impulses to "devour" children, as a manifestation of the adult fantasy of returning to childhood, or incorporating into themselves the innocence, purity, and "sweetness" that have become associated with childhood most strongly since the end of the nineteenth century.

The progression from kisses to licks and Manoela's triumphant response occurs on her fifth birthday, an important milestone marking the passage from infant/toddler to a more independent stage of childhood. This independence has traditionally been marked in the United States by a child's leaving the security of home and entering the world for a few hours a day through kindergarten. Though now Brazilian children often leave home for preschool at earlier ages, as in the United States, during Bohrer's childhood age five was a significant age because it was when a child entered society by attending the equivalent of kindergarten.

Moving from one developmental stage (infancy/toddler) to another more independent one creates a perceived ambiguity in Maneola's identity. Drawing on Mary Douglas's work on ambiguity and food prohibitions, Elisabeth Fürst repeats that acceptable foods are those that present no ambiguity: "Holiness requires that different classes of things not be confused with each other. It means order, integrity, and perfection. The dietary rules concerning clean and unclean beasts then, if we follow Douglas, are simply a development of the metaphor of holiness" (Fürst 114). While "holy" foods imply perfection in the sense of being whole, those foods that are often prohibited are those viewed as ambiguous. Ambiguous foods "are symbolically and hence practically 'out of control'" (Falk 62). Drawing the parallel between human development and foods, Fürst further comments on the implications of transitional states: "A person who must pass from one situation to another is in danger herself, and she emanates danger to others" (115). Because of this danger, young women, for example, who reach the age of menstruation must be excluded and separated in many societies: "The girl being neither child, nor grown woman, is ambiguous and hence unclean" (115).

Turning five puts Manoela into an analogous ambiguous state. She will begin school and possibly other activities that separate her from the family. The increase in oral affection given to Manoela can be seen as reluctance on the part of the family and friends to allow the baby of the family, the last reminder of "sweetness," and the last vehicle of childhood fantasy, to make this passage. Manoela's "natural" or unmodified taste is sugary, which places her into the "natural basis for the human diet" (Falk 59). However, Manoela's new flavor given to her by the pepper sauce does not fall into this category and demonstrates her desire to grow up and her ability to think and act independently—simultaneously asserting a chosen identity and rejecting the role her family would give her.

Specifically what bothers Manoela about the affection-fests is that they leave her sticky and her clothes crumpled. The aversion to the feeling of stickiness is a theme examined by Mary Douglas in her famous *Purity and Danger,* where she discusses the confrontation with anomaly. Relying on Sartre's remarks on the ambiguity of viscous matter, Douglas reaffirms that slimy or sticky substances are perceived as posing a danger of dissolving into themselves anyone who comes into contact with them. Using treacle, or molasses, as one example, Douglas discusses the aversion farther, stating that it is partially based on its ambiguous character, it is somewhere between solid and liquid. Thus it gives an "ambiguous sense impression" and "attacks the boundary between myself and it" (37–38). As a substance that can be manipulated somewhat, yet can also "attack" bodily boundaries, treacle is both object and subject. As Falk points out in his elaboration of Douglas's reflections,

> The sticky and slimy is something which threatens bodily integrity. . . . It creates on the level of sense-impression an ambiguous confrontation with the uncontrollable which may be specified as the "eat or be eaten by" situation: Am I taking that object/substance into possession or is it breaking my bodily boundaries and dissolving me into itself? (76)

Interestingly, the Portuguese adjective used to describe Manoela's sticky state is "melada," which in its noun form applies to syrup, molasses, or treacle. Also, the words used to describe the state of Manoela herself and her clothes after these affection sessions imply a loss of definition. The word "amassada" is twice used to describe the girl and has "massa" or dough as its root, and the verb "amassar" means to knead as dough, or to crush or smash. We read that her clothes are "amarrotada" or crushed, crumpled, or wrinkled—amorphous.

In her role of the baby girl of the family, Manoela endures these rituals and their sticky consequences with their implicit fear of dissolution and consumption, loss of form and definition, all of which can be seen as her individual identity. Her sweetness symbolically identifies her as everything a little girl should be, but her sugary taste, with its connotation of universal energy, also marks her symbolically as attractive as a comestible, as if she fulfills an urgent, perhaps biological, need of those around her, also bringing to mind the almost cultural universal of woman as food provider. As Carol Counihan highlights, the relation between female and food provider is nearly inevitable: "The predominant role of women in feeding is a cultural universal, a major component of female identity, and an important source of female connections to and influence over others" (52). Thus Manoela not only rejects her current conventional role as the infantile object of affection, but implies that in her future the stereotypical roles assigned to women will be vulnerable to the same fate.

Acting in a manner representative of the characters of Lobato, Manoela is unwilling to allow her individuality to be swallowed by the role imposed upon her by friends and family and changes her flavor. Her choice of hot pepper sauce is significant. Whereas sugar is recognized as immediate energy among most mammals, the pepper sauce is unendurable. In fact, it perfectly reverses Manoela's role from comestible to consumer. As the narrator tells us, the idea to use the sauce is one that can truly change the life of a little girl. Instead of savoring the pleasing sweet taste of Manoela, her guests find themselves being devoured internally, as by fire.

Falk contends that those foods that are considered "out of control" are those that blur the eater/eaten distinction—that is, those substances, wild animals, or even poisons that while under certain circumstances can be food, simultaneously threaten to eat or consume the consumer (63). The extreme spiciness of Manoela's new flavor internally consumes those who would devour her. Their eyes well with tears, the room is filled with their cries, and they beg for water to quench the burning within them. As they drink, the sound of flames being extinguished is heard and smoke is seen to drift from their mouths. By willfully changing her naturally consumable flavor to one that threatens to consume those who would treat her as object, Manoela exerts control over her environment becoming subject and hence "uncontrollable"—the common denominator of forbidden foods. She does so when she herself is in an ambiguous and hence dangerous transitional state. In choosing this flavor for herself, Manoela transforms herself from natural consumable to a forbidden consuming "food." It is this degree of uncontrollability that incenses the adults against her.

To the guests of the party the pepper sauce is not an acceptable or pleasing food, and yet Manoela finds it in the kitchen where it is used presumably as food. In explaining the development of taste preference, Paul Rozin offers two stances in humans regarding taste preferences: the desire for new tastes and variety of flavor experience, and the need to eat familiar foods (230). Falk refers to these positions as neophilia, the desire for the new and surprising; and neophobia, the desire to stick with what is known. He theorizes that over time, with repeated exposure and social pressure, people can become accustomed to substances that are initially irritating, such as hot chilies and tobacco. Falk problematizes Rozin's proposal somewhat because it "fails to explain the principle which pushes the taste preferences along ... from the negative (aversion) to the positive (liking, addiction)" (68). Falk proposes that for a food to shed its negative image and to become "good to taste," it has to "*stand for* something valued" and suggests that within the "modern condition of dynamic social hierarchies," where the elite are eternally seeking new means of differentiating themselves, it is possible to acquire the taste for certain foods that represent "the prestigious and valued—or 'good taste'" (69). Thus, foods such as strong spices that are initially unpleasant or irritating can acquire the status of desirability by being attached to higher social standing. For instance, highly spiced foods are generally enjoyed by adults rather than children, and the acquiring of a taste for such marks a progression towards more adult or socially superior taste. He reminds us that "those in dominant positions tend to monopolize the 'sweet things of life'" (69–72).

Manoela's parents and adult relatives, as the elite or dominant members of her familial society, have monopolized her and her function in that unit in assigning her the role of sugar girl, or consumable object. On her fifth birthday, Manoela changes her flavor from the consumed sweetness of the child into an "adult" flavor, which is no longer object, but a consuming subject, thus asserting her growth and independence. The disappointed adults are outraged; the other children in the same social position, perhaps equally potentially ambiguous, transitional, and dangerous, admire her as one of their own who has taken a step further towards individual assertion, control of self, and adulthood. Manoela does not seem to miss the affection associated with her former role and is pleased simply to wave her goodbyes. Just as Lobato took pains to demonstrate in his children's books, *A menina açucarada* demonstrates the potential negative consequences of actions that defy the social norm. Manoela incurs the anger of her adult relatives and relinquishes forever not only the security of infancy, but the exterior societal validation that comes with the acceptance of an assigned role. Yet she appears to be willing to accept these consequences, seemingly confident in her own will.

As has been iterated numerous times, from the earliest modern conception of stories for children, children's literature has traditionally been a literature that promotes conformity and seeks to perpetuate the values and norms of the society that produces it. Like the ballad and chapbook literature of Europe and the Americas from the early modern period through the eighteenth century, intended for both children and adults with rudimentary reading skills, contemporary children's literature seeks to instill the values and ideologies of the society that produces them by demonstrating the rewards of conformity and the dangers of rebellion. In some ways, *A menina açucarada* is no different. Though its message may be seen as nontraditional, in that it encourages a degree of rebellion, it reflects the high value placed on individuality and the occasional necessity of nonconformity by a society that suffered under repression for so long. Rather than diverging from societal values, *A menina açucarada* demonstrates more of a shift in those values.

In a recent Foucauldian analysis of Lowry's famous adolescent novel *The Giver*, Don Latham draws certain conclusions that portray this story as similar to those of the tradition of Brazilian children's literature. Latham points out that the story's protagonist, Jonas, rejects the role assigned him by his dystopian society and that the novel contradicts the notion typical of most novels for adolescents that contain as their message ways in which uncontrollable children can learn to function within their society's institutional limits. Like Manoela,

"Jonas should be admired precisely *because* he resists the institutional structures of his community" (Latham 135). Jonas's role as a giver-in-training is, similar to Manoela's as a sweet little girl, one that is prized and honored by the society, yet both protagonists reject roles that fulfill their respective society's needs in favor of one that reflects their own desires. As Latham suggests, Lowry creates a fictional dystopian society in order to create a situation in which it is admirable for the protagonist to rebel against it. But the society of Lobato, within Vargas's New State, and in the subsequent military dictatorship in which Brazilian children's literature matured, was a true-life dystopic society recognized as such by the populace, which came to value the courage to question dictates, whether societal or governmental. Like *The Giver*, *A menina açucarada* reflects the trend discussed by Reynolds, that children's literature in the late twentieth century increasingly deals with important issues of growing up in ways that break with the conventions of the past. But in the case of the Brazilian story, it reflects a tradition begun in the first quarter of the twentieth century by Monteiro Lobato rather than representing this tendency seen in English language children's literature in the late-twentieth century.

Notes

1   Getulio Vargas ruled Brazil in many capacities: as chief of the provisional government (1930–1934); president elected by Congress (1934–1937); dictator (1937–1945); and president elected by the people (1951–1954). Lobato was arrested for a time in 1941.

Works Cited

Bohrer, Ana Maria. "*Respostas*." E-mail to the author. 27 July 2005.
———. *A menina açucarada*. São Paulo: Editora FTD, 1994.
Counihan, Carole M. "Female Identity, Food, and Power in Contemporary Florence." *Anthropological Quarterly* 61 (1988): 51–62.
Douglas, Mary. *Purity and Danger*. London: Routledge, 1966.
Falk, Pasi. "The Sweetness of Forbidden Fruit: Towards an Anthropology of Taste." *Palatable Worlds: Sociocultural Food Studies*. Ed. Elisabeth L. Fürst, et al. Oslo, Norw.: Solum Forlag, 1991. 53–83.
Fenichel, Otto. *The Psychoanalytic Theory of Neurosis*. London: Routledge, 1982.
Fürst, Elisabeth L. "Food, Identity, and Gender. A Story of Ambiguity." *Palatable Worlds: Sociocultural Food Studies*. Ed. Elisabeth Fürst, et al. Oslo, Norw.: Solum Forlag. 111–130.
Latham, Don. "Discipline and Its Discontents: A Foucauldian Reading of *The Giver*." *Children's Literature* 32 (2004): 134–151.
Penteado, Filho, and José Roberto Whitaker. *Os filhos de Lobato : O imaginário infantil na ideologia do adulto*. Rio de Janeiro, Braz.: Dunya, 1997.
Reynolds, Kimberly. *Children's Literature in the 1890s and the 1990s*. Plymouth, UK: Northcote, 1994.
Rozin, Paul. "Human Food Selection: The Interaction of Biology, Culture and Individual Preference." *The Psychobiology of Human Food Selection*. Ed. Lewis M. Barker. Waco, TX: Baylor U, 1982. 225–254.

Part VI
Through Food the/a Self

Chapter Thirteen

Oranges of Paradise:
The Orange as Symbol of Escape
and Loss in Children's Literature

James Everett

Jane Eyre lost some favor in my eyes long ago when I first read that she "dismissed" the "little orphan" who served as her handmaid with "the fee of an orange" one evening at Morton (Charlotte Brontë 342). Still developing her writing style or not, Brontë was responsible, in my eyes, for the insensitivity of Jane's action. Hardly ten years earlier, Jane was a student herself at Lowood when one evening she and Helen Burns, hungry and with hands cold and a demeanor of "inexpressible sadness," crept into Miss Temple's quarters where they had been invited to share toast and tea and even a "good-sized seed-cake" (62, 65). Even that small meal became a sacrifice, we learn, when we see Miss Temple's request for more refused. But the midnight snack develops into something to cherish as the girls "feasted that evening as on nectar and ambrosia" (65), and the event lingers in the memories of many readers, I suspect, because of the literal warmth in food and in sheltered space Jane recalls, both treasures, if ever obtained at all, in a childhood devoid of such basic pleasures. *Jane Eyre*, for all its experienced and scholarly readers since, has also become a children's book, speaking to at least one audience (among many different ones) of young women maturing past their own ugly duckling stage and destined now for romance in a grown-up world. But for all readers young enough in heart to remember when a simple kindness from the adult world could mean rescue, or even salvation, *Jane Eyre* stands as validation. Why then is Jane so literally dismissive with the girl at Morton who most likely adores her? Why indeed, as such rapid turning away seems to obscure what it meant to lose Helen, whose lack of sustenance certainly contributed to her decline? So much depends on the value, real or perceived, of the orange.

Challenging Brontë's assessment of an orange could pertain to any study of food and children in Western literature, not only because Charlotte quite noticeably preoccupies herself with food in the novel, thus signaling, as has been argued, a food obsession that would loom large over her own deathbed, but also because the orange, as metonym, nicely encases the complex relationships among childhood and food and colonialism in Europe and its literature. In a broad sense, Jane's story represents at least one canonical English literary perspective on food and growing from childhood to adulthood. But there is more than the formal conception of *Bildungsroman* at issue here; wider elements than the literary suggest another Victorian contextual approach to studying fruit and children: oranges show a range of values until the middle of the nineteenth century and then, in many cases, lose metaphoric value because of literally increasing availability.

So it is chronology that matters: in the span of a particular one hundred years or so, oranges come and go in relative symbolic importance in the north of Europe, the broadly defined geographic area most pertinent to a study of children's literature in a Germanic language such as English. From its beginnings, the orange comes from the east (originating in China and India in most accounts) and from the south towards the west and north; in other words, from hot, southern Asia to colder regions in the north, where this orb of golden fire and sweet liquid ends up inspiring English poets: Andrew Marvell, for one, tells of the western "remote Bermudas" where "hangs in shades the orange bright, /like golden lamps in a green night." Ironic opposition here accompanies images of the orange; light in the darkness of a grove, for instance, shines brighter where oranges as little metaphorical suns puncture the emerald leaves in the scented night. To highlight the confluence of opposites inherent in the orange's origins set against its destinations, it is important to focus on children's literature written in English-speaking areas of the world where access to oranges was for some time not historically convenient. That the magic fruit has an expiration date for its symbolic value seems to be the real wonder. How does a symbol as rich as an orange lose literary value? And in its fall from grand symbol of an era to a sign of bleaker things ahead, is there recovery in store for the orange as perceived by young readers?

Deconstruction—even if no longer in its heyday spurred on by Jacques Derrida—remains useful beyond any golden age of criticism because of one of its tools. Hongyu Wang, in an intensive examination of *aporia* as it relates to pedagogical responsibility in multicultural education, draws from Derrida's own study of the term to explain a "state of impasse, nonpassage, or logical contradiction that can never be permanently resolved, a state of constant dilemma with no general or final solution" (45). Boundaries, a prominent theme in Victorian studies, between opposing places or states must be both crossed and not crossed; "in the passage and nonpassage of the borderline, aporia becomes the possibility of impossibility, and nonidentity becomes a part of identity" (Wang 47). The orange as both a source of delight and an emblem of the unreachable is aporetic because it both promises and denies escape and compensation.

Literary audiences may lean closer to a study of symbolism than to an appraisal of simple pleasure. But a focus on pleasure drives much of the children's literature criticism written by Jack Zipes and Perry Nodelman. Zipes warns of the intellectual pitfalls in discussing theory for theory's sake, which can lead easily to what he in 1990 called "academic gibberish" in the third edition of *Only Connect* (365), a title that not only reflects the theme of this study but that also anticipates E. M. Forster's role in my conclusion. In similar fashion, too much speculation on subtext or motive in the fairy tale (in particular for Zipes those collected by the Grimm brothers) can obscure the simplest subjects. Nodelman, though he points out Zipes's Marxist bias in interpreting fairy tales and Ruth Bottigheimer's comparable feminist bias, concedes that such personal observations do not interfere with his agreeing with the conclusions of these scholars (258). In fact, the general notion that the tales are not what they seem may be what most fully unifies scholars at odds with one another; a sort of harmony, then, exists because each interpreter acknowledges that there is pleasure in seeing how many differences can arise from the same source (259). This unifying aporia depends on difference: opposites are symbiotic. Nodelman's technique in his willingness to concede does not make him a fence-straddler; on the contrary, such an outlook prioritizes pleasure over the potentially misleading academic task of resolving inconsistencies. Embracing the unclear for the sake of pleasure puts symbolic significance in its place while also not rejecting it as unimportant; the orange contains such paradox. The orange in literature stands on a boundary between two states of being: it separates the everyday world from a place more wondrous, more exotic, but out of reach. One might ask whether the emblem spanning two sides unites more or divides more.

Because one major literary convention in the context of Christianity—fruit preceding a fall—gets depicted most often with apples instead of oranges, one might argue that there is, so to speak, no comparison between the two. In both prelapsarian and postlapsarian reference (which, seen in the right context, effectively covers all of time), the apple would seem to be the bigger star. However, the orange in literature for and about children holds a distinct edge over other fruit as symbol. Because of the orange's aporetic connection of promising escape while simultaneously calling attention to one's entrapment or while signifying deep values not immediately attainable, oranges, in at least this frame, may indeed be the only fruit. According to John McPhee in what certainly must be the definitive book on oranges, simply entitled *Oranges*, these are the only fruits which are sweeter when grown closer to the equator and which require northern latitudes for their distinctive tartness (4). The only common fruit with a wide range of growing latitude but not readily available in English-speaking countries, oranges remained uncommon in some of these regions until the eighteenth and even the nineteenth centuries, even in some states just outside the American Southeast. This inaccessibility, just a century or less ago, in northern areas where children's literature in English first developed, qualifies the orange as a symbol richer than the apple—how many things besides sin and temptation does the apple readily symbolize?

Like Wordsworth bounding as a roe among the mountains, McPhee moves quickly through the groves of his book with childlike delight, slowing down enough to sow golden images here and there for his readers. McPhee's romantic turn shows up especially well in his comparison of the bustle of "gas stations, Burger Queens, and shopping centers" of central Florida to the repose of the orange grove world where he encloses himself: "The groves, in absolute contrast, are both beautiful and quiet, at moments eerie. I retreated into them as often as I could. To someone who is alone in the groves, they can seem to be a vacant city, miles wide and miles long" (61). Seeing such dimension in the everyday seems to guide McPhee's delightful study, just as the subject of pleasure guides the criticism of Zipes and Nodelman. These various directions, in turn, form the basis at the heart of my analysis of the orange in literature.

Maguelonne Toussaint-Samat in her expansive *History of Food* points to how rare the orange was in Europe even as late as the nineteenth century: children dreamed of oranges all year, and most children, she says, "did not know what an orange tasted like, or even if they would dare to eat that golden, almost magical fruit" (659). But the medicinal value of the orange brought a new sense of "gold" to the fruit when shrewd doctors sold its juice to prospectors suffering from scurvy ("rife" among prospectors, Toussaint-Samat explains, who subsisted on a diet of canned food) in California in the late 1840s (665). Imported with "some difficulty" from Florida, the juice was sold by the spoonful: "Prospectors, horrified to find their teeth suddenly dropping out, could be seen offering a sardine can stuffed with gold dust for a consultation—equivalent to more than 200 dollars of the time" (665). As a means of compensation, the orange becomes bright currency, securing what is desired, and promising more to come in a better future or, as a token of dear times (such as Christmas, to be considered shortly), signifying values that surpass material riches. The hope of escape and compensation and the sign of that hope, the orange, create opposing states of being, one positive but the other dimmed by the very presence of the object signifying absence of real and full escape or compensation.

Naturally, oranges begin to appear more often in the literature of the day as more and more people become familiar with them. One reason for the increase of oranges in stories and articles was the new attention given to children as a whole. Laura Berry, in her study of children and government in the Victorian novel, points to the new realization of child welfare in 1859 when Herbert Spencer in a "sweeping and even startling statement" declared that "child welfare . . . was to be given pride of place over the more traditional projects and institutions of the state" (1). Now the home became, in Berry's words, "permeable territory" (2). The new status placed children on a higher plane, one in which their own literature could develop. Much of the critical regard for children's literature in English recognizes the eighteenth and nineteenth centuries as containing the first traces of such writing. Julia Briggs in the third edition of *Only Connect: Readings on Children's Literature* asserts, in fact, that the first serious literature intended for children was Sarah Fielding's *The Governess* in 1749 (28). From there it is not a long leap to Maria Edgeworth's tale of "The Orange Man," first published in 1796. In that story the oranges themselves serve mainly to supply that story's rising action. But the value of oranges stands out when we see how dearly this expensive fruit is defended by a boy who learns that accepting responsibility can lead to its own reward (the boy's desperate fight to protect the oranges leads to the Orange Man's admiration and ensuing decision to take the boy on as a business partner).

One Victorian study of Maria Edgeworth opens with the author's appraisal of Edgeworth's contribution to her own happy childhood (Oliver v). Edgeworth's didacticism matches the spirit of the age in which she writes, as indicated in the title of the collection containing "The Orange Man": *Parent's Assistant* (1796). But Grace Oliver's clear enjoyment of the tales she read as a child certainly sets delight over instruction. And though children may perceive the lesson in the boy's initial failure to safeguard the Orange Man's produce, the fun of the disasters that develop when the boy succumbs to the many pleas for "just one" orange makes the story memorable for the pleasure in reading it. Reading the story provides escape from the ordinary world, whether or not children see the orange as a symbol of the brighter, warmer world that provides the Orange Man's livelihood north of where the fruit grows.

The orange as magic, as a harbinger or token of another world, appears frequently in nineteenth-century literature for and about children in non-seasonal themes and especially in themes of the Christmas season. Charles Dickens's Christmas stories, most of which feature oranges in one way or another, did much to revive the celebration of Christmas that had been largely absent since the Puritans banned Christmas festivities during the 1649–1660 Interregnum (Schlicke 95). Because the austerity went on to influence many Christmases and because life suddenly took on more work and more work hours due to the rising Industrial Revolution, the sparseness of festival celebration lasted well into the 1830s (Schlicke 95). But the 1840s brought three distinct additions to the celebration: most importantly, the publication of Dickens's *A Christmas Carol* in 1843, but also the newly affordable Christmas cards for posting by mail in the 1840s, and finally, the Christmas tree's formal import from Germany by Prince Albert in 1841 (Schlicke 95–96). Dickens even invented a "Carol Philosophy" that especially valued the imagination of the child, the power of memory to restore moral sense, and "the need for human contact and compassion" (95). Feasting was a part of the celebration, but Dickens went to some length to show that luxurious food was never more important than compassion for others in need. In *Great Expectations*, for example, Pip (incidentally, the term for an orange seed) shares what would have been his Christmas dinner in the marsh with a convict while his family later eats their formal meal inside (Dickens 25, 33–37). Pip never even gets to taste the customary "nuts and oranges and apples" (32). In such mortal fear of both the convict and the soldiers pursuing him, Pip would be justified in refusing to look on any more oranges for a while. But Dickens does not fail to include oranges on the table of the feast uniting everyone at the end of *A Christmas Carol*, suggesting then that oranges may contain opposing symbolisms on either side of the orb.

Escaping to a magic world finds conflicting treatment in Christina Rossetti's "Goblin Market," where oranges are mentioned a couple of times along with a plethora of other fruits being sold by the elusive goblin men: "Come buy, come buy: / Apples and quinces, / Lemons and oranges, . . . / Figs to fill your mouth, / Citrons from the South, / Sweet to tongue and sound to eye; / Come buy, come buy" (Rossetti ll. 4–6, 28–31). Pleasure reigns in the poem's beginning yet does not triumph in the end. The fruits promise escape to a world that the sisters both long for and fear. Here, Derrida's aporia describes the irresolvable confluence of both desire for the forbidden enchanted world and relinquishment of that desire for the mature world that ought to be embraced. If it is not pleasurable to lose the one world where pleasure dominates, there may be at least some compensation for loss in the sisterly love that will face all odds to come. In Rossetti's "At Home," the speaker has already lost all contact with the living as her spirit cringes at the friends who are "Feasting beneath green orange boughs" and sucking "the pulp of plum and peach" without ever thinking of or even speaking once of the departed: her spirit leaves "Like the rememberance of a guest / That tarrieth but a day" (17).

Sometimes the magic orange indicates the gap between northern and southern worlds as it represents the delight of the South come to dwell in the midst of northern things. In *Life on the Mississippi,* Mark Twain notes that even Mrs. Trollope had to confess the charms of the land where "palmetto and orange" flourish; oranges can even "ripen in the open air" as far north as Natchez, she says (Twain 233). But Fanny Trollope may have been fed a tall tale, like one of Twain's own, by a proud farmer with a secret greenhouse in this town just north of the 31st parallel, certainly not ideal growing country for oranges. In *A Tramp Abroad* Twain tells how Scots islanders in the wild north of Scotland were given a shipwreck's remaining load of oranges; one of the men, having never seen an orange, replied some time later on being asked how he liked the oranges, that the strange fruit was tough when baked and even when boiled did not make up much for a hungry man to eat (148). Ignorance of a southern thing could not be clearer.

Earlier than Twain, Walt Whitman in a section from *Leaves of Grass* marvels at how fast orange trees can arrive up North: "Now here their sweetness through my room unfolding / A bunch of orange buds by mail from Florida" (Book XXXIV). A sign of brotherly love and compassion whether symbolism pertains or not, twenty or thirty oranges, bright edible symbols of warmth and peace, pass from Whitman's hand to the wounded soldiers he visits in one of the countless Civil War hospitals in the North. After coming into a hospital from the snow outside following one particular Christmas, Whitman wants to eat one of his oranges but fears that he will come up short as he hands them out later. He tells his friend Ellen Calder one day that he has met "soldiers from the West who had never seen an orange till he carried them to the hospital," and he adds that "the aroma of a lemon held in the hand was often most grateful to a fever patient" (Calder 2). It is clear wherever Whitman goes that these wounded soldiers are boys; it is also clear that these tales of Whitman's constant visits of mercy easily qualify as literature about children. When Walt peels an orange, the soldiers' heads "began to turn in their beds as the smell drifted over the ward" (Adrian 3). Their youth is sadly obvious in the next line: "Some asked if he had any for them" (3). Oranges minister to heartache and the horrors of war, but the following imagery suggests animation, buoyancy even: a soldier, proud to have known Walt for some time, replies, "'Course he does," and Walt stands up with a whole coatful of oranges (3). One wonders if Whitman put those orange buds sent from Florida to good use somewhere inside and away from the north winds.

When Robert Louis Stevenson arrived in New Jersey in 1880, he bought oranges on the street because they and nuts were the "only refection to be had" (13). Stevenson casually eats his orange and then throws the peel under the train car and is shocked to see "grown people and children groping on the track after my leavings" (13). Oranges at this juncture of the rich and the poor can take on sinister qualities of symbolism. To return to Charlotte Brontë for a moment, the fruit that Rochester encounters in the Caribbean is burdened with suggestiveness: he walks under the "dripping orange-trees" of the wet garden and beneath "drenched pomegranates" (Charlotte Brontë 131). In Jean Rhys's conception of the same place, Rochester resigns himself to "Rain, for ever raining. Drown me in sleep. And soon" (Rhys 94). In the jungle nearby, orange trees grow wild with dark leaves as backdrop, and a snake lives there, but the danger, even in its modern depiction, does not overshadow Brontë's Victorian heaviness. In *Wuthering Heights,* Emily Brontë seems to have the same regard for oranges as her sister does when she has Nelly using them as "propitiation" to keep Hareton from throwing a rock at her again (Emily Brontë 254). Once again the orange is a bribe, something that the adult will not miss but that attracts the child because of its inaccessibility.

The orange's currency continues to expire rapidly through the remainder of the century. Dickens has oranges thrown indiscriminately along with half-pence to the young Toodles in *Dombey and Son* (73). In *Oliver Twist,* orange peels are objects of amusement, little scraps to cause someone to slip and fall (123). In the prettiness of transparent liqueurs and "violet spinals" and "orange bitters" in Dorian Gray's garden, the orange is reduced to essence, a distillation of its wholeness, and everyone knows where such pure decadence will get you (Wilde, *Picture* 14). Kenneth Grahame's Harold in *Dream Days* manages to suck orange juice through a sugar cube inserted into the orange and then runs off full of "orange-juice and iniquity," as if the juice is more vinegar or cheap whiskey than the golden drink bought so dearly as medicine in the past (Grahame 43).

Changes in a modern world were expected by the Victorians. But the extent of carnage wrought by new technology could not be foreseen. Yet, the first World War seemed to be in a No Man's Land itself between the centuries: Victorian in its fading codes of honor and in its last cavalry charges but horribly modern in its rain of fire from airplanes and lumbering metal tanks and machine guns, all directed on the young men of many nations. The first and last battlefield Christmas truce in 1914 brought soldiers of both sides together in No Man's Land to exchange cigarettes and food, notably oranges and nuts and marmalade. One writer has called this truce the last "puff" of Victorianism.

Paul Fussell begins a chapter about British soldiers in the freezing weather of 1917 France with the observation that the men discover that "Two oranges this morning were as hard as cricket balls" (Fussell 4). Frozen oranges, Fussell explains, become "an emblem not just of the terrible winter of 1917 but of the compensatory appeal of the sun-warmed, free, lively world elsewhere, mockingly out of reach of those entrenched and immobile, apparently forever, in the smelly, freezing mud" (4). The soldiers, again most of them in their teens, grow up fast in war but also in the time after the war, in the new tourist age of leaving the dampness and cold at home and heading towards hotter places through faster and cheaper transportation. One war veteran, Osbert Sitwell, decides to follow the orange tree wherever it grows because oranges point to the best climate anywhere and, unlike the apple, Sitwell declares (mistakenly) that "the orange has never been associated with evil, only with warmth, civility, taste, beauty" (4).

Only the complexity of the aporia can lead to some sense of understanding how such opposite forces can coexist in one space. The orange in literature and in reality connects contraries repeatedly in its appearance in soldiers' letters and in diaries, but it also connects people separated by war. One Second World War veteran recalls that he and his men found a young Italian boy who wouldn't eat the orange they had given him because he wanted to take it home to share the luxury with his family. The soldiers manhandled him to the ground and filled his pants legs with oranges before turning him loose to go home (Ronningen 4). In a grand sense, the orange does occasionally exemplify E. M. Forster's often quoted line from *Howard's End* to "only connect" (21). Many foods may do this, but next to candy and other sugar products equally hard to find in tough times, oranges are often the sweetest sort of treat that children can get, when they can get it. Children need no symbolism to accompany the oranges; the value lies in quick consumption.

In his reply to a letter from a young scholar obsessed with figuring out every possible meaning in *A Passage to India*'s Marabar Caves, Forster surprises the student with a sense of frankness and pleasure that clearly dominates any heavy, academic treatment. Robert Selig, the student who never expected a personal reply from the novelist himself, explains how Forster pointed out to him in the letter that symbols can also be playthings that are not always to be taken seriously (Selig 476). One can get caught up in finding significance everywhere. Forster uncovers the obvious for the student writer: symbols may not always be there in any text. In this sense, the orange at times certainly may reflect a lack of effectual symbolism. It can correspond partially to something but at the same time fail to achieve weighty meaning and harmony. Sometimes simple enjoyment matters most, and letting go of mastering everything can ease one into that joy. Matthew Arnold, in wrestling with how to explain the function of criticism, decides that criticism involves seeing an object in itself as it really is (583). Oscar Wilde, leaping at any chance to glorify art as pleasure and nothing useful, responds years later to Arnold's earnest attempts by a reversal: the better judgment is seeing the thing as it really is not (Wilde, *Complete* 1028–30). Wilde presses the symbolic over the practical.

Oranges are mixed with war and other darkness and confusion in Jeanette Winterson's *Oranges Are Not the Only Fruit*, a coming-of-age story set in England's north, near Manchester. The cold and dark feature almost as characters themselves who surround the main character, Jeanette, as she tries to decide throughout the story literally where to go. She is trapped in a northern world but jolted out of it repeatedly by her mother's constant offerings of oranges. The opposition of North and South occurs commonly enough in literature to gain status as a convention, although both ends of the spectrum, or axis in this case, contain conflicting characteristics. In western Europe, the South plays opposition to the orderly North, a binary so powerful historically that entire systems arose from racist interpretations: Social Darwinism and geographic determinism recognized more favorable traits in peoples of northern and western Europe and less desirable traits in all points southward. Northern order and energy square off against southern passion and exoticism; thinkers indoors in the cold North are set against dancers outside in the Trade Winds. The binary works in justifying colonialism; the organized world can improve those peoples who live in ignorance and wild abandon in the hot countries.

Philip Dodd, reviewing writings concerning "the North," observes that the north part of England once held a certain status or aura that it now no longer has, as there are fewer factories in the region. Dodd's term "Northernness" depends on relationship with an opposite; the novel of "the North" differs from the norm, the novel of "the South," which for Dodd is "simply the novel" (Dodd 18). (Transposing the binary to the United States, the reverse holds true: Americans have a Southern literature but nothing called a "Northern literature.") Dodd observes that the delight of *Oranges Are Not the Only Fruit* has less to do with the "defiantly comic" working-class story than it does with the author's conflation of time in two distinct worlds or periods. Winterson shifts her setting back and forth, Dodd explains, mixing details of the Second World War homefront with the contemporary world of Jeanette's hometown. Oranges show up in both eras, connecting disparate things spatially as well as chronologically but never coming across as easily understandable symbols.

Dodd opens his discussion by referring to Yorkshire and the gloomy north of the Brontës without extending his analysis forward to any connection with Winterson's novel, which depends heavily on *Jane Eyre* as context in its role as the protagonist's formative novel. Already confused about love and men and women and sexual orientation in general, Jeanette learns one day that the tale of Jane Eyre told to her as a bedtime story did not actually end as her mother had ended it. Jeanette had believed for years that Jane had gone off happily with St. John to India at the end, assisting him as he hacked and hewed his way through caste and creed in the hot southlands. Jeanette is devastated to learn that the novel did not end so neatly and piously, and she feels horribly betrayed by her mother. The pairing of North and South, ice and passion, asserts itself in Jane's life as it does in Jeanette's, who can never escape the ubiquitous oranges proffered by her mother at every junction. Neither Dodd nor Winterson points to the orange as it actually appears in Brontë's novel at Morton. Jane chooses the cold North, not unusual, it seems, as the hot countries are thick with too much luxuriance and sensual delight. But the primary block of ice in her life has gone southward and eastward to India as a missionary, and she is free in the bracing northern air. The conflicting readings of Jane's independence and power at the novel's end come into play when we consider her future. She may not need to remember the orange; it was a mere subtropical thing anyway, nothing from the golden tropics, nothing that she will fail to encounter again. It can be, however, a useful fee to pay someone casually.

Sometimes the orange in recent children's books or coming-of-age stories signifies both the ineffable joy and pain associated with growing up. Patricia Polacco's *An Orange for Frankie* tells a sad and happy story that is fairly subdued in its portrayal of the Victorian Christmas spirit so often revived, successfully or not, for today's audiences. Frankie, in this wonderfully illustrated book for parents to read to their kids, loses his Christmas orange and gets a "new" one returned to him through a careful wrapping of each of eight segments from each of the other eight family members. Sentiment figures prominently, but any heaviness in theme gets counteracted by the realistic detail that the author provides from her own family history. The setting, in wintertime Illinois during the Great Depression, dominates the action. These are hard times, the story shows, when men without jobs and sometimes without shirts—and always longing for something to eat—ride on trains through the Illinois winter, stopping at the author's grandparents' house-turned-eatery by the tracks. The setting is laden with the burdens and obstacles of a poor economy in a remote northern location where even people, much less oranges, have a hard time getting across the white landscape. Just getting home, for the father, is an accomplishment in itself. But he gets there, bringing the family's traditional Christmas oranges from the city. The oranges are valuable for their brightness and sweetness but also for what they signify: the unity of family and the bond that will never break. In the family's future Christmases, there is always an orange set aside, "Frankie's orange," which represents the real gold, the real brightness, in any dark winters to come.

But sometimes the orange signals bad art ahead, the best intentions train-wrecked by straining sentimentality and overwrought nostalgia. Too many oranges in too many Christmas stories over the years can end up leaving a bad taste: one little book entitled *Christmas Oranges* presents a maudlin account of how orphans unite to enjoy the holiday despite the meddling of an orphanage director, a cardboard character who has no redeeming traits whatsoever. The story's vague setting enables the author to draw again from Victorian values about children, Christmas, and oranges, but this is the rosy Victoriana of current house decorating magazines. The story relies on the same reconstruction of an orange by uniting its separated segments as we saw in *An Orange for Frankie*, but it lacks any sense of character development and it presents a cartoon rivalry between the good kids and the bad orphanage director, thus pulling for sentiment where none has been established. We are expected to have good feelings stemming from bad writing.

On the other hand, a different sort of misery appears in good writing about bad times. One of the most disturbing illustrations of the orange as a Christmas gift, a compensation for what is missing, occurs in Richard Wright's *Black Boy:*

> Christmas came and I had but one orange. I was hurt and would not go out to play with the neighborhood children who were blowing horns and shooting firecrackers. I nursed my orange all of Christmas Day: at night, just before going to bed, I ate it, first taking a bite out of the top and sucking the juice from it as I squeezed it; finally I tore the peeling into bits and munched them slowly. (67)

This orange in its brightness and sweetness reminds the character of what he does not have and cannot get. Yet his grasp of the emblem is sure: he consumes the object that inflicts his pain, refusing to allow any sort of connection with other children or with hope itself.

It is certainly not difficult to find thousands of Christmas orange stories more joyful than Richard Wright's. With the new sense of connecting made possible by computers, one can bring up countless Internet stories that portray sentiment and nostalgia and spiritual joy through the Christmas orange. Online church newsletters frequently use these orange stories to remind readers of the values that matter most. Blogs everywhere present older people recounting their early Christmases when they were happy just to get an orange. Even more significantly, other sites have younger people recounting the nostalgia over their elders' stories of oranges. And like stories where human nature prevails heroically in the end, these stories end in brightness. Because new children's literature does show the orange in new light, can we say that the orange will retain its symbolic stature? I do know that it is steadily losing one kind of status: surely I am in one of the last generations whose members have heard firsthand accounts of Christmas oranges or who have actually received oranges for Christmas. Those of us who know such stories close at hand are growing fewer; those who read this and really did get only an orange for Christmas may be among the oldest readers, ones who understand the depth of symbolic value more than the rest of us. Of course class and culture must be taken into account, but it is probably safe to say that in many ways the orange has gone the way of Christmas peppermint sticks and butterscotch candies in a glass dish on the coffee table: candy canes are for decorating the tree rather than for saving to eat, and butterscotch candies are for grandparents.

In the end, there are at least two possible interpretations of an orange's symbolic value. One of these recognizes the infinite depths of meaning inherent in the orange and seeks to fully embrace its exotic nature and golden light and literary and cultural significance. This object of art proves the aesthetic value gained by Oscar Wilde's sharp response to Matthew Arnold's concept of judging a thing as it really is in life. The first approach to the orange mirrors Wilde's object in seeing art, in seeing the thing as it really is not. The other approach stops short of such well-meaning comprehensiveness and views the orange as rough, incomplete, a subtropical thing rather than some sort of purely tropical escapee hardly ever accessible to common people out of its precise range. It is not difficult to get to Gulf Shores, Alabama, where sweet satsumas thrive. There is no need to cross the Tropics to find the ideal golden fruit. Children see both the pleasure and the lessons behind the object. But they beat adults hands down in seeing the real object, grabbing it, and in the spirit of Matthew Arnold, eating the thing in itself as it really is.

Works Cited

Adrian, Chris. *Gob's Grief.* New York: Vintage, 2003. Online. <http://www.ereader.com/product/book/excerpt/11644?book=Gobs_Grief>.

Arnold, Matthew. "The Function of Criticism at the Present Time." *Critical Theory Since Plato.* Ed. Hazard Adams. New York: Harcourt, 1971. 583–595.

Berry, Laura C. *The Child, the State, and the Victorian Novel,* Charlottesville: UP of Virginia, 1999.

Bethers, Linda. *Christmas Oranges.* American Fork, UT: Covenant, 1999.

Briggs, Julia. "Reading Children's Books." *Only Connect: Readings on Children's Literature.* Ed. Sheila Egoff, Gordon Stubbs, Ralph Ashley, and Wendy Sutton. 3rd ed. Oxford: Oxford UP, 1989.

Brontë, Charlotte. *Jane Eyre.* 1847. New York: Norton, 1987.

Brontë, Emily. *Wuthering Heights.* 1847. London: Penguin, 1985.

Calder, Ellen. "Personal Recollections of Walt Whitman." *Atlantic Monthly* 99 (1907): 825–834. <http://www.jlc.net/~rwright/pages/wwcalder.html>.

Dickens, Charles. *Dombey and Son*. 1848. London: Penguin, 1988.

———. *Great Expectations*. 1861. New York: Signet, 1980.

———. *Oliver Twist*. 1838. London: Penguin, 2003.

Dodd, Philip. "Lowryscapes: Recent Writings about 'the North.'" *Critical Quarterly* 32.2 (1990): 17–29. Online. Available HTTP: <http://web.ebscohost.com> (accessed 2 June 2007).

Edgeworth, Maria. *The Parent's Assistant*. London: Johnson, 1796.

Forster, E. M. *Howard's End*. 1910. Boston: Bedford, 1997.

Fussell, Paul. *Abroad: British Literary Traveling Between the Wars*. New York: Oxford UP, 1980.

Grahame, Kenneth. *Dream Days*. London: John Lane, 1898. <http://www.online-literature. com/grahame/dream-days/>.

McPhee, John. *Oranges*. New York: Farrar, 1967.

Nodelman, Perry. *The Pleasures of Children's Literature*. 2nd ed. White Plains, NY: Longman, 1996.

Oliver, Grace A. *A Study of Maria Edgeworth: With Notices of Her Father and Friends*. Boston: Williams, 1882.

Polacco, Patricia. *An Orange for Frankie*. New York: Philomel, 2004.

Rhys, Jean. *Wide Sargasso Sea*. New York: Norton, 1966.

Ronningen, Thor. Interview with Joseph James. *Voices: Through the Eyes of the Cape Fear*. 1 July 1998. Online. Available HTTP: <http://capefearww2.uncwil.edu/voices/ronningen002. html> (accessed 3 May 2007).

Rossetti, Christina. *Goblin Market and Other Poems*. 1862. New York: Dover, 1994.

Schlicke, Paul. *Oxford Reader's Companion to Dickens*. New York: Oxford UP, 1999.

Selig, Robert L. "'God si Love': On an Unpublished Forster Letter and the Ironic Use of Myth in *A Passage to India*." *Journal of Modern Literature* 7.3 (1979): 471–487. Online. Available HTTP: <http://web.ebscohost.com> (accessed 2 June 2007).

Stevenson, Robert Louis. *Across the Plains: With Other Memories and Essays*. London: Chatto, 1892.

Toussaint-Samat, Maguelonne. *A History of Food*. Trans. Anthea Bell. Oxford, UK: Blackwell, 1994.

Twain, Mark. *Life on the Mississippi*. 1883. New York: Signet, 1961.

———. *A Tramp Abroad*. 1880. New York: Signet, 1963.

Wang, Hongyu. "Aporias, Responsibility, and the Im/Possibility of Teaching Multicultural Education." *Educational Theory* 55 (2005): 45–49.

Whitman, Walt. "Orange Buds by Mail from Florida." *Leaves of Grass*. Book XXXIV. <http:// www.daypoems.net/poems/2213.html>.

Wilde, Oscar. *Complete Works of Oscar Wilde*. Ed. Vyvyan Holland. London: Collins, 1966.

———. *The Picture of Dorian Gray*. 1891. London: Penguin, 1976.

Winterson, Jeanette. *Oranges Are Not The Only Fruit*. New York: Grove, 1985.

Wright, Richard. *Black Boy: A Record of Childhood and Youth*. New York: Harper, 1937.

Zipes, Jack. "Taking Political Stock: New Theoretical and Critical Approaches to Anglo-American Children's Literature in the 1980s." *Only Connect: Readings on Children's Literature*. Ed. Sheila Egoff, Gordon Stubbs, Ralph Ashley, and Wendy Sutton. 3rd ed. Oxford: Oxford UP, 1990.

Chapter Fourteen
Trials of Taste: Ideological "Food Fights" in Madeleine L'Engle's *A Wrinkle in Time*

Elizabeth Gargano

Written during the height of the Cold War, Madeleine L'Engle's *A Wrinkle in Time* constructs individuality as an essentialized concept, one that enables life in a democratic society, lays the groundwork for artistic and scientific accomplishments, and stands against the rise of the modern totalitarian state. At the same time, however, L'Engle's work is far more than a simple defense of mid-century American democracy. The text's rich ambiguities result in part from the parallels that it draws between twentieth-century totalitarian governments and the excesses of capitalist consumerism. In L'Engle's monitory parable of conformity and individual resistance, the monstrous brain known as "IT" aims to devour all living beings, fusing individual hearts and minds into a uniform, flat, and textureless existence. Yet IT can only consume other beings if they are willing to become mindless "consumers" of the deceptive nourishment that IT generates and purveys. The rhetoric used to describe IT's agenda evokes mid-century American fears about the "communist threat," and the inhabitants of IT's home planet of Camazotz live in a dystopian version of American suburbia, their bland, boxlike houses fronting tidy lawns edged with flowers. Furthermore, in one of the novel's central scenes, IT produces a quintessentially American feast, a parodic Thanksgiving dinner, for the novel's young protagonist Meg Murry.

In fact, though often overlooked, scenes involving food and eating play a crucial role in the novel's exploration of both totalitarian and capitalist models of consumerism. Set against the giant brain's appetite to consume all conscious beings, a series of related tableaux explore hunger and food on three different planets: Earth, the "dark" planet of Camazotz, and the mysterious and redemptive planet of Ixchel. Each of these scenes of eating exemplifies a key stage in Meg's development towards a mature understanding of her relation with others. As Meg learns to trust her own sense of "taste" (a word that operates on more than one level), she comes to realize that her own eccentricities, the traits that she formerly feared and disavowed, will serve as her best protection against coercive ideologies imposed from without. Thus, cultivating an allegedly authentic taste plays a crucial role in the formation of Meg's identity, just as her participation in the shared meal signals her socialization into a community of equals. The twentieth-century revolution in so-called synthetic and instant foods serves as a context for L'Engle's construction of the shared meal as a jeopardized arena of authenticity. By drawing on a growing unease about widely available, highly processed foods, L'Engle subtly enmeshes her totalitarian dystopia within images of American conformity and consumerism.

I.

L'Engle's concern with food as an index of authenticity spans her career and pervades much of her writing. In *Two-Part Invention* (1988), a memoir of her family life covering some forty years, she laments that we currently "live in an uprooted society" (200), a world "that seems to be less and less concerned with reality. We drink instant coffee and reconstituted orange juice. We buy our vegetables on cardboard trays covered with plastic" (104). L'Engle's memoir records her struggle to find human connectedness and spiritual significance in such an "uprooted" cultural milieu. For her, a sense of rootedness resides primarily in the rituals and customs of family life, centering on the comity of the shared family meal: "Food is part of [our family's] rootedness. . . . Much of what we eat comes from the garden, and the evening meal is a special part of the rootedness, when we linger at the table, lighting candles or oil lamps as the sky darkens" (201). Writing lyrically of "tomatoes and green peppers, sprinkled with basil and chives" and "young corn" planted by her husband (201), L'Engle depicts the shared meal as an emblem of a rich family life.

Rich in familial associations, the foods grown in L'Engle's garden stand in contrast to the supermarket's "vegetables . . . covered in plastic," an image that she goes on to link with modern America's marketing of "[p]lastics and synthetics," as well as "[p]lanned obsolescence." "The word *synthetic*," she contends, suggests something "*unreal*" (104). For L'Engle, capitalist consumerism not only disempowers individuals, forcing them to buy shoddy products that will self-destruct on schedule; even more ominously, it also erodes their relationship with their own physicality. Thus, the replacement of homegrown foods with pallid *simulacra* lacking both aroma and savor serves as one salient example of an increasing detachment from the realm of visceral experience.

L'Engle's attack on synthetic foods draws on the debate about processed and so-called natural foods in cookbooks, advertisements, and treatises on nutrition during the mid-twentieth century. "The day is coming," Eleanor Early wrote in the 1940s, "when you'll serve the girls a bridge luncheon of dehydrated meat and potatoes with powdered potatoes and powdered onions, a dehydrated cabbage salad, and custard made with powdered eggs and powdered milk for dessert."[1] Early's celebration of processed food as emblematic of a Utopian scientific future was not new. After commercial canning was introduced into America in 1910, producers of canned, condensed, and dehydrated foods claimed that their scientifically manufactured products were in fact tastier and more healthful than their homemade counterparts. As Katherine Parkin writes, advertisements in the early twentieth century "asserted that Campbell's soup was a superior product to what women could hope to achieve," in part because of its mass production in the company's "antiseptic kitchen" (58). Similarly, giant food processing companies advertised highly refined products as more healthful than less processed foods. The American Sugar Refining Company, which had established a virtual monopoly on the refining process, launched a marketing campaign against brown sugar, claiming that it was unsanitary and riddled with dangerous microbes.[2]

Cookbooks of the 1940s and 1950s increasingly endorsed the value of canned soups, cake mixes, and frozen juices, stressing their modernity and time-saving qualities. As one 1953 cookbook asserted, "packaged food cookery is virtually foolproof."[3] In the late 1950s, a newspaper food column carried a recipe for "crab bisque" that involved mixing "one can each asparagus soup, mushroom soup, tomato soup, and split pea soup" and then adding a can of crab meat.[4] As some historians of food have argued, the myth of scientific cookery also thrived in a climate of veiled misogyny. Although overtly offering women help in the kitchen and more leisure time, the rhetoric of advertising suggested that male scientists knew more about food preparation than generations of housewives.[5] Even though women remained the purveyors of meals, male experts could now be seen as the creators and evaluators of the best and most nutritious food products. In this specific sense, the factory and the laboratory replaced the kitchen as the center of food production.

At the same time, however, an undercurrent of nostalgia for unprocessed foods also began to manifest itself during the postwar period, becoming ever more insistent in the late 1950s and early 1960s. In 1962, the same year that *A Wrinkle in Time* appeared, one cookbook author laments, "I hate to see our children missing out on the pleasures of old-fashioned baking," acknowledging mournfully that cake mixes "cannot come up to the perfection of the old-fashioned variety" (qtd. in Endrijonas 162). During these years, when the natural foods movement was in its infancy and often an object of satire, the argument against food processing took on a wistful tone, as the march towards scientific food production seemed both inevitable and desirable. As is frequently noted, the bland breakfast drink Tang suffered from lackluster sales after it was introduced in 1959 but suddenly became a household staple in 1965 when it was used on the Gemini 4 space mission. Now known as the "breakfast drink of the astronauts," Tang partook of the glamour associated with scientific food production.

As Warren J. Belasco writes in *Appetite for Change*, "More than a mixture of nutrients, food is also a metaphor for what we like most or least about our society." Thus, the proliferation of food processing in the early twentieth century spawned a "critique of processed foods during the Progressive Era (1910–1914)" that reflected a "widespread concern about irresponsible corporations and dangerous urban-industrial conditions." More recently, in the late 1960s and early 1970s, the organic foods movement partnered with the emerging counterculture and the ecology movements. Clashes between mainstream culture and subversive movements can result in what Belasco identifies as "food fights" that dramatize "grassroots political struggles" (15). Formulated long after the early twentieth-century Progressivist critique of food processing and well before the natural foods movement hit its stride, L'Engle's attack on synthetic foods was both more original and more challenging than it might seem today. As we will see, her celebratory depiction of the shared meal, the emblem of human mutuality, not only harkens back to a sense of lost authenticity but also challenges widespread assumptions about gender in the early 1960s. Most importantly, however, L'Engle conducts her own ideologically freighted "food fight." She deploys food imagery to add a visceral dimension to her argument that totalitarian government and American consumerism enforce conformity in similar and parallel ways.

II.

At the beginning of *A Wrinkle in Time*, 14-year-old Meg Murry is distraught. Tormented by her difference from "Everybody Else" (4), Meg decides she must be a "monster" (6). Unlike her athletic twin brothers Sandy and Dennys, described by one of her neighbors as "nice, regular children," she and her 5-year-old brother Charles Wallace are viewed by acquaintances as "subnormal" or "unattractive" (9). To some extent Meg's "oddball" status is associated with her violations of common mid-century assumptions about gender (12). Unusually talented in math, she is not conventionally pretty, likes to "roughhouse," and engages in fistfights with boys who criticize her eccentric family (4). If Meg's confusion and angst seem typical of adolescent self-doubt, L'Engle nevertheless takes pains to emphasize that both she and her brother Charles Wallace differ substantially from the norm as defined by their small American town and conventional school. As her scientist father explains, the two children's "development has to go at its own pace. It just doesn't happen to be the usual pace" (9). Charles Wallace is a budding genius with strikingly rare mental powers, including telepathy; Meg is simply unusually bright and emotionally intense. Yet even these traits are enough to isolate her in her conventional small town.

Meg's torment over her difference is eased by her participation in an impromptu family gathering, which paradoxically cures her isolation while affirming her difference. In this deftly drawn scene, the Murry family enjoys a midnight feast with the charmingly eccentric Mrs. Whatsit, a disguised alien. The family's idiosyncratic food choices become the basis for the comity of the shared meal, just as, for L'Engle, human connectedness can only occur when individual differences are freely accepted. Thus, the simple meal takes on a substantial thematic significance. Not only does this scene dramatize the process whereby oddness and eccentricity are converted from negative to positive qualities, it also serves as Meg's introduction to Mrs. Whatsit, who will lead her and her brother on an interplanetary quest to rescue their missing father. In a world of supposedly contented nuclear families, Meg's teachers and classmates view Mr. Murry's absence as both a sign of shame and a confirmation of the family's abnormality. The children's ultimate reunion with their father—a scientist imprisoned by IT on the planet of Camazotz—not only helps erase the stigma of negative difference imposed by the community; it also affirms positive differences, revealing to Meg and Charles Wallace that their father is a heroic astronaut on a government mission.

The scene begins with Meg brooding about her supposed faults in her attic bedroom, while a storm rages through the night sky. Frightened by the storm's violence, which mirrors her inner tumult, Meg seeks refuge in the kitchen downstairs, where she shares hot chocolate with her mother and Charles Wallace. Gifted with a mysterious telepathy—at least where she and her mother are concerned—Charles Wallace has anticipated their arrival within a few minutes of each other and has already begun heating milk on the stove. His uncanny ability to anticipate their thoughts and feelings infuses an aura of almost mystical sympathy into the prosaic meal. In *Two-Part Invention*, L'Engle writes of "the special poignancy" with which she and her family enjoy food in times of grief and trouble.[6] Here too the warm, fragrant kitchen serves as a refuge from the storms, both external and internal, that frighten and torment Meg:

> The warmth and light of the kitchen had relaxed her so that her attic fears were gone. The cocoa steamed fragrantly in the saucepan; geraniums bloomed on the window sills. . . . The furnace purred like a great sleepy animal; the lights glowed with steady radiance; outside, alone in the dark, the wind still battered against the house, but [its] angry power . . . was subdued by the familiar comfort of the kitchen. (11)

Filled with light and warmth, the shared meal in the kitchen is also associated with images and metaphors of the natural world, including the blooming geraniums and the "animal" purr of the furnace. Just as she does in *Two-Part Invention*, L'Engle links food and its pleasures with an appreciation for nature. As the

*Food's role in religion (Christianity).

imagery invokes the senses of smell, sight, sound, and, implicitly, taste, readers become aware that we are moving into a visceral realm of bodily comfort.

Soothing as it may be, however, the meal is also decidedly unconventional. Cookbooks of the day frequently waxed lyrical about the joy experienced by women preparing food for their families.[7] During the Murrys' midnight feast, however, Meg's mother prepares nothing. Instead, she is waited on by 5-year-old Charles Wallace. As he happily takes on a role normally reserved for adult women, Charles Wallace's behavior unsettles conventional assumptions about age and gender. Both nurturing and bossy, he carefully prepares sandwiches for both Meg and his mother. Making each order distinctive, he asks a litany of questions about their preferences: "Lettuce on your sandwich, Mother?" "Onion salt?" (13), "How about you, Meg? . . . All right if I use [the last tomato] on Meg, Mother?" (11). Significantly, the three Murrys all select different foods. Mrs. Murry wants onion salt but not lettuce. Meg, who dislikes the liverwurst and cream cheese that Charles Wallace has made for their mother, insists on lettuce and tomato. Charles Wallace himself chooses jelly.

When the family welcomes the mysterious Mrs. Whatsit to their midnight feast, Meg takes over Charles Wallace's task of food preparation. Clearly, creating the shared meal is also a shared task, not a drudgery to be performed by a dutiful housewife. Freely sharing their thoughts and feelings, the Murrys willingly prepare each others' food. Like the other characters, Mrs. Whatsit shows distinctive preferences. She longs for the caviar in the refrigerator (which she spots through her own telepathic powers) but settles instead for tuna salad and sweet pickles. As L'Engle humorously emphasizes the characters' idiosyncratic food choices, we are reminded of their stubborn individuality and eccentric tastes. They all eat together, but they each eat differently, cheerfully arguing, sympathizing, and running through the gamut of messy human emotions.

To further emphasize the meal's invigorating oddity, Mrs. Whatsit flagrantly violates the gender conventions that Meg and Charles Wallace have transgressed in small ways. Wearing a man's hat and a woman's pink stole, Mrs. Whatsit is so "bundled up" in layers of scarves that her "age or sex [is] impossible to tell" (16). Later, of course, on the planet Uriel, the ridiculously dressed old lady will metamorphose into a powerful male centaur, who still insists on retaining her (or his?) "female" name. Willfully violating gender norms, Mrs. Whatsit demonstrates for Meg (and for readers) that identity need not be solely defined by gender. Mrs. Whatsit breaks other taboos as well; she admits to stealing sheets from a neighbor who is prosperous enough to "spare" them, in order to create stage-prop ghosts to frighten neighbors away from her house (18). Apparently agreeing with Emerson, that early apostle of American individualism, that "[g]ood men"—or women—"must not obey the laws too well" (427), Mrs. Whatsit airily justifies what her neighbors would clearly regard as antisocial behavior. Even more importantly, perhaps, Mrs. Whatsit explicitly formulates the novel's implicit valorization of eccentricity.

At the midnight feast, she praises Mrs. Murry for not "trying to squash down" the unusually gifted Charles Wallace but, instead, "letting him be himself," despite the criticisms of censorious neighbors (19).

Speaking to what she clearly regards as a mid-century culture of conformity, L'Engle suggests that Meg is reviled at school for the very qualities that make her most interesting: her intelligence and creativity, her stubborn honesty, and her honest anger. As L'Engle wrote in another context, "What is a good characteristic at one moment may be intolerable at another, and what is a dreadful characteristic may be all that saves us" ("Believing Impossible Things" 264). In part, the dangers of conformity reside in our inability to identify which qualities are ultimately of value. By repressing those traits that are not currently valued, we diminish ourselves and impair our ability to adapt to changing conditions. Later in the novel, Meg's obstinacy and even, to a degree, her anger will serve to gird her against the psychological attacks of IT on Camazotz. At school, however, these qualities separate her starkly from the more easygoing popular girls, who are serenely untroubled by anxiety and self-doubt.

If the shared meal embodies a Utopian synthesis of individualism and community, this ideal balance nevertheless remains unstable. The notion of community rests on the implicit assumption of exclusion. In other words, as not everyone can belong, the question is always: how far can or should the concept of community extend? L'Engle tacitly acknowledges this dilemma, revealing that the community of the midnight feast is based, to a degree, on exclusion. If Meg and Charles Wallace are marginalized by their conventional neighbors, their midnight feast also allows them to exclude others, especially those so-called normal children who make them feel inadequate. When Mrs. Murry mentions the possibility of waking their twin brothers Sandy and Dennys, Charles Wallace asserts, "Let's be exclusive. . . . That's my new word for the day. Impressive, isn't it?" (11). By showing the 5-year-old's understandable pride in mastering an adult vocabulary, L'Engle deflects the more negative implications of the word "exclusive." Charles Wallace's pride in learning a new word masks a more profound and problematic pride, his feeling of innate superiority over his so-called average brothers. At times, L'Engle's novel comes close to hinting that the pleasures of nonconformity are reserved for the exceptionally talented few. Like the "exclusive" Charles Wallace, his older friend Calvin O'Keefe dismisses his own average siblings with the comment, "They all have runny noses." Proud that he has skipped at least two years in school, Calvin emphatically asserts his difference from his ordinary family, announcing "I'm a [biological] sport" (31).

Not only excluded from the midnight feast, the "normal" Sandy and Dennys also miss out on the adventure in outer space that will unite Meg, Charles Wallace, and the gifted Calvin in a new familial relation.[8] Here, at the very beginning of the narrative, L'Engle celebrates "difference" in the face of conformity, not so much by affirming it as a state available to all children but, rather, by equating it with an innate intellectual or artistic superiority. "Sure,

I can function on the same level as everybody else," Calvin asserts. "I can hold myself down, but it isn't me" (44). Thus, the comity of the shared meal is also, in part, a product of exclusivity; to state the case even more strongly, L'Engle suggests that only eccentric individualists are ready for this level of exuberant *comitas*.

Calvin's inclusion as a virtual member of the Murry family is signaled by a second meal with eccentric overtones, when Mrs. Murry prepares dinner in the home laboratory where she conducts chemical experiments. Entering the house together, Meg and Calvin find Mrs. Murry "watching a pale blue fluid move slowly through a tube from a beaker to a retort. Over a Bunsen burner bubbled a big, earthenware dish of stew." Refreshingly, Mrs. Murry is able to fulfill her domestic responsibilities without compromising her intellectual vocation: "I had an experiment I wanted to stay with," she explains serenely. This striking scene deftly overturns an array of mid-century assumptions concerning food, gender, and science. Whereas contemporary cookbooks, commentaries, and advertisements often differentiated between housewives cooking in the kitchen and male experimenters developing new foods in the laboratory, L'Engle playfully combines both realms, giving women the run of both. At the same time, L'Engle underlines the unconventional nature of Mrs. Murry's cooking by emphasizing that the all-too-conventional Sandy and Dennys would not approve: "Don't tell Sandy and Dennys I'm cooking out here," Mrs. Murry warns. "They're always suspicious that a few chemicals may get in with the meat" (39). Once again, the twins must be excluded from the inner circle of the Murry family, replaced in the first instance by Mrs. Whatsit and in this instance by Calvin.

Welcomed into the Murry household, Calvin enthusiastically describes his new experience of belonging: "How did all this happen? Isn't it wonderful? I feel as though I were just being born! I'm not alone anymore!" (44). Calvin's participation in the life of the family is signaled by the gusto with which he partakes of the Murrys' meal: "Calvin ate five bowls of stew, three saucers of Jello, and a dozen cookies" (45). (Even the Murrys' bountiful homemade meal includes at least one prepackaged item.) At the same time, it is worth noting that Calvin eats as the Murrys eat, selecting and savoring his idiosyncratic choices. For Calvin and the Murrys, food selections are an exuberant emblem of individual tastes.

The Murrys' communal meals contrast with food consumption in the oppressive world of Camazotz. Approximately midway through the novel, the monstrous IT, ruler of Camazotz, stages yet another shared meal, one designed to replace fellowship with mindless conformity. IT manufactures a turkey dinner described in tantalizing detail and redolent with the connotations of the quintessentially American Thanksgiving feast. In fact, however, the turkey is a synthetic foodstuff that tastes like "sand" and seems flavorful only because IT, the giant brain who dominates the planet of Camazotz, is controlling taste centers in the brains of the Murry children and Calvin

(130). In an era of new synthetic foods made glamorous by advertising, IT's use of mind control to induce appetite suggests a subtle but telling social critique. As food advertisers insistently hammered home the idea that processed foods were more appetizing than home-cooked meals, they also recognized the limitations of their own arguments. Because the taste and smell of frozen, canned, or dehydrated, foods could never equal the aroma and savor of home-cooked meals, food processing companies sought to emphasize the visual appearance of their prepackaged foods. Thus, the packages of Swanson's TV dinners carried vivid images of luminously green peas and potatoes oozing with shiny gravy. In a similar way, IT's synthetic turkey dinner is described in vivid detail. Visually, IT has clearly taken pains to recreate the appearance of an authentic homemade meal, featuring "[t]urkey and dressing and mashed potatoes and gravy and little green peas with big yellow blobs of butter melting in them and cranberries and sweet potatoes topped with gooey browned marshmallows and olives and celery and rosebud radishes" (129). Stringing together a catalogue of colorful images with a series of conjunctions, L'Engle creates a feeling of bountiful excess. Yet, in the end, the food is almost too perfect. Unlike the Murrys' individualized meals—including such treats as cream cheese and liverwurst sandwiches with onion salt—every aspect of IT's meal is conventional and familiar.

Conventional as it appears, however, the meal tastes familiar only because IT can exert a measure of mind control over the hungry children. Thus, tasteless and vapid synthetic food is rendered appetizing by a species of conjuring trick. Even while eating this illusory food, Meg recognizes the trick being practiced on her; nevertheless, she eats eagerly, preferring the illusion of satiety to the reality of hunger. Tellingly, it is the aggressive Meg who first demands that IT feed the children: "It might help if you give us something to eat. . . . We're all starved. If you're going to be horrible to us you might as well give us full stomachs first" (126). Speaking through his human mouthpiece, the eerie man with glowing, "reddish" eyes (120), IT asserts that it could control the children by starving them but chooses to feed them instead. The message is clear: IT prefers to seduce rather than coerce, to undermine defenses rather than crush them, in part because the giant brain finds this approach easier and in part because this suits IT's methods. Engaging in Orwellian doublespeak, IT wishes to blur the boundary between the real and the unreal in order to present totalitarian mind-control as a form of love and connectedness. As IT acknowledges to Meg, "Of course [the food] doesn't really smell, but isn't it as good as though it really did?" (128).

Initially, only the brilliant Charles Wallace can shut his mind to IT's telepathic powers. Thus, Meg and Calvin find themselves enjoying the feast. As the monstrous brain exults, "I can get in through the chinks [in their mental resistance]. Not all the way in, but enough to give them a turkey dinner" (130). When Charles Wallace finds his food savorless, Meg clearly misses the point, failing to see that the process of brainwashing has already begun for her and Calvin. "It tastes all right," she tells her brother. "Try some of mine, Charles" (130). Ironically, however, Meg is ultimately able to pull back from IT's mind control, and the overconfident Charles Wallace succumbs. Believing himself strong enough to resist IT's powers, Charles Wallace opens his mind to the giant brain, hoping to learn more about it. Significantly, Charles Wallace's defeat is signaled by his final acceptance of IT's meal: "Come on, Meg, eat this delicious food that has been prepared for us" (131). In contrast, Meg rebels by smashing Charles Wallace's plate on the floor. Rejecting IT's synthetic pabulum is a revolutionary act, a "food fight" that challenges both totalitarian oppression and the manipulations of consumerism.

Although IT claims that it only wishes to save the children "pain and trouble," allowing them to be "happy, useful people" as it assumes "all the burdens of thought and decision," the supposedly benevolent dictatorship on Camazotz leads to a mind-numbing conformity (121). The inhabitants live in identical houses on identical streets. Wearing a uniform of nearly identical clothing, they follow uniform time schedules: "The men all wore nondescript business suits, and though their features were . . . different . . . there was also a sameness to them" (116). Thus, the rhetoric that Orwell describes as "political language . . . designed to make lies sound truthful" merges with images of what L'Engle regards as the mindless conformity of mid-century capitalist America (Orwell 156). The rhetoric of synthetic food is central to this fusion, as L'Engle parodies the agenda and discourse of mid-century advertisements. As IT proclaims, "Of course our food, being synthetic, is not superior to your messes of beans and bacon and so forth, but I assure you that it's far more nourishing, and though it has no taste of its own, a slight conditioning is all that is necessary to give you the illusion that you are eating a roast turkey dinner" (127). IT's words echo the advertisements that strove to "condition" consumers to choose white sugar or Campbell's Soup, allegedly more "nourishing" and sanitary than homemade fare.

Pretending to serve the children with allegedly parental care, IT clearly perverts the human experience of the shared meal, a moment of comity associated with the exchange of individual thoughts and feelings. Thus, IT replaces free discussion and debate with a different kind of "sharing," in which the children are subsumed into IT's dominant consciousness. Consuming IT's food, they become consumed. IT's attempt to dehumanize the children is eerily similar to L'Engle's analysis of American marketing in *Two-Part Invention*: "perhaps the most dehumanizing thing of all is that we have allowed the media to call us consumers—ugly. No! I don't want to be a consumer. Anger consumes. Forest fires consume. Cancer consumes" (104). And, of course, according to the logic of L'Engle's narrative, IT also consumes the Murry children when they allow themselves to become mindless "consumers" of its synthetic nourishment. It should be noted that L'Engle's quarrel here is not with science itself, which she repeatedly celebrates as one of the most valuable human pursuits, but only with its application within a coercive ideology of consumerism.

The novel's first two major scenes of eating are well developed, with rich thematic significance and narrative parallels. In contrast, the two related scenes on the planet Ixchel near the end of the novel remain sketchy and mysterious. These scenes, which build on the previous two, exist in a hierarchical relation to them. If the first meal, the midnight feast, reveals an eccentric individuality that serves as the true basis for healthy *comitas*, the second perverts *comitas* into mindless conformity through a synthetic or unreal "sameness." Medicinal and redemptive, the meals on Ixchel serve as an antidote to IT's perverted communal feast. In fact, the food on Aunt Beast's planet contrasts with IT's food in a number of instructive ways.

Whereas IT, the giant brain, is associated with an intellect out of control, Aunt Beast is linked with visceral experience and the body. She cures Meg by metaphorically taking her back to a state of infancy: "Cradled in the [beast's] four strange arms, Meg, despite herself, felt a sense of security that was deeper than anything she had known since the days when she lay in her mother's arms. . . . She leaned her head against the beast's chest" (179). Aunt Beast offers Meg an unconditional love experienced only by infants: "this beast would be able to love her no matter what she said or did" (183). Reducing Meg to the status of a baby, L'Engle hints that she can only be saved from IT's dangerous influence by being reborn into her own body; "lapped" in "warmth and peace," Meg feels the touch of Aunt Beast's tentacle, "as tender as her mother's kiss." Aunt Beast herself underlines her maternal connection to Meg. "You are so tiny and vulnerable," she says. "Now I will feed you." In this instance, eating is a passive experience, one that hints at an amorphous oneness with the mother before individual identity develops: "Something completely and indescribably delicious was put to Meg's lips and she swallowed gratefully. With each swallow, she felt strength returning to her body" (183). The mysterious substance "put to Meg's lips," requiring her only to swallow, subtly evokes mother's milk, the first food, which sets the stage for profound associations between eating, pleasure, and human connectedness.

This crucial scene emphasizes the central importance of food within the world of the narrative. Associated with love and the body, the *comitas* of shared food is both the precondition for individuality and the fullest expression of it. Through the figure of Aunt Beast, L'Engle grounds individual sensibility firmly in the body and physical existence, in acts of touching and tasting, in the sensations of appetite and mutual sustenance. As noted earlier, in *Two-Part Invention,* L'Engle expresses her concern that market-driven consumerism risks alienating Americans from their own physicality. Something analogous happens to Meg on Camazotz when she initially buys into IT's synthetic feast and later finds herself losing physical vitality when faced with the all-consuming "disembodied brain" (158). Linked to mother's milk, a product and an extension of the body, Aunt Beast's food reconnects Meg with the realm of visceral experience.

Directing readers to engage with the food imagery that permeates the novel, L'Engle overtly links this scene to earlier scenes of eating. As Aunt Beast feeds her, Meg "realize[s] that she had had nothing to eat since the horrible fake turkey dinner on Camazotz, which she had barely tasted. How long ago was her mother's stew?" (184). Meg's meals on Earth, Camazotz, and Ixchel thus become separate links in a chain of images, each signifying a stage in Meg's emotional and physical development.

The infantile merging with Aunt Beast is quickly followed by another scene of eating in which a restored Meg reasserts her individuality. During this subsequent communal meal, the humans and aliens gather around a "huge, round, stone table" as they share food and plan how to rescue Charles Wallace from IT's clutches. When Meg arrives at the table, Calvin calls out to her happily, "Meg. . . . You've never tasted such food in your life! Come and eat!" (188). Ironically, Calvin's words recall Charles Wallace's earlier injunction to consume IT's parodic Thanksgiving feast: "Come on, Meg, eat this delicious food" (131).

Such linking devices further emphasize the connections and differences between the two meals. Brainwashed human minions serve IT's savorless turkey dinner, but Aunt Beast offers Meg food herself:

> Aunt Beast . . . heaped a plate with food, strange fruits and breads that tasted unlike anything Meg had ever eaten. Everything was dull and colorless and unappetizing to look at, and at first, even remembering the meal Aunt Beast had fed her the night before, Meg hesitated to taste, but once she had managed the first bite she ate eagerly; it seemed that she would never have her fill again. (188)

IT's food is primarily a visual experience, described in colorful detail, but the food on Aunt Beast's planet is colorless: a significant fact because the beasts can't see but perceive the world more profoundly through their sensitive tentacles. If IT's food appears appetizing but is later revealed to be without substance, Aunt Beast's initially unappetizing food actually tastes delicious. Furthermore, unlike IT's synthetic food, Aunt Beast's fruit and bread are natural and wholesome. Finally, in contrast to the earlier meal's carefully catalogued "little green peas with big yellow blobs of butter" and "sweet potatoes topped with gooey brown marshmallows," Aunt Beast's food is apparently indescribable and can only be imagined by readers.

Like the comically exuberant midnight feast that served to set the novel's eccentric tone, this meal also serves as an image of *comitas*, but now the stakes are dramatically higher. The meal not only recapitulates all previous ones; it also leads Meg to a new stage of development, as she moves from dependent childhood through angry adolescence to a new stage of maturity. Sitting with the beasts and her father at the round table—itself an image of nonhierarchical community—Meg begins by being childishly dependent then grows resentful because her father was unable to save Charles Wallace on Camazotz. Finally, she accepts that it is her responsibility to rescue Charles because the bond between them is so strong.

As her self-righteous anger at her father dissolves, Meg rises to a new level of self-knowledge and finally recognizes her own particular strengths—for L'Engle, a precondition for mature love. Thus, the *comitas* of this last shared meal helps Meg realize that her best weapon against IT's tyranny is the love that one individual feels for another. Specific and concrete, located in the body, this love, for L'Engle, is stronger than IT's abstract verbal formulae mandating a generalized oneness and harmony based on the elision of differences. If the novel's first major scene of eating depicts Charles Wallace and Mrs. Whatsit happily challenging conventional gender roles, this meal reinforces the message that identity cannot be defined and limited solely by gender. As Meg comes to understand during this final communal feast, she must have the courage to do battle with IT, taking action herself rather than relying on her father to solve all the problems facing her family.[9]

Woven deftly through a series of major scenes, the novel's food imagery allows L'Engle to summon up the realm of bodily experience in order to "flesh out" her parable of resistance to abstract ideologies—whether associated with mid-century capitalism or the totalitarian modern state. Images of food and sustenance both begin and close the novel. Significantly, when Meg and her companions save Charles Wallace and return to earth, they land in the vegetable garden in their backyard amid the "broccoli," smelling the "sweet . . . autumnal earth" (209). Reclaiming food from the factory and the supermarket, L'Engle grounds it in the rich culture of home and the nurturing spaces of the garden. Valorizing the communal feast, L'Engle lays out a feast of difference.

Notes

1   Eleanor Early, *American Cookery*, 1942, np. Qtd. in Stern and Stern 243.
2   The American Sugar Refining Company, which marketed its product under the Domino label, went so far as to blow up photographs of harmless microbes sometimes found in less refined sugars in order to scare potential customers into buying white sugar. See Levenstein, *Revolution* 32.
3   Michael Reise, *The 20-Minute Cook Book* (New York: Crown, 1953) 2, qtd. in Endrijonas 159.
4   See Weiss's discussion of Kay Walsh's food column, 218–219.
5   According to Parkin, "Convenience food ads . . . focused on women's desire to be good homemakers and their fears of inadequacy. . . . Advertisements counseled women that to avoid humiliating themselves" by serving unappetizing food, "they ought to have a supply of Campbell's soup on hand" (Parkin 56–57).

6 L'Engle, *Two-Part Invention* 169. L'Engle describes eating with her grown children and how they prepare a meal for her after she has spent hours in the hospital with her seriously ill husband.

7 Irma S. Rombauer's classic *Joy of Cooking*, a mainstay for mid-century housewives, was only one of many cookbooks celebrating the pleasures of cooking for one's family.

8 In the sequel *Many Waters*, L'Engle finally allows Sandy and Dennys to pursue their own adventure, when they are transported to a mysterious world as a result of their mother's scientific experiments.

9 For a different interpretation of Meg's final battle with IT, see Katherine Schneebaum's engaging essay, "Finding a Happy Medium: The Design for Womanhood in *A Wrinkle in Time*." For Schneebaum, Meg's rescue of Charles Wallace is "noble" but nevertheless "impl[ies] a lack of freedom" as "she is operating in the traditionally feminine sphere of maternal love as a redeeming force" (36).

Works Cited

Belasco, Warren J. *Appetite for Change: How the Counterculture Took on the Food Industry.* 2nd ed. Ithaca, NY: Cornell UP, 2007.

Emerson, Ralph Waldo. "Politics." *The Complete Essays and Other Writings of Ralph Waldo Emerson.* Ed. Brooks Atkinson. New York: Modern Library, 1940. 422–434.

Endrijonas, Erika. "Processed Foods from Scratch: Cooking for a Family in the 1950s." *Kitchen Culture in America: Popular Representations of Food, Gender, and Race.* Ed. Sherrie A. Inness. Philadelphia: U of Pennsylvania P, 2001. 157–173.

L'Engle, Madeleine. "Believing Impossible Things." *Children's Literature.* Spec. issue of *Theory into Practice* 21:4 (Autumn 1982): 264–265.

———. *Two-Part Invention: The Story of a Marriage.* New York: Harper, 1988.

———. *A Wrinkle in Time.* New York: Yearling, 1962.

Levenstein, Harvey A. *Paradox of Plenty: A Social History of Eating in Modern America.* New York: Oxford UP, 1993.

———. *Revolution at the Table: The Transformation of the American Diet.* New York: Oxford UP, 1988.

Orwell, George. "Politics and the English Language." *George Orwell: A Collection of Essays.* New York: Harvest, 1981. 156–171.

Parkin, Katherine. "Campbell's Soup and the Long Shelf Life of Gender Roles." *Kitchen Culture in America: Popular Representations of Food, Gender, and Race.* Ed. Sherrie A. Inness. Philadelphia: U of Pennsylvania P, 2001. 51–67.

Schneebaum, Katherine. "Finding a Happy Medium: The Design for Womanhood in *A Wrinkle in Time*." *The Lion and the Unicorn* 14 (1990): 30–36.

Stern, Jane and Michael Stern. *Square Meals.* New York: Knopf, 1984.

Weiss, Jessica. "She Also Cooks: Gender, Domesticity, and Public Life in Oakland, California, 1957–1959." *Kitchen Culture in America: Popular Representations of Food, Gender, and Race.* Ed. Sherrie A. Inness. Philadelphia: U of Pennsylvania P, 2001. 211–226.

Wolf, Virginia L. "Readers of Alice: My Children, Meg Murry, and Harriet M. Welch." *Children's Literature Association Quarterly* 13:3 (Fall 1988): 135–137.

Chapter Fifteen

A Consuming Tradition: Candy and Socio-religious Identity Formation in Roald Dahl's *Charlie and the Chocolate Factory*

Robert M. Kachur

In the forty years since its publication, Roald Dahl's *Charlie and the Chocolate Factory* has sold almost as well as the craze-inducing candy bars it describes. In their 2001 compilation of "All-Time Bestselling Children's Books," Diane Roback and Jason Britton rank paperback and hardback sales of *Charlie and the Chocolate Factory* at 65 and 172 respectively among all children's books, noting that a total of 3,739, 631 copies had been consumed by that time and that the novel perennially appears on the children's top ten backlist. And as Jason Zasky has noted in his article, *"Willy Wonka and the Chocolate Factory*: From Inauspicious Debut To Timeless Classic," modest box office sales of the novel's film adaptation in 1971 gave way to video and laser disc and DVD sales that continue to grow exponentially—a strong factor, no doubt, in Warner Brothers's decision to produce another film adaptation starring Johnny Depp, *Charlie and the Chocolate Factory*, in 2005. The development of Dahl's story into a "cult classic"—*Entertainment Weekly* recently ranked *Willy Wonka* 25th in its "Top 50 Cult Movies" of all time (Bal, et al.)—has perplexed many readers: why does this narrative stir such strong responses in both children and adults? David Gooderham, one of the few scholars to tackle this question, notes that the simple explanations offered by educators and reviewers, which tend to center on *Charlie*'s punishment of vice and its subversion of adult authority,[1] "do not quite catch the intensity of those early passions that the books raised" in him

221

and his children (113). What, then, lies behind the enduring power of this children's text about candy?

Gooderham, Hamida Bosmajian, and William Todd Schultz have attempted to answer that question using various Freudian approaches. Bosmajian's "*Charlie and the Chocolate Factory* and Other Excremental Visions" analyzes the tale from a Freudian perspective, explaining that it allows "the child reader to indulge ... amorally in [a] liberating and libidinal satiric fantasy ... and releases a child's anxieties about bodily functions, physical injury and death" (47). Gooderham also argues that *Charlie* "is a text marked by strong anality," appealing to the "linguistically conceived Freudianism of Kristeva" as well as the "imaginal themes" of Erik Erikson to explain why adults as well as children continue to respond to the "primordial and resonating elements" of the text. (114–119). Most recently, Schultz has taken a psychobiographical approach to the question, arguing that in *Charlie*, Dahl "dreamed of a father who made a world that was fair and wonderful"; the text stems from what Silvan Tomkins has called a "nuclear script" in which Dahl attempts to overcome early trauma by recovering the father who died when he was three.

In diverging from Bosmajian and Gooderham's emphasis on psychosexual development, Schultz's reliance on the idea of a nuclear script as central to *Charlie* is intriguing but raises an obvious question in relation to readers' strong responses to the text. Although we may all be "self-dramatizers engaged from the earliest weeks of life in a constant dramaturgical process of constructing personal worlds," most readers of *Charlie* do not share Dahl's traumatic experience of losing a father at an early age (Schultz). What the majority of Dahl's readers do share, however, as John Stephens and Robyn McCallum have argued, is a social heritage transmitted through retold storylines, or metanarratives; and in this essay, I would like to argue that such a culturally reinforced metanarrative, one involving both food and the loss and recovery of a father, permeates *Charlie and the Chocolate Factory* and helps account for its power (3). Examining *Charlie* in conjunction with Dahl's own screenplay adaptation, it becomes clear that candy operates as a means by which children identify themselves and their desires with the resonant biblical metanarrative of creation, paradise, fall, and redemption. In this way, Dahl's story about a child who discovers his true identity and gains a father by finding a right relationship to food participates in the longstanding Western socioreligious tradition of linking food and identity.

In *Retelling Stories, Framing Culture: Traditional Story and Metanarratives in Children's Literature*, Stephens and McCallum explain why a biblical metanarrative such as the story of creation, fall, and redemption woven through *Charlie* is so powerful: "Such traditional materials ... come with predetermined horizons of expectation and with their values and ideas about the world already legitimized" (6). Despite declamations by some critics that *Charlie* is immoral and even dangerous,[2] then, the effect is largely conservative: the biblical story of creation, fall, and redemption is one of a number of "major narrative domains which . . . have the function of maintaining conformity to socially determined and approved patterns of behavior, which they do by offering positive role models, proscribing undesirable behavior, and affirming the culture's ideologies, systems, and institutions" (Stephens 3–4).

Food and Identity in the Judeo-Christian Tradition

The strong relationship between food and identity that is central to Judeo-Christian tradition has been well documented. Building on the work of Lévi-Strauss in her analysis of "The Semiotics of Food in the Bible," Jean Soler summarizes the logic of food-conscious religious quests this way:

> For man knows that the food he ingests in order to live will become assimilated into his being, will become himself. There must be, therefore, a relationship between the idea he has formed of specific items of food and the image he has of himself and his place in the universe. (55)

In the biblical account of creation, one of the few human activities to which the writer specifically calls attention is eating. Dominating God's first words to the newly created human pair are instructions concerning food:

> And God said, "Behold, I have given you every plant yielding seed which is upon the face of all the earth, and every tree with seed in its fruit; you shall have them for food. And to every beast of the earth, and to every bird of the air, and to everything that creeps on the earth, everything that has the breath of life, I have given every green plant for food. . . ." And the LORD God commanded the man, saying, "You may freely eat of every tree of the garden; but of the tree of the knowledge of good and evil you shall not eat, for in the day that you eat of it you shall die." (Genesis 1:29, 2:16–17)

In *The Lord's Table: The Meaning of Food in Early Judaism and Christianity*, Gillian Feeley-Harnik examines how Genesis establishes a biblical pattern concerning the meaning of food: "The power of the Lord is manifested in his ability to control food. . . . Rejection of the power and authority of the Lord is symbolized by seeking after food he has forbidden. . . . Eating joins people with the Lord or separates them" (72)

Although Dahl's tale begins in earnest with Wonka's announcement of the five Golden Tickets, the text offers background information about Wonka as creator and regulator of food that links him to this God of the Old Testament. As Grandpa Joe relates, Wonka is an extravagant and extraordinary creator: "a magician with chocolate" who "can make *anything*—anything he wants!" (12). As the oldest person in the text, Grandpa Joe acts as the conveyer of earlier oral traditions, in which both Wonka's idea as preeminent creator and his temporary alienation from humanity is explained. As God once walked with Adam and Eve in the Garden, so Wonka once mixed freely with humanity, he tells us. But at the time that the novel's action begins, the world is in a postlapsarian state. Like Adam and Eve, spies stole (in the form of Wonka's recipes) forbidden knowledge associated with food; consequently, he shut the gates of his factory, much like God shut the gates to paradise, banning not only the specific transgressors but the whole human race from his glorious factory. "He told *all* the workers that he was sorry, but they would have to go home," laments Grandpa Joe. "Then, he shut the main gates and fastened them with a chain" (19–20). Although Wonka continues to provide food for people, even as God does after Adam and Eve's transgressive eating, he no longer communicates with them face to face.

It is in this context—eating as the foundational activity most emphatically associated with expressing one's God-given human identity—that the centrality of food in *Charlie and the Chocolate Factory* is most deeply rooted. Because the world Dahl creates is a postlapsarian one, however, the characters' relationships to food are disordered from the start. Dahl vividly dramatizes Leon R. Kass's premise in *The Hungry Soul* that through correct eating human nature can once again be perfected. At the outset of *Charlie and the Chocolate Factory*, everyone seems to be unhealthily preoccupied with food—from the starving Buckets to the gluttonous Augustus Gloop to the compulsive chewer Violet Beauregarde. In short, the entire world (and Dahl is careful to emphasize that the search for golden tickets is a global event) recognizes that their deepest desires are bound up in food, but those desires have become frustrated and distorted by the fallen human condition. This is most vividly portrayed in ongoing descriptions of the Buckets', and especially Charlie's, bodily wasting away, counterpointed by descriptions of obese overeaters such as Augustus Gloop and the candy shopkeeper, whose "fat neck . . . bulged out all around the top of his collar like a rubber ring," and the conspicuous consumption of the Salts who buy, only to discard, hundreds of thousands of candy bars (48, 29).

The overarching metanarrative of the Bible, of course, lingers only briefly on the creation and loss of paradise in order to focus on its gradual restoration, and in that movement lies the heart of Dahl's story of how identity can be reconstructed through eating habits. *Charlie*'s main action begins when Wonka opens the door to communion with humanity once more by issuing five Golden Tickets. As the story of the children's entrance into the chocolate factory unfolds, the Old Testament story of creation and fall is recapitulated yet again but this time with the addition of the New Testament narrative of redemption and restoration. Echoing Jesus's words that you must become like a child to enter the kingdom of God,[3] only children, five lucky children, find Golden Tickets allowing them into the factory and a personal audience with Willy Wonka. Like salvation, you can't exactly buy Golden Tickets. Grace—the invitation to redemptive experience—can only be initiated by God, and the children who find tickets range from Veruca Salt, who buys hundreds of thousands of bars, to Charlie Bucket, who buys four, two of them with providentially provided money, which underscores God's initiating role. Like Ignorance in *Pilgrim's Progress* or the goats in Jesus's parable of the sheep and the goats, many expectantly make their way to the gates of Wonka's heavenly kingdom, but few are chosen to enter:

> Charlie glanced back over his shoulder and saw the great iron entrance gates slowly closing behind him. The crowds on the outside were still pushing and shouting. Charlie took a last look at them. Then, as the gates closed with a clang, all sight of the outside world disappeared. (64)

Once inside Wonka's "kingdom," these five children reenact the biblical story of humanity. Appropriately, their journey begins in the Chocolate Room, a paradise described by Wonka as "the nerve center of the whole factory, the heart of the whole business! And so beautiful!" (68). The narrator goes on to describe the garden setting in Edenic terms:

> Five children and nine grownups pushed their ways in—and oh, what an amazing sight it was that now met their eyes! They were looking down upon a lovely valley. There were green meadows on either side of the valley, and along the bottom of it there flowed a great brown river. What is more, there was a tremendous waterfall halfway along the river—a steep cliff over which the water curled and rolled in a solid sheet. (68)

Like the Garden of Eden, in which Adam and Eve are told they may "freely eat of every tree of the garden" except one, the Chocolate Room is dominated by delicious edibles. In fact, Wonka's guests have permission to eat anything, from the tops of the trees to the grass beneath their feet, with the biblically analogous exception of one important item—the chocolate river. Augustus's violation of this eating taboo is foundational to the story. Not only he but all the children and their parents get ushered out of paradise after Augustus's literal and metaphorical fall; although all the children except for Charlie are later punished for their own illicit consumption, they are tainted, it would seem, by his "original" sin.

In addition to being the scene of Augustus's fall, the Chocolate Room is also significant as the setting for one other event that precedes it—the introduction of the Oompa-Loompas, a race of beings related to but so different from Wonka's guests that Charlie exclaims, "they can't be *real* people" (73). Like angels in God's kingdom, these numerous alternate beings accomplish Wonka's bidding, always working behind the scenes despite the fact that they are unseen by fallen human perception. Like the cherubim who appear at the threshold of the Garden of Eden to signal and ensure Adam and Eve's exit from it in Genesis 3, the Oompa-Loompas appear whenever a child's transgression gets him or her ejected from the factory. Additionally, in much the same way that the angel Raphael appears to Adam in *Paradise Lost*, expounding on the relationship between spiritual development and physical eating, the Oompa-Loompas provide morality lessons in song on the effects of illicit consumption with each child's demise.

After Wonka and the rest bid the Gloops farewell, the notion of falling from paradise into spiritual death is heightened when the remaining guests exit via a boat ride into a "pitch-dark tunnel" (90). The chocolate river, contaminated by Augustus's transgression, becomes Styx-like, frightening its passengers out of their wits as their journey takes them into a symbolic experience of the underworld. Wonka himself seems temporarily to transform into a devil figure, hooting with laughter as he confirms the distressing significance of their ride away from paradise: "*Not a speck of light is showing, / So the danger must be growing, / For the rowers keep on rowing, / And they're certainly not showing / Any signs that they are slowing*" (90). How will humanity, represented by the passengers in Wonka's ship, make their way out of the spiritual darkness caused by original sin?

The answer, in part, is revealed in the next stop, Wonka's Inventing Room, "the room he loved best of all," which he describes as "the most important room in the entire factory" (95, 93). What is singular about Wonka's inventions is that they are not simply sensationally tasting candies, which are fleetingly glimpsed in so many of the factory's other rooms. The room which means the most to Wonka is one in which products are created that solve humanity's problems of scarcity, toil, and loss, the primary punishments meted out to humanity as a result of their disobedience in the Garden. Of the three products singled out in this room—Everlasting Gobstoppers, Hair Toffee that cures hair loss, and magic chewing gum that provides a three-course dinner—the Everlasting Gobstoppers most explicitly recall God's redemptive plan to overcome death, loss, and lack. As their name implies, Everlasting Gobstoppers defy the postlapsarian curse of time bringing decay and death: "They *never* get any smaller! They *never* disappear! *NEVER*!" Echoing God's special compassion in both Old and New Testament for the poor and poor in spirit, Wonka points out that he created the Everlasting Gobstopper with children "who are given very little pocket money" in mind (95). Wonka is devising a way for those who recognize their spiritual poverty to be eternally satisfied by him, represented here by his creation of the Everlasting Gobstopper.[4] As one of Wonka's "most secret new inventions"—so secret that "nobody else, not even an Oompa-Loompa, has ever been allowed in" the room—the Gobstopper also recalls the New Testament's emphasis on the surprising nature of God's plans for human salvation, described in 1 Peter 1:12 as a mystery into which even the angels have merely longed to look (93).

Ironically, it is in this Inventing Room associated with everlasting life that Violet's journey ends, a result of her grabbing a piece of magic chewing gum over Wonka's objections. Violet's action extends the role that food plays in the text by bringing more sharply into focus how *Charlie* reenacts the biblical metanarrative of redemption through both eating and restraint. As Jonathan Brumberg-Kraus explains, images of eating, in the form of symbolically charged feasts in both Old and New Testaments, come to take center stage over images of restraint as culminating events of spiritual identity formation:

> The authors of the early Christian eucharistic traditions and the early rabbinic seder make a point of explaining the symbolism of the food and wine they eat and drink . . . They are not "bread alone," but are also coded with cognitive contents to be internalized, that is, "ingested" just like the foods on which their meanings are conveyed. . . . The groups who ingest these incarnate "experiences" of a person or persons separated from them by time and/or circumstances take them on; they become what they eat. To the extent that each of these collective historical experiences are understood also as decisive revelations of God, eating the foods that embody these experiences also becomes in effect a means of union with God. (168)

Significantly, the gum Violet chews is not just gum, but a *meal*, reminiscent of the highly condensed sacramental eating of the Eucharist: in addition to its wafer-like "thin grey strip" being associated with Wonka and created by him to fill humanity's needs, its first two ingredients—tomato soup and roast beef—recall the blood and body of Christ. Violet's unauthorized and disrespectful consumption of Wonka's special meal thus becomes a blasphemous spectacle, and she too must be punished, echoing the New Testament's warnings against taking the Eucharist unworthily, and thereby suffering both bodily and spiritual harm.[5]

In the sense that Violet's transgression mocks the sacramental meal invented to sustain those left spiritually hungry by the fall, it builds on and intensifies Augustus's transgression. As a gum-chewing world champion and self-proclaimed gum expert, there is a sense of godlike pride inherent in Violet's act missing in Augustus's merely sensuous indulgence. As the tour through the factory continues and Veruca and Mike also meet their demise, this pattern of intensification continues. The last two children's acts of disobedience, though not directly involving eating, involve illicit consumption in increasingly prideful, blasphemous ways. Veruca and Mike, rather than stealing the edible ends of Wonka's production, attempt to obtain the control of the means of his production—a nut-sorting squirrel and a teleporting television camera—and thus continue the escalation from disobeying God for selfish pleasure alone to actually attempting to become like God apart from Him, both part of Eve's primal temptation:

> But the serpent said to the woman, 'You will not die. For God knows that when you eat of it your eyes will be opened, and you will be like God, knowing good and evil.' So when the woman saw that the tree was good

for food, and that it was a delight to the eyes, and that the tree was to be desired to make one wise, she took of its fruit and ate . . . (Genesis 3: 4–6)

Significantly, Dahl places the Television Room last, suggesting that the most dangerous type of consumption of all is humanity's latest vice, the consumption of virtual reality, which allows people, godlike, to move away most completely from God's creation toward what Jean Baudrillard has famously termed "hyperreality." Mike Teavee directs and stars in his own television production, but physically and symbolically he is the most diminished of all of the four disobedient children.

It is worth noting here that, in one sense, the journeys of *all* the disobedient children through Wonka's factory function as parodies of the Eucharist experience. In *The World as Sacrament*, Alexander Schmemann explains that the sacrament of Christian Eucharist has traditionally been conceived of as a "journey" into a very literal experience of God's kingdom that transforms pilgrims into the perfected people bearing the image of God that they were meant to be (32–33). Whereas popular understandings of the sacrament tend to focus on what happens to the bread and wine, Schmemann clarifies that "we must understand that what 'happens' to bread and wine, happens because something has, first of all, happened" to the participants (43). Rather than uniting with God, as believers do when they supernaturally become part of God's kingdom during the Eucharist meal, the disobedient children grotesquely merge with the objects of their own fleshly, transgressive desires—Augustus with chocolate, Violet with chewing gum, Veruca with the factory's workings itself, and Mike with a television screen. As in the Eucharist, the children's journey ends in their being literally consumed by, taken up into, what they consume.

Charlie's On-Screen Transformation from Christ Figure to Everyman

With Mike Teavee's exit, the reader is left with Charlie, who brings *Charlie and the Chocolate Factory*'s retelling of the biblical metanarrative to its climactic conclusion. Charlie alone completes his journey through the factory, but his destiny is more than a place; it is an identity as Wonka's heir:

> You see, my dear boy, I have decided to make you a present of the whole place. As soon as you are old enough to run it, the entire factory will become yours. . . . I'm much older than you think. . . . I've got no children of my own, no family at all. So who is going to run the factory when I get too old to do it myself? . . . A grownup won't listen to me; he won't learn. . . . I want a good sensible loving child, one to whom I can tell all my most precious candy-making secrets—while I am still alive. (156–157)

By making Charlie Wonka's *heir*, Dahl engages a prominent trope used in the New Testament to describe the transformed identity of believers.[6] He also reemphasizes the childlike quality cited by Christ as a prerequisite for entering the kingdom of God.

It is important to note, however, that in Dahl's novel, Charlie functions more as a Christ figure than a representative Christian. Without exception, he resists the temptation of transgressive eating, even when literally starving, as Jesus does during his divinely ordained fast in the wilderness at the beginning of his public ministry. Also like Christ, Charlie's story ends with an ascension, blasting off in Wonka's glass elevator. The narrative literally ends the same way as the gospels of Mark and Luke, with its hero disappearing into the open sky, united with the father figure who has declared him victor and heir.

The 1971 screenplay of the novel, *Willy Wonka and the Chocolate Factory*, however, changes Charlie from a Christ figure who resists all temptation and is ultimately exalted by the Father to an Everyman figure who also sins in relation to food and must be redeemed. Turning Charlie into an ordinary (albeit unusually good-natured) child with whom viewers can more closely identify actually works to intensify the text's emphasis on food as a means of socio-religious identity construction, and making him fatherless more overtly recalls the biblical trope that people come into the world as orphans, needing to be adopted by their heavenly Father.[7]

In between Violet's and Veruca's final scenes, Charlie joins Grandpa Joe in a sip of forbidden fizzy-lifting drinks and floats toward the factory's distant ceiling, almost getting his head chopped off by the powerful fan blades pulling him upward. His escapade seems to go unnoticed, but Wonka, of course, is omniscient; at the end of the tour, Wonka informs Charlie that he knows the boy "broke the rules" and thus doesn't get his promised lifetime supply of chocolate (much less the factory). Charlie's response is unique among the transgressors, however, even different from Grandpa Joe's: he implicitly acknowledges his sin against Wonka by returning the Everlasting Gobstopper he has been given as a gift. In terms of the film's biblical subtext, he acknowledges that he has forfeited eternal life by his own actions. And when he confesses his sin this way, proving his repentance by giving up the chance to sell the Gobstopper to Slugworth, everything changes at once. "You've won!" Wonka cries, freely offering forgiveness. He then blasts off with Charlie, his new heir, in the Glass Elevator, a scene which redemptively recapitulates Charlie's earlier attempt to fly. Symbolically, his desire to overcome his human limitations autonomously by drinking fizzy lifting drinks, to be like God, is replaced by a desire to ascend with God.

Although, as director Mel Stuart writes, "the most important alteration [to the book] was to emphasize the moral fallibility that exists in all of us" by making Charlie disobey Wonka's rules, other changes involving candy also strengthen *Charlie*'s relation to the biblical metanarrative in *Willy Wonka and the Chocolate Factory* (22). One subplot involves the newly created Everlasting

Gobstoppers, which rival candymaker Slugworth tempts the children to obtain for him. In foregrounding Slugworth (who only gets a brief mention in the novel) as the film's villain, *Willy Wonka* acknowledges the role of the devil/tempter figure in the biblical story. Slugworth's name recalls the serpent in the garden, cursed to creep along the ground as his punishment as a slug does, even as the tunnel in which he tempts Charlie recalls the underworld. Of all Wonka's edible inventions, Everlasting Gobstoppers, symbolic of God's plan to offer humanity eternal life, is the one that unnerves the author of death the most: "If he succeeds," Slugworth says, "he'll ruin me," which is of course how the biblical metanarrative of Christ winning eternal life for mankind by overcoming death plays out. It is also significant that, at the end of the tour, Wonka reveals that Slugworth works for him. Similarly, even the devil ultimately serves God's purposes, and is not destroyed in the biblical story until his purpose in testing mankind is accomplished.

Consuming *Charlie* in a Postmodern Context

Stuart's 1971 film adaptation of *Charlie and the Chocolate Factory* ultimately strengthened the ways in which Dahl's book positions food as central to the biblical quest for salvation, but more recent productions of the text have not. In 2005, director Tim Burton released another film adaptation, also titled *Charlie and the Chocolate Factory*, which diminishes the story's relationship to the biblical metanarrative. Burton and screenplay writer John August decline to retain any of the alterations in *Willy Wonka* that heighten associations between food and Judeo-Christian identity formation (gone are the scenes foregrounding Everlasting Gobstoppers and fizzy-lifting drinks). More striking, however, is the way in which Burton's film changes Dahl's book, substituting the biblical metanarrative for what Jean-François Lyotard calls a less universal "little narrative" also centered around food and reconciliation with a father (60). In the latter *Charlie*, it's not Charlie who must discover his true identity by regaining an alienated father but Wonka himself. Wonka, far from showing glimpses of a loving, fatherly nature behind his edgy mannerisms, barely tolerates even Charlie in this version, developmentally hindered from showing affecting because of his poor relationship with his own sadistic, candy-denying father. Like an amateur psychotherapist, Charlie helps Wonka through his unresolved childhood conflict, diminishing Wonka's godlike associations. Charlie's spiritual pilgrimage gives way to Wonka's psychological journey.[8]

This change should not surprise us. The move away from universalizing metanarratives of any kind is, according to Lyotard, one of the defining qualities of what he dubbed the postmodern condition, and it is worthwhile pondering how the relationship between food (and, more generally, consumption) and identity is changing in postmodern productions marketed to children (xxiv). Determining what exactly constitutes postmodernity is a highly complex and sometimes contentious matter, and a thorough response to what kinds of identities food in postmodern literary texts is helping children construct lies far beyond the boundaries of the present essay. But, as our present tour of the Wonka's factory comes to an end, it seems important to reflect briefly on the accumulating cultural meanings of *Charlie and the Chocolate Factory* during the four decades since its first reproduction as a film, in a postmodern era increasingly marked not only by skepticism of totalizing metanarratives, but also by the acceleration of technological advances and accompanying increases in the power and pervasiveness of media-generated images.

The mass reproduction of Dahl's text into the 1971 and 2005 films, their subsequent videos and DVDs, and a Wonka line of candies all, I would argue, complicate *Charlie*'s messages about consumption in what Frederic Jameson has described as postmodern consumer culture, "in which the earlier distinctions between cultural representations and economic activities have broken down" (Connor 16). Richard Appignanesi notes that in this current cultural climate, free market capitalism is the only widely accepted metanarrative left; in such a context, everything "real" is commodified or at least commodifiable (182). This is perhaps most vividly portrayed in reality shows where personal identities and private lives serve as raw material for scripted realities, which viewers end up consuming as "reality." Coupled with the ability to make virtual reality more attractive than experiences of reality available to most people—reviewer Jeff Shannon notes that "elaborate visual effects make [Burton's film] an eye-candy overdose"—our economy becomes, as Jameson has argued, increasingly driven by the production, exchange, marketing and consumption of media-generated images which eclipse, rather than refer to, the "real" unmediated world (Connor 46). In such an economy, even food products such as Nestle's line of Wonka candy derive primary value from their association with a media-generated experience rather than from the gastronomic qualities of the candy itself.

As *Charlie and the Chocolate Factory* enters the twenty-first century, its identity as a family of diverse, mass-marketed products rather than as a single text attests to the effects of commodification on its messages about consumption. Inevitably, the consumption of food dramatized *in* Dahl's text is swallowed by the proliferating activity of consuming the products associated with it: the films on DVDs which allow endless replay and offer bonus features, including interviews with 1971 cast members of Willy Wonka for nostalgic fans and glimpses of Johnny Depp for younger devotees of Burton's recent production; the Willy Wonka line of candy, relaunched by Nestle in 1998 for $20 million and targeted in 1999 to become its signature children's brand of candy worldwide with an ad budget exceeding $10 million; and the brand's Web site, Wonka.com, which averages 1 million hits a month (Pollack & Cuneo; Thompson, "Now Kids"). Increasingly, reading the book, or even watching the original film adaptation, is just one event in an interrelated group of events which become self-referential, pointing not to a cultural and religious identity outside of themselves but to the very act of ingesting media as a perpetually satisfying endeavor. One of the most startling landmarks in this repositioning of Dahl's text occurred in 2006 with Nestle's introduction of the WonkaZoid:

> In what's believed to be a category first, the confection giant this fall introduces a combination video game/candy dispenser called WonkaZoid . . . Touted as a "boredom buster" for kids, the product will be distributed not only in candy stores but also in toy stores such as Toys R Us. It's the first of an aggressive slate of new products planned over the next few years to invigorate the company's Willy Wonka brand. . . . In sales materials, Nestle cites research showing there were 248 million computer and video games sold in 2004 (almost two per American household) and people spend an average of 65 minutes a day playing them. . . . Games give you a more intimate relationship with the brand and, in the case of a game/dispenser, every time you go to play the game, the candy is there," Mr. Belcher [senior analyst at eMarketer] said. As people's media patterns shift, that one-on-one relationship becomes priceless. (Thompson "Now Kids")

In developing the priceless one-on-one relationship to which Mr. Belcher refers, food plays as central a part as it did in Dahl's original text. But the relationship being facilitated by food is between a consumer and a brand, not between a reader and a larger cultural tradition. With the WonkaZoid, eating is boldly paired with gaming, and the players, mostly children, learn through that pairing who they are: postmodern consumers of an "everlasting" supply of profit-generating virtual images, which Nestle promises to refresh every six months (Thompson "Now Kids"). These most recent developments in *Charlie*'s journey make Dahl's positioning of Mike Teavee's excessive media consumption as the last and most egregious violation of Wonka's rules look prophetic indeed. In an age when Dahl's text about food is spawning more and more consumables designed to grab and hold children's attention—to "brand" them—*Charlie and the Chocolate Factory* continues to bring us face to face with the inextricability of consuming and being consumed.

Notes

1 See, for example, Margaret Talbot, "The Candy Man: Why Children Love Roald Dahl's Stories—and Many Adults Don't," *The New Yorker* (July 11, 2005).
2 See, for example, Eleanor Cameron, "McLuhan, Youth and Literature," *Crosscurrents of Criticism, Horn Book Essays 1968–1977*, Ed. Paul Heins

(Horn Book, 1977) and David Rees, "Dahl's Chickens: Roald Dahl," *Children's Literature in Education* (September 1988).

3   See Matthew 18:3, Mark 10:14–15, and Luke 18:16–17.

4   Examples of the Bible's valorization of spiritual poverty and its representation as hunger are numerous. See especially Matthew 5:6: "Blessed are those who hunger and thirst for righteousness, for they shall be satisfied."

5   See 1 Corinthians 11:26–28: "Whoever, therefore, eats the bread or drinks the cup of the Lord in an unworthy manner will be guilty of profaning the body and blood of the Lord. Let a man examine himself, and so eat of the bread and drink of the cup. For any one who eats and drinks without discerning the body eats and drinks judgment upon himself. That is why many of you are weak and ill, and some have died."

6   References to believers as "heirs" are numerous in the New Testament. See, for example, Romans 8:15–17 and James 2:5.

7   See Galatians 4:4–5: "But when the time had fully come, God sent forth his Son, born of woman, born under the law, to redeem those who were under the law, so that we might receive adoption as sons."

8   Although Freudian psychosexual theories also function as metanarratives, Wonka's story of alienation from his father does not follow Freud's universalizing developmental narrative of Oedipal rivalry ending in identification. Rather, it is a more localized story in which a variety of Freudian and post-Freudian psychological theories come into play to explain a particular individual's experience.

Works Cited

Appignanesi, Richard, et al. *Introducing Postmodernism*. 1999. Royston, UK: Icon, 2004.

Bal, Sumeet, et al. "The Top 50 Cult Movies." *Entertainment Weekly* 23 May 2003: 26– 35. MasterFILE Premier. CD-ROM. EBSCOhost.

Baudrillard, Jean. "Simulacra and Simulations." *Jean Baudrillard: Selected Writings*. Ed. Mark Poster. Stanford, CA: Stanford UP, 1988. 166–184.

Bible, Revised Standard Version. *The Electronic Text Center*. Ed. Robert A. Kraft. Alderman Lib., U of Virginia. <http://etext.virginia.edu/rsv.browse.html>.

Bosmajian, Hamida. "*Charlie and the Chocolate Factory* and Other Excremental Visions." *The Lion and the Unicorn* 9 (1985): 36–49.

Brumberg-Kraus, Jonathan. "'Not by Bread Alone . . . ': The Ritualization of Food and Table Talk in the Passover *Seder* and in the Last Supper." *Semeia* 86 (1999): 165–193.

Charlie and the Chocolate Factory. Dir. Tim Burton. Perf. Johnny Depp and Freddie Highmore. 2005. DVD. Warner Home Video, 2005.

Connor, Steven. *Postmodernist Culture: An Introduction to Theories of the Contemporary*. Oxford: Blackwell, 1989.

Dahl, Roald. *Charlie and the Chocolate Factory*. New York: Puffin Books, 1988.

Feeley-Harnik, Gillian. *The Lord's Table: The Meaning of Food in Early Judaism and Christianity*. Washington, DC: Smithsonian Inst. P, 1981.

Gooderham, David. "Deep Calling unto Deep: Pre-oedipal Structures in Children's Texts." *Children's Literature in Education* 25:2 (1994): 113–123.

Kass, Leon R., M.D. *The Hungry Soul: Eating and the Perfecting of Our Nature*. New York: Free P, 1994.

Lyotard, Jean-Francois. *The Postmodern Condition: A Report on Knowledge.* 1979. Trans. Geoff Bennington and Brian Massumi. Theory and History of Literature. 10. Minneapolis: U of Minnesota P, 1984.

Pollack, Judann, and Alice Z. Cuneo. "Nestle Pours $20 Mil into Relaunch of Wonka Line." *Advertising Age* 11 May 1998 (69:19). *Communication & Mass Media Complete.* CD-ROM. EBSCOhost.

Roback, Diane and Jason Britton, eds. Comp. Debbie Hochman Turvey. "All-Time Bestselling Children's Books." *Publisher's Weekly* 17 Dec. 2001. 15 March 2004. http://www.publisher-sweekly.com/index.asp?layout=article&articleid=CA186995&publication=publishersweekly

Schmemann, Alexander. *The World as Sacrament.* London: Darton, 1966.

Schultz, William Todd. "Finding Fate's Father: Some Life-History Influences on Roald Dahl's *Charlie and the Chocolate Factory.*" *Biography* 21:4 (Fall 1998): 463–481. Literature Online. CD-ROM.

Shannon, Jeff. Rev. of *Charlie and the Chocolate Factory,* dir. Tim Burton. 2005. Amazon.com. 10 June 2007. <http://www.amazon.com/Charlie-Chocolate-Factory-Full-Screen/dp/B000BB1MHS/ref=pd_bbs_sr_3/103-5774506-1351002?ie=UTF8&s=dvd&qid=11818386 64&sr=1-3>.

Soler, Jean. "The Semiotics of Food in the Bible." *Food and Culture: A Reader.* Ed. Carole Counihan and Penny Van Esterik. New York: Routledge, 1997. 55–66.

Stephens, John, and Robyn McCallum. *Retelling Stories, Framing Culture: Traditional Story and Metanarratives in Children's Literature.* New York: Garland, 1998.

Stuart, Mel, with Josh Young. *Pure Imagination: The Making of* Willy Wonka and the Chocolate Factory. New York: St. Martin's, 2002.

Thompson, Stephanie. "Nestle Works to Build *Wonka* Brand." *Advertising Age* 15 Nov. 1999 (70:47). *Communication & Mass Media Complete.* CD-ROM. EBSCOhost.

———. "Now Kids Can Really Play with Food." *Advertising Age* 29 May 2006 (77:22). *Communication & Mass Media Complete.* CD-ROM. EBSCOhost.

Willy Wonka and the Chocolate Factory. Dir. Mel Stuart. Perf. Gene Wilder, Jack Albertson and Peter Ostrum. 1971. DVD. Warner Home Video, 2001.

Zasky, Jason. "*Willy Wonka and the Chocolate Factory*: From Inauspicious Debut to Timeless Classic." *Failure Magazine* Jan. 2003. 15 March 2004. <http://www.failuremag.com/arch_arts_willy_wonka.html>.

Chapter Sixteen

Prevailing Culinary, Psychological, and Metaphysical Conditions: *Meatballs* and Reality

Martha Satz

The current paperback edition of Judi Barrett's *Cloudy with a Chance of Meatballs* carries a banner proclaiming, "Over one million copies sold!" Indeed, the book has achieved the status of a classic, regularly read by children individually and in the classroom; the story is even widely incorporated into lesson plans. The whimsy of the title brings a smile to the faces of adults and ignites the imaginations of children. But on a more profound level, the book nurtures children—striking unconscious chords from their infancy, relishing the loving and lavish aspects of their childhoods, reassuring them about their trek to adulthood, and offering them the consolations of enterprise, art, and the imagination for the more troublesome aspects of reality. The book likewise appeals to adults, in particular fulfilling the homemaker's dream of dinner without shopping, preparation, or cleanup, and more generally the human fantasy of life without effort: in short, portraying a fanciful Edenic existence. Interestingly, the work develops the critic Christopher Bollas's view linking the child's first nurturing experience to the aesthetic moment. But most profoundly, the book promises that even after childhood, imagination and art can return us to the rapturous world of infancy. In the narrative, food spills out as a complex signifier with an ever-expanding relation to the Real in both its yielding and unyielding aspects.

Bruno Bettelheim offers a hint about the power of this book. In his groundbreaking work, *The Uses of Enchantment*, Bettelheim invokes Lewis Carroll's term, "love-gift," to characterize the fairy tale because " . . . [it] reassures, gives hope for the future, and holds out the promise of a happy ending" (26). The premise underlying Bettelheim's book, which is heavily indebted to a Freudian perspective, is that the fairy tale works on an unconscious level to comfort the child regarding his primal concerns of love, attachment, and separation. The present essay ventures that *Cloudy with a Chance of Meatballs* does so as well. Encompassed in this simple picture book are messages of comfort for loss of the primal state of ecstasy and for the problems of maturing and eventual death. Both in form and content, *Cloudy with a Chance of Meatballs* invokes art and imagination as recompense for the child's renouncing her most primitive satisfactions. It builds on Maurice Sendak's innovative work in picture books, which evoke the child's fantasy and dream world as an unconscious means of resolving psychological problems. Additionally, the work is complexly multilayered. It deals with gender politics as well as philosophical issues. On an aesthetic level, it invokes a Schopenhauerian and Nietzschian perspective on the role of art. Art and imagination may permeate the prosaic world and redeem it. As Nietzsche proclaims in *Birth of Tragedy*, "It is only as an *aesthetic phenomenon* that existence and the world are *eternally justified*" (32). In a subtle manner, the work also promotes an existential, human-centered view of life rather than a theocentric one. Thus, this marvelously compact picture book blends psychoanalytic, feminist, and philosophical perspectives in an enchanting manner.

The structure of the book suggests the close affinity of the real and the imaginative. The story consists of a frame narrative ostensibly grounded in reality and a "tall tale" told by the Grandfather, the jovial head of the family depicted in the framing structure. The illustrations of the frame narrative appear in black and white contrasted by brightly colored boxes of text; the pictures depicting Grandpa's "tall tale" appear in color. As the book makes a transition from the frame narration to that of the tall tale, spots of yellow, seemingly emanating from the sun that hovers over the fictional land the Grandfather creates, touch the heads of the children listening to the story. Thus, graphically, the children are connected to their Grandfather's fantasy. Additionally, Grandfather or versions of him appear both in the frame narrative and the "tall tale." Likewise, on the last page of the book, the black and white illustrations of the realistic frame narrative sport a yellow ellipse conjuring recollections of the fantasy that Grandfather has evoked. The use of color in the illustrations, particularly the yellowish glow in the black and white illustrations, narratively connects the world of reality and aesthetic creation in a manner more complex and subtle than the text. As Opal Moore, in her article about children's picture books, remarks, "The visual image is the most engaging of sensory images, imprinting its outlines upon the subconscious like an acid etch. The imprint is often indelible—defying the forgetfulness of the conscious mind. . . . This is particularly important for picture books aimed at the young child. Pictures are the primary message vehicle . . ." (183).

Both the frame tale and the tall tale suggest the primal ecstatic state. The opening page of the book portrays a spirited family, their kitchen suffused with comfort, warmth spilling over the scene like the pancake batter dripping from the mixing bowl. An open window and an overhead light illuminate the children's teasing banter. The girl narrator characterizes the situation, "It was Saturday morning. Pancake morning. Mom was squeezing oranges for juice. Henry and I were betting on how many pancakes we each could eat. And Grandpa was doing the flipping" (Barrett). The black and white illustration portrays the two children, mouths agape, challenging each other in playful dialogue, their mother looking on with approving pleasure. A cat contentedly sleeps on one of the chairs. A rather comical-appearing grandfather intently flips pancakes at the stove, his tongue hanging out in concentration, the family dog eyeing him attentively. The kitchen emanates a sense of order with each appliance in its place, but the children suggest an enthusiasm teetering on the edge of decorum, and the corner where Grandfather prepares the pancakes exudes a comfortingly messy aura. The scene resonates with M. F. K. Fisher's remarks: "It seems to me that our three basic needs, for food and security and love, are so mixed and mingled and entwined that we cannot straightly think of one without the others. So it happens that when I write of hunger, I am really writing about love and the hunger for it, and warmth and the love of it and the hunger for it . . . and then the warmth and richness and fine reality of hunger satisfied . . . and it is all one" (ix). Indeed, Barrett's kitchen scene radiates warmth, love, and nurturance.

The family is a nontraditional one: no father is present, and the grandfather who would presumptively head the family does not bear the traits traditionally associated with a patriarch. Rather, he has a humorous and reassuring appearance with a bulbous nose, goggle eyeglasses, balding hair, a tongue hanging out of his mouth, and a paunch. And the illustrated scene subtly plays with gender categories. The pancake mix box bears the brand name "Aunt Jim's Pancake Mix." And as the children argue about their acumen in eating pancakes, the girl's hand is held slightly above that of the boy's, thereby disrupting the usual gender hierarchy. And on the second page, when "something flew through the air headed toward the kitchen ceiling" (Barrett), the grandfather assumes a pose of acute helplessness and distress as the dog begins to pursue the previously peacefully sleeping cat. The mother appears somewhat startled, but the grandfather looks positively undone. No fearless, protective male here. Likewise, the pancake lands on the boy's head, and the illustration portrays him with his mouth agape and his visible eye agog, as opposed to his sister who sits with a relatively calm but quizzical expression on her face.

After the disruption of the flying pancake, the happy and harmonious relationship of the family is restored, all four members of the family sitting happily at the breakfast table eating pancakes. The girl feeds a bit of her pancake to the cat. The dog tries to edge his nose to the table. The adults smile benevolently at the children. The boy is utterly engaged with his grandfather. Thus, in many ways, the first four pages of the frame narrative parallel and summarize the "meat" of the book, the tall tale the grandfather will tell: an idyllic scene is disrupted by an ostensible disaster, but then the world is restored to a functional state, providing happiness and comfort.

As Grandfather relates his story, "That night, touched off by the pancake incident at breakfast, Grandpa told us the best tall-tale bedtime story he'd ever told" (Barrett), the black and white real world pictorially merges with the world of fantasy. The transition recalls the famous illustration in Maurice Sendak's *Where the Wild Things Are*, when Max's room becomes "the world all around," both pictures representing that nether unconscious realm, where fantasy and reality fuse. Grandfather tells the story of the "tiny town of Chewandswallow" (Barrett), a technicolor town in which an ever-so-slightly younger version of Grandfather appears, living with facsimiles of the cat and the dog. The town is one in which manna (or in this case hamburgers, mashed potatoes, and peas) rain down from the sky. There are no food shops, no preparation, no cleanup. The cosmos, even without any imprecations, provides everything needed: "Dinner one night consisted of lamb chops, becoming heavy at times, with occasional ketchup. Periods of peas and baked potatoes were followed by gradual clearing, with a wonderful Jell-O setting in the west" (Barrett). The page with this text is illustrated by a glorious palace-like structure of golden Jello illuminating the country side.

The scene described on these pages recalls what many psychologists and theoreticians, beginning with Freud, describe as the primal experience. Carolyn Daniel, in *Voracious Children*, describes this state: "Imagine a Land where hunger and anxiety are unknown, where there is only constant warmth, comfort, satiety, and satisfaction. There is no self and other, no inside and outside, and no desire because nothing is lacking. This is a place of total fulfillment" (87). Traditionally, this state is that of the infant at the mother's breast, the state where mother and child merge, where the anxiety of separation and desire do not exist, where no effort is required to have needs fulfilled. Interestingly, our mythology and tales of origin echo this developmental state, most familiarly in the Garden of Eden, when humanity is placed in the position of the infant, where all desires are satisfied without exertion. Thus, the infant's loss upon maturing and the consequent longing for the mother parallels human loss and the desire to return to a state in which effort, toil, and anxiety are absent.

We may speculate that the allure of *Cloudy* for adults comes from the resonant nostalgic chords it strikes of the primal state, developmentally and metaphysically, when all is provided, before growing up, before the Fall. For children, the appeal of this book may initially be less profound, namely the fanciful pictures it paints—meatballs, orange juice, and pancakes raining down from the sky. The book provides many absurd images deliciously amusing to contemplate. And yet the book is also deeply consoling for children, offering answers to their most acute, often unacknowledged fears— how will I live as an adult, without my parents providing for me, or when my parents are gone?

Notably, Grandpa's tall tale is not one of just unmitigated fulfillment, although perhaps this aspect is the one most recalled. For unknown reasons, meteorological conditions in Chewandswallow change; there is disaster. Once again Barrett provides us with fanciful images, in this case, of culinary weather disasters: "One day there was nothing but Gorgonzola cheese all day long. The next day there was only broccoli, all overcooked. And the next day there were brussel sprouts and peanut butter with mayonnaise" (Barrett). In this comical fashion, a metaphysical problem is posed: what does one do when an unanticipated, inexplicable catastrophe occurs? Grandpa's tall tale provides an answer: one copes as best as one can with the talents and materials at hand: "So a decision was made to abandon the town of Chewandswallow. . . . The people glued together the giant pieces of bread sandwich-style with peanut butter . . . took the absolute necessities with them, and set sail on their rafts for a new land" (Barrett). This scene once again recalls a scene from Sendak. Mickey in *In the Night Kitchen* takes the bread dough in which he had formerly been submerged and from it fashions an airplane in which he flies to his chosen destination. This is an important moment in *In the Night Kitchen*, an existential moment if one will, when Mickey individuates himself and out of amorphous matter shapes his life to suit his intentions. If we recall the phrase "existence precedes essence," Jean-Paul Sartre's cryptic formulation of existentialist philosophy in *Existentialism Is a Humanism*, then we ponder Sartre's view that values and purposes are not inherent in the design of the universe or part of God's plan but must be chosen by each person. In crafting and flying his airplane, Mickey symbolically chooses his destiny. Likewise in *Cloudy*, the people of Chewandswallow decide not to be at the mercy of capricious and at times hostile cosmic forces but to set their own path. They fashion their vehicles out of whatever presents itself and set out, thereby defining their purpose. They arrive at a land that resembles our own, a reality more difficult than their former realm, but one in which they have more control, as evidenced by the fact that they can choose what to eat instead of simply accepting whatever falls from the sky. Thus, within Grandpa's "tall tale" resides the implicit message that there is compensation for giving up the primal, rapturous state, namely more autonomy. When one leaves infancy or the Edenic state, one is not entirely at the mercy of the cosmos, but one steers one's own course.

What is the effect of Grandpa's story on the children? Clearly, it changes the world for them, imbuing it with a fantastical, magical quality. The next morning, as the children sled down the snow-covered hill, they remark: "It's fun, but even as we were sliding down the hill we thought we saw a giant pat of butter at the top, and we could almost smell mashed potatoes" (Barrett). The illustration accompanying this text, the last page of the book, contains, amidst the otherwise black and white illustration, a golden sun just behind the small figure of the grandfather in the background at the top of the hill. He waves in salute at the large figures of the children in the foreground at the bottom of the hill, who wave back to him.

This illustration with the accompanying text is suggestive on a multiplicity of levels. In the illustration, the substantial presence of Grandfather throughout the book has visibly receded. He is small compared with the much larger figures of the children in the foreground. Undoubtedly, the illustration presages Grandfather's death and portrays the progression of the generations as well as their connection. The children perched on their sleds are apparently ready for the ride of their lives, or whatever ride life will bring them. The marks of their sleds visibly demonstrate that they have journeyed from their grandfather's orbit and are now going to an unknown destination. However, the importance of Grandpa's influence remains as the children wave to him from below in acknowledgment. They are going forth strengthened by the wisdom Grandpa has provided them. In the illustration, Grandfather has the rising sun at his back, illuminating him, suggesting either the golden aura of memory or the divine grace of the next world.

Yet, this last page generates other meanings as well. The children see the sun not only as a sun but also as a giant pat of butter, for their grandfather has transformed their world, enabling them to see it in a novel way. Their senses take in the snow at one and the same time as snow and mashed potatoes. Imagination has provided them with plentitude, warmth, and satisfaction and the means to recover the primal ecstatic state. If, at least under one interpretation, this book is about the secure and fulfilled state of the infant and its inevitable disruption, then Grandfather, with his tale, has shown how to recover in some way that rapturous infantile state through art and imagination. Christopher Bollas points out an affinity between the child's earliest ecstatic moments at his mother's breast and aesthetic experience: "The mother's idiom of care and the infant's experience of this handling is the first human aesthetic. . . . The uncanny pleasure of being held by a poem, a composition, a painting, or for that matter any object rests on those moments. . . . This human aesthetic informs the development of personal character and will predispose all future aesthetic experience that place the person in subjective rapport with an object" (41). Bollas quotes Murray Krieger in distinguishing the aesthetic: "What would characterize the experience as aesthetic rather than either cognitive or moral would be its self sufficiency, its capacity to trap us within itself, to keep us from moving beyond it to further knowledge or to practical efforts" (40). Indeed, the aesthetic experience is *sui generis* and has no further end. In *Cloudy*, the children's aesthetic experience (listening to their grandfather's story) has transformed their world to one that seizes them in its thrall and provides a primal warmth. Their Grandfather's tale has not only transformed their environment but it has demonstrated how art and imagination can transform the world.

Grandfather's tall tale, the heart of *Cloudy with a Chance of Meatballs*, is triply enlightening and reassuring for the children in the story and the children who read the story as well. It provides them with the gift of imagination and art to reenvision the world and to recall and reinstate the plenitude of the universe. But within the tale also lie the tools to cope with the vicissitudes of the universe—to do the best one can, shaping one's life with what one has and discovering that maturity or autonomy has its compensations. The tale also subtly reassures that although one may not always have sustaining parental figures in one's life, one will have the wisdom and love they have imparted.

The book as a whole reassures on another level as well. The figure of Grandfather, not mother, dominates this book. He provides not only the pancakes, connoting love in the frame narrative, but the artistic rendering and wisdom in the tall tale. As suggested in the earlier discussion, Grandfather is an androgynous figure, nurturing, heading the family, and providing wisdom. Thus, for children in all varieties of families, the implicit message is that one can receive unconditional love and nurturing from whoever is there to provide it. The family structure is less important than what is provided. And in the family portrayed, love, food, laughter, and wisdom are doled out in generous portions.

Judi Barrett's book is deservedly popular and famous for its wonderful, comical vision of meatballs falling from the sky and its evocation of a world of love, ease, and humor. But its underlying messages enhance its value. It imparts the view that such a world is already present for children as portrayed in the cocoon-like breakfast scene that opens the book, where everyone is ensconced in love and warmth. It recognizes and exalts the role of art and imagination in transfiguring the world to restore the most reassuring of states. It instructs and empowers children, informing and encouraging them to shape their own lives. It emphasizes and endorses tradition and continuity within the family and offers flexibility in gender roles. *Cloudy with a Chance of Meatballs* offers children, and incidentally adults who happen upon it, a way to preserve a glimmer of a totally satiated state in their lives.

Works Cited

Barrett, Judi. *Cloudy With a Chance of Meatballs*. New York: Simon, 1978.

Bettelheim, Bruno. *The Uses of Enchantment: The Meaning and Importance of Fairy Tales*. New York: Knopf, 1976.

Bollas, Christopher. "The Aesthetic Moment and the Search for Transformation." *Transitional Objects and Potential Spaces: Literary Uses of D. W. Winnicott*. Ed. Peter L. Rudnytsky. New York: Columbia UP, 1993.

Daniel, Carolyn. *Voracious Children: Who Eats Whom in Children's Literature*. New York: Routledge, 2006.

Fisher, M. F. K. *The Gastronomical Me*. San Francisco: North Point, 1943.

Moore, Opal. "Picture Books: The Un-Text." *The Black American in Books for Children: Readings in Racism*. Ed. Donnarae MacCann and Gloria Woodard. Metuchen, NJ: Scarecrow, 1985.

Nietzsche, Friedrich. *Birth of Tragedy*. Trans. Shaun Whitside. London: Penguin, 1993.

Sartre, Jean-Paul. *Existentialism Is a Humanism*. Trans. Carol Macomber. New Haven: Yale UP, 2007.

Sendak, Maurice. *In the Night Kitchen*. New York: Harper, 1970.

———. *Where the Wild Things Are*. New York: Harper, 1963.

Chapter Seventeen
"The Attack of the Inedible Hunk!": Food, Language, and Power in the Captain Underpants Series

Annette Wannamaker

> The creamy candied carrots clobbered the kindergarteners. The fatty fried fish fritters flipped onto the first graders. The sweet-n-sour spaghetti squash splattered the second graders. Three thousand thawing thimbleberries thudded the third graders. Five hundred frosted fudgy fruitcakes flogged the fourth graders. And fifty-five fistfuls of fancy French-fried frankfurters flattened the fifth graders. (Pilkey, *Wrath* 66–67)

Food play and linguistic play in Dav Pilkey's Captain Underpants books are connected through excess: food flies and alliterations abound. Indeed, those moments in the series that are the most over-the-top in terms of the grotesque are also those moments when the language is most playful: alliteration, assonance, consonance, rhyme, puns, parody, and, of course, onomatopoeia all feverishly combine with images of food that is thrown, worn, squashed, stepped on, splattered, or transformed into a monstrous blob (the "inedible hunk") that devours the gym teacher. Food features prominently in this series for beginning readers, but it is rarely eaten. It is used as a tool to gross out or to humiliate adult characters; it is a focal point for linguistic playfulness; and it is a source of much of the carnivalesque humor in the books. Food functions differently in these books than it does at the dinner table. Foods that please the child characters in the books are precisely those of which adults disapprove (ice cream, cake, and gummy worm sandwiches); food that is flung for comic effect is chosen for its color, texture, and sound effect potential (butterscotch pudding); and food that is used for linguistic play is chosen for the delicious sounds the food words make as they pour from the mouth of the reader: say "fifty-five fistfuls of fancy French-fried frankfurters flattened the fifth graders" three times fast.

243

These excesses of language about food can be interpreted in multiple ways. On one level, food in the Captain Underpants books serves as a site for fantasies of power and control. As Kara Keeling and Scott Pollard note, "The functions of food, as well as the rituals of eating and the rituals of the table, are compact metaphors for the power struggle inherent to family dynamics" (132). Children, who are continuously told what, when, how much, and what not to eat, can see food as a focal point of power struggles in their lives, and the Captain Underpants books depict an inversion of these power struggles. On another level, the constant conflation between play with food and play with language could be seen as a narrative device working to seduce the beginning reader into the Symbolic in ways that make reading seem inviting and mildly subversive of adult control over child bodies and mouths. At the same time, however, these narratives and their readers exist within larger systems of family, school, and consumer culture that mediate the texts and that may not allow the books in the Captain Underpants series to be wholly subversive. The excesses of the text, after all, may be a way to fulfill adult and societal expectations of the child in the process of learning self-control, who needs safe, fictive outlets, like silly comic books, in order to harmlessly release his frustrations at continuously being told "no." Finally, depictions of excessive consumption as pleasurable and subversive may also work to fulfill corporate expectations of the child as an excessively desiring consumer of both food and mass-produced series books marketed to children.

So far, Dav Pilkey has written and illustrated nine books for the Captain Underpants series (and several spin-off books). The protagonists are two mischievous boys, George and Harold, and their grouchy principal, Mr. Krupp, whom they have hypnotized into believing that he is the fictional hero Captain Underpants. These illustrated chapter books for beginning readers often ridicule adults, especially teachers, and rely mostly on scatological humor, parody, and word play to move forward their silly, far-fetched plot lines. Food plays a role in all the books and takes center stage in some of them. For example, the third Captain Underpants book is excessively titled *Captain Underpants and the Invasion of the Incredibly Naughty Cafeteria Ladies from Outer Space (and the Subsequent Assault of the Equally Evil Lunchroom Zombie Nerds)*, and in this installment of the series, food, eating, and the threat of being eaten are the main themes. The school lunch ladies, in an attempt to make a batch of cupcakes for Principal Krupp, create a vat of green ooze that "crashe[s] through the cafeteria doors and splashe[s] down the halls, swallowing everything in its path" (Pilkey, *Invasion* 34). A giant Venus fly trap-like plant from outer space is about to eat our hero, Captain Underpants, until he swallows some Extra-Strength Super Power Juice that gives him superhero powers. Once the school's lunch ladies quit their jobs in a huff, evil lunch ladies from outer space take over the lunchroom and turn kids into zombie nerds by feeding them cafeteria food. The zombified children (made docile by conceding to adult dictates) are cured when they drink some root beer spiked with "anti-evil zombie nerd juice," mixed up by our heroes, George and Harold. Much like the potions and cakes in *Alice's Adventures in Wonderland,* food in the Captain Underpants books is sometimes magical and able to transform the body of the careless or careful eater. The illustrations that accompany the text in this book, and others in the series, depict continuous challenges to the stability of bodily borders as people are transformed by food, covered with food, or disappear altogether when they are ingested as food. Food in this and the other Captain Underpants books is monstrous and excessive—it splatters, oozes, smothers, engulfs bodies, and even comes to life. It is also often associated with the feminine because it is served up by antagonistic Lunch Ladies in the elementary school cafeteria or fills the tables at a much-maligned female teacher's wedding.

Of course, food, prettily arranged on banquet tables at a wedding, doesn't stay on the tables long because—like a loaded gun that appears in the first act of a play, which is destined to go off in Act II—the comic book genre dictates that fancy food prettily displayed is destined to be thrown. In *Captain Underpants and the Wrath of the Wicked Wedgie Woman,* George and Harold's grouchy teacher, Ms. Ribble, is engaged to marry their oppressive principal, Mr. Krupp. The school's gymnasium is converted "into a beautiful wedding hall, complete with food, decorations, and even a six-foot-tall ice sculpture," and the children are, to their dismay, required to attend. "Man," says George, "I can't believe we have to go to school on SATURDAY!" (54). An accompanying illustration depicts rows of frowning children dressed in their Sunday best, sitting up straight, and looking miserable. When the wedding is foiled because the bride discovers that George and Harold tricked the principal into proposing, the bride becomes monstrous in her fury: "As George and Harold turned to leave the gymnasium, they heard the loud thumps of cleated wedding boots clomping down the aisle toward them. 'I'M GONNA GRIND THOSE KIDS INTO HEAD CHEESE!' screamed Ms. Ribble as she lunged for the two boys" (61). The food starts to fly when Ms. Ribble, in a rage, destroys the wedding banquet:

> With a horrible roar, she pushed the right pillar over. It landed on the back of the luncheon table, causing the front of the table to flip high into the air. Unfortunately, this sent all of the food flying into the crowd. (62)

As the visual and linguistic downpour of food cited as an epigraph to this chapter ensues, the ritual of the wedding and the bodily control required of the attending children is subverted. The teacher's threatening rage is transformed into slapstick comedy. Although she threatens to grind the boys into head-cheese, to turn them into food to be consumed, she instead ends up covering the children and herself in layers of food and drink, which no one will consume. She is foiled by food that is being used in ways that break the rules, violate rituals, and thwart her authority. At the end of the scene, just as she catches the tricksters George and Harold by their neckties, she is stopped when the wedding cake lands—"splat"—on her head. As they make their narrow escape, George says, "That's what we get for going to school on Saturday!" (68).

A food fight at a wedding makes perfect sense in the carnivalesque world of Captain Underpants, where societal expectations are often turned topsy-turvy. Food consumption is a highly ritualized and regulated social practice. Carolyn Daniel writes that "we must eat according to culturally defined rules in order to achieve proper (human) subjectivity. In other words it is vital, for the sake of individual and social order, that every human subject liter-ally embodies culture" (4). Food consumption is directly connected to subject formation, to technologies of the body, and to the workings of the social body. There are rules we must follow about when to eat, when to eat specific foods, how to eat, how to hold one's fork, which fork to use, how to chew, how to sip, and how to use a napkin. We must learn not to chew with our mouths open, not to burp at the table, not to put our elbows on the table, not to eat cold pizza for breakfast, not to eat cotton candy for dinner, not to slouch at the table, and not to reach across the table. Talk at the table is also regulated because dinnertime is when children are often pressed to talk about their day at school, yet admonished not to talk with food in their mouths, not to inter-rupt the adults, and not to talk excessively. Eating, then, is conflated with bodily and linguistic control, with stifling social conventions and with rigid sets of rules that children must learn to follow. If the dinner table is a site for nightly battles between parents and children, then a wedding, where children must exhibit their very best behavior in a public, formal, and ritualized set-ting, is the epitome of such adult control, and an ideal fictional site for fanta-sies of subversion and excess that involve eating, language, and the body.

Keeling and Pollard write that "A child lives in a world where giant adults seem to have no other purpose than limiting the child's options" (127). In such a world, they argue, it is no wonder that food, bodies, and eating rituals are often depicted in children's texts in ways that are excessive: "To become large, larger than one's parents. To become monstrous, beyond adult con-trol. To reject the food on one's plate. To eat something else, anything else, everything else, anywhere else but at the table. To reject parental food. To feel revulsion, then to act on it, in spite of the taboos. To eat and eat and eat" (127). These tropes of excess, common in much children's literature, seem to be even more exaggerated in the Captain Underpants books, where they are depicted through text and illustration in ways that directly link transgressive, excessive images of food to the subversion of various adult expectations—and that do so in ways that metafictionally parody adult expectations about eating, bodily control, language use, other texts, and sometimes the Captain Underpants texts themselves.

Mikhail Bakhtin's work on carnival is a useful tool to use to discuss the subversive pleasure the Captain Underpants books may provide for child read-ers, because they are texts characterized by scatological folk humor, inversions of hierarchies, parody, laughter, food, grotesque bodies, and mild curses: all characteristics that Bakhtin highlights in his work. Although Bakhtin focused much of his discussion in *Rabelais and His World* on the specific practices of the Renaissance carnival, he also notes that there are vestiges of carnival in modern texts—especially in humorous ones. Deborah Thacker argues that some works of children's literature are ideal examples of Bakhtin's observations:

> The parodic features of his notion of the carnivalesque and its roots in "low" culture, bodily functions, and notions of the "Other," continually challenging notions of bourgeois social conformity, resemble and include those child-like uses of language that repeatedly test the authority of imposed structures of meaning. (10)

Carnival has the potential to challenge the status quo by playfully turning hierarchies inside out in the ways it contests the borders between high and low, king and peasant, adult and child, and author and reader. It often does so by calling attention to the body and to bodily functions, like eating, thereby also contesting the borders between what is eaten and what is worn, what is inside the body and what is out, what is consumed by the self and what is consuming of the self.

The carnivalesque aspects of the Captain Underpants books also come from their deliberate and self-referential position as lowbrow literary junk food, of which many adults seem to disapprove. Taste in literature is acquired just as one acquires a taste for fine food—we refine our palates and our minds. Taste is also directly linked to other categories such as socioeconomic class and race. Lowbrow books are the equivalent of potato chips, corn dogs, and cotton candy and are often called junk food, the comparison implying that lowbrow texts are at best empty calories children can occasionally enjoy or, worse, they are artery-clogging garbage children must learn to reject in favor of spinach salad, tuna rolls, and whole wheat pasta, especially if they expect to be accepted as respectable members of the middle or upper class. The lowbrow status of a text like a Captain Underpants book is another site of struggle for parents and children. Battles over the dinner table move to the bookstore where adults say to children, "wouldn't you rather read *Charlotte's Web*?" in the same tone they might use to say, "wouldn't you rather choose broccoli?"

Dinner table battles over broccoli further connect to battles over language, not only in those discussions about which words a child is permitted to use but also in the types and the amount of speech parents allot to a child. Many children are told not to use certain words that are used in the Captain Underpants books in abundance: "poop," "turd," "peepee," "butt" and a host of other mild curses. In his essay about the grotesque and taboo in Roald Dahl's work, Mark I. West suggests that children deal with anxieties about parental control over their bodies through types of humor that make many adults uncomfortable. He writes, "For very young children, this form of humor is expressed without a hint of subtlety" (93), that younger children will simply blurt out words like "poop." Older children seek more sophisticated ways to vent frustrations, but they also "enjoy jokes and stories that poke fun at the moral authority of adults" (93). Children's speech is regulated in the same ways food consumption and bodily functions are regulated as they are told to hush, to watch their language, to stop asking so many questions, and to stop prattling on. Furthermore, food and eating also are metaphors we use for speaking, writing, and thinking: we eat our words, sweet talk one another, chew on our thoughts, devour books, and swallow those words we are afraid to utter. As children read the books in this series, they are testing the limits of social conventions regarding food while also testing the limits of language, of reading, and of the textual conventions of children's books, and they are doing so in ways that many adults may not understand or appreciate.

George and Harold take great pleasure in playing with language in the same ways they play with food. They run over and burst ketchup packets with their skateboards, and they write, reproduce, and distribute comic books that are confiscated by teachers. They splatter butterscotch pudding all over their peers, and they playfully change the letters around on signs at their school. They often subvert official school announcements by turning them into jokes: "Please wash your hands after using the toilet" becomes "Please wash your hands in the toilet" (Pilkey, *Big Bad Battle* 12–14); "Today's menu: Soy burgers, hot lime pie, apple juice" becomes "Please eat my plump, juicy boogers" (Pilkey, *Preposterous Plight* 38–40); and the school lunch menu changes from "New tasty cheese and lentil pot-pies" to "Nasty toilet pee-pee sandwiches" (Pilkey, *Invasion* 13–16). Words merge and jumble into one another, food is made grotesque and conflated with other bodily functions, and school authorities are thwarted in creative ways simply by moving a few letters around on school signs. In one scene, forced to eat lunch in the principal's office as a punishment, the boys use their brown bag lunches to subvert his authority by pushing the limits of both gastronomic and linguistic boundaries: "I'll trade you half of my peanut-butter-and-gummy-worm sandwich," says George, "for half of your tuna-salad-with-chocolate-chips-and-miniature-marshmallows sandwich," to which Harold adds, "Sure, Y'want some barbeque sauce on that?" The principal responds, saying, "You kids are DISGUSTING!" (Pilkey, *Invasion* 57). Here, the words about food, the boys' vivid descriptions of their lunches used in just the right rhetorical context, are what cause the principal's disgust and the reader's delight.

Thomas Newkirk writes that in children's books,

> Humor, and particularly parody, is not simply a genre coexisting innocently with other genres. It is a tool for those who feel themselves in a subordinate position; to the extent that those in authority must exert their authority through kinds of discourse (speeches, rules, forms,

advice, "good literature"), they leave themselves open to the mockery of these language forms. (154)

Through parody and humor, the Captain Underpants books work to highlight the relationships among food, language, and power and the ways these function together as part of a larger system of control working to police children's words and bodies until they learn to exercise such control over themselves. The final end of power, after all, is for subjects to exert control over their own bodies and discourse. Power, of course, is not always a negative force, and such self-control is necessary to function as a member of society, but a certain level of resistance against power is also necessary to maintain a sense of self, and, paradoxically, to maintain larger, diffused systems of power. Michel Foucault said,

> If power were never anything but repressive, if it never did anything but to say no, do you really think one would be brought to obey it? What makes power hold good, what makes it accepted, is simply the fact that it doesn't only weigh on us as a force that says no, but that it traverses and produces things, it induces pleasure, forms knowledge, produces discourse. It needs to be considered as a productive network which runs through the whole social body, much more than as a negative instance whose function is repression. (Rabinow 61)

This always unresolved tension between control and being controlled, between resisting and submitting, between pleasure and repression, and between self-control and desire plays itself out in the Captain Underpants books in ways that illustrate the many negotiations even younger children must make as they learn to navigate their place within larger systems of power that extend beyond their families into school and other social relations.

For example, in *Captain Underpants and the Invasion of the Incredibly Naughty Cafeteria Ladies from Outer Space (and the Subsequent Assault of the Equally Evil Lunchroom Zombie Nerds)*, food and language play combine in ways that parody adult control over consumption, adult dictates on language use, and even the adult author(ity) of the writer of Captain Underpants, but the text does so in ways that also result in closure and a reestablishment of order. After seeing their science teacher make a bubbly volcano using baking soda and vinegar, the boys decide to trick the lunch ladies at their school into making a doctored cupcake recipe containing these two ingredients. Unbeknownst to the boys, the lunch ladies multiply the ingredients by 100 so they can make enough for the entire student body. When they mix 200 bottles of vinegar with 200 boxes of baking soda, the mixture explodes, "KA-BLOOOOOSH!" (Pilkey, *Invasion* 33), in an excess of splattering food, illustrations, and language play. The lunch ladies are propelled through the air by a "giant wave of green goop" that covers three pages of text as it

> crashed through the cafeteria doors and splashed down the halls, swal-
> lowing everything in its path. Book bags, bulletin boards, lunch boxes,
> coat racks, trophy cases . . . nothing could stand in the way of the gigantic
> green glob o' goo. It traveled down to the north, east, and west wings of
> the school, covering everything from the drinking fountains to the text
> on this page. (34–35)

On the page, the oozing food literally covers over words and parts of words
so that part of the text is illegible. Here, food play and linguistic play converge in a wonderfully self-conscious way that works to mock the author's
own excesses, to call attention to the text as an object, and to directly address
and engage an active child reader, who is made aware of the conventions of
narrative as they are being subverted through humor.

When the lunch ladies quit, after being covered in exploding goop, they
cite a list of transgressions George and Harold have committed:

> Every day, they change the letters around on our lunch sign. They put
> pepper in the napkin dispensers and unscrew the caps of the salt shakers.
> . . . They start food fights. . . . They go sledding on our lunch trays. . . .
> They make everybody laugh so the milk squirts out their noses. . . . And
> they're *constantly creating these awful comic books about us!!!*" (38)

The tricksters, George and Harold, invert hierarchies by using both language
and food in inappropriate ways that subvert adult authority. They throw food
and cause food to fly out of kids' noses instead of into their stomachs. They
also rearrange texts adults have written and create new texts of their own,
writing and rewriting instead of just passively consuming adult-sanctioned
discourse. In a rustic, misspelled comic book within a comic book (story
within a story) that is written by the boys and titled "Captain Underpants
and the Living Lunch Ladies," the three lunch ladies are trapped inside the
school and forced to eat the cafeteria food they prepared. They die from eating the food, are buried on a haunted hill, they become zombies, and then
return to the school as cannibals in search of brains to eat. A woman screams,
"Help! The lunch ladys arosed from the dead! They're Hungry for brains and
they just attacked the gym teacher," to which the "principle" replies, "But I
thought you said they were hungry for 'brains'!" (40). The misspelled words
and incorrect grammar, supposedly penned by the fictional boys, combined
with crude drawings and even cruder jokes, subvert the expectations of some
educators and other adults who hope that children will read more sophisticated fare that models, if not proper behavior, then at least proper grammar,
correct spelling, and a more refined aesthetic.

The language play in the text and its ridicule of adult-sanctioned behaviors and textual conventions may be connected to its function as a book for
early readers. The Captain Underpants books are popular with children who

are just learning how to read and are often cited by teachers and parents as being one of the first books children are able to read independently. The books also, though, are often read to children by their teachers or parents, and they are books that younger readers just learning to read independently often read together with an adult. Karen Coats argues that when children first are learning to read, there are simultaneous feelings of both loss and pleasure. Children miss the comfort of being physically close to an adult reading to them but take great pleasure in finally having a more direct access to texts. They are torn between wanting to read themselves but still wanting to be read to. "Hence the Symbolic has to run a sort of PR campaign to convince the reluctant child that the space he is entering has as much if not more to offer than the space he is leaving behind" (60). As part of this "PR campaign" children must be seduced by playful language that gives them feelings of pleasure and power. The child protagonists of the books, George and Harold, perform ownership of various texts—they write, illustrate, and self-publish their own comic books, and they rearrange signs in ways that allow them to rewrite adult dictates—in ways that are inviting, funny, and that privilege the child's ability (both the fictional child and the implied child reader) to make meaning and to claim ownership over language.

Thacker also argues that a child reader, and adult readers as well, must feel a sense of mastery over a text in order to find it pleasurable. She argues, though, that for a child reader there is always a mediation, a negotiation of power between the adult writer and the adult reading a text to a child, listening to a child read, reading along with the child, or teaching the child to read. "The interactions between parents and children in the negotiation of power are various and contradictory, suggesting that the illusory nature of self-determination and authority are played out in a social context." She goes on to write that, "Book-reading is, thus, a social game in which the mother plays with the illusion of control" (6). Therefore, within this context, how subversive can any text for children be when it is written by an adult, published and marketed by adults, bought for children by adults and read to children by adults? The Captain Underpants books, in all their excess, are perhaps winking at the adult who is mediating the text for the child, are perhaps using language play and ridicule of adult authority to seduce the child into the Symbolic, and, in the process, perhaps they are even performing some of our adult expectations of the child reader. After all, we, as adults, take delight in children's laughter and gleeful expressions of mock disgust at flung food. We *expect* these reactions. We pause and wait for them, we encourage them, and we are delighted when the child reader fulfills these expectations and bemused when he doesn't.

Why do we have these expectations of voracious, excessive, consuming children that we reproduce in the texts we give to our children? Jacqueline Rose argues that adult desires shape the child (the fictional child, the imagined child reader, and, by extension, the actual child) who is depicted in the texts we write and read to our children. What adult desires, then, are being fulfilled through these depictions of excessive consumption of language and food? In what ways is the implied child reader being shaped through these expectations? Thacker writes that, "The need to test and challenge are [sic] finally controlled through social practices and adult mediations" and that a "revolutionary sense of resistance to the symbolic order of language is subsumed by the forces of bourgeois ideology, which treat these challenges as a 'safety valve for repressed impulses it denies in society'" (8–9). Do we read our children stories of excess in order to more effectively restrict their behavior? Keeling and Pollard argue that the message of many children's books depicting excessive consumption of food is that "The child can have his/her libidinal flings—they are even seen as natural and healthy—but, with the proper guidance, these flings need not threaten parental authority" (130).

Such safe books, which knowingly wink at the adult who is watching over the child's shoulder while mediating these "libidinal flings," should not then be perceived as threats to adult authority. However, the books in the Captain Underpants series are consistently listed among the most challenged and censored books in the United States, appearing regularly on the American Library Association's "most censored" lists (ALA 2007). Challenges to the books have come from adults concerned that they will entice children to disobey authority, that they are too violent, and that they will teach children incorrect spelling and language usage. Thacker argues that linguistic play is often curtailed in many children's texts by adults, who see fictional texts as a way to teach proper language usage. She writes that "linguistic subversion and parody is present in some of the most imaginative children's books, while the pressure to engage with 'correct' usage and conformist language contests the tendency to 'play'" in most others (8). As quite a few adults have objected to the books in the Captain Underpants series, could the food play and language play in the books actually present a threat to adult authority? Books in the Captain Underpants series do feature quite a bit of linguistic play but, like much nonsense, it is rule-bound and takes the form of excessive repetitions of sound—long strings of alliterations, rhyme, consonance, assonance, and onomatopoeia are used to highlight the sounds words make and to call attention to the pleasures of language. The depictions of food play are similarly rule-bound and even conventional: cafeteria food is disgusting, food fights are common, children are rewarded with pizza and ice cream, and boys are allowed a voraciousness that is not accessible to girls. These conventional depictions of fictional subversions of power may indeed mark the books as ones that maintain societal norms, although seeming to challenge them.

Daniel asks whether any texts depicting food in grotesque ways can ever be subversive or whether they are always reinforcing the status quo. She argues that carnivalesque texts have the potential to be subversive because "for children, carnivaleque-grotesque material can reveal what adults are trying to suppress and it makes a move toward deconstructing sociocultural systems and laying bare their values" (166). Parody only works, after all, if one is aware that it is a parody, and when conventions are subverted then our attention is called to those conventions. However, she goes on to argue that one value not laid bare in much carnivalesque children's literature is "the underlying misogynistic discourses" that often shape representations of the grotesque and carnivalesque (166). This is also a key argument in my book, *Boys in Children's Literature and Popular Culture: Masculinity, Abjection, and the Fictional Child,* where I write that many of the grotesque depictions in the Captain Underpants series work to construct women, girls, and feminized boys and men as "others" or as abject. I will not discuss the problematic depictions of gender in the series in detail here, except to note that in these texts fantasies of power, control, and subversion of adult authority seem much more accessible to male characters than to female or feminized characters. If boys are the ones throwing food and re-writing signs, then where are the girls in the text? Girls are often shown frowning and covered in food, and women in the books are often depicted as monstrous. A girl reader, then, must choose between two difficult choices: she can be the "other," the object ridiculed and splattered with food, or she can learn to identify with the boys—but, of course, never fully (Wannamaker 96–101).

We seem more willing to tolerate voracious, excessive, and grotesque boys in children's texts because these constructs of boys conform to our expectations of boy behavior and are part of a long tradition of "bad boy" texts. Kenneth Kidd argues that in the "bad boy" genre of children's books the "boy subject is the author's young self in thin disguise, which implies that the boy will grow (has already grown) into a special kind of man, the man of letters" (53). This clearly is the case with the Captain Underpants books, where the assumption is that George and Harold are just mischievous little boys who will eventually grow up to be smart, literate adults like the author, who claims in a variety of autobiographical accounts to have been a mischievous little boy himself. This assumption, however, is one based in a sense of entitlement. As Kidd points out, "the Bad Boy's delinquency is safely middle-class" (54). The boys in such narratives can afford to be naughty and disruptive because they can count on inheriting a position of privilege when they grow into men— their "boys will be boys" antics are tolerated because we believe they will one day become safe, middle-class men who have learned self-control, and who have become respectable members of society.

What we tolerate or do not tolerate in the texts we give to our children may also depend on our awareness of and attitudes about child consumerism. In mass-produced texts, like the Captain Underpants books, there is a relationship between depictions of the consumption of food and the consumption of the text as a product. The Captain Underpants texts are, after all, a series of books meant to be collected. Children able to purchase every book in the series can gain a certain cultural capital and that comes from consuming correctly. One cynically could view the spattering food, linguistic play, and inversions of hierarchies depicted in the books as marketing ploys meant to interpellate child readers as willing and docile consumers of literary junk food. For example, television commercials for children's food or toys often offer a promise of power to the child able to purchase the product. Bill Osgerby writes that,

> since the late 1960s modern capitalist economies have undergone a fundamental transformation—moving from a "Fordist" era of mass production for mass consumer markets, into a new, "post-Fordist" epoch of flexible production for a profusion of differentiated market segments. . . . These kinds of developments have been evidenced especially clearly in the field of youth marketing. (46)

This identification of children as a "market segment" makes many adults nervous, perhaps because, when we notice the ways in which the child is directly addressed in advertisements, it clearly makes visible the ways in which our children are being enticed to desire products they don't need: the ways they are deliberately being constructed as consumers. Some adults mistakenly believe that children can, at least for a little while, exist outside of global consumer culture and can be protected from the discourses and influences of commercialism. In her discussion of the Pokémon phenomenon, Christine R. Yano writes that such fears of child consumerism "express Euro-American and other ambivalences toward global (late) capitalism—here fanatic consumerism—even as we adults live, create, and sometimes glorify a world of consumption." She goes on to say that, "An attack on [children's] consumer desires takes a stab at policing our own" (133). As food becomes a metaphor child readers use to learn to navigate discourse, adult authority, and complex systems of power, it also serves as a metaphor for negotiating the power structures of contemporary consumer culture. Specifically, the consumption of food and of books as products that one voraciously devours is depicted, without irony, as a way to circumvent adult restrictions, as subversive, and as empowering. Perhaps, when adults object to the Captain Underpants books, which depict flying, splattering, wasted food produced and consumed in excess, and which depict conspicuous consumption as both pleasurable and subversive, it is because we are made aware of our own adult excesses.

Works Cited

American Library Association Web site. <http://ala.org> (accessed 24 June 2007).

Coats, Karen. *Looking Glasses and Neverlands: Lacan, Desire, and Subjectivity in Children's Literature.* Iowa City: U of Iowa P, 2004.

Daniel, Carolyn. *Voracious Children: Who Eats Whom in Children's Literature.* New York: Routledge, 2006.

Keeling, Kara K., and Scott Pollard. "Power, Food and Eating in Maurice Sendak and Henrik Drescher: *Where the Wild Things Are, In the Night Kitchen,* and *The Boy Who Ate Around.*" *Children's Literature in Education* 30.2 (1999): 127–143.

Kidd, Kenneth. *Making American Boys: Boyology and the Feral Tale.* Minneapolis: U of Minnesota P, 2004.

Newkirk, Thomas. *Misreading Masculinity: Boys, Literacy, and Popular Culture.* Portsmouth, NH: Heinemann, 2007.

Osgerby, Bill. *Youth Media.* New York: Routledge, 2004.

Pilkey, Dav. *Captain Underpants and the Big, Bad Battle of the Bionic Booger Boy, Part 1: The Night of the Nasty Nostril Nuggets.* New York: Scholastic, 2003.

———. *Captain Underpants and the Invasion of the Incredibly Naughty Cafeteria Ladies from Outer Space (and the Subsequent Assault of the Equally Evil Lunchroom Zombie Nerds).* New York: Scholastic, 1999.

———. *Captain Underpants and the Preposterous Plight of the Purple Potty People.* New York: Scholastic, 2006.

———. *Captain Underpants and the Wrath of the Wicked Wedgie Woman.* New York: Scholastic, 2001.

Rabinow, Paul, ed. *The Foucault Reader.* New York: Pantheon Books, 1984.

Rose, Jacqueline. *The Case of Peter Pan; or, the Impossibility of Children's Fiction.* London: Macmillan, 1984.

Thacker, Deborah. "Disdain or Ignorance? Literary Theory and the Absence of Children's Literature." *The Lion and the Unicorn* 24.1 (2000): 1–17.

Wannamaker, Annette. *Boys in Children's Literature and Popular Culture: Masculinity, Abjection, and the Fictional Child.* New York: Routledge, 2007.

West, Mark I. "The Grotesque and the Taboo in Roald Dahl's Writings for Children." *Psychoanalytic Responses to Children's Literature.* Ed. Lucy Rollin and Mark I. West. Jefferson, NC: McFarland, 1999. 91–96.

Yano, Christine R. "Panic Attacks: Anti-Pokémon Voices in Global Markets." *Pikachu's Global Adventure: The Rise and Fall of Pokémon.* Ed. Joseph Jay Tobin. Durham, NC: Duke UP, 2004.

Contributors

Genny Ballard is an Assistant Professor at Centre College. Her publications include: "Approaching *Calila y Dimna* as Children's Literature" in *The Image of the 20th Century* (2000), and entries for José Martí, Hilda Perera, Graciela Montes, and Juana de Ibarbourou in the *Oxford Encyclopedia of Children's Literature* (2006). Her book, *Hispanic Children's Literature of the EnCuento Series*, is in press at The University Press of Kentucky.

Holly Blackford is an Assistant Professor of English at Rutgers University-Camden. She teaches and publishes literary criticism on American, children's, and adolescent literature, as well as literatures in English. She has published articles on Louisa May Alcott, Emily Brontë, J. M. Barrie, Carlo Collodi, Anita Diamont, Julia Alvarez, Shirley Jackson, Margaret Atwood, Henry James, Mark Twain, and Harper Lee. Her book *Out of this World: Why Literature Matters to Girls* (2004) analyzes the empirical reader responses of girls to literature. From 2004–2006 she held an International Reading Association research award for the study of teen responses to *The Adventures of Huckleberry Finn* and *To Kill a Mockingbird*. For term 2005–2008 she holds an elected position as article award committee member for the Children's Literature Association.

Winnie Chan teaches post/colonial Anglophone literatures at Virginia Commonwealth University. Her current project, *Imperial Gastronomy*, examines the relationships among gastronomic consumption, imperial power, and post/colonial identity in Anglophone writing; her book, *The Economy of the Short Story in British Periodicals of the 1890s*, was published by Routledge in 2007.

Lan Dong is Assistant Professor of English at the University of Illinois at Springfield where she teaches Asian American literature and comparative literature. She has published articles on Asian American literature, films, and children's literature, including "Writing Chinese America into Words and Images: Storytelling and Re-telling of 'The Song of Mu Lan'" in *The Lion and the Unicorn* 30.2 (April 2006). She is working on a book manuscript on the cross-cultural transformation of *Mulan*.

James Everett is an Associate Professor of English at Mississippi College. He earned his PhD in English at the University of Washington in Seattle. His major fields of interest are Victorian travel writing and film studies.

Leona W. Fisher is at Georgetown University. Her publications include *Lemon, Dickens, and "Mr. Nightingale's Diary: A Victorian Farce"* (U of Victoria 1988); "Mark Lemon's Three Farces on the 'Woman Question'" in *Studies in English Literature* (1988); "Mystical Fantasy for Children: Silence and Community" in *The Lion and the Unicorn* (1990); "Bridge Texts: The Rhetoric of Persuasion in American Children's Realist and Historical Fiction" in *Children's Literature Association Quarterly* (2002); "Focalizing the Unfamiliar: Laurence Yep's Child in a Strange Land" in *MELUS* (2002); "'I'm thinking how nothing is as simple as you guess': Narration in Phyllis Reynolds Naylor's *Shiloh*" in *Children's Literature Association Quarterly* (2003); "*The Adventures of Tom Sawyer* and *The Great Brain*: Language, Ritual, Race, and the Construction of the 'Real' American Boy" in *Rituals and Patterns in Children's Lives*, ed. Kathy Merlock Jackson, U of Wisconsin P (2005); "Race and Xenophobia in the Nancy Drew Novels" (forthcoming McFarland, 2009). She is also working on a book manuscript, *Is Nancy Drew a Girl Scout?: Constructions of American Girlhood in the Twentieth Century*.

Lisa Rowe Fraustino is an Associate Professor of English at Eastern Connecticut State University, a Visiting Associate Professor in the Hollins University Graduate Program in Children's Literature, and a 2006 Fulbright Scholar to Mahasarakham University, Thailand. Her children's books have received numerous honors, among them the American Library Association's Notable Book designation for *The Hickory Chair* and an ALA Best Book for Young Adults designation for *Ash: A Novel*. She has edited three short story anthologies for young adults, including *Dirty Laundry: Stories about Family Secrets*; *Soul Searching: Thirteen Stories of Faith and Belief*; and *Don't Cramp My Style: Stories about That Time of the Month*. Her historical novel, *I Walk in Dread: The Diary of Deliverance Trembley, Witness to the Salem Witch Trials*, was on the final list of Scholastic's popular Dear America series.

Elizabeth Gargano is an Assistant Professor at the University of North Carolina-Charlotte. Her publications include "The Education of Brontë's New Nouvelle Heloise in *Shirley*" in *SEL Studies in English*

Literature 44.4 (Autumn 2004) and "Death by Learning: Zymosis and the Perils of School in E. J. May's *Dashwood Prior*" in *Children's Literature* 33 (2005).

Robert M. Kachur is Associate Professor at McDaniel College. His publications include "Buried in the Bedroom: Bearing Witness to Incest in Poe's 'The Tell-Tale Heart'" (*Mosaic*, March 2008); "Elizabeth Gaskell, Gender, and the Apocalypse" in *Reinventing Religion: Nineteenth-Century Contexts* (2001); and "Envisioning Equality, Asserting Authority: Women's Devotional Writings on the Apocalypse, 1845–1900" in *Women's Theology in Nineteenth-Century Britain: Transfiguring the Faith of Their Fathers* (1998).

Kara K. Keeling has published articles on food and children's literature in *Children's Literature in Education and Beatrix Potter's Peter Rabbit: A Children's Classic at 100*. She and Scott Pollard are working on their own book-length study of the topic. She teaches in the English Department at Christopher Newport University, specializing in children's and young adult literature.

Jacqueline M. Labbe is at Warwick University in the United Kingdom. She has published *Romantic Visualities: Landscape, Gender and Romanticism* (1998); *The Romantic Paradox: Violence, Death, and the Uses of Romance, 1760–1830* (2000); an edition of Charlotte Smith's novel *The Old Manor House* (2002); *Charlotte Smith: Romanticism, Poetry and the Culture of Gender* (2003); and an edition of the poems of Charlotte Smith (2007). She is currently researching a new book on Smith, Wordsworth, and Romanticism.

Karen Hill McNamara is an Adjunct Assistant Professor of Children's Literature in the Caspersen School of Graduate Studies at Drew University in Madison, New Jersey. She was a contributing author in *Hungry Words* (2006). Other publications include "From Fairies to Famine: How Cultural Identity is Constructed through Irish and Irish-American Children's Literature" in *Children's Folklore Review* and "Children's Literature of the Great Irish Famine" in *Foilsiu: An Interdisciplinary Journal of Irish Studies*.

Scott T. Pollard has published articles on food and children's literature in *Children's Literature in Education and Beatrix Potter's Peter Rabbit: A Children's Classic at 100*. He and Kara Kelling are working on their own book-length study of the topic. He teaches in the English Department at Christopher Newport University, specializing in world literature and critical theory.

Martha Satz is at Southern Methodist University. Her publications include "Genetic Counseling and the Disabled: Feminism Examines the Stance of Those Who Stand at the Gate" (with Annette Patterson) in *Hypatia* (2002), reprinted in *Genetics: Science, Ethics, and Public Policy* (2005); "Implicated in a Color Change: Darkening the Picture of Jane Lazarre's Maternal Transracial Memoir" in *Motherself: Theories and Narratives of Maternal Subjectivities* (forthcoming); "Finding Oneself: Images in Adoption in Children's Literature" in *Adoption & Culture* (forthcoming); "Teaching *Native Son*: A Missionary to Her People" in *Approaches to Teaching Richard Wright's Native Son* (1997); and "The Death of the Buddenbrooks: Four Rich Meals a Day" in *Disorderly Eaters: Texts in Self-Empowerment* (1992).

Jodie Slothower's interests in food and culture developed from teaching courses in popular culture and graphic design as a communication professor at Kansas State University, Eureka College, and Heartland Community College. As president of the Herb Guild of McLean County, she demonstrated cooking techniques and wrote a short cookbook. Slothower collects cookbooks, particularly those created for children. While teaching her son to cook, they decided their favorite cookbooks are based on Roald Dahl's children's books and *Star Wars*. She has published on children's television, technology, and picture book illustrators.

Jan Susina is a Professor of English at Illinois State University where he teaches courses in children's and adolescent literature and Victorian Studies. He has published in *Children's Literature, The Lion and the Unicorn, Children's Literature in Education, Children's Literature Association Quarterly*, and *Marvels & Tales: A Journal of Fairy-Tale Studies*. His research interests include illustrated texts for children and adults, Victorian children's literature, graphic novels, and folk and literary fairy tales.

Richard Vernon is at the University of North Carolina-Chapel Hill. His current book project treats a corpus of forty-five eighteenth-century Portuguese chapbooks, currently out of print but found in the Lisbon National Library. The work examines how, at the end of the eighteenth century, in a country restricted by severe inquisitorial and royal censorship, the street literature forum was appropriated as a forum for social debate. A portion of this study is forthcoming in *Santa Barbara Portuguese Studies*. He has also published on the twentieth century Portuguese poet Mario de Sá Carneiro (*Romance Notes*) and the Brazilian novelist Lima Barreto (*Hispanófila*).

Annette Wannamaker is Assistant Professor at Eastern Michigan University. Her publications include *Boys in Children's Literature and Popular Culture: Masculinity, Abjection and the Fictional Child* (2007); "Marking Time: Bertolt Brecht's Antigone as Tragedy of Revolution and Exile" in *The Brecht Yearbook* (31); "Reading in the Gaps and Lacks: (De)Constructing Masculinity in *Holes*" in *Children's Literature in Education* (37.1); "Men in Purple Cloaks, Men Wielding Pink Umbrellas: Witchy Masculinities in the Harry Potter series" in *The Looking Glass: Alice's Academy* (10.1); "Present(ing) Historical Memory: Beah Richards's 'A Black Woman Speaks,' Performance, and a Pedagogy of Whiteness" in *Theatre Topics* (14.1); "Specters of Potters: Inheritance in the Harry Potter Series" in *Elsewhere: Selected Essays from the "20th Century Fantasy Literature: From Beatrix to Harry" International Literary Conference* (2003); "'Memory Also Makes a Chain': The Performance of Absence in Griselda Gambaro's Antigona Furiosa" in *Journal of The Midwest Modern Language Association* (Fall 2000/Winter 2001).

Jean Webb, whose professorship is in International Children's Literature, is Director of the International Center for Research in Children's Literature, Literacy and Creativity at the University of Worcester, United Kingdom. She is also program leader for the M.A. in Children's Literature: An International Perspective. In addition to supervising PhD students, she teaches the generic Research Student Training program at Worcester. Her publications include *Text Culture and National Identity in Children's Literature* (2000); with Deborah Cogan Thacker, *Introducing Children's Literature: Romanticism to Postmodernism* (2002); ed., *The Sunny Side Of Darkness: Children's Literature in Totalitarian and Post-Totalitarian Eastern Europe* (2005); "Genre and Convention" in Butler, C. (ed.) *Teaching Children's Fiction* (2006); "Beyond the Knowing: The Frontier of the Real and the Imaginary in David Almond's *Skellig* and *The Fire-Eaters*" in Justyna Deszcz-Tryhubczak and Marek Oziewicz's *Towards or Back to Human Values. Spiritual and Moral Dimensions of Contemporary Fantasy* (2006); ed., *"A Noble Unrest": Contemporary Essays on the Work of George MacDonald* (2007).

Index